Alan Bold

Longman Dictionary of

POETS

The lives and works of 1001 poets
in the English language

Longman

Longman Group Limited,
Longman House, Burnt Mill, Harlow,
Essex CM20 2JE, England
and Associated Companies throughout the world.

First published 1985

Bold, Alan
    Longman dictionary of poets
    1. Poets — Biography
    I. Title
    809/1   PN1111

ISBN 0-582-55570-1

Set in 9/11pt Quadritek 1400 Garamond
Printed in Great Britain
by Hazell, Watson & Viney Ltd, Aylesbury.

Introduction

POETS have rarely come to common conclusions about the purpose of poetry. When WH Auden, in his 'In Memory of WB Yeats', asserted that 'poetry makes nothing happen' he was rationalising a change of position, rejecting the political label that had stuck to him throughout the 1930s. Shelley, of course, had claimed that 'Poets are the unacknowledged legislators of the world' and Hugh MacDiarmid, in our own time, claimed that 'any utterance that is not pure / Propaganda is impure propaganda for sure!' Clearly, opinions differ and remind the reader that the poet is, above all, an idiosyncratic individual. That, at any rate, is the assumption on which this dictionary is based.

Through the centuries, critics have tried to contain poetry by devising a number of exclusive categories, some of them more useful than others. We have Metaphysical poetry, Augustan poetry, Romantic poetry, Georgian poetry, Modernist poetry, Pylon poetry, Movement poetry, Confessional poetry, Martian poetry – to name but a few. I have used some of these terms as a convenient shorthand in preparing the entries. I have also, however, used an illustrative quotation in each entry so that every poet can speak for himself or herself. Ultimately, the singular poetic voice is what we want to hear.

Wherever possible the exact dates of birth and death have been given and key works have been cited. The geographical placing of a poet is just that and indicates a national rather than a linguistic fact. Thus the term 'Welsh poet' means a poet associated with Wales and not one who writes in Welsh. Similarly, 'Irish poet' refers to a poet of Ireland and not a poet writing in Irish. For reasons of space the dictionary has been limited to English-language poets though the use of dialect has been enthusiastically acknowledged.

Preparing this book has been an educational experience and I have been impressed at the immense variety of poetry over the centuries. I believe that a dictionary admitting the very new as well as the very old, and including the intellectual ingenuity of Donne as well as the doggerel energy of McGonagall, can claim to be fairly exhaustive. If some poets are conspicuous by their absence then readers should (via Longman) inform me of this fact which may be utilised in a future edition. Meanwhile, I hope the reader will find the work entertaining as well as informative and will enjoy keeping the company of the poets in the following pages.

Alan Bold

About the author

Alan Bold was born in Edinburgh in 1943 where he attended university and trained as a journalist. Since 1966 he has been a full-time writer and visual artist. In addition to over twenty-five books of poetry, stories and nonfiction he has edited many anthologies, including *The Penguin Book of Socialist Verse*, The *Cambridge Book of English Verse 1939–75*, and *The Bawdy Beautiful*.

Books by Alan Bold

Poetry

Society inebrious
The voyage
To find the new
A perpetual motion machine
Penguin modern poets 15 (with Braithwaite and Morgan)
The state of the nation
The auld symie
He will be greatly missed
A century of people
A pint of bitter
Scotland, yes
This fine day
A celtic quintet (with Bellany)
In this corner: selected poems 1963–83
Haven (with Bellany)
Summoned by Knox
Homage to MacDiarmid (with Bellany)

Stories

Hammer and thistle (with Morrison)
The edge of the wood

Nonfiction

Thom Gunn & Ted Hughes
George Mackay Brown
The ballad
The sensual Scot
Modern Scottish Literature
MacDiarmid: The terrible crystal
True characters (with Giddings)
The book of rotters (with Giddings)

As editor

The Penguin book of socialist verse
The martial muse: Seven centuries of war poetry
Cambridge book of English verse 1939–75
Making love: The Picador book of erotic verse
The bawdy beautiful: The Sphere book of improper verse
Mounts of Venus: The Picador book of erotic prose
Drink to me only: The prose (and cons) of drinking
Smollett: Author of the first dimension
The sexual dimension in literature
A Scottish poetry book
Scott: The long-forgotten melody
Byron: Wrath and rhyme
The thistle rises: A Macdiarmid miscellany
Macdiarmid: Aesthetics in Scotland
The letters of Hugh Macdiarmid
The poetry of motion
Muriel Spark; An odd capacity for vision
Harold Pinter: You never heard such silence
Auden: The far interior

Acknowledgements & Bibliography

First of all I would like to thank all the contemporary poets who cooperated in this project and gladly gave me permission to use illustrative quotations from their work. I would also like to thank Fleur Adcock, Bill Costley, Robert Crozier, Catherine Froud, Hayden Murphy, Trevor Royle and Meic Stephens for lending me books and/or suggesting authors for inclusion. In preparing the text I found the books in the following list helpful and have pleasure in warmly recommending them.

Adcock, Fleur (ed) *The Oxford Book of Contemporary New Zealand Poetry* (Auckland: Oxford University Press 1982)

Beier, Ulli and Moore, Gerald (eds) *The Penguin Book of Modern African Poetry* (Harmondsworth: Penguin Books 1963, 1984)

Bernikow, Louise (ed) *The World Split Open: Four Centuries of Women Poets in England and America 1552–1950* (London: the Women's Press 1979)

Bold, Alan (ed) *Cambridge Book of English Verse 1939–75* (Cambridge: Cambridge University Press 1976)

Bold, Alan *Modern Scottish Literature* (Harlow: Longman 1983)

Bradbury, Malcolm and Mottram, Eric (eds) *The Penguin Companion to Literature 3: USA* (Harmondsworth: Penguin Books 1971)

Browning, D C (ed) *Everyman's Dictionary of Literary Biography* (London: Pan Books 1972)

Carruth, Gorton and Ehrlich, Eugene *The Oxford Illustrated Literary guide to the United States* (New York: Oxford University Press 1982)

Chapman, Abraham (ed) *Black Voices* (New York: Mentor 1968)

Daiches, David (ed) *The Penguin Companion to Literature 1: Britain and the Commonwealth* (Harmondsworth: Penguin Books 1971)

Dale-Jones, Don and Jenkins, Randal (eds) *Twelve Modern Anglo-Welsh Poets* (London: University of London Press 1975)

Dawe, Gerald (ed) *The Younger Irish Poets* (Belfast: Blackstaff Press 1982)

Fiacc, Padraic (ed) *The Wearing of the Black: An anthology of contemporary Ulster poetry* (Belfast: Blackstaff Press 1974)

Gardner, Helen (ed) *The New Oxford Book of English Verse 1250–1950* (Oxford: Clarendon Press 1972)

Garlick, Raymond and Mathias, Roland (ed) *Anglo-Welsh Poetry 1480–1980* (Bridgend: Poetry Wales Press 1984)

Gustafson, Ralph (ed) *The Penguin Book of Canadian Verse* (Harmondsworth: Penguin Books 1958,1984)

Hall, Donald (ed) *Contemporary American Poetry* (Harmondsworth: Penguin Books 1962, 1972)

Heseltine, Harry (ed) *The Penguin Book of Australian Verse* (Harmondsworth: Penguin Books 1972)

Johnson, James Weldon (ed) *The Book of American Negro Poetry* (New York: Harcourt, Brace and World 1931)

Kennelly, Brendan *The Penguin Book of Irish Verse* Harmondsworth: Penguin Books 1970, 1981)

MacBeth, George (ed) *The Penguin Book of Victorian Verse* (Harmondsworth: Penguin Books 1969)

MacQueen, John and Scott, Tom (eds) *The Oxford Book of Scottish Verse* (Oxford: Oxford University Press 1966)

Mahon, Derek (ed) *The Sphere Book of Modern Irish Poetry* (London: Sphere Books 1972)

Moore, Geoffrey (ed) *The Penguin Book of American Verse* (Harmondsworth: Penguin Books 1977, 1983)

Morrison, Blake and Motion, Andrew (eds) *The Penguin Book of Contemporary British Poetry* (Harmondsworth: Penguin Books 1982)

O'Sullivan, Vincent (ed) *An Anthology of New Zealand Poetry* (Oxford: Oxford University Press 1970)

Royle, Trevor *The Macmillan Companion to Scottish Literature* (London: Macmillan 1983)

Turner, Michael R (ed) *Parlour Poetry* (London: Michael Joseph 1967)

Untermeyer, Louis (ed) *An Anthology of the New England Poets from Colonial Times to the Present Day* (New York: Random House 1948)

Welch, Robert *Irish Poetry from Moore to Yeats* (Gerrards Cross: Colin Smythe 1980)

Abse, Dannie

Welsh poet *born* Cardiff 22 September 1923

Brought up in a family of doctors, Dannie Abse qualified in 1950 and has practised as a chest physician in London. In his work he brings together his twin passion for medicine and poetry; his deeply emotional concern for life's casualties is expressed in precisely crafted verse. He is an exceptionally intelligent poet and 'Pathology of Colours' is characteristically contemplative; 'I know the colour rose, and it is lovely, / but not when it ripens in a tumour; / and healing greens, leaves and grass, so springlike, / in limbs that fester are not springlike.' Abse is also a fine prose stylist whose autobiography, *A Poet in the Family* (1974), is illuminating.

Acorn, Milton

Canadian poet *born* Charlottetown, Prince Edward Island 1923

After his military service in the Second World War, Milton Acorn worked as a carpenter. He then decided to abandon his trade to concentrate on writing poetry full time. He was given the Governor General's Award for poetry in 1975; in 1983 he published his selected poems under the title *Dig Up My Heart*. His imagination is always open to everyday experience and in 'Knowing I Live in a Dark Age' he describes his poems as follows: 'they show / pale bayonets of grass waving thin on dunes; / the paralytic and his lyric secrets; / my friend Al, union builder and cynic, / hesitating to believe his own delicate poems / lest he believe in something better than himself.'

Adams, Arthur Henry

New Zealand poet *born* Lawrence 6 June 1872 *died* 4 March 1936

Adams was educated at Otago High School and University before becoming a journalist in Sydney in 1898. He was in South Africa during the Boer War, covering the action as a special correspondent. For much of his life he worked in Australia, producing novels and plays as well as poems. From his collection *Maoriland* (1899) comes his 'The Dwellings of our Dead' in which he catalogues the graves of humankind: 'For some the common trench where, not all fameless, / They fighting fell who thought to tame the tameless, / And won their barren crown; / Where one grave holds them nameless – / Brave white and braver brown.'

Adams, Francis Lauderdale
Scottish poet *born* Malta 27 September 1862
died 4 September 1893

Son of a Scottish scientist, Adams was educated at a private school in Shrewsbury and in Paris. After working as a schoolteacher in England, he went to Australia and joined the staff of the *Sydney Bulletin* which published many of his poems. Suffering from an incurable lung disease, he committed suicide. He published *Leicester* (1884), an autobiographical novel, and *Australian Essays* (1886). His finest poems appear in *Songs of the Army of the Night* (1888) which includes 'To the Christians': 'Take, then, your paltry Christ, / Your gentleman God. / We want the carpenter's son, / With his saw and hod. / We want the man who loved / The poor and oppressed, / Who hated the rich man and king / And the scribe and priest.'

Adams, Léonie
American poet *born* New York 9 December 1899

Educated at Barnard College, Léonie Adams published her first book, *Those Not Elect*, in 1925. Her third collection, *Poems*, appeared in 1954. She was elected to the Chair of Poetry at the Library of Congress and to membership of the National Institute of Arts and Letters. In 1955 she was (with Louise Bogan) awarded the Bollingen Prize. She taught at various universities and was on the creative writing staff of Columbia University. Her work is romantic in mood and vividly descriptive, as in 'Grapes Making': 'Noon sun beats down the leaf; the noon / Of summer burns along the vine / And thins the leaf with burning air, / Till from the underleaf is fanned, / And down the woven vine, the light.'

Adcock, Fleur
New Zealand poet *born* Papakura, near Auckland
10 February 1934

A classics graduate of the University of Wellington, Adcock has lived in England since 1963 and her poetry suggests a highly emotional exile: 'Letter to Alistair Campbell', for example, cites a friendship comprising 'five years of marriage, twenty of divorce'. Her poems recall distressing experiences and record disturbing dreams. Though thematically sombre, she is stylistically bright as in 'Send-Off': 'Half an hour before my flight was called / he walked across the airport bar towards me / carrying what was left of our future / together: two drinks on a tray.' Adcock's poetry is not entirely autobiographical for she is adept at inventing entertainingly odd situations.

Aiken, Conrad Potter
American poet *born* Savannah, Georgia 5 August 1899 *died* 1973

When Aiken was eleven his father – a doctor interested in the arts – killed the poet's mother, then committed suicide. As Aiken acknowledged, this traumatic event haunted him for the rest of his life. Taken to live with relatives, Aiken attended Harvard where his contemporary was T S Eliot. After producing some derivative volumes Aiken came into his own with *Preludes for Mennon* (1931) in which he considers, majestically, the destruction of innocence by the inevitability of death. His poem 'Obituary in Bitcherell' recreates his obsessive nightmare: 'And the morning quarrel, and shots, and then / four orphaned children taken north again.'

Alabaster, William
English poet *born* 1567 *died* 1640

Educated at Trinity College, Cambridge, where he became a Fellow, Alabaster was chaplain to the Earl of Essex on the Cadiz Expedition of 1596. Returning to England, he acknowledged his conversion to Catholicism and wrote his divine sonnets in prison. He subsequently went to Rome where his attitude offended the Inquisition; when he came back to England he returned to the Protestant fold then married and became a country parson. In his later years he published his theological conclusions in cabbalistic works. His sonnet 'Upon the Ensignes of Christes Crucifyinge' states: 'My tongue shall be my pen, mine eyes shall rain / Tears for my ink, the cross where I was cured / Shall be my book.'

Aldington, Richard
English poet *born* Hampshire 8 July 1892 *died* 27 July 1962

Educated at the University of London, Aldington was drawn to the Imagist idiom and in 1913 married the American Imagist Hilda Doolittle (the couple being divorced in 1937). During the First World War he served on the Western Front and was gassed. His poem 'Bombardment' vividly recalls the combative conditions he endured: 'Four days the earth was rent and torn /By bursting steel, / The houses fell about us; / three nights we dared not sleep, / Sweating, and listening for the imminent crash / Which meant our death.' He never fully recovered from the trauma of war and eventually abandoned poetry for prose protesting against the military mentality.

Aldrich, Thomas Bailey
American poet *born* Portsmouth, New Hampshire 11 November 1836 *died* Boston, Massachusetts 19 March 1907

Aldrich, thirteen when his father died, took a job as a clerk in his uncle's office in New York. He was nineteen when he published his first collection *The Bells*, and twenty when he was appointed editor of the *Home Journal*; subsequently he edited the *Atlantic Monthly* (1881–90). He abandoned his editorial career to devote himself to creative writing, publishing *The Story of a Bad Boy* in 1870. In short poems, for example 'Maple Leaves', he uses images effectively: 'October turned my maple's leaves to gold; / The most are gone now; here and there one lingers. / Soon these will slip from out the twig's weak hold, / Like coins between a dying miser's fingers.'

Alexander, Sir William

Scottish poet *born* Menstrie, Logie, Clackmannanshire *c*1567
died London 12 September 1640

After the death of his father, Alexander was raised by his greatuncle in Stirling. Educated at the universities of Glasgow and Leiden he became a tutor of the Earl of Argyle who introduced him to the court of James VI. He was Prince Henry's tutor and one of the Castalian Band of poets patronised by the King. He was knighted in 1609 and in 1621 obtained the plantation of Nova Scotia. He became Secretary of State for Scotland in 1626 and Earl of Stirling in 1633. *Aurora* (1604) contains his sonnets, number 26 beginning: 'Cleare moving cristall, pure as the Sunne beames, / Which had the honor for to be the glasse, / Of the most daintie beautie ever was.'

Allingham, William

Irish poet *born* Ballyshannon, Donegal 19 March 1824
died 18 November 1889

Son of a banker, Allingham moved to London where he met Leigh Hunt and Carlyle and published several collections, culminating in *Collected Poems* (6 vols, 1888–93). After retiring from the civil service in 1870 he worked on *Fraser's Magazine*, succeeding Froude as editor in 1874. His wife was the watercolourist Helen Paterson and he was friendly with the Pre-Raphaelites. 'The Winding Banks of Erne' is his farewell to his birthplace; 'Adieu to Ballyshannon! where I was bred and born / Go where I may, I'll think of you, as sure as night and morn, / The kindly spot, the friendly town, where everyone is known, / And not a face in all the place but partly seems my own.'

Alvarez, A

English poet *born* London 5 August 1929

Educated at Oxford, Alvarez became an influential literary critic, contributing to the *Observer* and *New Statesman*. His anthology *The New Poetry* (1962) demonstrated his faith in Confessional poetry and he was the leading English advocate of the late work of Sylvia Plath and the psychologically brittle poetry of Robert Lowell. *The*

Savage God (1971) is a study of suicide which concludes with the author's recollection of his own attempted suicide, an experience that informs 'Back': 'I recall / Nothing of death but the puzzled look on your face, / Swimming towards me, weeping, clouded, uncertain, / As they took the tube from my arm / And plugged the strange world back in place.'

Amabile, George
Canadian poet *born* New Jersey 1936

Founding editor of *The Far Point* and *Northern Light*, George Amabile was educated at the universities of Minnesota and Connecticut. His collection *The Presence of Fire* appeared in 1982. Like many of the Canadian poets, he is fascinated by the appearance of a landscape uncontaminated by urban artefacts. 'Prairie' lyrically explores the implications of the title: 'a light word / filled with wistful spokes / of sun through the overcast at dusk / or smoke totems bent at the top / wisping away into beige emulsions // an earth word / a moist darkness turning / stones and roots / fossils and tiny lives / up to the sun.'

Amis, Kingsley
English poet *born* Clapham 16 April 1922

Educated at Oxford, with his contemporary Philip Larkin, Kingsley Amis was a university teacher of English until 1963. His novel *Lucky Jim* (1954), a spectacular success, established him as a witty enemy of pomposity. His poetry shows similar qualities of clarity and control and he has emerged as one of the best modern exponents of light verse. Using traditional rhythms and rhymes, Amis has produced a series of sharp verse commentaries on the shabbiness of the modern world. His sardonic sense of humour is well expressed in 'Delivery Guaranteed': 'Death has got something to be said for it: / There's no need to get out of bed for it; / Wherever you may be, / They bring it to you, free.'

Ammons, A R
American poet *born* Whiteville, North Carolina 1926

Ammons was a businessman before he became a lecturer at Cornell University. He published several volumes of verse including *Selected Poems* (1971) and *Six-Piece Suite* (1979). His highly subjective accounts of his experience project him as an individual confronting the elements of the natural world. 'Corsons Inlet' begins with a morning walk by the sea then reaches out to a conclusion about the nature of poetic perception: 'I will try / to fasten into order enlarging grasps of disorder, widening / scope, but enjoying the freedom that / Scope

eludes my grasp, that there is no finality of vision, / that I have
perceived nothing completely, / that tomorrow a new walk is a
new walk.'

Anderson, Patrick

Canadian poet *born* England 1915 *died* 1979

Educated at Oxford and Columbia, Anderson came to Montreal
in 1940 and earned his living by teaching. A member of the
'Preview' group of Montreal writers, he published his selected
poems, under the title *Return to Canada*, in 1977. His long 'Poem
on Canada' brings a strong social concern to bear on the
landscape of Canada which older poets had applauded
uncritically: 'Mine are the violet tones of the logs in rivers, / my
tallness is the tallness of the pines and the grain elevators /tubular
by the scarps of coal, at Quebec. / My caves are the caves of ice
but also the holes of Cartier / where the poor squat, numb with
winter, / and my poverty is their rags and the prairies' drought.'

Andrew of Wyntoun

Scottish poet *born c*1355 *died* 1422

Andrew of Wyntoun was canon regular at St Andrews and from
1395-1413 was Prior of St Serfs Inch, the island on Lochleven
(where Mary Queen of Scots was imprisoned in 1567). For his
patron, Sir John Wemyss, he composed the *Orygynale Cronykil of
Scotland* (published 1795), a verse history from the Creation to the
reign of Robert the Bruce. Written in octosyllabic couplets, in
nine books, it comments on such characters as Macbeth: 'In till
this tyme that I of tell, / That this tressoune in Ingland fell, / In
Scotland fell neire the like cais / Be Fynlaw Makbeth that than
was, / Quhen he had murtherist his aune eme / Throu hope at he
had of a dreme.'

eme uncle; *at* that

Arnold, Sir Edwin

English poet *born* Gravesend 10 June 1832 *died* 24 March 1904

Son of a Sussex magistrate, Arnold was educated at Oxford where
he won the Newdigate Prize for 'The Feast of Belshazzar'. He
became a teacher at King Edward's School, Birmingham and was,
in 1856, appointed Principal of the Government Deccan College,
Poona. Returning to England in 1861, he worked for, and
eventually edited, the *Daily Telegraph*. His experience of the East
led him to write *The Light of Asia* (1891), a poem on the life of
Buddha: 'So saying the good Lord Buddha seated him / Under a
jambu-tree, with ankles crossed – / As holy statues sit – and first

began / To meditate this deep disease of life, / What its far source
and whence its remedy.' He also wrote *The Light of the World*
(1891), a poem about Christ.

Arnold, Matthew
English poet   *born* Laleham-on-Thames 24 December 1822
died Liverpool 15 April 1888

From his father, the famous headmaster of Rugby School,
Matthew Arnold acquired a reverence for learning and his
intellectual clarity made him one of the ablest critics of the
century, as witness *Culture and Anarchy* (1869). Believing that
poetry should be a 'criticism of life', and that the man of letters
should spread 'sweetness and light', he wrote poems that were
both shrewd and sensitive. 'Thyrsis', a monody in memoriam
Arthur Hugh Clough, commemorates a friendship in Oxford,
'that sweet city with her dreaming spires'. 'Dover Beach' is a more
direct statement of his sense of isolation in a faithless world
'Swept with confused alarms of struggle and flight, / Where
ignorant armies clash by night.'

Ashbery, John
American poet   *born* New York 28 July 1927

Ashbery has been active as an art critic, as editor (of *Art News*), as
a dramatist and as one of America's most distinguished poets. The
technical polish of his poetry presents disturbing incidents in an
artistically acceptable way. The title poem of his collection *A
Wave* (1984) is a successful attempt to write a triumphant
refutation of the idea of death as a defeat. With its references to
'a man and his wife' and 'Our story', the poem is a remarkably
objective account of a relationship that has ended abruptly. In
stressing the importance of survival, Ashbery insists 'Much that
has drained out of living / Returns, in those moments, mounting
the little capillaries / Of polite questions and seeming concern. I
want it back.'

Asquith, Herbert
English poet   *born* 1881   *died* 1947

Son of the Liberal Prime Minister replaced by Lloyd George in
1916, Herbert Asquith was associated with the Georgian
movement in poetry. A friend of Rupert Brooke's, he served with
the artillery on the Western Front during the First World War
and wrote romantically of those who died in action. 'The
Volunteer' is a tribute to a clerk killed in battle: 'he lies content /
With that high hour, in which he lived and died. / And falling thus
he wants no recompense, / Who found his battle on the last

7

resort; / Nor needs he any hearse to bear him hence, / Who goes to join the men of Agincourt.'

Atherstone, Edwin
English poet *born* Nottingham 17 April 1788
died Bath 29 January 1872

A dramatist and novelist as well as an epic poet, Atherstone published 'The Last Days of Herculaneum' in 1821. It tells, in blank verse, of the destruction of the city by the eruption of Mount Vesuvius in AD 79: 'Soon the storm / Burst forth: the lightnings glanced: – the air / Shook with the thunders. They awoke: – they sprung / Amazed upon their feet. The dungeon glowed / A moment as in sunshine, – and was dark: – / Again a flood of white flame fills the cell'. Atherstone's main work, *The Fall of Nineveh*, appeared in thirty books from 1828–68. He also wrote *The Sea Kings of England* (1830), an historical romance; and *The Handwriting on the Wall*(1858), a prose account of the fall of Babylon.

Atwood, Margaret
Canadian poet *born* Ottawa 18 November 1939

Internationally known as a novelist with books like *Life Before Man* (1979), Margaret Atwood has also written *Survival: a Thematic guide to Canadian Literature* (1972). Her first collection of poems, *The Circle Game* (1966), won the Governor General's Award for Poetry. Her *Selected Poems* came out in 1976. Her poems luxuriate in lyricism and she takes a highly subjective approach to experience. Her 'Variation on the Word *Sleep*' is a tender expression of love: 'I would like to follow / you up the long stairway / again and become / the boat that would row you back / carefully, a flame / in two cupped hands / to where your body lies / beside me, and you enter / it as easily as breathing in'.

Auden, W H
English poet *born* York 21 February 1907
died Vienna 29 September 1973

A doctor's son, Wystan Hughes Auden was educated at Oxford where he met Spender, Day Lewis and MacNeice – who all adhered to the Leftist principles Auden expounded in the 1930s – and renewed his friendship with Christoper Isherwood with whom he collaborated on three verse plays including *The Ascent of F6* (1936). Auden's return to Christian ideals is expressed in *New Year Letter* (1941): 'We can love each because we know / All, all of us, that this is so: / Can live since we are lived, the powers / That we create with are not ours.' In later years he lived in Austria, wrote poems in praise of his domestic life with Chester Kallman

(*About the House*, 1966) and continued to pursue his vision of the
Just City.

Austin, Alfred
English poet   *born* Headingley, near Leeds 30 May 1835
died 2 June 1913

A wool–stapler's son, Austin was educated at Stonyhurst and
Oscott College and was called to the Bar in 1857. He switched
from law to literature, reporting for the *Standard* and editing the
National Review. He was appointed Poet Laureate in 1896 in
recognition of his deeply traditional views. In poems such as 'The
Last Night' he combines his conservatism with his love of rural
England: 'O, Winnie, I do not want to go / From the dear old
home; I love it so. / Why should I follow the sad sea-mew / To a
land where everything is new, / Where we never bird-nested, you
and I, / Where I was not born, but perhaps shall die?' He also
wrote novels and an *Autobiography* (1911).

Avison, Margaret
Canadian poet   *born* Galt, Ontario 1918

After an education at the University of Toronto, Margaret Avison
earned her living as a secretary and librarian. Her collection
Sunblue appeared in 1978. She is a poet who finds herself
fascinated by the extraordinary appearance of everyday events,
like 'Janitor Working on Threshold' (to cite one of her titles).
'Tennis' is an ingenious sonnet that combines the athletic and the
aesthetic: 'Purpose apart, perched like an umpire, dozes, /Dreams
golden balls whirring through indigo. / Clay blurs the whitewash
but day still encloses / The albinos, bonded in their flick and
flow. / Playing in musicked gravity, the pair / Score liquid Euclids
in foolscaps of air.'

Aytoun, Sir Robert
Scottish poet   *born* Kinaldie, near St Andrews 1570
died London February 1638

Educated at St Andrews University, Aytoun studied law in Paris.
He went, with the court of James VI and I, to London and became
secretary to the Queen. He was knighted in 1612. A brilliant
linguist, he wrote poems in Latin, Greek and French and was one
of the first Scottish poets to write in English – under the influence
of the Metaphysical poets. His sonnet 'Upone Tabacco' begins:
'Forsaken of all comforts but these two, / My faggott and my
Pipe, I sitt and Muse / On all my crosses, and almost accuse / The
heavens for dealing with me as they doe.' He wrote a poem 'Old
Long Syne' which was later reworked by Burns with international
success.

Aytoun, W E

Scottish poet *born* Edinburgh 21 June 1813
died Edinburgh 4 August 1865

Although he aspired to write heroic poems in the manner of
Macaulay – as witness his *Lays of the Scottish Cavaliers* (1849) –
William Edmonstoune Aytoun is best remembered for his
humorous verse. He was a lawyer who contributed regularly to
Blackwood's Magazine; a Scottish nationalist who played a leading
part in the Association for the Vindication of Scottish Rights
(1853). As his poem on 'The Scottish Christmas' shows, he was an
enemy of Calvinistic grimness. His own irreverent attitude is seen
to advantage in his light verse on Scottish subjects, such as 'The
Massacre of the Macpherson'; 'For he did resolve / To extirpate
the vipers, / With four-and-twenty men / And five-and-thirty
pipers.'

Baldwin, James

American poet *born* Harlem, New York 1924

As a novelist James Baldwin explores the human predicament of
the black citizens of America. As a polemicist he has articulated
the anger of American blacks in powerful works such as *The Fire
Next Time* (1963). His poetry, like his prose, alternates between
savagery and well organised black humour. 'Staggerlee wonders',
for example, addresses a US president ironically: 'Oh, towering
Ronnie Reagan, / wise and resigned lover of redwoods, / deeply
beloved, winning man-child of the yearning Republic, / from
diaper to football field to Warner Brothers sound-stages, / be
thou our grinning, gently phallic, Big Boy of all the ages!'

Baldwin, Michael

English poet *born* 1 May 1930

Baldwin has worked in radio and television as a broadcaster and
presenter. His sequence *King Horn* (1983) was written, at
Montolieu in old Languedoc, during a period of convalescence,
when Baldwin was sensitive to the sights and sounds of the area.
Regarding the local peasants as a crude 'unforgiving people' he
turned to the flora and fauna and produced poems that bring the
landscape to life vibrantly. In the first poem there is a glimpse of
'a whole crop of vipers / With others in their belly'; thereafter he
contemplates the special creatures (including the peasants) of the
area in poems that constantly put language under poetic pressure.

Baraka, Imamu Amiri

American poet *born* Newark, New Jersey 7 October 1934

The poet was born LeRoi Jones and served in the Air Force from

1954–7. He scored a great success with his off-Broadway play *Dutchman* (1964) and was widely regarded as an explosive new literary talent. In 1968 he was arrested, in Newark, on a charge of illegally possessing a gun and he has increasingly taken a black militant stand against the authorities. His change of name spells out his rejection of white American culture. He is a sharp, witty writer capable of making a political point in a poetic way, as in 'A guerilla handbook': 'We must convince the living / that the dead / cannot sing.' Baraka has encouraged black community theatre and is an artistic as well as a political activist.

Barbour, John
Scottish poet *born* Aberdeen *c*1320 *died* Aberdeen 13 March 1395

Archdeacon of Aberdeen, Barbour extended his education at Oxford and in Paris. He was made a member of the Scottish royal household by Robert II, founder of the Stewart dynasty. In honour of his grandfather Robert the Bruce, Robert II commissioned Barbour to write *The Bruce* a narrative poem in octosyllabic couplets comprising twenty books and 13,550 lines. In celebrating a Scottish hero Barbour expressed, in powerful vernacular verse, the notion of independence, as in the celebrated lines on freedom: 'A! Freedom is a noble thing! / Freedom makis man to have liking; / Freedom all solace to man givis: / He livis at ease that freely livis!'

Barham, Richard Harris
English poet *born* Canterbury 6 December 1788
died 17 June 1845

A country gentleman's son, Barham was educated at Oxford and took holy orders; he was Divinity Lecturer and minor canon of St Paul's. He originally contributed *The Ingoldsby Legends* to *Bentley's Miscellany* before they were collected in three series (1840–7). These hugely popular humorous narratives included the tale of 'The Jackdaw of Rheims' who took the Lord Cardinal's ring with surprising consequences, for when he died 'The Conclave determined to make him a Saint; / And on newly-made Saints and Popes, as you know, / It's the custom, at Rome, new names to bestow, / So they canonised him by the name of Jim Crow!' Barham also contributed a novel, *My Cousin Nicholas*, to *Blackwood's Magazine*.

Barham, R H Dalton
English poet *born* Westwell, Kent October 1815
died Dawlish 28 April 1886

Son of R H Barham, author of *The Ingoldsby Legends*, Richard Harris Dalton Barham was educated at St Paul's School and Oxford. Like his father he took holy orders, and was presented with the living of Lolworth, near Cambridge, where he remained until 1863. Subsequently he pursued his geological interests in Dawlish. He published the *Life and Remains* (1849) of Theodore Hook and the *Life and Letters* (1870) of his father. He also contributed humorous verse to *Bentley's Magazine*. 'The Temptations of St Anthony' is typical: 'St Anthony sat on a lowly stool, / And a book was in his hand; / Never his eye from its page he took, / Either to right or left to look'.

Barker, George
English poet *born* Loughton, Essex 26 February 1913

Educated in London, Barker was Professor of English Literature at the Imperial Tohuku University in 1939 and from 1940–3 lived in the USA. During the 1930s he was known as a leading English surrealist but his prolific output has shown him in command of various modes from the lyrical to the didactic. Fundamentally romantic by temperament, Barker has composed many moving love poems. His sonnet 'To My Mother' reveals his compassion for a woman 'Sitting as huge as Asia, seismic with laughter, / Gin and chicken helpless in her Irish hand, / Irresistible as Rabelais, but most tender for / The lame dogs and hurt birds that surround her.'

Barlow, Joel
American poet *born* Reading, Connecticut 1754
died near Cracow, Poland 22 December 1812

A farmer's son, Barlow was educated at Dartmouth College and Yale where he was one of the Connecticut Wits. Radical by inclination, he worked as a lawyer and bookseller as well as writing poetry. For some time he lived in France where he was made a citizen in recognition of his support of the Revolution. Barlow became President Monroe's minister to France and was with Napoleon during the retreat from Russia; he died of a fever as a result of the conditions in the rout. His address to 'Freedom' embodies his enthusiasm: 'Sun of the moral world; effulgent source / Of man's best wisdom and his steadiest force, / Soul-searching Freedom! here assume thy stand, / And radiate hence to every distant land'.

Barnes, William
English poet *born* Rushley, Dorset 20 March 1801
died Came, Dorset 7 October 1886

A farmer's son, Barnes married Julia Mills in 1827 and took orders at Cambridge in 1838. He was rector of Came, Dorset, from 1862. Devoted to his region and determined to 're-saxonise' the English language he used the Dorset dialect in his *Poems of Rural Life* (1844, 1859, 1863). When the poet's wife died in 1852 he was overwhelmed by grief and wrote a series of poems in her memory. 'The Wife A-Lost' is particularly poignant: 'Since you noo mwore be at my zide, / In walks in zummer het, / I'll goo alwone where mist do ride, / Drough trees a-drippen wet; / Below the rain-wet bough, my love, / Where you did never come, / An' I don't grieve to miss ye now, / As I do grieve at hwome.'

Barnfield, Richard
English poet *baptised* 13 June 1574 *buried* 6 March 1627

Educated at Oxford, Barnfield was greatly influenced by the poetry of Shakespeare, his acknowledged master. His *The Affectionate Shepherd* (1594) is clearly inspired by Shakespeare's *Venus and Adonis*; his sonnets are thematically, as well as stylistically, indebted to Shakespeare; and in *The Encomium of Lady Pecunia* (1598) he included lines on the genius of Shakespeare. Barnfield's most distinctive poem is a contemplative lyric on the song of the nightingale. It begins: 'As it fell upon a day / In the merry month of May, / Sitting in a pleasant shade / Which a grove of myrtles made, / Beasts did leap and birds did sing, / Trees did grow and plants did spring'.

Baughan, Blanche Edith
New Zealand poet *born* Putney, Surrey 1870
died Akaroa 20 August 1958

Daughter of a London stockbroker, Blanche Edith Baughan was educated at London University. In London she joined the Suffragette movement and worked with the poor of the East End. She went to New Zealand around 1900 and became an active penal reformer. In 1924 she formed a Christchurch branch of the Howard League and in 1928 formed the New Zealand Howard League for Penal Reform. Her book *People in Prison* was published anonymously in 1936. She also worked on behalf of the handicapped. Her poem 'The Old Place', a dramatic monologue, describes New Zealand thus: 'Oh, it's a bad old place! Blown out o' your bed half the nights, / And in summer the grass burnt shiny an' bare as your hand, on the heights'.

Baxter, James K
New Zealand poet *born* Dunedin 1926 *died* 1972

Educated at the universities of Otago and Victoria, Baxter spent most of his life in Dunedin and Wellington. In 1969 his horror of materialism persuaded him to set himself up as a Christian sage in his community at Jerusalem on the Wanganui River. An enormously productive writer, his stylistic range is impressive. His ballad 'Lament for Barney Flanagan' shows his command of a popular idiom: 'Barney Flanagan, sprung like a frog / From a wet root in an Irish bog – / May his soul escape from the tooth of the

dog! / God have mercy on Flanagan.' His *Jerusalem Sonnets*
(1970) are quietest by comparison: 'As the cross is lifted and the
day goes dark / Rule over myself He has taken away from me.'

Bayly, Thomas Haynes
English poet *born* Bath 13 October 1797 *died* 22 April 1839

A lawyer's son, educated at Oxford, Bayly was a prolific writer
from an early age. He contemplated a career in the church and as
a lawyer but eventually turned to writing plays and lyrics (and
sometimes the music for these lyrics). His income from his
literary work was supplemented by his wife's dowry. One of his
best-known lyrics, 'Oh, No! We Never Mention Her', has dated
though the second stanza retains its charm: 'They bid me seek in
change of scene the charms that other see; / But were I in a
foreign land, they'd find no change in me. / 'Tis true that I behold
no more the valley where we met, / I do not see the hawthorn-
tree; but how can I forget?'

Beardsley, Doug
Canadian poet *born* Montreal 1941

A design and editing service partner in Victoria, British
Columbia, Beardsley was educated at the universities of Victoria
and York, Toronto. His collection *Kissing the Body of My Lord* came
out in 1982. His viewpoint is that of an individual who turns from
the city to study the natural life that gathers in his garden.
'Birdbath' observes that 'Sometimes you can't see the trees for
birds' while 'Natural Selection' contemplates the phenomenon of
fruition: 'For nine weeks now I've watched them / Grow to
perfection in the sun. / I've seen sights too incredible to tell, / I've
been through the whole harrowing thing, / From bud to blossom,
through flower, / To green pellet no bigger than your thumb.'

Beattie, James
Scottish poet *born* Laurencekirk, Kincardineshire 25 October
1735 *died* Aberdeen 18 August 1803

A shopkeeper's son, Beattie was educated at Aberdeen University
and returned there as Professor of Moral Philosophy (1760-90).
His attempted philosophical refutation of David Hume, *Essay on
Truth* (1770), was widely read and he also wrote *The Evidences of the
Christian Religion Briefly and plainly Stated* (1786). Though he
published, in 1779, a list of 'Scotticisms' to be avoided, his best
work is in Scots. 'To Mr Alexander Ross', indeed, enthuses over
the Scottish tradition: 'The Southland chiels indeed hae mettle, /
And brawley at a sang can ettle, / Yet we right couthily might

settle / O' this side Forth. / The devil pay them wi' a pettle / That slight the North.'

chiels fellows; *ettle* attempt; *couthily* cosily; *pettle* plough-staff; *brawley* excellently

Beaumont, Joseph
English poet *born* Hadleigh, Suffolk 13 March 1616
died 25 September 1699

Son of a clothier, Beaumont was educated at Peterhouse, Cambridge, where he became a Fellow. He was ejected in 1644 as a Royalist and returned to Hadleigh where he composed *Psyche* (1648), an immense epic of 30,000 lines. After the Restoration he became Master of Jesus College in 1662 and Master of Peterhouse in 1663. He was appointed Professor of Divinity in 1674. *Psyche* makes great demands on the reader's stamina but Beaumont has excellent moments such as his description of Paradise: 'Within, rose hills of spice and frankincense, / Which smiled upon the flowery vales below, / Where living crystal found a sweet pretence / With musical impatience to flow'.

Beckett, Samuel
Irish poet *born* Dublin 13 April 1906

One of the great stylists of the century, Beckett worked for a time as James Joyce's secretary and applied Joyce's linguistic experiments to the drama. His *Waiting for Godot* (1954) is recognised as a modern classic and in 1969 Beckett's eminence was confirmed by the award of the Nobel Prize for Literature. Since 1932 he has lived mainly in Paris and writes in both French and English. His vision of life is bleak and in poems such as 'What Would I Do', as well as in novels and plays, he stresses the isolation of the individual: 'what would I do what I did yesterday and the day before / peering out of my deadlight looking for another / wandering like me eddying far from all the living'.

Beddoes, Thomas Lovell
English poet *born* Clifton, Somerset 30 June 1803
died Basle 26 January 1849

A nephew of novelist Maria Edgeworth, Beddoes – son of a doctor – studied medicine in Germany where he also absorbed German literature. Ambitious to revive the Elizabethan mode of drama he wrote *The Bride's Tragedy* (1822). After a quarrel with his friend Degen, a Swiss baker, Beddoes dramatically cut an artery in his leg; as a result he suffered amputation. His next suicide attempt, using poison, was successful. His morbid outlook is expressed in his Gothic tragedy, *Death's Jest Book* (1850) which contains fine lyrics: 'a storm of ghosts shall shake / The dead, until they wake / In the grave'.

Beers, Ethel Lynn
American poet *born* Goshen, New York 13 January 1827
died 11 October 1879

A desceundant of the Indian missionary John Eliot, Ethel Lynn
Eliot was the daughter of a druggist. She married W H Beers in
1846 and in 1861 published her Civil War poem 'The Picket
Guard' in *Harper's Magazine*. The poem expresses sympathy for
the unsung casualties of war: '"All quiet along the Potomac,"
they say, / "Except now and then a stray picket / Is shot, as he
walks on his beat to and fro, / By a rifleman hid in the thicket. /
'Tis nothing – a private or two now and then / Will not count in
the news of the battle; / Not an officer lost – only one of the
men, /Moaning out, all alone, the death-rattle."' The author's
Collected Poems were published the day before she died.

Behn, Aphra
English poet *born c*1640 *died* London 16 April 1689

Possibly an illegitimate child, the details of Aphra Behn's early
life are obscure but she embarked on a spectacular career. She
went to Antwerp in 1666 to spy for Charles II, she was imprisoned
for debt in 1668, she became the first English woman to support
herself by writing, and she was buried in Westminster Abbey. Her
prose romances helped establish the novel form and as a poet she
put her feminist point of view forward. Her lines 'To Alexis'
consider men ironically: 'They fly if honour take our part, / Our
virtue drives 'em o'er the field. / We lose 'em by too much
desert, / And Oh! they fly us if we yield.'

Belloc, Hilaire
English poet *born* Paris 27 July 1870 *died* 16 July 1953

A barrister's son, Belloc studied history at Oxford. His first
collection *Verses and Sonnets* appeared in 1895 and was followed by
several volumes of light and nonsense verse. He was Liberal MP
for South Salford from 1906–10; in the First World War he was a
driver with the French artillery. In 1934 he was made Knight
Commander of the Order of Gregory by the Pope. His humorous
poems, such as 'Matilda, Who told Lies, and was Burned to
Death', have touches of black humour. At the end of the poem
Matilda, the girl who cried wolf (or 'Fire!'), is ignored: 'And
therefore when her Aunt returned, / Matilda, and the House,
were burned.'

Benedikt, Michael
American poet *born* 26 May 1935

Benedickt was educated at the universities of New York and
Columbia and subsequently taught at various colleges. In 1975 he
was poet in residence at Boston University and he worked as an

editorial assistant on *Art News*. His interest in surrealism is reflected in such poems as 'The European Shoe' which has its own irrational logic: 'The European Shoe is constructed of grass and reed, bound up and wound around so that it may slip easily over the wearers' head. / In case you are an aircraft pilot, you must take care that the European Shoe does not creep off your foot, and begin to make its way carefully along the fuselage.'

Benét, Stephen Vincent
American poet *born* Bethlehem, Pennsylvania 22 July 1898
died 13 March 1943

Educated at Yale and the Sorbonne, Benét returned to France in 1926 on a Guggenheim Fellowship. While in France he wrote *John Brown's Body*, a long poem on the Civil War, which won him the Pulitzer Prize in 1928. He wrote novels, such as *Spanish Bayonet* (1926) and short stories including 'The Devil and Daniel Webster' (1937) which won the O. Henry Award and was made into a play. His *Selected Works* appeared in 1942. 'A Song of Breath' has the cumulative force of a catalogue: 'The harsh gasp of the runner, / The long sigh of power / Heaving the weight aloft, / The grey breath of the old. / Men at the end of strength / With their lungs turned lead and fire, / Panting like thirsty dogs'.

Bennett, William Cox
English poet *born* Greenwich 14 October 1820 *died* 4 March 1895

A watchmaker's son, Bennett became a businessman who took an active interest in public affairs. He contributed to the *Weekly Dispatch* and the London *Figaro* and published such works as *War Songs* (1855), *Baby May, and other Poems on Infants* (1861) and *Poems* (1862). 'Baby May' retains its period charm: 'Cheeks as soft as July peaches; / Lips whose dewy scarlet teaches / Poppies paleness; round large eyes / Ever great with new surprise. / Minutes fill'd with shadeless gladness, / Minutes just as brimmed with sadness, / Happy smiles and wailing cries, / Crows and laughs and tearful eyes / Lights and shadows swifter born / Than on windswept autumn corn, / Ever some new tiny notion, / Making every limb all motion'.

Berryman, John
American poet *born* McAlester, Oklahoma 25 October 1914
died Minneapolis 7 January 1972

When John Berryman was eleven his father committed suicide, a tragic pattern that was repeated when the poet jumped off the Washington Avenue Bridge over the Mississippi River. Throughout his life Berryman, an idiosyncratic and original writer, suffered from depression and was several times treated for chronic alcoholism. Influenced by the work of his friends Saul

Bellow and Robert Lowell, Berryman created *The Dream Songs* (1969) in which the semi-autobiographical hero, Henry, tries to cope with the world (as in Song 285): 'Henry peered quite alone / as if the world / would answer to a code / just around the corner, down gelid dawn, / beckoning like a moan.'

Bethell, Mary Ursula
New Zealand poet *born* Surrey 1874 *died* 1945

Educated in England, Mary Ursula Bethell was a social worker in London and Scotland from 1898–1902. In 1924 she returned to her girlhood home in New Zealand. Much of her work is inspired by her garden in the Cashmere Hills, Christchurch, which she regarded with a mystical reverence. In 'Trance' she describes her garden thus: 'So still it lay, it suffered an enchantment. / It was the dimly mirrored image of a grove laid up in heaven, / Or the calm mirage of a long–since–lost oasis, / Or the unflickering dream of a serene midnight / Dreamt by one falling into a profound sleep.' Her *Collected Poems* appeared in 1950.

Betjeman, Sir John
English poet *born* London 28 August 1906 *died* Trebetherick, Cornwall 19 May 1984

Appointed Poet Laureate in 1972, Betjeman was one of the most popular poets of his time. His *Collected Poems* of 1958 sold 100,000 copies and he was a successful television pundit, especially on the subject of Victorian architecture. Technically conservative, he relied on regular rhymes and well-worn rhythms. His poems do, however, convey a sense of adventure as Betjeman upholds the values of the English middle-class with gentle irony. His ability to encapsulate a scene in a quatrain is shown in 'A Subaltern's Love-song': 'The Hillman is waiting, the light's in the hall, / The pictures of Egypt are bright on the wall, / My sweet, I am standing beside the oak stair / And there on the landing's the light on your hair.'

Binyon, Laurence
English poet *born* Lancaster 10 August 1869 *died* 10 March 1943

A clergyman's son, Binyon was educated at Oxford and began work at the British Museum in 1893. From 1913 to 1933 he was the Keeper of the Oriental Paintings and Prints. After retiring from the British Museum in 1933, he was for a year Professor of Poetry at Harvard. His poem 'For the Fallen' first appeared in *The Times* of 21 September 1914, two years before Binyon went to the front as a Red Cross orderly. Its elegiac quality made an enormous impact and the fourth stanza is an obligatory part of the popular perception of the First World War: 'They shall not grow old, as we that are left grow old: / Age shall not weary them, nor the years condemn. / At the going down of the sun and in the morning / We will remember them.'

Birney, Earle
Canadian poet *born* Calgary, Alberta 13 May 1904

In his childhood, Birney was confronted with the mountains of Alberta and British Columbia and retained this visionary experience thereafter. He was educated at the University of British Columbia where he became Professor of English in 1946. During the 1930s, Birney responded enthusiastically to socialist ideals and edited the *Canadian Forum* energetically. He was with the Canadian Army during the Second World War and in 1945 published his collection *Now is Time*. His *Collected Poems* appeared in 1975. His poem 'Bushed' shows his verbal panache: 'He invented a rainbow but lightning struck it / shattered it into the lake-lap of a mountain / so big his mind slowed when he looked at it'.

Bishop, Elizabeth
American poet *born* Worcester, Massachusetts
8 February 1911 *died* 1979

Elizabeth Bishop's father died when she was an infant and her mother was taken to a mental institution. Painfully aware of death and defeat she grew up in Nova Scotia and Boston and began to write poems as a schoolgirl before going to Vassar College, New York: 'To a Tree', with its reference to 'tiny tragedies and grotesque grieves', is an extremely assured performance for a girl of sixteen. The mature 'Song' expresses Bishop's feelings of isolation as she measures the distance between herself and others: 'The friends have left, the sea is bare / that was strewn with floating, fresh green weeds.' For Bishop life is a gift that always seems just out of reach.

Bishop, John Peale
American poet *born* Charles Town, West Virginia
21 May 1892 *died* 1944

Educated at Princeton where he was friendly with Edmund Wilson and F Scott Fitzgerald, who used him as the model for D'Invilliers in *This Side of Paradise* (1920), Bishop was a First Lieutenant of Infantry in the First World War. In New York he succeeded Edmund Wilson as managing editor of *Vanity Fair* and worked on the staff of Paramount Pictures. After living at Cape Cod he returned to New York in 1941 as Publications Director of the Office of the Co-ordinator and Inter-American Affairs. He died of heart failure. 'The Hours' has his characteristically grandiose tone: 'I cannot animate with breath / syllables in the open mouth of death.'

Bishop, Samuel

English poet *born* London, 21 September 1731
died 17 November 1795

Bishop, a clergyman and a master of Merchant Tailors' School in London, wrote a volume of Latin verse (*Feriae Poeticae*) and several English poems. His address 'To Mrs Bishop', on giving his wife a knife, has much uxorious enthusiasm: 'The knife, that cuts our love in two, / Will have much tougher work to do; / Must cut your softness, truth, and spirit, / Down to the vulgar size of merit; / To level yours, with modern taste, / Must cut a world of sense to waste; / And from your single beauty's store, / Clip what would dizen out a score.' Another poem to his wife, 'To the Same', cites the present of a ring: 'With this I wed, till death us part, / Thy riper virtues to my heart'.

Bissett, Bill

Canadian poet *born* Halifax Nova Scotia 1939

Bill Bissett (who uses the lowercase style 'bill bissett' when writing) settled in Vancouver and became involved with the Blewointment Press. An experimental poet he published his selected poems, *beyond even faithful legends*, in 1980; and *seagull on yonge street* in 1983. He writes concrete poems as well as socially concerned statements that have a conversational tone: 'as well as not telling peopul thers evn an alert / in vankouver theyve decidid not to advise / heart nd lung patients to stay indoors / during this time evn tho th scale is 11 / points above dangrous bcoz th worry mite / make them wors'

Black, David

Scottish poet *born* Wynberg, South Africa 8 November 1941

Black was educated at the universities of Edinburgh and Lancaster and settled in London to work as a Jungian analyst. His work is impressively inventive, a fluent catalogue of Gothic and surrealistic images. In the 1960s he was recognised as a distinctive voice with his freeflowing fluent verse that turned dreamlike and nightmarish incidents into incisive narratives. His stylish dramatic monologues bring disturbing figures to mind: the Red Judge, the Black Judge, the Hangman. Even a location like 'Leith Docks' (in Edinburgh) is given an eerie atmosphere: 'I / run spinning in the / wet lights, past / morose burghers. An / amazing length, Leith Walk.'

Blacklock, Thomas
Scottish poet *born* Annan, Dumfriesshire 1721 *died* 7 July 1791

A bricklayer's son, Blacklock lost his sight after becoming ill with smallpox at the age of six months. Despite this disability, he was educated at Edinburgh University and was licensed to preach in 1759. Three years later he married a Miss Johnstone of Dumfries. His *A Collection of Original Poems* (1760) revealed competent use of neoclassical conventions. His self-portrait in 'The Author's Picture' is shrewdly observant: 'Self is the grand pursuit of half mankind; / How vast a crowd by self, like me, are blind! / By self the fop in magic colours shown, / Though scorned by every eye, delights his own'. Blacklock was an early champion of Robert Burns.

Blackmore, Sir Richard
English poet *born c* 1650 *died* 8 October 1729

Blackmore graduated from Oxford in June 1676 and practised as a doctor in Padua then London. He was physician-in-ordinary to William III and Queen Anne. His epic poems, such as *King Arthur* (1697), were criticised by several contemporaries including Pope who referred (in the *Dunciad*) to 'Blackmore's endless line'. Addison, however, admired *Creation: a Philosophical Poem* (1712) which is ambitious in theme: 'I meditate to soar above the skies, / To heights unknown, through ways untried, to rise; / I would the Eternal from his works assert, / And sing the wonders of creating art.' Blackmore's affable nature survived the attacks on his work.

Blake, William
English poet *born* London 28 November 1757
died London 12 August 1827

A hosier's son, Blake began six years' apprenticeship as an engraver in 1772 and ten years later married Catherine Boucher. After the death of his brother in 1787 Blake had visions in one of which his brother Robert revealed to him the method of illuminated printing. Blake used this method in the production of his books from *Songs of Innocence* (1787) onward. Though neglected in his lifetime Blake is now recognised as one of the most imaginative of English poets. His hope for a spiritual awakening in England is contained in his preface to the visionary poem *Milton* (1804): 'I shall not cease from Mental Fight, / Nor shall my Sword sleep in my hand: / Till we have built Jerusalem, / In England's green and pleasant Land.'

Blamire, Susanna
English poet *born* Dalston, near Carlisle January 1747
died Carlisle 5 April 1794

Susanna Blamire, the 'Muse of Cumberland', was brought up by

her aunt, Mrs Simpson of Thackwood. In 1764 she went to
Scotland with her sister Sarah, who married Colonel Graham of
Gartmore; while in the country she responded enthusiastically to
Scottish traditional songs. Her own songs are in Scots, English
and the Cumbrian dialect. 'The Nabob', written around 1788,
begins 'When silent time, wi' lightly foot, / Had trod on thirty
years, / I sought again my native land / Wi' mony hopes and
fears: / Wha kens gin the dear friends I left / May still continue
mine? / Or gin I e'er again shall taste / The joys I left langsyne.'
Susanna Blamire's great friend Catherine Gilpin was also a fine
songwriter.

Blind Harry the Minstrel
Scottish poet *born c*1440 *died c*1492

In 'Lament for the Makaris', his catalogue of death, Dunbar notes
that death has 'Slain [Blind Harry] with his showr of moral haill'.
Little is known of Blind Harry's life though the Accounts of the
Lord High Treasurer of Scotland reveal that, between April 1490
and January 1492, James IV made five payments to the poet.
Wallace (*c*1477), is his heroic narrative in twelve books and 11,877
lines about the life of the great Scottish patriot Sir William
Wallace. Blind Harry describes his hero thus: 'Wallace stature of
greatness, and of hicht, / Was judgit thus, by discretioun of
richt, / That saw him baith dissembill and in weid: / Nine quarters
large he was in lenth indeed'.

dissembill undressed; *in weid* dressed; *quarters* quarter-ells

Bloomfield, Robert
English poet *born* Honington, Suffolk 3 December 1766
died Shefford, Bedfordshire 19 August 1823

When Bloomfield was one his father died and he was raised and
educated by his mother, who kept the village school. While
working for a shoemaker in London he wrote his celebrated 'The
Farmer's Boy' which sold 26,000 copies in the three years after its
publication in 1800. The Duke of Grafton helped him get a job in
the Seal office and, when he resigned through ill-health, gave him
a pension of one shilling a day. His attempts to establish himself
as a bookseller came to nothing and he died in poverty. His comic
ballad 'The Fakenham Ghost' turns on this crucial quatrain: 'An
ass's foal had lost its dam / Within the spacious park; / And,
simple as the playful lamb, / Had followed in the dark.'

Blunden, Edmund
English poet *born* Yalding, Kent 1 November 1896
died 20 January 1974

Educated at Christ's Hospital, Blunden fought at the Somme and the Ypres salient with the Royal Sussex Regiment and was awarded the MC. After the war he studied at Oxford, then taught English at Tokyo University before returning to Oxford as a Fellow. He was Professor of Poetry at Oxford from 1966–8. A prolific poet over a long period, Blunden remained faithful to the Georgian principles of formal clarity and fine description. At his best he evokes the English countryside in a delicate diction, as in 'October Comes': 'I heard the graybird bathing in the rill, / And fluttering his wings dry within thorn boughs / Which all embowered the rill; with tiny bill / The robin on red-berried spray bade rouse / One whom I could not see, a field away'.

Bly, Robert
American poet *born* Madison, Minnesota 23 December 1926

Educated at St Olaf's College and at Harvard, Bly has been active as an editor, publisher and translator: his versions of Pablo Neruda's verse helped bring the great Chilean poet to prominence in the USA. Bly writes with both sensitivity and political passion. Several of his poems celebrate the rural calm of Minnesota while others have ridiculed American foreign policy. When Bly was given the National Book Award in 1968 he donated the prize money to those who wished to 'defy the draft authorities' over the Vietnam War. 'Awakening' is a delicate evocation of his favourite landscape: 'The small farmhouse in Minnesota / Is hardly strong enough for the storm. / Darkness, darkness in grass, darkness in trees.'

Boake, Barcroft
Australian poet *born* Sydney 1866 *died* Sydney 1892

Boake left his native Sydney to confront the challenge of the Australian bush: he was a surveyor in the Monaro and a drover in Western Queensland. What he discovered was the reality, not the romance of the bush and his poems powerfully embody his pessimistic conclusions, as in 'Where the Dead Men Lie': 'Strangled by thirst and fierce privation – / That's how the dead men die! / Out on Moneygrub's farthest station – / That's how the dead men die! / Hardfaced greybeards, youngsters callow; / Some mounds cared for, some left fallow; / Some deep down, yet others shallow; / Some having but the sky.' Boake committed suicide by hanging himself with his stock whip on the shores of Sydney's Middle Harbour.

Bogan, Louise
American poet *born* Livermore Falls, Maine 1897 *died* 1970

Educated at the Boston Girls' Latin School and (for one year) Boston University, Louise Bogan published her first collection, *Body of This Death*, in 1923. She moved to New York and was, from 1929, regular poetry reviewer for the *New Yorker*. In 1944 she was elected a Fellow in American letters, Library of Congress and in 1955 she and Léonie Adams shared the Bollingen Prize. She was a visiting lecturer at the universities of Washington, Chicago and Arkansas. Louise Bogan eschewed the innovations of modernism and preferred to accept the English tradition in lyrics such as 'Fiend's Weather': 'And even tomorrow / Stones without disguise / In true-coloured fields / Will glitter for your eyes.'

Boland, Eavan
Irish poet *born* Dublin 1944

Educated in London, New York and at Trinity College, Dublin, Eavan Boland later taught at Trinity. She published *New Territory* in 1967 and the following year received the Macaulay Fellowship for poetry. With Micheál MacLiammóir she wrote *WB Yeats and His World* (1971) and subsequently published *The War Horse* (1975), *In Her Own Image* (1980) and *Night Feed* (1982). In her poem 'Belfast Vs Dublin', addressed to Derek Mahon, she writes: 'Cut by the throats before we spoke / One to another, yet we breast / The dour line of North and South, pressed / Into action by the clock. Here we renounce / All dividend except the brilliant quarrel / Of our towns'.

Bold, Alan
Scottish poet *born* Edinburgh 20 April 1943

After attending Edinburgh University and working as a journalist Bold became, in 1966, a full-time writer. He has published many critical books including *Modern Scottish Literature* (1983); has edited many anthologies including *Making Love* (1978); and has written extensively on Hugh MacDiarmid whose *Letters* he edited in 1984. The political tone of his early verse altered after he settled in rural Fife in 1975 and his *In This Corner: Selected Poems 1963–83* (1983) contains contemplative poems such as 'Markinch Triptych': 'The wood looks deserted, and the wind / Starts up again and scatters leaves / Through the darkness, down and around / The hill, past forgotten graves.'

Bontemps, Arna
American poet *born* Alexandria, Louisiana 13 October 1902 *died* 1973

Raised in California, Bontemps was educated at Pacific Union College. He came to Harlem and became one of the prominent figures in the 'Harlem Renaissance'. In 1926 he won the *Opportunity* Poetry Prize and the following year won it again along with first prize in a *Crisis* poetry contest. During the Depression he did graduate studies at Chicago University and was Librarian at

Fisk University from 1943–65. In 1966 he joined the staff of the
University of Illinois, Chicago Circle. His *Story of the Negro* won
the Jane Adams Children's Book Award in 1966. 'A Black Man
Talks of Reaping' ends: 'small wonder then my children glean in
fields / they have not sown, and feed on bitter fruit'.

Booth, Martin
English poet *born* Lancashire 7 September 1944

Educated in Hong Kong and (as a student) in London, Booth was
secretary of the Poets' Workshop in London, from 1967–71, and
actively involved on the general and executive councils of the
Poetry Society and the National Poetry Centre. In the early 1970s
he was a fellow commoner and tutor at St Peter's College, Oxford
and in the 1980s he held a fellow commonership at Corpus Christi
College, Cambridge. He was elected a fellow of the Royal Society
of Literature in 1980. Influenced by American verse he writes, in
'Trying to Explain the Goldenrod' (from *Killing the Moscs*, 1984),
of 'the gold sea seeping / pollen waves over / the entire universe'.

Bottomley, Gordon
English poet *born* Keighley, Yorkshire 20 February 1874
died 25 August 1948

Bottomley, the son of a Yorkshire businessman, was well
described (by C C Abbot) as 'a Victorian whose roots were in the
'nineties'. He was introduced to Scottish themes by his mother,
Ann Maria Gordon, and in 1918 wrote *Gruach* as a retrospective
prelude to Shakespeare's *Macbeth*. The verse play was presented
with success by the Scottish National Players in 1923. Gruach,
the future Lady Macbeth, is about to marry her cousin Conan
when she meets Macbeth. When Conan is left behind he says: 'If I
touch Gruach / I feel her body go hard beneath my hand, / And
danger crouching there: if she does nothing, / She makes me feel
outside her.'

Bottrall, Ronald
English poet *born* Cambourne, Cornwall 2 September 1906

In *New Bearings in English Poetry* (1932) F R Leavis pronounced
Ronald Bottrall, then aged twenty-six, 'the voice of a generation'.
After this judgement Bottrall made a career as a British Council
Representative in Sweden, Italy, Brazil, Greece and Japan. Using
his considerable cultural sophistication, his international
experience and his technical virtuosity Bottrall has written poems
of the utmost exactitude. 'Old Age', an autobiographical poem,
illustrates Bottrall's passion for precision: 'I can't walk or breathe

properly, but my brain / And senses work as sharply as ever. / I
don't need spectacles, crutches or a lover, / Balding I've few grey
hairs. Yet I feel the strain.'

Bowering, George
Canadian poet *born* Penticton, British Columbia
1 December 1937

A writer of several accomplishments who has published criticism
and, for example, the stories in *Flycatcher* (1974), Bowering was
educated at the University of British Columbia. He became a
professor at Simon Fraser University and founding editor of *Tish*.
In 1982 he published his selected poems under the title *West
Window*. Influenced by the Objectivist approach of William Carlos
Williams, he eschews rhetoric in his verse. His presentation of
facts is, of course, selective, as in 'In the Elevator': 'Everyone in
the box / knows where / he's going, // he only looks / at the
others / when the elevator stops / between floors.'

Bowers, Edgar
American poet *born* Georgia 1924

Educated at the universities of North Carolina and Stanford
(where he studied with Yvor Winter) Bowers taught at the
University of California, Santa Barbara. His work is technically
traditional, using stanzaic patterns and an essentially iambic
rhythm. Bowers likes to make large ontological statements about
life and death, as in 'The Mountain Cemetery'; 'For on the grass
that starts about the feet / The body's shadow turns, to shape in
time, / Soon grown preponderant with creeping shade, / The final
shadow that is turn of earth; / And what seems won paid for as in
defeat.'

Bowles, William Lisle
English poet *born* King's Sutton, Northamptonshire
24 September 1762 *died* 7 April 1850

Vicar of Bremhill, Wiltshire, for most of his life, Bowles was a
vicar's son. He made a tour of the north of England and Scotland
and published an influential collection of fourteen *Sonnets* (1789)
as a result. Appealing to such as Wordsworth as well as the
general public, Bowles's sonnets represented a reaction against
the classicism of Pope (whose work Bowles criticised in his *Life of
Pope* in 1806). His sonnet dated 18 July 1787 is an address to
Time: 'On Thee I rest my only hope at last, / And think, when
thou hast dried the bitter tear / That flows in vain o'er all my soul
held dear, / I may look back on many sorrows past, / And meet
life's peaceful evening with a smile'.

Boyd, Mark Alexander

Scottish poet *born* Penkill, Ayrshire 13 January 1563
died Ayrshire 10 April 1601

After the death of his father, Boyd was educated by his uncle
James Boyd who became Archbishop of Glasgow in 1573. A
combative character fond of fighting duels, he fled to Paris in
1581 and studied civil law at Orleans and Bourges before moving
to Italy. He fought in Henry III's army in France and was
wounded at Toulouse. He returned to Scotland in 1596. His Latin
poems were published in 1637. His single 'Sonet' in Scots,
described as 'the most beautiful sonnet in the language' by Ezra
Pound, ends: 'Unhappie is the man for evirmaire / That teils the
sand and sawis in the aire; / Bot twyse unhappier is he, I lairn, /
That feidis in his heart a mad desire, / And follows on a woman
throw the fyre, / Led be a blind and teichit be a bairn.'
teils tills; *teichit* taught

Bradstreet, Anne

American poet *born* Northampton *c*1612
died 16 September 1672

Daughter of Thomas Dudley, steward to the Earl of Lincoln,
Anne married Simon Bradstreet in 1628. Two years later she
moved to New England, living first at Ipswich then at North
Andover: Anne's father and husband both became Governors of
the Province of Massachusetts Bay. Her volume *The Tenth Muse
Lately Sprung Up in America* (1650) appeared in London. Later
poems, such as 'Some Verses upon the Burning of Our House
July 10th, 1666', reveal her at her most original: 'Here stood that
trunk, and there that chest; / There lay that store I counted best: /
My pleasant things in ashes lye, / And them behold no more shall
I. / Under thy roof no guest shall sitt, / Nor at thy Table eat a
bitt.'

Branch, Anna Hempstead

American poet *born* New London, Connecticut 1875
died New London 8 September 1937

A lawyer's daughter, Anna Hempstead Branch was brought up in
New York where she ran the Poet's Guild and directed their
activities at Christadora House on the Lower East Side. She
believed that poetry was a collective experience that could save
the world. In some of her sonnets her imagery is abandoned and
euphoric: 'Into the void behold my shuddering flight, / Plunging
straight forward through inhuman space, / My wild hair backward
blown and my white face / Set like a wedge of ice. My chattering
teeth / Cut like sharp knives my swiftly freezing breath. / Perched
upon straightness I seek a wilder zone. / My Flying Self – on this
black steed alone – / Drives out to God or else to utter death.'

Brasch, Charles
New Zealand poet *born* Dunedin 1909 *died* 1973

Educated at Waitaki and in England at Oxford, Brasch worked as an archaeologist in Egypt and, later, as a teacher of problem children. During the Second World War he was in England as a civil servant. When he returned to New Zealand he founded, in 1947, the quarterly *Landfall* which became the most important literary journal in New Zealand. The title poem of *Ambulando* (1964) suggests that imaginative adventure is an antidote to the onset of age: 'I cannot set boundaries to experience. / I know it may open out, enlarged suddenly, / In any direction, to unpredictable distance, / Subverting climate and cosmography, / And carrying me far from tried moorings'.

Brathwaite, Edward
Caribbean poet *born* Bridgetown, Barbados 11 May 1930

Educated in the West Indies and at Barbados, Brathwaite taught in Ghana from 1955–62 and became a Lecturer in History at the University of the West Indies. His poetic trilogy – *Rights of Passage* (1967), *Masks* (1968), *Islands* (1969) – is an exploration of the world from a Caribbean viewpoint. 'The Twist' uses the rhythm of a popular song in the interests of a realistic vision: 'watch her move her wrist / and feel your belly twist / feel the hunger thunder / when her hip bones twist // try to hold her, keep her under / while the juke box hiss / twist the music out of hunger / on a night like this.' By contrast the meditative 'South' recalls the islands and celebrates 'the strength of that turbulent soil'.

Brennan, Christopher
Australian poet *born* near Darling Harbour, Sydney 1870
died Sydney 1932

Educated at Jesuit School and Sydney University, Brennan – the son of an Irish brewer – was an expansive individual whose uninhibited behaviour shocked many friends and colleagues. In 1925 his self-destructive drinking led to his dismissal from the post of Associate Professor of German and Comparative Literature at Sydney University. A physically large and intellectually impressive man, Brennan was given to bouts of depression and his alcoholism led to the breakup of his marriage. He eventually returned to the Roman Catholic faith that had once sustained him. His poems are technically assured though thematically obsessed by the fear of failure. In 'The Wanderer' he speaks of 'the lone hours when only evil wakes'.

Brereton, John le Gay
Australian poet *born* 1871 *died* 1933

Brereton's father was a prominent member of the Swedenborgian

community in Sydney and he introduced a sensitive note to
Australian poetry at a time when it was dominated by the bush
balladists. He became the first Challis Professor of English
Literature at Sydney University and was an accomplished critic of
literature. Influenced by Whitman, and his friend Christopher
Brennan, Brereton wrote rhapsodically about the creative
impulse, in (for example) 'The Silver Gull': 'In me is the manifold
urge, / The shedding of leaves, the upward push of the seed, / Of
all the life upon earth / The scramble and fury and fret'.

Breton, Nicholas
English poet *born* Oxford *c*1545 *died c*1626

Son of a London merchant, Breton was educated at Oxford and
afterwards established himself as a satirist, pamphleteer, and
prose-writer. Eight of his lyrics appeared in *England's Helicon*
(1600), the Elizabethan miscellany. 'Wooing in a Dream', one of
these poems, shows his ability to put rhyme to an attractively
subjective purpose: 'Shall we go learn to woo, to woo? / Never
thought came ever to, / Better deed could better do. // Shall we
go learn to kiss, to kiss? / Never heart could ever miss / Comfort,
where true meaning is. // Thus at base they run, they run, / When
the sport was scarce begun. / But I waked, and all was done.' His
mother married the poet George Gascoigne.

Brewster, Elizabeth
Canadian poet *born* Chipman, New Brunswick 26 August 1922

Educated at the universities of New Brunswick and London,
Elizabeth Brewster became a professor of English at the
University of Saskatchewan. She published various volumes
including *Sometimes I Think of Moving* (1977) and has written fiction
as well as verse. Poems such as 'Where I Come From' show her
drawing on the Canadian tradition of vividly descriptive agrarian
verse: 'Where I come from, people / carry woods in their minds,
acres of pine woods; / blueberry patches in the burned-out bush; /
wooden farmhouses, old, in need of paint, / with yards where
hens and chickens circle about, / clucking aimlessly; battered
schoolhouses / behind which violets grow.'

Bridges, Robert
English poet *born* Walmer, Kent 23 October 1844
died 21 April 1930

Bridges, who became Poet Laureate in 1913, was educated at
Eton and Oxford before going on to study medicine at St
Bartholomew's Hospital. He was a surgeon until 1870 when he
abandoned his profession and devoted himself to writing. As a
friend of Gerard Manley Hopkins, he was responsible for the
1918 edition of Hopkins's poems and though the two men

differed over religion they shared a dedication to the craft of
verse. In 'London Snow' Bridges produces a memorable verbal
picture of a city coming to life: 'For now doors open, and war is
waged with the snow; / And trains of sombre men, past tale of
number, / Tread long brown paths, as towards their toil they go'.

Bringhurst, Robert
Canadian poet *born* Los Angeles 1946

Raised in the Canadian Rockies, Bringhurst settled in Vancouver.
An experienced traveller he published his selected poems under
the title *The Beauty of the Weapons* in 1982. He scrutinises the
surface of the external world in his poems and approaches the
problem of perception through images: 'Some days the sun, like a
fattening goose, crosses over in ignorant stupor. / Other days,
watch: you will see him shudder and twitch, like a rabbit / caught
in the snare – but what / does it matter? / One way / or the other,
his death is the same. // We must learn to be thought by the gods,
not to think them.'

Brock, Edwin
English poet *born* London 1927

After serving with the Royal Navy in the Pacific, Brock worked as
a trade journalist, a London policeman, and as an advertising
copy-writer. His novel *The Little White God* (1961) draws on his
experience as a policeman. His collection *With Love from Judas*
(1963) contains his catalogue of death, 'Five Ways to Kill a Man'.
After describing a crucifixion, a medieval battle, scenes from the
First and Second World Wars, Brock concludes ironically: 'These
are, as I began, cumbersome ways / to kill a man. Simpler, direct,
and much more neat / is to see that he is living somewhere in the
middle / of the twentieth century, and leave him there.'

Brontë, Charlotte
English poet *born* Thornton, Yorkshire 21 April 1816
died 31 March 1855

The third child of Patrick Brontë, the curate, Charlotte was
brought up at Haworth Parsonage on the Yorkshire Moors. As
her novel *Jane Eyre* (1847) shows, she and her sisters were
unhappy at the school they went to at Cowan Bridge.
Subsequently she worked as a governess and (with Emily) studied
in Brussels. She married the Reverend A B Nicholls in 1854 and
died of an illness connected with childbirth. Her poems, such as
'Evening Solace', are sombre and sonorous: 'The human heart has
hidden treasures, / In secret kept, in silence sealed; / The
thoughts, the hopes, the dreams, the pleasures, / Whose charms
were broken if revealed.'

Brontë, Emily
English poet *born* Thornton, Yorkshire 20 August 1818
died 19 December 1848

Most of Emily's life was spent in the Haworth Parsonage on the
Yorkshire Moors: her novel *Wuthering Heights* (1847) shows how
she transformed her environment into an extraordinary
imaginative world. Her poems too have unique qualities and the
formal structure barely contains the emotional power of which
Emily was capable. An example of her intensity of feeling is her
contemplation of death in 'Remembrance': 'Cold in the earth,
and the deep snow piled above thee! / Far, far removed, cold in
the dreary grave! / Have I forgot, my Only Love, to love thee, /
Severed at last by Time's all-wearing wave?' She died of
consumption after catching a cold at her brother's funeral.

Brooke, Rupert
English poet *born* Rugby 3 August 1887
died Skyros, Greece 23 April 1915

Brooke was educated at Rugby School, where his father was a
housemaster, and at Cambridge where he was the darling of the
aesthetes. In 1914 he was commissioned in the Royal Naval
Division and, after seeing action at the defence of Antwerp, spent
his Christmas leave at home where he wrote five sonnets
including 'The Soldier': 'If I should die, think only this of me: /
That there's some corner of a foreign field / That is for ever
England.' Brooke's schoolboyish good looks and patriotic
romanticism made him the perfect martyr and when he died, after
contracting food poisoning, Winston Churchill, First Lord of the
Admiralty, described him as being 'all that one would wish
England's noblest sons to be'.

Brooks, Charles Shirley
English poet *born* London 29 April 1816 *died* 23 February 1874

Articled to his maternal uncle, as a solicitor, Brooks studied law
for five years before turning to journalism. He represented the
Morning Chronicle in the gallery of the House of Commons, wrote
leaders for the *Illustrated London News*, edited the *Literary Gazette*,
Home News and (from 1870) *Punch* to which he contributed his
'Essence of parliament' column. His novels include *Aspen Court*
(1855) and *The Gordian Knot* (1860). His light verse was
posthumously collected in *Poems of Wit and Humour* (1875) and
include 'To My Beloved Vesta': 'Miss, I'm a Pensive Protoplasm, /
Born in some pre-historic chasm, / I, and my humble fellow-men /
Are hydrogen, and oxygen, / And nitrogen and carbon too, / And
so is Jane and so are you.'

Brooks, Gwendolyn
American poet *born* Topeka, Kansas 17 June 1917

Brought up on the South Side of Chicago, Gwendolyn Brooks was encouraged to write by her father, who gave her a writing desk, and her mother, who presented her with the work of Paul Laurence Dunbar as an appropriate poetic hero. She attended a poetry class, in Chicago, for young blacks and gradually established a literary reputation: her collection *A Street in Bronze* (1945) impressed white readers and her novel *Annie Allen* (1949) won the Pulitzer Prize. In 1968 she was named Poet Laureate of Illinois. Poems such as 'Kitchenette Building' apply her descriptive gift to squalid sights such as 'yesterday's garbage ripening in the hall'.

Brough, Robert
English poet *born* 10 April 1828 *died* 26 July 1860

Son of a businessman, Brough went to London where he was a successful writer of burlesque dramas and humorous articles. In 1855 his more serious side was expressed in *Songs of the Governing Classes*, an assault on upperclass England. 'My Lord Tomnoddy', a characteristically caustic portrait, ends: 'My Lord in the Peers will take his place: / His Majesty's councils his words will grace. / Office he'll hold, and patronage sway; / Fortunes and lives he will vote away – / And what are his qualifications? – ONE! / He's the Earl of Fitzdotterel's eldest son.' Brough hoped his songs would 'arrive at the dignity of being whistled in the streets'.

Brown, Christy
Irish poet *born* Dublin 5 June 1932
died Somerset 7 September 1981

One of twenty-three children born to his mother in the Dublin slums, Brown was a spastic so severely handicapped that few realised he could contemplate, let alone communicate. However it was discovered that part of his brain linked directly with his left foot, hence the title of his autobiography *My Left Foot*. His verse has a poignantly personal character as it seeks to escape from crippling physical limitations. He celebrates oddity and embodies it amusingly (in 'Slug Song'): 'O how I envy snail, termite and slug / snug as God willed it in the proverbial rug / all petty guile lacking and unassuming / never once knowing what it is to be human.'

Brown, T E
English poet *born* Douglas, Isle of Man 5 May 1830
died 30 October 1897

A vicar's son, Thomas Edward Brown was educated at Oxford and later taught at Clifton for thirty years. He wrote narrative poems

in the Manx dialect, to the great delight of Victorian readers. His
declaration that 'A garden is a lovesome thing, Got wot!' has
entered the English language. His sequence 'In the Coach' is an
exceptionally spirited example of his dialect verse, especially the
section 'Conjergal Rights': 'Conjergal rights! Conjergal rights! / I
don't care for the jink of her and I don't care for the jaw of her, /
But I'll have the law of her. / Conjergal rights! yis, yis, I know
what I'm sayin' / Fuss-rate, Misthress Corkhill, fuss-rate, Misther
Cain, / And all the people in the coach . . .'

Browne, Isaac Hawkins
English poet *born* Burton-on-Trent 1705 *died* 1760

Browne was educated at Cambridge and studied law at Lincoln's
Inn. A wealthy man, he was a Member of Parliament for Wenlock,
Shropshire. Browne wrote imitations of his favourite poets on the
subject of tobacco. His 'Imitation of Pope' is particularly
impressive: 'Poison that cures, a vapour that affords / Content,
more solid than the smile of lords: / Rest to the weary, to the
hungry food, / The last kind refuge of the wise and good. /
Inspired by thee, dull cits adjust the scale / Of Europe's peace,
when other statesmen fail. / By thee protected, and thy sister,
beer, / Poets rejoice, nor think the bailiff near. / Nor less the
critic owns thy genial aid, / While supperless he plies the
piddling trade.'

Browne, William
English poet *born* Tavistock *c*1590 *died c*1645

Educated at Oxford and the Inner Temple, Browne produced
Britannia's Pastorals (1613), a narrative poem in couplets
punctuated with lyrics; and *The Shepherd's Pipe* (1614). He wrote,
in considerable descriptive detail, under the influence of Spenser
and the rhythmic fluency of his work was admired by such poets
as Milton, Keats and Elizabeth Barrett Browning. From the *Inner
Temple Masque* (first printed in *Works* of 1772) comes his seductive
sirens' song: 'For swelling waves our panting breasts, / Where
never storms arise, / Exchange, and be awhile our guests: / For
stars gaze on our eyes. / The compass Love shall hourly sing, /And
as he goes about the ring, / We will not miss / To tell each point
he nameth with a kiss.'

Browning, Elizabeth Barrett
English poet *born* Coxhoe Hall, Co Durham 6 March 1806
died Florence 29 June 1861

Eldest of twelve children of Edward Moulton Barrett and Mary
Graham Clarke, Elizabeth was brought to London by her father in
1835. A spinal injury incurred in a riding accident made her an
invalid and her isolation was increased by her father's hostility to

Robert Browning with whom Elizabeth eloped, marrying him on 12 September 1846. A strong-willed and conspicuously intelligent woman, she earned a considerable literary reputation with her *Poems* of 1844. Her novel–poem *Aurora Leigh* (1856) has powerfully feminist sentiments: 'Never flinch, / But still, unscrupulously epic, catch / Upon the burning lava of a song / The full-veined, heaving, double-breasted Age'.

Browning, Robert
English poet *born* Camberwell 7 May 1812
died London 12 December 1889

Browning, a bank clerk's son, married Elizabeth Barrett in 1846 and the couple lived in Italy until her death in 1861. Browning never entirely recovered from the loss of his wife but returned to England and introduced a new conversational strength to English verse. His dramatic monologues, such as 'My Last Duchess', have psychological subtlety; his verse drama *The Ring and the Book* (1868–9) uses multiple viewpoints. 'A Toccata of Gallupi's' closes on a characteristic note of longing: 'Dear dead women, with such hair, too – what's become of all the gold / Used to hang and brush their bosoms? / I feel chilly and grown old.'

Brownjohn, Alan
English poet *born* London 28 July 1931

Alan Brownjohn read history at Oxford and later taught in schools and colleges. He has taken an active interest in politics and produced a number of topical poems, including 'William Empson at Aldermaston'. Brownjohn treats poetry as a responsible art capable of documenting events as well as conveying emotions. Consequently he writes in an uncluttered, conversational style. He can transform an ordinary scene by the intensity of his response to it. 'Sadly on Barstools' renders a public house romantically: 'The drinks, the bar, the barman, the fast bar clock / Are spun away to nothing among a cat's cradle / Of lovely information and speculation'.

Bruce, George
Scottish poet *born* Fraserburgh 10 March 1909

Educated at Aberdeen University, Bruce was a schoolteacher and then joined the BBC as a producer from 1946–70. His first book *Sea Talk* (1944) established him as the poet of the Buchan area. Drawing on the spare sculptural solidity of Ezra Pound's *Hugh Selwyn Mauberley* (1920), Bruce pared his language to the bone, writing (in 'Inheritance'): 'This which I write now / Was written years ago / Before my birth / In the features of my father.' In a later poem, 'Laotian Peasant Shot', he retained his characteristic tautness: 'When he fell the dust / hung in the air / like an empty container / of him.' His *Collected Poems* appeared in 1970.

Bruce, Michael
Scottish poet *born* Kinnesswood, Kinross-shire 27 March 1746 *died* Kinnesswood 5 July 1767

The 'poet of Lochleven' is associated with the landscape at the foot of the Lomond Hills by the northern shore of Lochleven. Bruce's brief life was dominated by the faith of his father – a weaver who was an elder of the Secessionist Church – and the fact of his own consumptive illness. Bruce studied for the ministry and produced metrical paraphrases that still circulate in the Church of Scotland. His best–known poem is 'Ode to the Cuckoo' but some of his finest lines occur in his longest poem, 'Lochleven', which depicts 'Irriguous vales, where cattle low, and sheep / That whiten half the hills'.

Brutus, Denis
South African poet *born* Salisbury 1924

Brutus, a prominent campaigner against racism in sport, was shot in Johannesburg by South African police and jailed for eighteen months in Robben Island. In 1966 he left South Africa, moved to London, then became a professor at North-Western University, Chicago. His poems are fiercely critical of white supremacist regimes yet he expresses himself with a lyrical feeling for language. 'This Sun on this Rubble' ends: 'but now our pride-dumbed mouths are wide / in wordless supplication / – are grateful for the least relief from pain / – like this sun on this debris after rain.'

Bryant, William Cullen
American poet *born* Cummington, Massachusetts 3 November 1794 *died* New York 12 June 1878

Son of a country doctor, who had to treat the infant Bryant's abnormally large head, he was precocious enough to master neo-classical mannerisms by the age of thirteen. He was called to the bar in 1819 and two years later married Frances Fairchild. From 1829 he edited, with distinction, the New York *Evening Post*. He died after collapsing at a ceremony in Central Park. His Wordsworthian approach to the American landscape produced thoughtful poems. He is best–remembered for 'Thanatopsis', a poem written at the age of seventeen and beginning 'To him who in the love of nature holds / Communion with her visible forms, she speaks a various language'.

Buchanan, Robert
English poet *born* Caverswall, Staffordshire 18 August 1841
died 10 June 1901

Buchanan was nine when his father took him to Glasgow and he
was educated at Glasgow University. Moving to London in 1860,
he became friendly with Dickens, Browning and George Eliot.
From 1866–74 he lived in Oban and wrote *The Land of Lorne*
(1871) about a yachting tour. His article 'The Fleshly School of
Poetry', in the *Contemporary Review* of October 1871, offended the
Pre-Raphaelites and in a libel action Buchan was awarded £150
though he subsequently withdrew his allegations. He settled in
Rossport, County Mayo, in 1874 and later returned to London to
write his novel *God and the Man* (1881). Eventually he went
bankrupt and died in poverty. His *London Poems* (1866) include a
portrait of 'The Bookworm' with his 'coat of dingy brown'.

Buckley, Vincent
Australian poet *born* Victoria 1925

Educated by the Jesuit Fathers in Melbourne, then at Melbourne
University, Buckley was with the Royal Australian Air Force
during the Second World War. Later he became a Professor of
English at Melbourne University. Buckley combines his scholarly
standards with a commitment to Roman Catholicism, invariably
evident in his poems – for example, 'Places' with its mention of
Mass. It closes with an anecdotal shudder: 'I think how once, /
Hardly thinking, in a strange church, / A man, forgetting the
common rubric, prayed / "O God, make me worthy of the
world", / And felt his own silence sting his tongue.'

Bukowski, Charles
American poet *born* 1920

Bukowski left Germany at the age of two and settled in Los
Angeles. A fluent and prolific poet he published *Flower, Fist and
Bestial Wail* in 1960, *Dangling in the Tournefortia* in 1981. His verse is
full of the emotional debris of American life which he frequently
treats with contempt in poems such as 'something for the touts,
the nuns, the grocery clerks and you': 'days like this. like your day
today. / maybe the rain on the window trying to / get through to
you. what do you see today? / what is it? where are you? the best /
days are sometimes the first, sometimes the middle and even
sometimes the last. / the vacant lots are not bad, churches in /
Europe on postcards are not bad.'

Bunting, Basil
English poet *born* Scotswood on Tyne 1900
died Hexham, Northumberland 17 April 1985

Educated at the London School of Economics, Bunting went to

prison as a conscientious objector during the First World War. Under the influence of Ezra Pound he began to publish his poems in the 1930s. During the Second World War he abandoned his conscientious objection and went to Persia with the British diplomatic service. After being expelled from Persia, he worked as a journalist in Newcastle. His work was neglected in England until the 1960s when *Loquitur* (1965) appeared and then the autobiographical long poem *Brigflatts* (1966) which celebrates the Northumbrian landscape: 'Ripe wheat is my lodging. I polish / my side on pillars of its transept, / gleam in its occasional light.'

Burns, Robert
Scottish poet *born* Alloway, Ayrshire 25 January 1759
died Dumfries 21 July 1796

Son of a tenant-farmer, Burns developed his incisive mind from an early age thanks to his father's insistence on education. This, combined with his experience of manual work, gave him an unusual poetic tone – both earthy and erudite. When the Kilmarnock edition of his *Poems, Chiefly in the Scottish Dialect* appeared on 31 July 1786 he was acclaimed as a 'ploughman poet' though he was, in fact, a consummate artist with a good knowledge of English as well as Scots poetry. Influenced by Robert Fergusson, he created emotionally intense poems that have a global appeal. Yet he claimed, with excessive modesty in 'Epistle to J Lapraik', 'I am nae poet, in a sense; / But just a rhymer like by chance'.

Butler, Samuel
English poet *born* Worcestershire February 1612
died 25 September 1680

Son of a farmer, Butler was educated locally before beginning a career as a clerk and secretary. He was employed by the Countess of Kent; by Sir Samuel Luke, a colonel in the parliamentary army; by the Earl of Carberry after the Restoration; by the Duke of Buckingham. His *Hudibras* appeared in three parts (1663, 1664, 1678) to the delight of royalists, from Charles II downwards, who relished its satirical treatment of Puritanism. In Part One, Canto 11, Butler has the quixotic Sir Hudibras engage in a mock-epic battle after the following observation: 'It is a heavy case, no doubt, / A man should have his Brains beat out, / Because he's tall, and has large Bones: / As men kill Beavers for their stones.'

Byrom, John
English poet *born* Broughton, near Manchester
29 February 1692 *died* 26 September 1763

Educated at Cambridge, where he was a Fellow, Byrom studied medicine abroad. After his marriage in 1721 he invented a new

system of shorthand and taught it, under an oath of secrecy, to
such as Horace Walpole. A mystic as well as an enthusiastic
Jacobite, he wrote the hymn 'Christians, awake! Salute the happy
morn' and the epigram (concerning Handel and Bononcini)
'Strange all this difference should be / 'Twixt Tweedledum and
Tweedledee!' His diary was edited in four volumes, by
R Parkinson, from 1854-7. His poems tend to offer expressions
of piety: 'My spirit longeth for thee / Within my troubled breast, /
Although I be unworthy / Of so divine a guest.'

Byron, Lord
Anglo-Scottish poet *born* London 22 January 1788
died Missolonghi, Greece 19 April 1824

Son of a notoriously decadent gentleman and a Scottish heiress,
Catherine Gordon, George Gordon became sixth Baron Byron
on the death of his great-uncle in 1798. Educated at Aberdeen,
Harrow and Cambridge he achieved instant fame with the
publication in 1812 of the first two Cantos of *Childe Harold*. He
married Anne Milbanke in 1815 and their separation after a year –
combined with his romantic attachment to his half-sister Augusta
Leigh – so outraged public opinion that Byron left England for a
life of exile that ended with his participation in the Greek
struggle for independence. *Don Juan* (1819-24) is the classic comic
masterpiece of English poetry: 'Let us have wine and women,
mirth and laughter, / Sermons and soda-water the day after.'

Callanan, Jeremiah Joseph
Irish poet *born* Cork 1785   *died* Lisbon, Portugal 1829

Educated at Trinity College, Dublin, Callanan rooted his work in
West Cork and for a while he was a tutor in Millstreet, a village in
northwest Cork. He fell in love with Alicia Fisher, a Cork
Methodist, but parted from her in 1827. Eventually he took up a
post as a tutor with a Cork businessman living in Lisbon where he
died as the result of a throat infection. He translated
imaginatively from the Gaelic and wrote folksy poems such as
'The Outlaw of Loch Lene': 'O many a day I have made good ale
in the glen, / That came not of stream, or malt, like the brewing
of men. / My bed was the ground, my roof, the greenwood
above, / And the wealth that I sought –one far kind glance from
my love.'

Calverley, C S
English poet *born* Martley, Worcestershire 22 December 1831
died Folkestone 17 February 1884

Son of Henry Blayds, a clergyman who changed his name to
Calverley in 1852, Charles Stuart Calverley was educated at
Oxford (where he was sent down because of his irreverent

behaviour) and Cambridge (where he became a Fellow of Christ's College). Called to the Bar in 1865, he contracted concussion of the brain in a skating accident the following year and was a semi-invalid for many years. *Fly Leaves* (1872) includes his brilliant parodies such as 'The Cock and the Bull' which puts Browning's *The Ring and the Book* in a comic context: 'You see the trick on't though, and can yourself / Continue the discourse *ad libitum*. / It takes up about eighty thousand lines, / A thing imagination boggles at'.

Cameron, George Frederick
Canadian poet *born* New Glasgow, Nova Scotia 1854 *died* 1885

Educated at Boston University and Queen's University, Cameron was – for the last three years of his short life – editor of the Kingston *News*. His *Lyrics on Freedom, Love and Death* (1887) came out two years after his death. In poems such as 'My Political Faith' he expresses his romantic faith in individual freedom: 'It is in the extreme begins / And ends all danger: if the Few / Would feel, or if the Many knew / This fact, the mass of fewer sins / Would shrive them in their passing through: // O'er all God's footstool not a slave / Should under his great glory stand, / For men would rise, swift sword in hand, / And give each tyrant to his grave / And freedom to each lovely land.'

Cameron, Norman
Scottish poet *born* Bombay 1905 *died* April 1953

A friend of Robert Graves, Cameron was educated at Fettes College, Edinburgh, and at Oxford. From 1929–32 he was an educational officer in Nigeria and he later went to live with Graves and Laura Riding in Mallorca. Thereafter he worked as an advertising copy-writer and served, as a political officer, in North Africa during the Second World War. Towards the end of his life he converted to Roman Catholicism. From his *Collected Poems* (1957) comes 'The Dirty Little Accuser', an entertainingly indignant poem: 'Who invited him in? What was he doing here, / That insolent little ruffian, that crapulous lout? / When he quitted a sofa, he left behind him a smear. / My wife says he even tried to paw her about.'

Campbell, Alistair
New Zealand poet *born* Rarotonga 1925

Campbell's father was of Scottish extraction and his mother came from Tongareva in the Northern Cook Islands. He was educated at Victoria University and pursued a career in educational publishing in Wellington. His collections include *Sanctuary of Spirits* (1963), *Wild Honey* (1964), *Dreams, Yellow Lions* (1975) and *Collected Poems* (1982). A poet with a wide stylistic range, he is thematically at home reflecting on his origins as in 'My Mother' which begins: 'Rebellion was in her character. / Sullenly beautiful, of *ariki* / Descent, childbearing utterly wrecked her, /So that she died young in Tahiti / Where she was buried.'

Campbell, David

Australian poet *born* Ellerslie Station, near Adelong, New South Wales 1915

Educated at Sydney and at Cambridge, Campbell played for England in football matches against Ireland and Wales. A pilot with the Royal Australian Air Force during the Second World War, he was awarded the DFC. He subsequently farmed his land near Canberra. Campbell's verse, in the tradition of the bush ballads, celebrates his life on the land though he has also written some appealingly erotic poems such as 'Windy Nights': 'O what do lovers love the best, / Upstairs naked or downstairs dressed? / Windy nights and hot desire / Or an old book and a steady fire? / Ask your mistress. Should she pause, / She has a lover out of doors.'

Campbell, Joseph

Irish poet *born* Belfast 1879 *died* 1944

Campbell left Ireland to become Director of Studies at Fordham University, New York, but later came home. Influenced by the Imagist movement, he published *The Mountainy Singer* in 1900, *Irishry* in 1913 and *Earth of Cualam* in 1917; his *Complete Poems* appeared in 1963. In 'Days' he projects images of days full of incident: 'One is a black valley, / Rising to blue goat-parks / On the crowns of distant hills. / I hear the falling of water / And the whisper of ferns' tongues, / And, still more, I hear / The silence.' The poem opens and closes with the statement: 'The days of my life / Come and go.'

Campbell, Roy

South African poet *born* Durban 2 October 1901 *died* near Setúbal, Portugal 23 April 1957

A complicated and confused man, Roy Campbell (a doctor's son) cultivated the image of a hard-drinking, hell-raising tough guy ready to flatten any literary foes in England. In fact he was a sensitive man who suffered for his feelings of insecurity. Nevertheless he managed to alienate the English literary Left by his determination to champion Franco's forces in the Spanish Civil War. In his *Flowering Rifle* (1939) he projects himself as a fierce warrior-poet: 'So where you thought to slash the bulging nape / It is a face you widen in its gape, / To whose fierce shock your jolted elbow rings / And like a tuning-fork, your forearm sings'. He was killed in a car crash.

Campbell, Thomas
Scottish poet *born* Glasgow 27 July 1777
died Boulogne 15 June 1844

After abandoning his legal studies, Campbell got a job tutoring in
Mull and it was there he conceived *The Pleasures of Hope* (1799)
which went through four editions in a year. Although his shorter
poems, such as 'Ye Mariners of England', were popular he was (as
his friend Byron noted) unable to repeat the romantic power and
meditative fluency of *The Pleasures of Hope* with its many
memorable lines, including these from the opening stanza; 'Why
do those cliffs of shadowy tint appear / More sweet than all the
landscape smiling near? – / 'Tis distance lends enchantment to the
view, / And robes the mountain in its azure hue.'

Campbell, Wilfred
Canadian poet *born* Kitchener, Ontario 1858   *died* 1918

Educated in Toronto and Cambridge, Massachusetts, Campbell
worked in the Civil Service, Ottawa, but was best known for the
literary column – 'At the Mermaid Tavern' – he, Archibald
Lampman and Duncan Campbell Scott ran in the Toronto *Globe*.
Like Lampman and Scott, Campbell was taken with the idea of
expressing the Canadian landscape in a visionary manner. His
'How One Winter Came in the Lake Region' ends euphorically:
'That night I felt the winter in my veins, / A joyous tremor of the
icy glow; / And woke to hear the north's wild vibrant strains, /
While far and wide, by withered woods and plains, / Fast fell the
driving snow.' His *Poetical Works* appeared in 1922.

Campion, Thomas
English poet *born* Witham, Essex 12 February 1567
died 1 March 1619

A musician as well as a poet, Campion composed the music for
many of the lyrics collected in his four books of *Ayres* (1610–12).
He was educated at Cambridge and at Gray's Inn but gave up the
law for the practice of medicine. Though he criticised a reliance
on rhyme in his *Observations on the Art of English Poesie* (1602)
Campion put rhyme to impressively euphonic use in lyrics such as
the celebrated 'Cherry-Ripe': 'There is a garden in her face, /
Where roses and white lilies grow; / A heavenly paradise is that
place, / Wherein all pleasant fruits to flow. / There cherries grow
which none may buy, / till "Cherry-ripe" themselves do cry.'
Campion had a considerable influence on the evolution of
English lyricism.

Canning, George
English poet *born* London 11 April 1770
died Chiswick 8 August 1827

Best known as the Tory statesman who, as Foreign Secretary in 1809, fought a duel with Castlereagh (then War Secretary). Canning again became Foreign Secretary on the death of his rival in 1822 and in 1827 Prime Minister for a few months before his death. He was also an enthusiastic man of letters, founding the *Anti-Jacobin* (1797-8) in defence of the English system of government. The humorous verse he contributed to the journal shows his intelligence and metrical ingenuity, as in 'Elegy, or Dirge': 'Poor John was a gallant Captain, / In Battles much delighting; / He fled full soon / On the *First of June* – / But he bade the rest keep fighting.' His *Collected Poems* appeared in 1823.

Carew, Richard
English poet *born* West Wickham 1595 *died* 22 March 1640

A lawyer's son, Carew was educated at Oxford and at the Inner Temple. He went to Venice as secretary to Sir Dudley Carleton but was sent back to England in disgrace after offending his employer with a satirical sketch. He subsequently went to Paris with Sir Edward Herbert and became Gentleman of the Privy Chamber and Sewer to the King in 1630. He used the Metaphysical style brilliantly in some erotic poems, such as 'A Rapture' which was widely circulated in manuscript: 'I'll behold / Thy bared snow, and thy unbraided gold. / There my enfranchised hand, on every side / Shall o'er thy naked polished ivory slide.' He had a considerable reputation as a libertine though his lyrical skill was also acknowledged.

Carey, Henry
English poet *born c*1687 *died* 1743

Carey was a dramatist and accomplished songwriter. His use of the term *Namby Pamby* (1726), to describe the sickly sentimentality of Ambrose Philips, gave a new expression to the English language. He has been wrongly credited with writing the words of 'God Save the King' but 'Sally in Our Alley' is all his own work and his most endurable lyric: 'Of all the girls that are so smart, / There's none like pretty Sally; / She is the darling of my heart, / And she lives in our alley. / There is no lady in the land /Is half so sweet as Sally: / She is the darling of my heart, / And she lives in our alley.' F. T. Wood published an edition of Carey's *Poems* in 1930.

Carleton, Will
American poet *born* Hudson, Michigan 21 October 1845 *died* 18 December 1912

A farmer's son, Carleton was educated at Hillsdale College before becoming a journalist. He edited the Hillsdale *Standard* and the Detroit *Weekly Tribune* and later moved to Boston. A skilled performer, he gained great popularity by giving recitals of his work which included the sentimental dialect ballad 'Over the Hill to the Poor-House': 'Over the hill to the poor-house I'm trudgin' my weary way – / I, a woman of seventy, and only a trifle grey – / I, who am smart an' chipper, for all the years I've told, / As many another woman that's only half as old.' Carleton published *Farm Ballads* in 1873 and *Rhymes of Our Planet* in 1896.

Carman, Bliss
Canadian poet *born* Fredericton, New Brunswick
15 April 1861 *died* 8 June 1929

Educated at the universities of New Brunswick, Edinburgh and Harvard, Carman and his friend Richard Hovey agreed to devote their lives to literature and together produced three volumes of *Songs from Vagabondia* (1894, 1896, 1902). In 1897 he began his long relationship with Mrs Mary King who encouraged the philosophical aspects of his art; after 1908 Carman lived with Dr and Mrs King in New Canaan, Connecticut. One of the Group of the Sixties, he expressed a transcendental empathy with nature, as in 'Low Tide on Grand Pré': 'Then all your face grew light, and seemed / To hold the shadow of the sun; / The evening faltered, and I deemed / That time was ripe, and years had done / Their wheeling underneath the sun.'

Carroll, Lewis
English poet *born* Daresbury, near Warrington 27 January
1832 *died* Guildford 14 January 1898

A clergyman's son, Charles Lutwidge Dodgson was educated at Oxford where he took double honours in Classics and Mathematics; his working life was spent as a Fellow of Christ Church. His books *Alice's Adventures in Wonderland* (1865) and *Through the Looking Glass* (1872) quickly became classics of children's literature and immortalised the original of the heroine – Alice Liddell, daughter of the Dean of Christ Church. Dodgson, who used the pseudonym Lewis Carroll to protect his privacy, punctuated his prose with verse as linguistically adventurous as 'Jabberwocky' from *Through the Looking Glass*: ''Twas brillig, and the slithy toves / Did gyre and gimble in the wabe; / All mimsy were the borogoves, / And the mome raths outgrabe.'

Cartwright, William
English poet *born* September 1611
died Oxford 29 November 1643

Cartwright's father kept an inn at Cirencester after exhausting his financial resources. Educated at Oxford, Cartwright took orders in 1635 and earned a reputation as a verbose preacher. A fervent Royalist, he preached the victory sermon, in 1642, on the King's return to Oxford after Edgehill. When he died of camp fever Charles I, according to John Aubrey, 'dropt a teare at the newes of his death'. He wrote four plays as well as the poems in his collected *Works* (1651). A Metaphysical poet he wrote a stirring tribute 'On the Queen's Return from the Low Countries', in 1642: 'Courage was cast about her like a dress / Of solemn comeliness; / A gathered mind, and an untroubled face / Did give her dangers grace.'

Cary, Phoebe
American poet *born* near Cincinnati 4 September 1824
died 31 July 1871

With her sister Alice (1820–71), Phoebe Cary published the *Poems of Alice and Phoebe Cary* (1849). In 1850 Alice and Phoebe met Whittier in New York where they settled and set up a lively literary circle. Less prolific than her sister, Phoebe published *Poems and Parodies* (1845) as well as *Poems of Faith, Hope, and Love* (1868). Her account of 'The Leak in the Dyke' is suitably sentimental; ''Tis many a year since then; but still, / When the sea roars like a flood, / Their boys are taught what a boy can do /Who is brave and true and good. / For every man in that country / Takes his son by the hand, / And tells him of little Peter, / Whose courage saved the land.' Phoebe died five months after Alice's death.

Casey, John Keegan
Irish poet *born* 1846 *died* 1870

A Fenian, Casey was imprisoned in 1866 and died four years later as a direct result of the vicious treatment he received at the hands of the authorities. The poems he wrote are motivated by a passionate interpretation of Irish history. 'The Rising of the Moon AD 1798' celebrates a heroic ideal of nationalist struggle: 'Well they fought for poor old Ireland / And full bitter was their fate / (Oh! what glorious pride and sorrow / Fill the name of Ninety-Eight.) / Yet, thank God, e'en still are beating / Hearts in manhood's burning noon, / Who would follow in their footsteps / At the risin' of the moon!'

Cato, Nancy
Australian poet *born* Adelaide 1917

Educated at Adelaide University, Nancy Cato worked as a journalist. She helped found, in 1948, the Lyre-Bird Writers who promoted the cause of Australian poetry. Her poems are delicately descriptive yet persuasively assert the feminine principle of creativity against the conventional notion of the domesticated woman. Her meditative lines on 'The Shelter' show her exploring a subject often taken for granted: 'In this square box men call a house / My body hides, a frightened mouse / Snug in its close confining hole, / And would deny its questing soul; / But the black cat, dark Infinity, / Waits still outside to pounce on me.'

Caudwell, Christopher
English poet *born* London 1907 *died* Spain 1937

Educated at the Benedictine School, Ealing, Christopher St John Sprigg (his real name) became a reporter with the *Yorkshire Observer* then a director in a firm of aeronautical publishers. He joined the Communist Party in 1935 and went to Spain to fight for the International Brigade; like John Cornford, he was one of the casualties of the Spanish Civil War. Caudwell's verse, in *Poems* (1965), is didactic though 'The Progress of Poetry' evolves through images. At the end of the poem the Gardener says: 'In evening's sacred cool, among my bushes / A Figure was wont to walk. I deemed it angel. / But look at the footprint. There's hair between the toes!'

Causley, Charles
English poet *born* Launceston, Cornwall 1917

Causley served with the Royal Navy during the Second World War, an experience that is explored in several poems. He worked as a teacher and broadcaster, being Literary Editor of BBC West Region magazines in the 1950s. Influenced by the traditional ballads and by Auden and Betjeman, he has written a large number of literary ballads, distinguished by metrical skill and rhythmic control. 'Death of a Poet' shows him personalising the ballad metre: 'Over the church a bell broke like a wave upended. / The hearse left for winter with a lingering hiss. / I looked in the wet sky for a sign, but no bird descended. / I went across the road to the pub; wrote this.'

Chamberlain, Brenda
Welsh poet *born* Bangor 1912 *died* 1971

Educated at the Royal Academy, Brenda Chamberlain was both painter and poet. With Alun Lewis, she helped produce the 'Caseg Broadsheets' (poems plus wood engravings) during the Second World War. She lived for fifteen years on Ynys Enlli, Bardsey Island, off the tip of Llŷn, Caernarvonshire; also in Snowdonia. Her collections – *The Green Heart* (1958), *Poems with Drawings* (1969) – show a deep sympathy with crofting and fishing communities. 'Islandman', for example, is a vivid account of a character: 'Full of years and seasoned like a salt timber / The island fisherman has come to terms with death. / His crabbed fingers are coldly afire with phosphorus / From the night-sea he fishes for bright-armoured herring.'

Chamberlayne, William
English poet *born* 1619 *died* January 1689

Chamberlayne was a doctor at Shaftesbury. He joined the Royalists on the outbreak of Civil War and fought at the second battle of Newbury in 1644. His tragi-comedy *Love's Victory* appeared in 1658 and, a year later, he published his epic *Pharonnida*. In the following passage the heroic Argalia has been taken prisoner by the Turks: 'Argalia lies in chains, ordained to die / A sacrifice unto the cruelty / Of the fierce bashaw, whose loved favourite in / The combat late he slew; yet had not been / In that so much unhappy, had not he / That honoured then his sword with victory, / Half-brother to Janusa been, a bright / But cruel lady'.

Channing, William Ellery
American poet *born* Boston, Massachusetts 29 November 1817 *died* Concord, Massachusetts 23 December 1901

Known as William Ellery Channing II – to distinguish him from his namesake uncle, the clergyman – he was educated at Harvard. He moved to Concord to be close to Emerson and was drawn into the Transcendentalist circle. After working for some time in New York as an editor he returned to Concord though was something of a recluse after Thoreau's death in 1862. Channing then produced the first biography of *Thoreau, the Poet-naturalist* (1873). In, for example, 'Hymn of the Earth' he affirms the Transcendentalist approach: 'No leaf may fall, no pebble roll, / No drop of water lose the road; / The issues of the general Soul / Are mirrored in its round abode.'

Chapman, George
English poet *born* near Hitchin *c*1559 *died* 12 May 1634

A dramatist as well as a poet, Chapman's most celebrated achievement is his translation of Homer's *Iliad* (1611) and *Odyssey* (1616): Keats, 'On First Looking into Chapman's *Homer*', was transported when he 'heard Chapman speak out loud and bold'. He collaborated with Johnson in *Eastwood Ho!* (1605) and completed Marlowe's *Hero and Leander* (1598), contributing such outstanding items as the song beginning: 'O! Come, soft rest of cares, come Night, / Come, naked Virtue's only tire, / The reapèd harvest of the light, / Bound up in sheaves of sacred fire. / Love calls to war; / Sighs his alarms, / Lips his swords are / The field his arms'. His patrons were Prince Henry and, after 1612, the Earl of Somerset.

Chatterton, Thomas
English poet *born* Bristol 20 November 1752 *died* London 25 August 1770

Chatterton – 'the marvellous boy, / The sleepless soul that perished in his pride' as Wordsworth called him –grew up beside the church of St Mary Redcliffe where his uncle was sexton. Fascinated by the ecclesiastical archives, Chatterton began to create, complete with antique spelling and vocabulary, poems by an imaginary medieval monk Thomas Rowley. Horace Walpole was initially persuaded of the authenticity of the Rowley poems but Thomas Gray realised they were a modern fabrication. Discouraged and depressed, Chatterton poisoned himself with arsenic. In the minstrel's song from *Aella* he reveals his genuine poetic gift: 'Black hys cryne as the winter nyghte, / Whyte hys rode as the sommer snowe'.

Chaucer, Geoffrey

English poet *born* London 1340 *died* London 25 October 1400

The son of a vintner, Chaucer served as a page before going to the French wars in 1359. Captured near Reims he was released on payment of a ransom by Edward III. His marriage to Philippa Roet, a knight's daughter, helped his career and he was Controller of Customs for Wool then (in 1389) Clerk of the King's Works. Chaucer began work on his masterpiece, *The Canterbury Tales*, in 1387 but never completed the work. Nevertheless his status as father of English poetry is confirmed by its poetic quality which shines through the opening lines: 'Whan that Aprill with his shoures soote / The droghte of March hath perced to the roote, / And bathed every veyne in swich licour / Of which vertu engendered is the flour'.

Chesterton, G K

English poet *born* London 29 May 1874 *died* 14 June 1936

An estate agent's son, Chesterton studied at the Slade School of Art before embarking on his successful life as a versatile literary journalist. Enormously overweight, he was one of the leading figures in English letters achieving immense popularity with his detective stories featuring Father Brown and his humorous poems. Chesterton's collection *Wine, Water, and Song* (1915) contains some comic classics such as 'The Song Against Grocers': 'The wicked Grocer groces / In spirits and in wine, / Not frankly and in fellowship / As men in inns do dine; / But packed with soap and sardines / And carried off by grooms, / For to be snatched by Duchesses / And drunk in dressing-rooms.'

Chettle, Henry

English poet *born* London *c*1560 *died c*1607

A dyer's son, he became an apprentice printer in 1577 and subsequently a partner in a printing firm. He edited Robert Greene's *Groatsworth of Wit* (1592), wrote thirteen plays and collaborated in more than thirty joint productions. In 1599 he was imprisoned for debt. The Elizabethan anthology *England's Helicon* (1600) contains his lyric beginning: 'Diaphenia, like the daffodowndilly, / White as the sun, fair as the lily, / Heigh ho, how I do love thee! / I do love thee as my lambs / Are beloved of their dams; / How blest were I if thou wouldst prove me!' His only play to survive is *The Tragedy of Hoffman* (1602) which has some innovative touches.

Churchill, Charles
English poet *born* Westminster February 1731
died 4 November 1764

By secretly marrying at the age of seventeen, Churchill ruined his academic career and so took holy orders. In 1758 he succeeded his father as curate of Westminster. A reckless and argumentative man, he left his wife and offended his colleagues to such an extent that he had to resign his preferments. He published, in 1761, the *Rosciad*, in which he attacked the theatrical establishment of his time with satirical savagery: 'A Motley Figure, of the FRIBBLE Tribe, / Which Heart can scarce conceive, or pen describe, / Came *simp'ring* on; to ascertain whose sex / Twelve, sage *impannell'd* Matrons would perplex. / Nor *Male*, nor *Female*; *Neither*, and yet both; / Of *Neuter* Gender, tho' of *Irish* growth'.

Clare, John
English poet *born* Helpston, Northamptonshire 13 July 1793
died Northampton Lunatic Asylum 20 May 1864

Clare, whose father was a semi-literate labourer and whose mother was illiterate, was put to work on the land at the age of twelve. His teenage love for Mary Joyce, a farmer's daughter, was forbidden by her family; this emotional trauma further disturbed him and though he married, and had seven children, he continued to talk to Mary, after her death, and write poems to her. His depression deepened by drinking bouts; he spent the last twenty-three years of his life in an asylum. His descriptive poems of rural life have a quietly tragic tone: 'I long for scenes where man has never trod; / A place where woman never smiled or wept' he wrote in 'I am'.

Clark, Tom
American poet *born* 1941

Raised in Chicago, Clark was educated at the universities of Michigan, Cambridge and Essex. He returned to the USA in 1967 and settled in California. His first collection *Stones* (1969) was well received on account of poems such as 'Doors' which obsessively explores the theme of belonging: 'Something is the matter with the doors but no one stops / We rush through the joys that were there / The same weight of confusion leads me / To pick up everything I find / I turn this over in my hand and find you /Your hands are behind your head /Forming a grave on the pillows / Reality only listens when your words are true'.

Clarke, Austin
Irish poet *born* Dublin 1896 *died* 1974

Educated in Dublin at the Jesuit Belvedere College and the University, Clarke worked as a lecturer then as a journalist in England. He returned in 1937 to Dublin where he formed the Dublin Verse Speaking Society and the Lyric Theatre Company (which performed his own verse plays). Like Irish writers before him, he wanted to simulate Gaelic rhythms in English verse. His 'Martha Blake' shows his penetrating ability to portray character: 'She trembles for the Son of Man, / While the priest is murmuring / What she can scarcely tell, her heart / is making such a stir; / But when he picks a particle / And she puts out her tongue, / That joy is the glittering of candles / And benediction sung.'

Clarke, Gillian
Welsh poet *born* Cardiff 1937

Educated at University College, Cardiff, Gillian Clarke became a teacher in a technical college. Her poetry first appeared in *Poetry Wales* in 1970 and she became editor of the *Anglo-Welsh Review*. Her finest poems are informed by an insight into suffering and a powerfully descriptive diction. 'Lunchtime Lecture' contemplates the remains of a young woman from the third millenium BC: 'Some plague or violence / Destroyed her, and her whiteness lay safe in a shroud / Of silence, undisturbed, unrained on, dark / For four thousand years.' In the final stanza the woman is compared to 'a tree in winter, stripped white on a black sky, / Leafless formality, brow, bough in fine relief.'

Clemo, Jack
English poet *born* St Stephen's, St Austell,
Cornwall 11 March 1916

Clemo, who became blind in 1955, was the son of a clay labourer. A lifetime spent in St Stephen's, in Cornwall, provides the content of his verse. His poems are highly individual explorations of a landscape that holds for him evidence of spiritual survival. 'Christ in the Clay-Pit' insists: 'I see His blood / In rusty stains on pit-props, waggon-frames / Bristling with nails, not leaves. There were no leaves / Upon His chosen Tree, / No parasitic flowering

over shames / Of Eden's primal infidelity.' At the end of the poem
Clemo rejects 'worshippers of beauty' and opts for the pit which
must be 'rendered fit / By violent mouldings through the
tunnelled ways / Of all He would regain.'

Cleveland, John

English poet *baptised* Loughborough 20 June 1613
died London 29 April 1658

A clergyman's son, Cleveland was educated at Cambridge where,
in 1634, he became a Fellow of St John's and Reader in Rhetoric.
He opposed Cromwell's election as Member for Cambridge in
1640, and was consequently ejected from his college two years
later. From 1645-6 he was Judge Advocate at Newark and
defended the town against the Scots. Imprisoned in 1655-6 he
successfully appealed to Cromwell for his release. He later lived
in London. A Metaphysical poet, his sensuous work, such as his
poem 'To the State of Love, or the Senses Festival', was greatly
admired: 'Is not the Universe strati-lac't, / When I can claspe it in
the Waste? / My amorous foulds about thee hurl'd, / With Drake,
I compass in the world.'

Clough, Arthur Hugh

English poet *born* Liverpool 1 January 1819
died Florence 13 November 1861

Clough was the son of a cotton merchant who, in 1823, took his
family to the USA. Sent back to England for his education Clough
was Dr Thomas Arnold's outstanding pupil at Rugby School and a
close friend of Matthew Arnold's at Oxford. In 1852 he was
engaged to Florence Nightingale's cousin Blanche Smith and,
after an unsuccessful year in America, returned to England to
marry Blanche and become an examiner in the Education Office.
Amours de Voyage was written in Rome in 1849 in Clough's own
version of the classical hexameter. Hesitant in tone and satirical
in style, it demonstrates Clough's modernity: 'So, I have seen a
man killed! An experience that, among others!'

Coatsworth, Elizabeth

American poet *born* Buffalo, New York 31 May 1893

Best known as the author of children's books, such as *The Cat Who
Went to Heaven* (1930), Elizabeth Jane Coatsworth was educated at
Vassar. In 1929 she married Henry Beston, author of *The
Outermost House* (1928), and lived with him in their summer house
at Hingham, Massachusetts and at Chimney Farm in Maine.
(Henry Beston died in 1968.) Her verse, like her prose, is
engagingly direct and expresses a sense of wonder at the variety
of natural and animal life. 'Song of the Rabbits Outside the

Tavern' begins: 'We who play under the pines, / We who dance in the snow / That shines blue in the light of the moon / Sometimes halt as we go, /Stand with our ears erect, / Our noses testing the air, / To gaze at the golden world / Behind the windows there.'

Coffin, Robert P T

American poet *born* Brunswick, Maine 18 March 1892 *died* 1955

Coffin was educated at Bowdoin and Oxford (where he was a Rhodes Scholar); he taught English at Wells College, New York, for thirteen years before going back to Bowdoin as Pierce Professor of English. A prolific writer he won the Pulitzer Prize in 1936 for his collection *Strange Holiness*. He wrote sentimentally in praise of the people of New England but his verse has a formal tautness. 'New Englanders Are Maples' begins; 'New Englanders are like the pasture slopes / Behind their barns. You put them down as sober, / And then one day you wake up, and you find them / Red and golden maples of October.' Coffin also wrote biographies and novels, and about the qualities of New England.

Cogswell, Fred

Canadian poet *born* 1917

Fred Cogswell settled in Fredericton where he taught English and published Fiddlehead Poetry Books. After his daughter, Carmen, died of cancer on 28 December 1981, he wrote the poems in his collection *Pearls* (1983). Here the poet tries to confront an unbearably painful experience by acknowledging his anguish in conventionally crafted verse. 'The Death', for example, begins by describing a visit to his daughter's bedside as she tried to hold on to life: 'At last her breathing stopped. She died. / My giving done, I walked outside / And felt the world's vacuity / Merge with the emptiness in me.'

Cohen, Leonard

Canadian poet *born* Montreal 1934

Cohen is a singer-songwriter with a large following who flock to his professional performances. He was educated at McGill University and did postgraduate work at Columbia. He has published two novels, *The Favourite Game* (1963) and *Beautiful Lovers* (1966). His poems project his personality as that of an individual anguished in a hostile world, as in 'What I'm Doing Here': 'I do not know if the world has lied / I have lied / I do not know if the world has conspired against love / I have conspired against love / The atmosphere of torture is no comfort / I have tortured / Even without the mushroom cloud / still I would have hated / Listen / I would have done the same things / even if there were no death'.

Cole, Barry
English poet *born* 1936

Barry Cole left his London school at fifteen and pursued a career in the Central Office of Information. He published several novels, including *A Run Across the Island* (1968), *Joseph Winter's Patronage* (1969) and *The Search for Rita* (1970). His poems, in (for example) *The Visitors* (1970), offer imaginative scenarios drawn from the domestic and emotional details of his life. 'Reported Missing' beings: 'Can you give me a precise description? / said the policeman. Her lips, I told him, / were soft. Could you give me, he said, pencil / raised, a metaphor? Soft as an open mouth, / I said. Were there any noticeable / peculiarities? he asked. Her hair hung / heavily, I said.'

Coleridge, Mary
English poet *born* London, 23 September 1861
died 25 August 1907

Mary Coleridge's father was a lawyer friendly with Tennyson and Browning so she was familiar with the leading literary figures of the Victorian age. She passed most of her time at home though she was drawn into the literary circles formed by Victorian women. She published novels as well as poems signed with a Greek pseudonym meaning 'The Wanderer'. There is a profoundly visionary quality to some of her poems, such as 'The Other Side of a Mirror': 'I sat before my glass one day, / And conjured up a vision bare, / Unlike the aspects glad and gay, /That erst were found reflected there – / The vision of a woman, wild / With more than womanly despair.'

Coleridge, Samuel Taylor
English poet *born* Ottery St Mary, Devon
21 October 1772 *died* 25 July 1834

A clergyman's son, Coleridge was educated at Cambridge. He formed a friendship first with Southey then with Wordsworth before marrying Sara Fricker as part of his unsuccessful plan to set up a Pantisocratic commune in America. In 1796 he settled at Nether Stowey and two years later published *Lyrical Ballads* with Wordsworth. In 1800 he moved to Keswick where he became addicted to opium and separated from his wife and his beloved Sara Hutchinson. His work explores intellectual issues but sometimes soars majestically, as in 'Kubla Khan' (prompted by an opium-induced dream): 'Weave a circle round him thrice, / And close your eyes with holy dread: / For he on honey-dew hath fed, / And drunk the milk of Paradise.'

Coles, Don
Canadian poet *born* Woodstock, Ontario 1928

Before joining the Humanities Division of York University, Toronto, Coles lived and studied in England, Italy, Scandinavia and Central Europe. He published *The Prinzhorn Collection* in 1982. For all his technical sophistication and cultural references, Coles writes a lyrical poetry that has its roots in Canadian romanticism. In his sequence 'Landsides' he says (section XIII) 'Sometimes I'll rant, or grieve, / But rather now would sidestep / Eternitywards and glimpse a sort of / Comfort there, out under the stars / where every man's // In soul-motion, / And know the private life's / Motley and generous / And in its manifoldness flies / Finally above pity'.

Collins, Anne
English poet *flourished* 1653

On the title page of *Divine Songs and Meditations* (1653) 'An. Collins' is given as the name of the author. A prologue explains only that the author has suffered from sickness and has written some of her poems when ill. The songs, such as the first one, convey courage in a situation of stress: 'He therefore that sustaineth / Affliction or distress, / Which every member paineth, / And findeth no release: / Let such therefore despair not, / But on firm hope depend, / Whose griefs immortal are not, / And therefore must have end. / They that faint / With complaint / Therefore are to blame: / They add to their afflictions, / And amplify the same.'

Collins, Mortimer
English poet *born* Plymouth 29 June 1827
died Richmond 28 July 1876

A solicitor's son, Collins became a teacher of mathematics at Queen Elizabeth's College, Guernsey. In 1856 he decided to devote himself to fulltime writing and turned out fifteen novels (including *A Fight with Fortune*, 1876) and a mass of journalistic work. His books of verse range from *Idyls and Rhymes* (1855) to the satirical *The British Birds* (1872) in which he ridicules (for example) 'The Positivists': 'If you are pious, (mild form of insanity,) / Bow down and worship the mass of humanity. / Other religions are buried in mists; / We're our own gods, say the Positivists.' Collins was known as the 'King of the Bohemians' because of his sartorial style.

Collins, William
English poet *born* Chichester 25 December 1721
died Chichester 12 June 1759

The author of several memorable Odes, William Collins endured mental instability and was considered insane at the time of his death. A hatter's son, he was educated at Oxford and gained a rakish reputation which he survived as the result of a legacy of 1749. His poetry has formal strength and a subtle suggestion of sensitivity. His 'Ode to Evening' is delicately descriptive and his 'Ode, Written in . . . 1746' demonstrates the melodic balance of his verse: 'How sleep the brave, who sink to rest, / By all their country's wishes blest! / When Spring, with dewy fingers cold, / Returns to deck their hallow'd mould, / She there shall dress a sweeter sod, / Than Fancy's feet have ever trod.'

Colum, Padraic
Irish poet *born* Longford 8 December 1881 *died* 1972

Educated locally, Colum worked in Dublin as a railway clerk. With Yeats, G W Russell and Synge he promoted the Irish Literary Renascence and wrote plays, such as *The Land* (1905), for the Abbey Theatre. He helped found the *Irish Review* and was its editor for a period. He visited the USA in 1914 and settled in New York in 1939: in 1952 he received the award of the American Academy of Poets and, in 1953, the Gregory Medal of the Irish Academy of letters. His 'A poor Scholar of the Forties' ends ironically: 'And what to me is Gael or Gall? / Less than the Latin or the Greek. / I teach these by the dim rush-light, / In smoky cabins night and week.'

Congreve, William
English poet *born* Bardsey, near Leeds February 1670
died 19 January 1729

Congreve's father, an army officer, was garrisoned in Ireland and the poet was educated at Trinity College, Dublin. He returned to England in 1688 and brilliantly extended the range of Restoration comedy with successes such as *The Way of the World* (1700). He was criticised for the erotic content of his work but enjoyed the admiration of the Court. Blind during the last years of his life, he was buried in Westminster Abbey. He wrote fine lyrics, as witness: 'False though she be to me and love, / I'll ne'er pursue revenge; / For still the charmer I approve / Though I deplore her change. // In hours of bliss we oft have met: / They could not always last; / And though the present I regret, / I'm grateful for the past.'

Connor, Tony
English poet *born* 1930

After leaving school at the age of fourteen, Connor worked as a textile designer in Manchester for several years. He later lived in the USA as a professor of English at Wesleyan University. His approach is direct as he documents the most relevant incidents from his own life rather than speculating on abstractions. Connor always provides a wealth of detail as when he writes, for example, of 'Lodgers': 'Some boozed and came in late, and some / kept to their bedrooms every night, / some liked a joke, and some were glum, / and all of them were always right. / Unwitting fathers; how their deep / voices come back to me in sleep!'

Conquest, Robert
English poet *born* Malvern 15 July 1917

After an Oxford education, Conquest was in the British Army during the Second World War and then worked for ten years in the Foreign Service in Sofia and London. A distinguished academic he has written persuasively about the iniquities of Stalinism and has also promoted the serious study of science fiction. His anthology *New Lines* (1956) brought 'the Movement' into being and he has continually observed the conservative conventions of English verse. In poems such as 'Man and Woman' he examines human emotions from a formal distance: 'Other tensions rasp the brain and body / Rougher, stitch the tic on eyelid or in cheek: / Desperations of money, fears / Of torn flesh, of death.'

Conran, Anthony
Welsh poet *born* India 1931

Conran came to Wales at the age of eight and became a tutor in English at Bangor. His translations in *The Penguin Book of Welsh Verse* (1967) were highly acclaimed as was his discussion of the tradition of Welsh praise-poetry. His own work in English verse treats the notion of tradition ironically, as in 'Death of a Species': 'Talk of old families: / Among the teacups flowing into me / My ancestors! The tundra settles. / Huge snow against the wide plain blows. / Wool on my mammoth back stiffens with icicles / And wearily my awkward trunk gropes for mere moss / And my enormous knees kneel into sharp mud.'

Cook, Eliza
English poet *born* Southwark 24 December 1818
died 23 September 1889

The daughter of a brazier, Eliza Cook was one of eleven children. She began to write verse at the age of fifteen and published her first collection, *Lays of a Wild Harp*, in 1835. In 1836 the *Weekly Dispatch* published her 'The Old Arm-Chair' anonymously though its popularity compelled her to acknowledge it. The poem is a sentimental eulogy to an armchair that is treated as a sacred object because the narrator's mother died in it: 'Say it is folly, and deem me weak, / While the scalding drops start down my cheek; / But I love it! I love it! and cannot tear / My soul from a mother's old arm-chair.' From 1849 to 1854 Eliza edited *Eliza Cook's Journal*.

Corbet, Richard
English poet *born* Ewell, Surrey 1582 *died* 28 July 1635

A gardener's son, Corbet was educated at Oxford. After taking
holy orders he became Dean of Christ Church, Bishop of Oxford
(where his chaplain was the poet William Strode) and Bishop of
Norwich. Corbet's poems put his considerable wit to a moralistic
purpose, as witness the second stanza of his poem 'Farewell,
rewards and Fairies': 'Lament, lament, old Abbies, / The fairies'
lost command; / they did but change priests' babies / But some
have changed your land; / And all your children sprung from
thence / Are now grown Puritans, / Who live as changelings ever
since / For love of your domains.' His *Certain Elegant Poems*
appeared in 1647.

Cornford, John
English poet *born* Cambridge 27 December 1915
died Córdoba 28 December 1936

Cornford was a research student at Cambridge where his father
was Laurence Professor of Ancient Philosophy. A brilliant
scholar, he became a leader of the Cambridge University
Communist Party and joint-secretary of the Socialist Club. He
was the first Englishman to go to the front in the Spanish Civil
War and was killed in action the day after his twenty-first
birthday. His poem 'Full moon at Tierz; before the storming of
Huesca' was written in the year of his death and contains his
credo: 'Our fight's not won till the workers of all the world /
Stand by our guard on Huesca's plain / Swear that our dead
fought not in vain, / Raise the red flag triumphantly / For
Communism and for liberty.'

Corso, Gregory
American poet *born* New York 26 March 1930

Brought up by foster parents, Corso was an insecure youth whose
violent moods were transformed into poetic energy when he met
Allen Ginsberg. Under Ginsberg's influence he became one of
the leading Beat poets, writing poems of emotional power and
radical discontent. His meditative poem on 'Marriage' shows a
powerful use of incidental detail as he thinks of himself as a father
in 'hot smelly tight New York City / seven flights up roaches and
rats in the walls / a fat Reichian wife screeching over potatoes Get
a job! / And five nose running brats in love with Batman / And the
neighbours all toothless and dry haired'.

Cory, William
English poet *born* Torrington, Devon 9 January 1823
died 11 June 1892

Son of a Devon squire, William Johnson was educated at Eton

and Cambridge, where he became a Fellow of King's College. From 1847–71 he was an assistant master at Eton; in 1863 he wrote the 'Eton Boating Song' which appeared in the school magazine of 1865. Under his own name William Johnson he published *Ionica* (1858), a collection of lyrics. When he inherited an estate in 1872 he took the surname Cory and settled at Hampstead. Several of his poems have a forced poetic diction but 'Mimnermus in Church' reveals his intelligence: 'You bid me lift my mean desires / From faltering lips and fitful veins / To sexless souls, ideal quires, / Unwearied voices, wordless strains'.

Cotton, Charles
English poet *born* Beresford Dale, Staffordshire 28 April 1630 *died* London 14 February 1687

As his father was a courtier, heavy-drinker and friend of the leading English writers, Charles Cotton grew up in Beresford Hall in an easy atmosphere of cultural and convivial over-indulgence. During the Commonwealth he developed his appetite for burlesque poetry to express tastes acquired from his father. An 'Ode' concludes: 'Let me have sack, tobacco store, / A drunken friend, a little whore, / *Protector*, I will ask no more.' He married his cousin, Isabella Hutchinson, and produced nine children and formed such a close friendship with Izaak Walton that he was asked to write the second part of *The Compleat Angler* (published in 1676).

Courthope, William John
English poet *born* South Malling, near Lewes, Sussex 17 July 1842 *died* 10 April 1917

Son of the rector of South Malling, Courthope was educated at Oxford where he won the Newdigate Prize for Poetry. He was appointed an examiner in the Education Office in 1869 and from 1887–1907 was a Civil Service Commissioner. He was elected Professor of Poetry at Oxford in 1895. His critical *History of English Poetry* (1895–1900) was much admired in its time. His talent for humorous verse is shown in his *The Paradise of Birds* (1869), an imitation of the *Birds* of Aristophanes. Here Maresnest expounds the theory of evolution: 'And though Man has a place from the Sponge at the base in variety farthest removed, / And has managed to reach what he calls soul and speech, yet his blood is by language approved.'

Coward, Sir Noel
English poet *born* Teddington, Middlesex 16 December 1899 *died* Jamaica 26 March 1973

After making his stage *debut* in 1911 (in *The Goldfish*) Coward pursued a hugely successful career as a complete man of the theatre. A gifted actor, he wrote classic comedies such as *Hay Fever* (1925) and also composed memorable songs such as 'Some Day I'll Find You' and 'Mad Dogs and Englishmen' which he performed in cabaret. His collection of verse, *Not Yet the Dodo* (1967), has the inventive verbal quality that made Coward one of the most admired writers of his time. 'The Boy Actor' ends: 'I never cared who scored the goal / Or which side won the silver cup, / I never learned to bat or bowl / But I heard the curtain going up.'

Cowley, Abraham

English poet *born* London 1618 *died* Chertsey 28 July 1667

A stationer's son, Cowley was educated at Cambridge and became a Fellow in 1640. Before the Puritans could eject him he moved to Oxford in 1643 and later served, in France, as secretary to Queen Henrietta Maria. On his return to England in 1654 he was imprisoned as a Royalist spy but survived by pretending to conform to Cromwell's regime. After the Restoration he leased land from Henrietta Maria. An immensely erudite man he wrote an extremely sophisticated Metaphysical poetry and introduced the Pindaric ode to English verse. His poem 'On the Death of Mr Crashaw' begins by asserting: 'Poet and Saint! to thee alone are given / The two most sacred names of Earth and Heaven.'

Cowley, Malcolm

American poet *born* Belsano, Pennsylvania 24 September 1898

A graduate of Harvard, Cowley spent two years (1920–2) at the University of Montpelier on an American Field Service Fellowship. He came back to Paris in 1924 and joined other expatriates of the so-called 'Lost Generation'. Cowley helped edit two experimental magazines *Broom* and *Secession* and was literary editor of the *New Republic* from 1920–44. A poet who tends to draw on literature for his material, he exploits the theme of the double in 'William Wilson', a variant of Poe's story of the same title: 'As red as wine, as white as wine, / his face which is not and is mine / and apes my face's pantomime.' Cowley's *Think Back on Us* (1967) collects his writings from the 1930s.

Cowper, William

English poet *born* Great Berkhamsted, Hertfordshire 26 November 1731 *died* East Dereham, Norfolk 25 April 1800

Cowper, a rector's son, was called to the Bar in 1754 but depression led to attempted suicide and treatment in a St Albans asylum. In 1765 he went to live with the Rev Unwin in Huntingdon, then with Unwin's widow in Olney where he came under the evangelical influence of the Rev John Newton with whom he produced *Olney Hymns* (1779). In 1773 another attack of

insanity prevented his marriage to Mrs Unwin and further attacks
followed. At the suggestion of his friend Lady Austin he wrote the
comic ballad 'The Diverting History of John Gilpin' and *The Task*
(1785), a discursive poem in blank verse. His last poem contrasts
his fate with that of 'The Castaway': 'But I beneath a rougher
sea, / And whelm'd in deeper gulfs than he.'

Crabbe, George
English poet *born* Aldeburgh, Suffolk 24 December 1754
died Trowbridge 3 February 1832

Son of a salt-tax collector, Crabbe worked as a surgeon before
moving to London where he was championed by Edmund Burke.
He was, from 1782–5, domestic chaplain at Belvoir Castle and in
1783, the year of *The Village*, married Sarah Elmy. When Sarah
died in 1813 Crabbe went to Trowbridge as rector. He was an
inventive narrative poet who undermined the pastoral tradition
with his metrical realism, as in Book I of *The Village*: 'Can poets
soothe you, when you pine for bread, / By winding myrtles round
your ruin'd shed? / Can their light tales your weighty griefs
o'erpower, / Or glad with airy mirth the toilsome hour?'

Crane, Hart
American poet *born* Garrettsville, Ohio 21 July 1899
died Gulf of Mexico 26 April 1932

After the divorce of his parents Crane was raised by his father, a
candy manufacturer determined to 'drive the poetry nonsense'
out of him. In 1920 Crane broke with his father and found a
patron, Otto H Kahn, who enabled him to complete *The Bridge*
(1930), his vision of America. A self-destructive drinker and
homosexual, Crane sought spiritual salvation in Mexico. When
he failed to find it he boarded the northbound steamer *Orizaba*
and, some three hundred miles north of Havana, jumped to his
death in the water. His symbolically charged verse is often
melancholy as in 'The Phantom Bark': 'So dream thy sails, O
phantom bark / that I thy drowned man may speak again'.

Crane, Stephen
American poet *born* Newark, New Jersey 1 November 1871
died 5 June 1900

Fourteenth child of a Methodist minister, Crane was educated at
military academy, Lafayette College and Syracuse University
(where he was captain of the baseball team). A war correspondent
who worked in Cuba and Greece, he used his experience to give a
realistic tone to his masterly novel *The Red Badge of Courage* (1895).
His collection *War is Kind* (1899) contains his opinion of
newspapers: 'A newspaper is a collection of half-injustices /
Which, bawled by boys from mile to mile, / Spreads its curious

opinion / To a million merciful and sneering men, / While families cuddle the joys of the fireside / When spurred by tale of dire lone agony.' Crane died, of tuberculosis, in Germany.

Crapsey, Adelaide
American poet *born* 1878 *died* Saranac Lake, New York
8 October 1914

Brought up in Rochester, New York, Adelaide Crapsey studied at Vassar College where she later taught poetry. Like Robert Louis Stevenson, who had been there in 1887, she came to the sanatorium at Saranac Lake to seek relief from a tubercular condition. Her poems appeared posthumously in *Verse* (1915) and her *Study of English Metrics* (1918) demonstrated her understanding of poetic technique. Her poem 'The Lonely Death' shows her direct treatment of a painful subject: 'In the cold I will rise, I will bathe / In waters of ice; myself / Will shiver, and shrive myself, / Alone in the dawn, and anoint / Forehead and feet and hands'.

Crashaw, Richard
English poet *born* London *c* 1612
died Loretto, Italy 21 August 1649

Son of a prominent Puritan, Crashaw became an Anglican priest at Peterhouse after leaving Cambridge University. When the chapel at Peterhouse was desecrated by the Parliamentary Commission, Crashaw moved to Europe where he became a Roman Catholic convert. In 1649 he was given a post at Loretto Cathedral. Influenced by Marino, the Italian baroque poet, he transformed the Metaphysical mode into an ecstatically ornamental expression of his faith. 'Hymn to Saint Teresa' reveals his rhapsodic approach to a sacred subject: 'O what delight, when revealed Life shall stand / And teach thy lips heaven with his hand, / On which thou now mayst to thy wishes / Heap up thy consecrated kisses.'

Crawford, Isabella Valancy
Canadian poet *born* Dublin 1850 *died* 1887

Isabella Valancy Crawford left Ireland, at the age of eight, and settled with her family in Ontario. Always financially insecure, Isabella lived with her mother in Toronto, constantly writing the poems that were posthumously assembled in *Collected Poems* of 1905. Her poems extend the landscape of Ontario into a vision of a land teeming with natural vitality, as in 'The Dark Stag': 'Red torches of the sumach glare, / Fall's council-fires are lit; / The bittern, squaw-like, scolds the air; / The wild duck splashes loudly where / The rustling rice-spears knit.' Her poetic example helped to form a Canadian national cultural consciousness.

Crawford, Robert
Scottish poet *died* 1733

Little is known about Crawford's life beyond a few facts. He was the brother of Colonel Crawford of Achinames and he was drowned when coming from France. He contributed two fine songs to Allan Ramsay's *Tea-Table Miscellany*. These were 'Tweedside' and 'The Bush Aboon Traquair' which begins: 'Hear me, ye nymphs, and every swain, / I'll tell how Peggy grieves me; / Though thus I languish and complain, / Alas! she ne'er believes me. / My vows and sighs, like silent air, / Unheeded, never move her; / At the bonnie Bush aboon Traquair, / 'Twas there I first did love her.' Another version of the song was produced in the nineteenth century by J C Shairp.

Creeley, Robert
American poet *born* Arlington, Massachusetts 21 May 1926

Educated at Harvard, Creeley served with the American Field Service in India and Burma during the Second World War. He later taught at Black Mountain College where he responded to the aesthetic of Charles Olson – whose *Selected Writings* he edited in 1966. Creeley constantly affirms the importance of emotional warmth in verse that is conversationally candid and rhythmically abrupt, as in 'For Love': 'Love, what do I think / to say. I cannot say it. / What have you become to ask, / what have I made you into, // companion, good company, / crossed legs with skirt, or / soft body under the bones of the bed.' Creeley's novel *The Island* (1963) has interesting autobiographical aspects.

Cronin, Anthony
Irish poet *born* County Wexford 1925

Educated at Trinity College, Dublin, Cronin moved to London where he worked as literary editor of *Time and Tide*. He subsequently lived in Spain before returning to Dublin. His novel *The Life of Riley* appeared in 1964, his *Collected Poems* in 1973. In his 'Elegy for the Nightbound' he expresses an urban anguish: 'Yet tonight as the twig-breaking winter creeps in through the garden / And the blasphemous Irish are fighting on Hammersmith Broadway / The living pray to the living to recognise difference: / For who can believe that we are but the sum of our actions? / Only the saint and the dead and the deer and the dog.'

Cruickshank, Helen B
Scottish poet *born* Hillside, Angus 15 May 1886
died Edinburgh 2 March 1975

After leaving school at fifteen, Helen Burness Cruickshank became a Civil Servant in London, staying there for ten years

before returning to Edinburgh for another thirty years in her
chosen profession. She was regarded as the first lady of Scottish
letters and her kindness was legendary: in his most difficult years
Hugh MacDiarmid received moral and material support from her.
She published work in both English and a dialect Scots that drew
on her upbringing in Angus. Her use of dialect is seen to
advantage in the lyric 'Shy Geordie': 'Up the Noran Water / In by
Inglismaddy, / Annie's got a bairnie. / That hasna got a daddy.'

Cullen, Countee
American poet *born* New York 30 May 1903
died New York 10 January 1946

Countee Porter was eleven when his mother died and he was
adopted by Reverence Frederick Cullen, pastor of the Harlem
mission of St Mark's Episcopal Church. He was educated at the
universities of New York and Harvard and later taught French at
his old junior high school in Harlem. Cullen's first collection *Color*
(1925), established him as an important poet and he was regarded
as the literary voice of Harlem: his funeral was attended by more
than 3,000 people. His poem 'Heritage' begins: 'What is Africa to
me: / Copper sun or scarlet sea, / Jungle star or jungle track, /
Strong bronzed men, or regal black / Women from whose loins I
sprang / When the birds of Eden sang?'

Cummings, E E
American poet *born* Cambridge, Massachusetts 14 October
1894 *died* New York 3 September 1962

Edward Eselm Cummings's father, who taught at Harvard and
subsequently became minister of Old South Church, Boston,
encouraged the academic talents of the poet. After graduating
from Harvard, though, Cummings quit academic life to work for
a mail order firm in New York. During the First World War,
Cummings went on active service to France where he was
detained, as a suspicious person, for three months in a prison
camp – *The Enormous Room* (1922) of his prose book. 'Mr
Lowercase Highbrow', as he was called, printed his name
e e cummings and used a distinctive typography as a visual means
to a lyrical end: 'a tall / wind / is dragging / the / sea / with /
dream / –S'.

Cunard, Nancy
English poet *born* 1896 *died* 1965

The daughter of Sir Bache and Lady Cunard, she moved, after an
unhappy first marriage, to Paris where she became one of the
cultural celebrities of the 1920s and 1930s. At her Normandy
home she founded the Hours Press which brought out Samuel
Beckett's first book and published poems by Pound and Graves.

She went to Spain, during the Civil War, as a correspondent for the Manchester *Guardian*. During the Second World War she worked for the Free French in London and published, under the imprint La France Libre, the anthology *Poems for France* (1940). Her First World War poem 'Zeppelins' ends: 'But in the morning men began again / To mock Death following in bitter pain.'

Cunningham, Allan
Scottish poet *born* Dalswinton, Dumfriesshire 7 December 1784 *died* London 30 October 1842

Cunningham was an apprentice stonemason whose enthusiasm for literature was stimulated through his father's friendship with Robert Burns. When R H Cromek was collecting Scottish songs for his *Remains of Nithsdale and Galloway Song* (1810) Cunningham passed off some of his own compositions as examples from the oral tradition. From 1811 onwards, he lived in London as a parliamentary reporter and superintendent of works to the sculptor Chantrey. His 'A Wet Sheet and a Flowing Sea' (sheet being the rope attached to the lower corner of a sail) ends enthusiastically 'The wind is piping loud, my boys, / The lightning flashing free - / While the hollow oak our palace is, / Our heritage the sea.'

Curnow, Allen
New Zealand poet *born* Timaru 1911

Educated at the universities of Canterbury and Auckland, and at St John's Theological College (Auckland), Curnow was (from 1935-8) a journalist with the Christchurch *Press* and in London. In 1951 he joined the English Department of Auckland University, retiring as Associate Professor in 1977. His many collections include *Enemies* (1937), *Jack Without Magic* (1946), *A Small Room With Large Windows* (1962), *An Incorrigible Music* (1979). Regarded as the most talented New Zealand poet of his generation, his 'The Unhistoric Story' reflects on the history of his country: 'Spider, clever and fragile, Cook showed how / To spring a trap for islands, turning from planets / His measuring mission'.

Curran, John Philpot
Irish poet *born* Newmarket, County Cork 1750 *died* London 1817

Celebrated as a raconteur and wit, Curran took an amused look at life in his verse. His most memorable poem, 'The Deserter's Meditation' was written after he had encountered a man on the run from the army. The second stanza (of two) has a jauntiness underscored by the internal rhymes: 'To joy a stranger, a way-worn ranger, / In every danger my course I've run; / Now hope all ending, and death befriending / His last aid lending, my cares are done. / No more a rover, or hapless lover, / My griefs are over –

my glass runs low; / Then for that reason, and for a season, / Let us be merry before we go.'

Daley, Victor
Australian poet *born* 1858 *died* 1905

Daley left Ireland to live in Australia where he earned very little money from his writing since his Celtic tone and world-weary aestheticism were not qualities greatly valued by the Australian reading public. His poem 'Dreams' shows how solemnly Daley received the notion of art for art's sake as he indulges his appetite for poetry: 'I have been dreaming all a summer day / Of rare and dainty poems I would write; / Love-lyrics delicate as lilac-scent, / Soft idylls woven of wind, and flower, and stream, / And songs and sonnets carven in fine gold.' In complete contrast to his self-consciously poetic stance is the polemical manner he adopted in the verse published under the pseudonym Creeve Roe.

Dallas, Ruth
New Zealand poet *born* Invercargill 1919

A writer of children's novels, as well as a poet, Ruth Dallas settled in Dunedin. Her collections include *The Turning Wheel* (1961), *Day Book* (1966), *Shadow Show* (1968). Her affirmation of natural grace is impressively expressed in 'Among Old Houses' where she contrasts the spectacle of mechanical debris with seasonal growth: 'No yard made hideous by discarded oil-drums, / Rusted scrap-iron, crates, collapsing sheds, / That is not visited by madcap Spring; / It's not just one old tree that glitters forth, / Not two, but tree on blossoming tree – / A fairytale procession, like the arrival / Of twenty sisters ready for a ball, / Or mermaids, voluptuous, glistening from the sea.'

Dana, Richard Henry
American poet *born* Cambridge, Massachusetts
15 November 1787 *died* 1879

Dana (who was descended, through his mother, from Anne Bradsteet) was forced to leave Harvard because of his participation in a student rebellion. He became a lawyer, then a politician, then a journalist: he helped found *The North American Review* and ran his own journal, *The Idle Man*, in New York. He is remembered for sentimental lyrics such as 'The Little Beach-Bird': 'Thou call'st along the sand, and haunt'st the surge, / Restless and sad; as if, in strange accord / With motion, and with roar / Of waves that drive to shore, / One spirit did ye urge – / the Mystery – the Word.' His son, Richard Henry Dana, Jr, wrote *Two years Before the Mast* (1840).

Daniel, Samuel
English poet *born* near Taunton 1562
died Somerset October 1619

Son of a music-master, Daniel was educated at Oxford before
becoming tutor to William Herbert, third Earl of Pembroke, then
to Anne Clifford, daughter of the Countess of Cumberland. From
1603–14 he composed four court entertainments, in 1615 he
helped form a Children's Company at Bristol, and from 1615–18
he was Inspector of the Children of the Queen's Revels. The first
four books of Daniel's *Civil Wars between the Two Houses of York and
Lancaster* appeared in 1595, the complete work of eight books in
1609. His description of the battle of Towton (1461) is
characteristically atmospheric: 'It was upon the twi-light of that
day / (That peacefull day) when the Religious beare / The Olive-
branches as they go to pray'.

Darley, George
Irish poet *born* Dublin 1795 *died* 23 November 1846

Educated at Trinity College, Dublin, Darley moved to London to
set himself up as a successful man of letters: under the
pseudonym 'John Lacy' he wrote for the *London Magazine* then
became a critical force on the *Athenaeum*. As well as writing novels
and plays he was a gifted mathematician. Perhaps because of his
stammer, he wrote poems, like 'Nepenthe', with extremely
flowing lines and strong alliteration: 'The glittering fountains
seemed to pour / Steep downward rills of molten ore, / Glassily
tinkling smooth between / Broom-shaded banks of golden green'.

Darnley, Lord
Scottish poet *born* c1545 *died* Kirk o'Field, near Edinburgh
10 February 1567

The cousin and (in 1565) second husband of Mary Queen of
Scots, Henry Stuart, Lord Darnley, was born in England. Though
he was capable of charm, he seemed 'an agreeable nincompoop'
to one of his contemporaries and his marriage to Mary was a
disaster for both of them. After the murder of Riccio, in 1566,
Darnley was expendable and he was assassinated (almost certainly
at Bothwell's bidding) while convalescing at the old provost's
house outside Edinburgh's town wall. His poem 'To the Queen'
shows metrical skill: 'Be governour baith guide and gratious; /
Be leill and luifand to thy liegis all; / Be large of fredome and no
thing desyrous; / Be just to pure for ony thing may fall'.
leill honest

Darwin, Erasmus
English poet *born* Elston, Nottinghamshire
12 December 1731 *died* 18 April 1802

Grandfather of Charles Darwin, the naturalist, Erasmus Darwin was educated at Oxford and Edinburgh where he qualified as a doctor. He settled in Lichfield where he was twice-married and persuaded his patients to drink water rather than wine (though he imbibed English wine). He formed his own botanical garden in 1778 and expressed his scientific thought in the couplets of *The Botanic Garden* (1795). Part two, 'The Loves of the Plants', contains the narrative of 'Eliza' and her demise: 'The red stream issuing from her azure veins / Dyes her white veil, her ivory bosom stains, / – "Ah me!" she cried, and sinking on the ground, / Kiss'd her dear babes, regardless of the wound'.

Daryush, Elizabeth
English poet *born* 1887 *died* 1977

The daughter of Robert Bridges, Elizabeth Daryush followed her father in taking a special interest in the metrics of modern verse. Though she wrote many poems using traditional techniques, she was also drawn to the expressive possibilities of the syllabic count. 'Throw Away the Flowers' combines syllabic metre with rhyme and excessive alliteration: 'Throw away the flowers, / they are no use, / the faery bowers / of the former truce; / fancy quickly dies / under fear's dark skies.' Her work generally moves from description to a projection of her affirmative aesthetic.

Davenant, Sir William
English poet *born* Oxford March 1606 *died* 7 April 1668

Educated in his native Oxford, Davenant may have been Shakespeare's godson and he was happy to live with the persistent rumour that he was also Shakespeare's illegitimate son. After some theatrical success he became Poet Laureate in 1638. A supporter of Charles I, Davenant was knighted at the siege of Gloucester (1643) and from 1650–2 was imprisoned in the Tower of London before being released through Milton's intervention. Davenant's best-known poem is 'The Souldier going to the Field', a tender expression of regret on leaving love for war: 'For I must go where lazy peace, / Will hide her drouzy head; / And, for the sport of Kings, encrease / The number of the Dead.'

Davidson, Donald
American poet *born* Campbellsville, Tennessee 18 August 1893 *died* 1968

Educated at Vanderbilt University, Davidson was one of the founders of the *Fugitive*, the Southern magazine which ran from 1922–5 and expressed agrarian ideals. With eleven other members of the Fugitive group, Davidson contributed to the collection of agrarian essays entitled *I'll Take My Stand* (1930). He was a Southern traditionalist who condemned the modern industrial state in *The Attack on Leviathan* (1938). His poem 'On a Replica of the Parthenon', about a celebrated building in Nashville, contrasts classical images with contemporary characters: 'Around the gables Athens wrought, / Shop-girls embrace a plaster thought, / And eye Poseidon's loins ungirt'.

Davidson, John
Scottish poet *born* Barrhead 11 April 1857
died Penzance 23 March 1909

Acclaimed as an important influence by both T S Eliot and Hugh MacDiarmid, Davidson was brought up in Greenock where his father was an Evangelical minister. In 1889 he went to London where he became a member of the Rhymers' Club and established himself as a fluent poet with a flair for conversational rhythms, as in 'Thirty Bob a Week' which Eliot declared 'a great poem for ever'. Though attracted by the Nietzschean concept of the artist as a superman, Davidson was subject to suicidal fits of depression and eventually drowned himself in the English Channel, recalling the fate of 'A Runnable Stag' – 'The stag, the buoyant stag, the stag / That slept at last in a jewelled bed / Under the sheltering ocean spread'.

Davie, Donald
English poet *born* 1922

Educated at Cambridge, Davie held various academic positions in Ireland, England and America before becoming Professor of English at Vanderbilt University in Tennessee. He wrote enthusiastically about the poetry of Ezra Pound and published such critical books as *Purity of Diction in English Verse* (1952). His verse is academically-orientated, invariably taking its themes and subjects from books the poet has read. His address 'To Thom Gunn in Lost Altos, California' begins: 'Conquistador! Live dangerously, my Byron, / In this metropolis / Of Finistère. Drop off / The edge repeatedly, and come / Back to tell us!' His *Collected Poems 1971–83* appeared in 1983.

Davies, Dudley G
Welsh poet *born* Swansea 1891 *died* 1981

Davies joined the Indian Civil Service but resigned in 1928 for reasons of health. He subsequently entered the Church and was, from 1935–55, rector of Bletchingdon. While he was living in India he wrote 'Carmarthenshire', an exile's evocation of Wales. Though the poem is formally unambitious it is pictorially persuasive: 'The roads between the villages / Are shy and shadowy

with trees, / And every turn to left or right / Brings a new picture
of delight, / / And hazel boughs are everywhere, / So that in
autumn, walking there / On any roadside hedge you'll find / The
brown nuts nodding to the wind.'

Davies, Edward
Welsh poet *born* Llandafff 1718 *died* 1789

Davies became prebendary of the cathedral in his home town. His
gift for combining contemplation with description is evident in
'Chepstow: A Poem'. Like Wordsworth after him, Davies was
greatly impressed by Tintern Abbey: 'Above Lancaut in a
sequestered dell / Where monks in former days were wont to
dwell. / Enclosed with woods and hills on every side, / Stands
Tintern Abbey, spoiled of all her pride, / Whose mournful ruins
fill the soul with awe, / Where once was taught God's holy saving
law; / Where mitred abbots fanned the heavenly fire / And shook
with hymns divine the heavenly choir. / Though now the fallen
roof admits the day / She claims our veneration in decay'.

Davies, Idris
Welsh poet *born* Rhymney, West Monmouthshire 1905
died 6 April 1953

Son of a miner, Davies was himself a miner for seven years after
leaving school at fourteen. He was appalled at the defeat of the
miners in the General Strike of 1926 and began to write verse
during his period of unemployment from 1926-9. He qualified as
a teacher and worked in London and in Wales. He died of cancer.
His work, which was admired by both Yeats and Eliot, draws on
his mining experience. 'I Was Born in Rhymney' states; 'And
there were strikes and lock-outs / And meetings in the Square, /
When Cook and Smith and Bevan / Electrified the air. // But the
greatest of our battles / We lost in '26 / Through treachery and
lying, / And Balwdwin's box of tricks.'

Davies, John
Welsh poet *born* Hereford *c*1565 *buried* 6 July 1618

John Davies, who was bilingual, was known as 'the Welsh Poet'. A
writing master, he was regarded as the best penman of his time.
His published works include *The Picture of a Happy Man* (1612) and
Wit's Bedlam (1617). His 'Cambria' includes lines in praise of
Henry Stuart, Prince of Wales; 'Then live with us, dear Prince,
and we will make / Our wildest wastes jet-coloured garden plots, /
So Flora will her flowered meads forsake / To set flowers there, in
many curious knots, / To please thee and our other selves the

Scots: / We'll turn our villages to cities fair / And share them
twixt the Scots and us by lots, / Whereto both one and other may
repair / To interchange commodities or air.'

Davies, Sir John
English poet *born* Tisbury, Wiltshire 1569 *died* 1626

Educated at Oxford, Davies became a barrister at the Middle
Temple in 1595. He was a member of Parliament and, from
1606–19, Attorney-General for Ireland. In 1613 he became
Speaker of the Irish Parliament and, returning to England in
1616, was made Chief Justice shortly before his death by
apoplexy. His *Orchestra* (1596) uses the dance as a symbol of
universal grace: 'Who doth not see the measure of the moon? /
Which thirteen times she danceth every year, / And ends her
pavan thirteen times as soon / As doth her brother, of whose
golden hair / She borroweth part, and proudly doth it wear. /
Then doth she coyly turn her face aside, / That half her cheek is
scarce sometimes descried.'

Davies, William Henry
Welsh poet *born* Newport, Monmouthshire 20 April 1871
died Nailsworth, Gloucestershire 26 September 1940

Davies was born in his father's tavern, The Church House, and
graduated into a life of tramping. In America, while train-jumping
his way to the Klondike, he injured his right leg so severely it was
amputated. On his return to England he published, at his own
expense, *The Soul's Destroyer* (1905) which Bernard Shaw thought
the work of 'a real poet . . . a genuine innocent'. He was
acclaimed in London but preferred to live away from it all. His
rudimentary rhymes convey an engaging personality: 'I am the
Poet Davies, William, / I sin without a blush or blink: / I am a
man that lives to eat; / I am a man that lives to drink.'

Davis, Thomas
Irish Poet *born* Mallow, County Cork 14 October 1814
died 16 September 1845

An army surgeon's son, Davis was educated at Trinity College,
Dublin, and called to the Irish Bar in 1838. A founder of *The
Nation* newspaper and a leader of the Young Ireland political
party, Davis was an important force in promoting the Irish
Revival. Characteristic of his patriotic balladry is his 'Lament for
the Death of Eoghan Ruadh O'Neill' (set in 1649): '"Did they
dare – did they dare, to slay Owen Roe O'Neill?" / "Yes, they slew
with poison him they feared to meet with steel." / "May God
wither up their hearts! May their blood cease to flow! / May they
walk in living death who poisoned Owen Roe!"'

Day Lewis, Cecil

Irish poet *born* Ballintubber, Ireland 27 April 1904 *died* 1972

A clergyman's son, Day Lewis was educated at Sherborne and Oxford before taking up schoolteaching. In 1935 he decided to devote himself to writing and produced poems, criticism and (as Nicholas Blake) detective novels. In 1968 he was appointed Poet Laureate. During the 1930s, Day Lewis was closely associated with Auden and often eclipsed by his friend's fame. However his best poems are not political but personal, like his 'Walking Away' dedicated to his son Sean: 'I have had worse partings, but none that so / Gnaws at my mind still. Perhaps it is roughly / Saying what God alone could perfectly show – / How selfhood begins with a walking away, / And love is proved in the letting go.'

De la Mare, Walter

English poet *born* Charlton, Kent 25 April 1873
died Twickenham 22 June 1956

Educated at St Paul's Cathedral Choir School (where he founded the *Chorister's Journal*) De la Mare worked as a clerk in an oil company. A Civil List pension in 1908 enabled him to devote his time to writing; he was also remembered in the will of Rupert Brooke. His work steadily increased in popularity and he was awarded the Order of Merit in 1953. The surface simplicity of his poetry, using attractive rhythm and rhymes, is complicated by an enigmatic content. Some of his poems have supernatural connotations and in 'Deadalive' he writes: 'Alas, through all Man's centuries / No wizard yet has forged the key / To unlock, at will, the cell where lies / The Mage of Dream, called Fantasy.'

Denham, Sir John

Irish poet *born* Dublin 1615 *died* 10 March 1669

Son of an Irish judge, Denham was educated at Oxford and called to the Bar in 1639. He fought for the Royalist side in the Civil War and was with Queen Henrietta Maria's exiled court in Paris after the triumph of Cromwell. At the Restoration he was knighted by Charles II and appointed Surveyor of the Royal Works. He was acclaimed on the publication of his topographical poem *Cooper's Hill* (1642) which describes the landscape near his home at Egham, Surrey. His lines on the River Thames show a deep sympathy with nature: 'O could I flow like thee, and make thy stream / My great example, as it is my theme! / Though deep, yet clear, though gentle, yet not dull, / Strong without rage, without ore-flowing full.'

De Tabley, Lord (John Byrne Leicester Warren)
English poet *born* Tabley House, Cheshire 26 April 1835
died 22 November 1895

Educated at Eton and Oxford, Lord de Tabley spent some of his
childhood in Italy and Germany and was for a while attached to
the British Embassy in Constantinople. He published verse under
the pseudonym George F Preston and wrote the tragedy
Philoctetes (1863); the failure of *The Soldier's Fortune* (1876) made
him live the life of a recluse in London. Towards the end of his
life, however, he received some recognition for poems such as
'Nuptial Song' with its effective internal rhymes: 'Sigh, heart, and
break not; rest, lark, and wake not! / Day I hear coming to draw
my Love away. / As mere-waves whisper, and clouds grow
crisper, / Ah, like a rose he will waken up with day.'

Deutsch, Babette
American poet *born* New York 22 October 1895
died 13 November 1982

Educated at the Ethical Culture School and Barnard College,
Babette Deutsch married Avrahm Yarmolinsky, the Slavonic
scholar, in 1921. She worked as secretary to Thorstein Veblen,
the influential economist, and participated in the Committee for
Cultural Freedom established by the philosopher John Dewey.
From 1944 to 1971 she taught in the School of General Studies at
Columbia University. A prolific writer, in poems such as 'Epistle
to Prometheus' she communicates her social concern: 'Let the
dead future / bury its dead. / After the funeral / return to the
empty house – / the door is open, / go into the unswept room, /
go in and face / the iron day.'

De Vere, Sir Aubrey
Irish poet *born* 1788 *died* 1846

Sir Aubrey de Vere was a liberal landlord who favoured Catholic
Emancipation. His son, Aubrey, described him as a 'Liberal Tory'.
He wrote a historical drama *Mary Tudor* (1847) but was most
successful with his sonnets which Wordsworth regarded as 'the
most perfect of our age'. 'The Rock of Cashel' begins: 'Royal and
saintly Cashel! I would gaze / Upon the wreck of thy departed
powers, / Not in the dewy light of matin hours, / Nor the
meridian pomp of summer's blaze, / But at the close of dim
autumnal days, / When the sun's parting glance, through slanting
showers, / Sheds o'er thy rock-throned battlements and towers /
Such awful gleams as brighten o'er Decay's / Prophetic cheek.'

De Vere, Aubrey

Irish poet *born* Adare, County Limerick 10 January 1814
died 21 January 1902

Son of Sir Aubrey de Vere, Aubrey de Vere was educated at
Trinity College, Dublin, and was an enthusiastic supporter of
Catholic Emancipation. At Oxford, in 1838, de Vere met
Newman whose theological approach impressed him: Newman
was received into the Roman Catholic church in 1845, de Vere in
1851 (at Avignon, on his way to Rome). He was friendly with
Wordsworth, Tennyson and Browning and wrote poems as
ecclesiastically earnest as 'The Year of Sorrow': 'Without a sound,
without a stir, / In streets and wolds, on rock and mound, / O
omnipresent Comforter, / By thee, this night, the lost are found!'
His prose work includes *English Misrule and Irish Misdeeds* (1848).

Devlin, Denis

Irish poet *born* 1908 *died* 1959

Devlin, born in Scotland of Irish parents, was raised in Dublin.
He was educated at the National University, Munich, and the
Sorbonne, then worked as a diplomat. At the time of his death he
was Irish Ambassador to Italy. His *Collected Poems* of 1965 show
the Continental influence on his verse. His poem 'Lough Derg' is
a powerfully contemplative work: 'The poor in spirit on their
rosary rounds, / The jobbers with their whiskey-angered eyes, /
The pink bank clerks, the tip-hat papal counts, / And drab, kind
women their tonsured mockery tries, / Glad invalids on
penitential feet / Walk the Lord's majesty like their village street.'

Dickey, James

American poet *born* Atlanta, Georgia 1923

Dickey taught at Rice University, the University of Florida and
the University of South Carolina. He also worked in advertising
and as a consultant in poetry for the Library of Congress. His
novel *Deliverance* (1970) was a great commercial and critical
success and his volumes of poetry have established him as one of
the most distinctive of modern American poets. In poems such as
'The Heaven of Animals' Dickey explores the natural world with
a sense of wonder: 'And those that are hunted / Know this as their
life, / Their reward: to walk / Under such trees in full knowledge /
Of what is in glory above them, / And to feel no fear, / But
acceptance, compliance.'

Dickinson, Emily

American poet *born* Amherst, Massachusetts 10 December
1830 *died* Amherst 15 May 1886

Daughter of a country lawyer, Emily Dickinson seemed content
to stay at home as a New England spinster. However she had

strong poetic and emotional ambitions. She sent her sharp, rhythmically brittle poems to T W Higginson and was upset but not silenced when he criticised her eccentric style. As a teenager she was close to law student Benjamin Franklin Newton; later she became passionately fond of the Rev Charles Wadsworth, a married minister. Both men rejected her and the anguish she felt is reflected in her posthumously published poems. In a characteristically terse quatrain she wrote: 'That Love is all there is, / Is all we know of Love; / It is enough, the freight should be / Proportioned to the groove.'

Dixon, Richard Watson
English poet *born* London 5 May 1833 *died* 23 January 1900

Son of a Wesleyan minister, Dixon was educated at Oxford where hewas friendly with William Morris. Ordained as an Anglican curate in 1858 he became vicar of Hayton, Cumberland, and Warkworth, Northumberland. His most famous work is his *History of the Church of England from the Abolition of the Roman Jurisdiction* (6 vols, 1878–1902) but he also wrote poems that have the imaginative quality of dreams, as in 'The Wizard's Funeral': 'For me, for me, two horses wait, / Two horses stand before my gate: / Their vast black plumes on high are cast, / Their black manes swing in the midnight blast, / Red sparkles from their eyes fly fast. / But can they drag the hearse behind, / Whose black plumes mystify the wind?'

Dobell, Sydney
English poet *born* Cranbrook, Kent 5 April 1824
died 22 August 1874

Son of a wine-merchant, Dobell was brought up in Cheltenham. At the age of fifteen he became engaged and at twenty he married. Like his friend Alexander Smith he was one of the poets condemned as the 'Spasmodic' school by W E Aytoun who objected to the headlong rush of words. In *England in Time of War* (1856), however, Dobell showed a more sensitive style in 'Tommy's Dead': 'There's nothing but cinders and sand, / The rat and the mouse have fled, / And the summer's empty and cold; / Over valley and wold, / Wherever I turn my head, / There's a mildew and a mould; / The sun's going out overhead, / And I'm very old, / And Tommy's dead.'

Dobson, Austin
English poet *born* Plymouth 18 January 1840
died Ealing 2 September 1921

Dobson, a civil engineer's son, was educated in Plymouth and the gymnase at Strasbourg before entering the Board of Trade where he worked from 1856 to 1901. He retired on a Civil List pension of £250. He excelled at light verse but was also capable of poems as measured and humane as 'Before Sedan': 'Look. She is sad to miss, / Morning and night, /His – her dead father's – kiss; / Tries to be bright, / Good to mamma, and sweet. / That is all. "Marguerite." // Ah, if beside the dead / Slumbered the pain! / Ah, if the hearts that bled / Slept with the slain! / If the grief died; – But no; – / Death will not have it so.'

Dobson, Rosemary
Australian poet *born* Sydney 1920

Rosemary Dobson, a granddaughter of Austin Dobson, was educated at Sydney University. She became an art teacher before moving to London to work in publishing. When she returned to Australia she lived first in Sydney then in Canberra. Her interest in visual art has shaped her poetry and a characteristic poem is 'The Mirror', a dramatic monologue spoken by Jan Vermeer. The final stanza is contemplative: 'There, it is done. The vision fades / And Time moves on. Oh you who praise / This tangled, broken web of paint, / I paint reflections in a glass: / Who look on Truth with mortal sight / Are blinded in its blaze of light.'

Donaghy, John Lyle
Irish poet *born* 1902 *died* 1946

John Lyle Donaghy was a contributor to Eliot's *Criterion*. He had some treatment for depression in 1931 and wrote, in his poem 'Grotesque' from *Wilderness Signs* (1942), 'I presented myself as a pathological case / but my extreme sanity put out the psycho-analysts'. He lived in England before settling in County Wicklow. In collections such as *Into the Light* (1934) and *Selected Poems* (1939) he applied modernist principles to Irish poetry. 'The Hermit' tells how the subject of the poem 'sat in the mouth of a cave / brooding on the waters, / on the four floods that meet without: / the flood of light, / the flood of darkness, / the flood of pain / and the flood of joy.'

Donne, John
English poet *born* London 1572 *died* London 31 March 1631

Son of an ironmonger, Donne was educated at Oxford, Cambridge and the Inns of Court. He sailed in Essex's expeditions to Cadiz (1592) and the Azores (1597) and in 1598 became secretary to Sir Thomas Egerton, Lord Keeper of England. In 1601 his secret marriage to Ann More, daughter of Egerton's brother-in-law led to his dismissal. After a period of poverty he took holy orders in 1615 and in 1621 became Dean of St Paul's. Donne's majestic command of language made him equally powerful as the erotic master of the Metaphysical manner or as a writer of divine poems. His 'The Triple Foole' opens amusingly 'I am two fooles, I know, / For loving, and for saying so / In whining Poetry'.

Doolittle, Hilda
American poet *born* Bethlehem, Pennsylvania 10 September 1886 *died* 27 September 1961

In 1913 H D – as Hilda Doolittle styled her literary self – married Richard Aldington and the couple issued a joint volume *Images, Old and New* (1915). Her early verse conforms to the Imagist ideal of pictorial clarity but she later introduced a more emotional mood to her poetry when recording her despair at the infidelity of her husband. Suffering from stress H D went to Vienna in 1933 to seek psychiatric help from Freud and her poem 'The Master', a tribute to the great analyst, shows H D in a prophetic mood as she affirms the feminine principle of creativity. H D dwells on the notion that 'woman is perfect' and so she hopes 'all men will feel / what it is to be a woman'.

Dorn, Edward
American poet *born* Illinois 1929

Educated at the University of Illinois and at Black Mountain College where he absorbed the aesthetic of Charles Olson, Dorn taught at Idaho State University and the University of Essex. From Pocatello, Idaho he edited the magazine *Wild Dog*. He has written critical prose as well as poetry but his major achievement is the Gunslinger sequence: *Gunslinger I* (1968), *Gunslinger II* (1969), *Gunslinger III* (1972), *Slinger* (1975). This sustained composition is a highly personal exploration of an American myth: 'I met in Mesilla / The Cautious Gunslinger / of impeccable personal smoothness / and slender leather encased hands / folded casually / to make his knock. / He would show you his map.'

Douglas, Lord Alfred
English poet *born* Ham Hill, near Worcester 22 October 1870 *died* 20 March 1945

Lord Alfred's name will always be linked to that of Oscar Wilde whom he met in 1891. It was the fury of his father, the Marquess of Queensbury, at his association with Wilde that led to Wilde's trial and imprisonment for homosexuality. After Wilde's death (in 1900) Douglas edited the *Academy*; later he went to prison for six months for publishing a libel on Winston Churchill. In 1911 he entered the Roman Catholic church. His poem 'Rejected', from *The City of the Soul* (1899), is psychologically revealing: 'Alas! I have lost my God, / My beautiful God Apollo. / Wherever his foosteps trod / My feet were wont to follow.'

Douglas, Gavin
Scottish poet *born c* 1474 *died* London September 1522

Son of the fifth Earl of Angus, Douglas was educated at the universities of St Andrews and Paris and became Bishop of Dunkeld in 1515. Imprisoned during the regency of the Duke of Albany, Douglas was back in favour by 1517 when he went to France to arrange a marriage between James V and a daughter of Francis I. Returning to Scotland he became involved in intrigue and was exiled to England in 1521. His greatest achievement is his *Eneados* (1513, first printed 1553), a translation of Virgil's *Aeneid* into Middle Scots. Each book is prefaced by a prologue and the seventh prologue is a splendid example of descriptive verse: 'The frosty regioun ringis of the year, / The time and season bittir, cald and paill'.

Dowden, Edward
Irish poet *born* Cork 3 May 1843 *died* Dublin 4 April 1913

Educated at Queen's College, Cork, and Trinity College, Dublin, he was Professor of English at Trinity from 1867 until his death. An outstanding Shakespeare scholar, he published *Shakspere: His Mind and Art* (1875) and his *Shakspere Primer* in 1877. He was friendly with Walt Whitman though his own poems, as 'In the Cathedral Close' shows, are traditional in feeling and form: 'Day after day the swallows sit / With scarce a stir, with scarce a sound, / But dreaming and digesting much / They grow thus wise and soft and round. // They watch the Canons come to dine, / And hear, the mullion-bars across, / Over the fragrant fruit and wine / Deep talk of rood-screen and reredos.'

Dowling, Basil
New Zealand poet *born* Southbridge, Canterbury 1910

Educated at Canterbury University, Knox Theological College (Dunedin) and Westminster College (Cambridge), Dowling was ordained as a Presbyterian minister. He subsequently worked as a labourer and as a librarian; from 1951 he was a schoolteacher in England. He settled in Rye, East Sussex. His collections include *A Day's Journey* (1941), *Signs and Wonders* (1944) and *Hatherley, Recollective Lyrics* (1968). His compassionate approach is seen to advantage in 'The Trapped Hare' which begins: 'This morning I found a hare gaoled alive in a gin, / One red forepaw held bitten in clenched iron. / With ears laid back and large eyes full of woe / He crouched on the scoured floor of his open prison'.

Dowson, Ernest
English poet *born* Kent 2 August 1867 *died* 23 February 1900

Dowson's father owned a dry-dock in the East End of London. The poet was educated at Oxford. In London he met his 'Cynara'

-a French restaurant-owner's daughter celebrated in Dowson's refrain 'I have been faithful to thee, Cynara! in my fashion' -and later lived in Paris and Dieppe. A consumptive, he was also a self-destructive drinker yet produced resonant lines as in his stanzas entitled 'Vita summa brevis spem nos vetat incohare longam': 'They are not long, the weeping and the laughter, / Love and desire and hate: / I think they have no portion in us after / We pass the gate. // They are not long, the days of wine and roses: / Out of a misty dream / Our path emerges for a while, then closes / Within a dream.'

Doyle, Charles
New Zealand poet *born* 1928

Educated at Auckland University, Doyle became Professor of English at the University of Victoria, British Columbia, Canada. He published *A Splinter of Glass* in 1956, *Messages for Herod* in 1965, *Earth Meditations: 2* (1968). He is a contemplative poet able to convey his conclusions through images, as in 'Starlings and History': 'Now I turn, find it is winter. Dreary birds / Make the grey air untidy, their rough-gutted screech / A hubbub that disturbs me. I suddenly know that all worlds / Are chequered and drab like these, that promise of rich / Permanent summer is false.' The poem ends by stating 'nothing is endless. / One does not die for ever.'

Doyle, Sir Francis
English poet *born* Nunappleton, Yorkshire 21 August 1810
died 8 June 1888

Doyle's father was a general and army traditions were strong in the family. However, Doyle studied law and was called to the Bar in 1837; he was appointed Commissioner of Customs in 1869. His ballad 'The Private of the Buffs' was published in *The Times* of 1860 with a note explaining that when an English private, Moyse, and some Sikhs were captured by the Chinese they were asked to prostrate themselves before the Chinese authorities. When Moyse refused he was killed and his body was thrown on a dunghill. Doyle commemorated this example: 'So let his name through Europe ring – / A man of mean estate, / Who died, as firm as Sparta's king, / Because his soul was great.'

Drake, Joseph Rodman
American poet *born* New York 7 August 1795
died 21 September 1820

Orphaned at an early age Drake, known as 'the American Keats', studied medicine (as did Keats). His marriage to the daughter of a marine architect brought him some financial security and he visited Europe. With his friend Fitz-Greene Hallek, he collaborated on *The Croaker Papers* (1819). His 'The American Flag' retains its patriotic appeal: 'When Freedom from her mountain height / Unfurled her standard to the air, / She tore the azure robe of night, / And set the stars of glory there. / She mingled with its gorgeous dyes / The milky baldric of the skies, / And striped its pure celestial white / With streakings of the morning light'. Drake died of consumption.

Drayton, Michael
English poet *born* Hartshill, Warwickshire 1563
died 23 December 1631

A page to Sir Henry Goodere, Drayton fell in love with his employer's daughter Anne and continued to worship her though she married Sir Henry Rainsford. Drayton's passion is expressed in the sonnets in *Idea's Mirror* (1594) in which Anne is addressed as idea: 'Since there's no help, come let us kiss and part. / Nay, I have done; you get no more of me, / And I am glad, yea, glad with all my heart, / That thus so cleanly I myself can free.' Drayton never married and was sustained by his patrons, such as Sir Walter Aston. His masterpiece is *Polyolbion* (1622), a topographical description of England.

Drennan, William
Irish poet *born* Belfast 1754 *died* 1820

Drennan wrote the original manifesto of the Society of United Irishmen and was a prominent supporter of the movement. An accomplished linguist, he published a translation of Sophocles in 1817 as well as the collection of his own poems entitled *Fugitive Pieces* (1815). His 'The Wake of William Orr' is animated by an obvious anger: 'Hapless Nation! hapless Land! / Heap of uncementing sand! / Crumbled by a foreign weight: / And by worse, domestic hate. // God of mercy! God of peace! / Make this mad confusion cease; / O'er the mental chaos move, / through it SPEAK the light of love.'

Dressel, Joe
Welsh poet *born* St Louis, Missouri 1934

Of Welsh descent, Dressel became (in 1976) Director of Studies for American students at Trinity College, Carmarthen. In 1979 his *Cerddi Ianws* was judged the best entry for the Crown at the National Eisteddfod but disqualified as it had been written in collaboration with T James Jones. His poems, such as 'The Drouth', comment wittily on Wales: 'two weeks of sun in Sept- / ember, sails blazing on the Tywi, // reading in a garden warm with stone, / going barefoot like we'd never left / Missouri; Christ, I said, if this // holds we'll be breaking out the mandolins, / taking siestas on the dike, drinking ouzo, / pinching girls' behinds at the market'.

Drummond, William
Scottish poet *born* Hawthorden, near Roslin, Midlothian 13 December 1585 *died* 4 December 1649

Son of a gentleman–usher to James VI, William Drummond of Hawthorden was familiar with the court from an early age. He was educated at Edinburgh University and studied law on the Continent; he abandoned his intention to practise law when he became laird of Hawthorden on the death of his father in 1610. A collection of his poems was published in 1614 and his *Flowers of Sion*, a second volume, confirmed his gifts as a Scotsman writing impressively in English. His 'Sonet to Sleepe' begins 'Sleepe, *Silence* Child, sweet Father of soft Rest, / Prince, whose Approach Peace to all Mortals brings, / Indifferent Host to Shepheards and to Kings, / Sole comforter of Minds with Griefe opprest'. He was known as the 'Scottish Petrarch'.

Drummond, William Henry
Canadian poet *born* near Mohill, County Leitrim 13 April 1854 *died* Cobalt, Ontario 6 April 1907

William Henry Drummond, 'The Poet of the Habitant', came to Canada as a boy and worked in the telegraph service at Bord-à-Plouffe before going on to study medicine at Bishop's University. He had medical practices in Stornoway and Knowlton; he then returned to Montreal and, in 1894, married May Harvey. In 1905 he joined his brothers in the exploitation of new mines at Cobalt, New Ontario. A physically large and robust man, his poetic celebration of French–Canadians, the *habitants*, brought him great popularity. In his poem 'The Habitant' he shows his skill with the French–Canadian dialect; 'De fader of me, he was habitant farmer, / Ma gran' fader too, an' hees fader also'.

Dryden, John
English poet *born* Aldwinckle, Northamptonshire 9 August 1631 *died* London 1 May 1700

Son of a country squire, Dryden was raised as a Puritan and educated at Cambridge. In succession Dryden produced 'Heroic Stanzas' on the death of Cromwell in 1659 and 'Astraea Redux' on the Restoration of 1660. He married Lady Elizabeth Howard in 1663 and in 1668 was appointed Poet Laureate. Dryden's conversion to Catholicism during James II's reign cost him his laureateship and pension on the accession of William and Mary in 1688. He was one of the greatest satirists in the English language and a technical virtuoso whose heroic couplets, as in the portrait

of Zimri (Buckingham) in *Absalom and Achitophel* (1681), are fluent
as well as forceful: 'A man so various that he seemed to be / Not
one, but all mankind's epitome'.

Du Bois, W E B
American poet *born* Great Barrington, Massachusetts 1868
died 1963

Educated at the universities of Fisk and Harvard, William Edward
Burghardt Du Bois established himself as author, editor, scholar,
historian, sociologist and advocate of human rights for American
blacks. In *The Souls of Black Folk* (1903) he examined the
phenomenon of black 'double-consciousness' (both African and
American) and in an article in the *Crisis*, April 1915, he insisted on
putting 'the black man before the world as both a creative artist
and a strong subject for artistic treatment'. His poem 'The Song
of the Smoke' has an incantatory rhythm: 'I am the smoke king, /
I am black. / I am swinging in the sky / I am ringing worlds on
high: / I am the thought of the throbbing mills / I am the soul
toil kills'.

Dudek, Louis
Canadian poet *born* Montreal 1918

Educated at McGill and Columbia universities, Dudek was active
in the world of Canadian publishing. With Irving Layton and
Raymond Souster, he founded the Contact Press of Toronto; he
also edited *Delta* magazine and Delta Press. He brought out
Collected Poetry in 1971 and *Continuation I* – the first part of an
experimental poem – in 1981. His poems, such as 'Europe',
affirm a natural aesthetic: 'All ugliness is a distortion / of the
lovely lines and curves / which sincerity makes out of hands / and
bodies moving in air. / Beauty is ordered in nature / as the wind
and sea / shape each other for pleasure; as the just / know, who
learn of happiness / from the report of their own actions.'

Dugan, Alan
American poet *born* New York 1923

Educated at Mexico City College, Dugan returned to New York
where he worked as a model-maker for a medical supply house.
His collection *Poems* (1961) won him the National Book Award
and the Pulitzer Prize for Poetry. His *Collected Poems* appeared in
1969, *Sequence* in 1976. His work expresses anger and indignation
as he projects himself as an individual contending with a hostile
environment, even in: 'Love Song; I and Thou' where he
describes the building of his house: 'This is hell, / but I planned it,
I sawed it, / I nailed it, and I / will live in it until it kills me. / I can
nail my left palm / to the left-hand cross-piece but / I can't do
everything myself.'

Duggan, Eileen
New Zealand poet *born* Tua Marina, Marlborough 1894 *died* 1972

Educated at Victoria University, Eileen Duggan spent one year
teaching in school and another year as a university lecturer in
history. Most of her life was concentrated in Wellington where
she was a journalist and poet. Her collections include *New Zealand
Bird Songs* (1929), *New Zealand Poems* (1940) and *More Poems* (1951).
Traditional in technique and nostalgic in tone, she wrote such
poems as 'Pilgrimage' in which the iambic pentameter is used
with distinction: 'Now are the bells unlimbered from their spires /
In every steeple-loft from pole to pole: / The four winds wheel
and blow into this gate, / And every wind is wet with carillons.'

Dunbar, Paul Lawrence
American poet *born* Dayton, Ohio 27 June 1872
died Dayton 9 February 1906

Dunbar, the son of former slaves, was educated locally. While
working in Dayton as an elevator operator, he published *Oak and
Ivy* (1893) and sold copies to those he encountered in his job. His
third collection, *Lyrics of Lowly Life* (1896) was published in New
York and established him as an outstanding black poet who could
use dialect with poetic intelligence as well as humour. The last
stanza of his 'A Death Song' runs: 'Let me settle w'en my
shouldahs draps dey load / Night enough to hyeah de noises in de
road; / Fu' I t'ink de las' long res' / Gwine to soothe my sperrit
bes' / If I's layin' 'mong de t'ings I's allus knowed.' He died, in his
home town, of tuberculosis.

Dunbar, William
Scottish poet *born c*1460*died c*1520

Dunbar's life, like Shakespeare's, is something of a closed book
though internal evidence gives the impression of a combative
personality. After the accession of James IV, in 1488, Dunbar
spent most of his life as a critical member of the king's court. In
1503 he was ordained a priest and his royal pension was gradually
increased to £80 per annum by 1510. Dunbar's poetry ranges
from the lyrical to the satirical and his language is by turns
aureate and austere. In 'Lament for the Makaris' he combines a
realistic catalogue with a ritual mood as he conducts his dance of
death: 'Our plesance heir is all vane glory, / This fals warld is bot
transitory, / The flesche is brukle, the Fiend is slee; / Timor
Mortis conturbat me.'

Duncan, Robert
American poet *born* Oakland, California 7 January 1919

Robert Duncan associated with the poets of San Francisco,
including Kenneth Rexroth; and also taught at Black Mountain

College where he enthusiastically explored the ideas of Charles Olson. Like many American poets of his generation he is concerned with poetry as an art of perception and he is a self-conscious and considerable craftsman. His 'Poetry, a Natural Thing' is a declaration, and demonstration, of his aesthetic principles: 'This beauty is an inner persistence / toward the source / striving against (within) down-rushet of the river, / a call we heard and answer / in the lateness of the world / primordial bellowings / from which the youngest world might spring'.

Duncan, Ronald
English poet *born* Rhodesia 1914

Educated in Switzerland and England, Duncan stayed with his mentor Gandhi when he was twenty-two and was also friendly with Pound and Eliot. He founded the English Stage Company and co-founded, with Benjamin Britten, the English Opera Company. Apart from his epic poem *Man*, he has written prolifically, often about death and ways of coping with it. A sequence of poems for his mother, Ethel Duncan, are painfully exact in their imagery and possess a dignity that informs the facts with feeling: 'Black earth whites her bones / Maggots make ringlets from her hair / Where I was weaned / worms move in.' 'Epitaph' states: 'Here lies my Mother / My loss, her profit. / My whole life's buried here / Chuck earth upon it.'

Dunn, Douglas
Scottish poet *born* Inchinnan, Renfrewshire 23 October 1942

Douglas Dunn, who worked as a librarian with Philip Larkin in Hull, is a descriptive poet of considerable emotional power. He cleverly combines images from childhood with observations from adulthood. His first collection, *Terry Street* (1969), used the understated style associated with Larkin but later collections have shown a moving elegiac quality. Dunn is especially adept at recalling figures from the past, like the old woman in 'Savings' who kept her money in a tea tin and when she died 'It wasn't death that I could see / In tea-leaves sifting from a spoon / That came out of a Chinese tin. / I saw the life she'd shovelled in.'

Durcan, Paul
Irish poet *born* Dublin 1944

The child of Mayo parents, Durcan studied Archaeology and Medieval history at University College, Cork. In 1974 he won the Patrick Kavanagh Award and he published *Teresa's Bar* (1976), *Sam's Cross* (1978), *Jesus, Break His Fall* (1980). His verse is frequently informed by the religious tensions of Ireland. In 'What is a Protestant, Daddy?' he approaches the subject sardonically: 'Protestants were Martians / Light-years more weird / Than

zoological creatures; / But soon they would all go away / For as a
species they were dying out. / Soon there would be no more
Protestants . . . / O Yea, O Lord, / I was a proper little Irish
Catholic boy / Way back in the 1950s.'

Dutton, Geoffrey
Australian poet *born* Kapunda, South Australia 1922

Dutton was a flight-lieutenant with the Royal Australian Air
Force during the Second World War then studied Arts at Oxford.
He lectured in English literature at Adelaide University and was
associated with *Australian Book Review* and *Australian Letters*. He is
skilled at evoking the Australian landscape but many of his poems
move beyond description to suggest an ominous presence.
'January' begins as a tribute to a 'dark-haired girl' before the
mood changes: 'The sun's blond fire turns red and black, / A
horrible army runs through hay / By flank of hill through hair of
tree / And the ashes fall upon the sea.'

Dyer, Sir Edward
English poet *born* Sharpham Park, Somerset 1545 *died* May 1607

After an education at Oxford, Dyer was taken to the Court by the
Earl of Leicester. He went on a mission to Denmark in 1589 and
in 1596 was knighted and made Chancellor of the Order of the
Garter. Though it has some jarringly complacent passages, his
most famous poem retains its contemplative quality: 'My mind to
me a kingdom is / Such perfect joy therein I find, / That it excels
all other bliss / That world affords or grows by kind. / Though
much I want which most would have, / Yet still my mind forbids
to crave.' The two lines that close the fifth stanza of the poem are
impressively emphatic; 'They poor, I rich; they beg, I give; / They
lack, I leave; they pine, I live.'

Dyer, John
Welsh poet *born* Llanfyndd, Carmarthenshire 13 August
1699 *died* 1758

Dyer studied painting with Jonathan Richardson and existed as an
artist in South Wales. Seeking more security he took orders and
served as vicar of Calthorp, Leicestershire. In 1727 he published
Grongar Hill, a description of the landscape of the Towy valley.
The poem appealed greatly to the Romantics who responded to
its wealth of natural detail: 'Below me Trees unnumber'd rise, /
Beautiful in various Dies: / The gloomy Pine, the Poplar blue, /
The yellow Beech, the sable Yew, / The slender Firr, that taper
grows, / The sturdy Oak with broad-spread Boughs'. Dyer also
published *The Ruins of Rome* (1740) and *The Fleece* (1757), an
account of sheep-raising.

Eberhart, Richard

American poet *born* Austin, Minnesota 5 April 1904

Educated at Dartmouth and Harvard, Eberhart taught naval gunnery in the Second World War. He founded the Poet's Theatre, worked in the Library of Congress, and won the Bollingen Prize in 1962. His *Collected Poems, 1930–76* appeared in 1976, *Ways of Light* in 1980. Eberhart's verse ranges from meditative responses to nature to verbal assaults on the reader's complacency. 'The Fury of Aerial Bombardment' invokes the issue of theodicy: 'Was man made stupid to see his own stupidity? / Is God by definition indifferent, beyond us all? / Is the eternal truth man's fighting soul / Wherein the Beast ravens in its own avidity?'

Edmond, Lauris

New Zealand poet *born* Hawkes Bay 1924

Educated at Victoria University, Lauris Edmond became a secondary schoolteacher of English and French. She edited the Post Primary Teachers' *Journal* and settled in Wellington. She came to poetry late in life, publishing her first collection, *In Middle Air*, in 1975. Other collections include *Wellington Letter* (1980) and *Salt from the North* (1980). Her contemplative quality is shown in such poems as 'the Names': 'my children who / were my blood and breathing I do not know you: / we are friends, we write often, there are / occasions, news from abroad. One of you is dead. // I do not listen fearfully for you in the night, / exasperating you with my concern'.

Edmond, Murray

New Zealand poet *born* Hamilton 1949

Educated at Auckland University, Edmond became involved in experimental and educational theatre. An actor and director as well as a writer, he associated with the Town and Country Players in Wellington. His collections include *Patchwork* (1978) and *End Wall* (1981). His poetic tone is confidential as he projects his own personality into various situations. 'My Return to Czechoslovakia' describes the otherness of Prague and Christchurch, then introduces a personal dimension: 'I watched the moon disappear / and thought of myself as the sum / of all the people who went into my making / – my father's stoop, my mother's hands, / grandmother's hips, my Scottish soul'.

Ehrmann, Max

American poet *born* Terre Haute, Indiana 26 October 1872
died 9 September 1945

Max Ehrmann, who studied law and philosophy at Harvard, practised as a lawyer and worked in the family manufacturing business. His prose-poem 'Desiderata' was written in 1927 and subsequently appeared anonymously on a mimeograph issued by Old St Paul's Church, Baltimore; as the church was founded in 1692 the poem was widely circulated, erroneously, as a seventeenth century text on posters and as a popular record. It has a gently reassuring tone: 'Beyond a wholesome discipline be gentle with yourself. You are a child of the universe no less than the trees and the stars.' The poem is ©Max Ehrmann 1927, reprinted by permission of Robert L Bell, Melrose, Massachusetts, USA.

Eliot, T S

Anglo–American poet *born* St Louis, Missouri 26 September 1888 *died* London 4 January 1965

Thomas Stearns Eliot was educated at Harvard, the Sorbonne and Oxford. In London he taught for a while in Highgate School then worked in Lloyd's Bank. *Prufrock and Other Observations* (1917) established him as an important poet with an ironic tone and a gift for urban images. *The Waste Land* (1922) is one of the greatest triumphs of the modernist movement –erudite, allusive, thematically profound in its concept of culture. As a publisher (with Faber and Faber), critic (of conservative views) and poet, Eliot – who became a naturalised British subject – had an enormous 'impact on modern literature. In 'East Coker', from *Four Quartets* (1943), he evoked 'a lifetime burning in every moment'.

Elliot, Alistair

English poet *born* Liverpool 1932

Educated at Edinburgh and Oxford, Elliot did various jobs before becoming a librarian at Newcastle University. He is an imaginative translator from various languages and a witty observer of his academic and urban environment. In 'A Northern Morning' he rejoices over a townscape transformed by the weather: 'I dodge to the High Street conscious of my fellows / damp and sad in their vegetable fibres. / But by the bus-stop I look up; the spring trees / exult in the downpour, radiant, clean for hours: / This is the life! This is the only life!' Though the texture of much of his poetry is self-consciously literary, he has several such touches of freshness.

Elliot, Jean

Scottish poet *born* Teviotdale 1727
died Edinburgh 29 March 1805

The third daughter of Sir Gilbert Elliot of Minto, Jean Elliot was devoted to her father and never married. Most of her life was spent in Edinburgh where she cultivated a love of French literature and corresponding hatred of French revolutionary politics. She is remembered solely for her lyric 'The Flowers of the Forest' which she is supposed to have written after her brother Gilbert challenged her to write a song about the battle of Flodden (1513), the tragic Scottish defeat: 'I've heard them lilting at our yowe-milking – / Lasses a-lilting before dawn of day; / But now they are moaning on ilka green loaning – / The Flowers of the Forest are a' wede away.'

Elliott, Ebenezer
English poet *born* Masborough, Yorkshire 17 March 1781 *died* 1 December 1849

After working at the iron-foundry where his father was a clerk, Elliott went to Sheffield in 1821 to set himself up as an ironworker. He had published *A Vernal Walk* in 1801 and *Night* in 1818 but it was his experience of working conditions in Sheffield that made him a powerful poet of social protest. His *Corn Law Rhymes* (1831), which earned him the title of the 'Corn Law Rhymer', are shaped by indignation, as in 'The People's Anthem': 'When wilt Thou save the people? / O God of mercy, when? / The people, Lord, the people! / Not thrones and crowns, but men! / God save the people; thine they are, / Thy children, as they angels fair; / Save them from bondage and despair! / God save the people!'

Emerson, Ralph Waldo
American poet *born* Boston, Massachusetts 25 May 1803 *died* Concord, Massachusetts 27 April 1882

Emerson's father, a Unitarian minister, died when the poet was eight and Emerson conformed to the family tradition by entering the ministry in 1827. However, the death of his wife, Ellen Louisa Tucker, in 1831 made him doubt his religious vocation and he determined instead to be a writer. After a European tour, during which he met Thomas Carlyle, Emerson settled in Concord and set forth his transcendental philosophy in lectures and *Poems* (1847). He had a memorable turn of phrase and an experimental attitude to prosody. His Concord 'Hymn' expresses his penchant for heroism: 'Here once the embattled farmers stood, / And fired the shot heard round the world.'

Empson, William
English poet *born* Howden, East Yorkshire 27 September 1906 *died* 15 April 1984

Son of A R Empson of Yokefleet Hall, Empson was educated at Winchester and Cambridge where he took a degree in mathematics before studying English under I A Richards who influenced his first critical book *Seven Types of Ambiguity* (1930). He taught in Tokyo and during the Second World War returned to London to work for the BBC. After the war he taught at

Peking National University then at Sheffield University until
1971. An ingeniously intelligent man, Empson applies the
Metaphysical manner to modern subjects, as in 'Legal Fiction':
'Law makes long spokes of the short stakes of men. / Your well
fenced out real estate of mind / No high flat of the nomad
citizen / Looks over, or train leaves behind.'

Enright, D J

English poet *born* Leamington 1920

Enright taught English – in, for example, the universities of
Alexandria and Singapore – then returned to England to work in
publishing. He built up a considerable British reputation by
avoiding rhetorical gestures and putting strict limits on language
so that his verbal tone is restrained even when his subjects are
arresting. His is a poetry that values irony above passion and
keeps an emotional distance from the reader. He projects an
aloof and pedagogic personality in poems that gently mock
philistinism, as in 'Buy One Now': 'this new Poem does the work
for you. / Just drop your mind into it / And leave it to soak /While
you relax with the telly / Or go out to the pub'.

Evans, Evan

Welsh poet *born* Lledrod, Cardiganshire 1731 *died* 1788

Evans became an Anglican curate in Manafon and elsewhere.
Known as *Ieuan Brydydd Hir*, he was a Welsh scholar and a
bilingual poet who wrote in Welsh as well as English. In 'The
Love of Our Country', Evans affirms the quality of Welshness:
'Let annals tell how Cambria's princes fought, / The Saxon
victories how dearly bought, / And how for liberty they bravely
strove / As if they had their sanction from above. / The bards
extolled in lasting verse their praise, / In lofty numbers and in
sweetest lays, / While to the lyre's sweet harmony they sung /
Each warrior's hall with feats heroic rung.' The poem includes a
warning – 'Beware of Saxons still, ye Cambrian swains'.

Evans, Sebastian

English poet *born* Market Bosworth 2 March 1830 *died* 1909

An exceptionally active individual, Evans was a practical man as
well as a poet and worked as a barrister, politician and factory
manager and also as a painter and journalist. He was skilled at the
creation of fluent monologues that are full of the most exact
detail. The title poem of *Brother Fabian's Manuscript* (1865) has an
impressive conversational flourish: 'Meanwhile, Ben Gogolai, –
What? – You don't know Ben? / The curst old Hebrew with the
wooden leg? / Why, he was half the income of the cell! / 'Twas
Blaize, of course, first saw the man's true worth, / Transmuted
him by alchemy to gold, / And minted him.'

Ewart, Gavin
English poet *born* London 1916

The sheer fluency that distinguishes Gavin Ewart's poems is a consequence of a special mimetic gift: he can pick up the pieces of any given style and put them together in his own way. Thus 'Jubilate Matteo' is a stylistic parody of Christopher Smart that retains the characteristic Ewart touch of irony: 'For Yorkshire indeed excels in all things, as Geoffrey Boycott is the best Batsman. / For the Yorkshire Ripper and the Hull Arsonist have their horns exalted in glory. / For Yorkshire is therefore acknowledged the greatest County.' His erotic poems are both witty and touching for Ewart puts women on a pedestal so high the troubadours would have approved.

Fairbridge, W S
Australian poet *born* Perth, Western Australia 1918 *died* 1950

Wolfe Seymour Fairbridge's father was the founder of the Fairbridge Farm Schools; the poet was educated in England before returning to Australia to study science at the University of Western Australia. A marine biologist by profession, he became Research Officer with the Commonwealth Scientific and Industrial Research Organisation in New South Wales. He died, of poliomyelitis, after settling into a new house with his wife. 'Consecration of the House' describes his pleasure at his new possession though the penultimate stanza has ominous overtones; 'Let this mortar be / Consecrate to death – a place where one / Gladly might wither to his glowing seed.'

Fairburn, A R D
New Zealand poet *born* Auckland 1904 *died* 1957

Like R A K Mason, Arthur Rex Dugard Fairburn was one of the New Zealand poets associated with the radical Left periodical *Phoenix* (1932–3) in Auckland. He was Secretary of a Farmers' Union, editor of a compositing society's magazine, a journalist, script-writer, English tutor and then lecturer in the history and theory of art at Auckland University. His *Three Poems* (1952) contains the satirical poem 'Dominion' in which he unleashes a verbal assault on complacency: 'In the suburbs the spirit of man / walks on the garden path, / walks on the well-groomed lawn, dwells / among the manicured shrubs.' R A K Mason published a tribute to Fairburn in 1962.

Fallon, Padraic
Irish Poet *born* Athenry, County Galway 3 January 1905 *died* Aylesford 8 October 1974

Son of a sheep-and-cattle dealer, Fallon began his career as a Customs and Excise official in Dublin. Early in his life he was encouraged by 'AE' (George Russell) and influenced by Yeats. His Celtic style was gradually extended by a study of French poetry and his individual manner was both Irish and international. When he died a translation of Rimbaud's 'O Saisons, O Châteaux' was found on his typewriter and two lines from this are engraved on his tombstone: 'I have made a magic study / Of the good thing that eludes nobody'. Fallon also wrote a number of verse plays: *Diarmuid and Grainne* (1950) is often revived in Ireland.

Fanshawe, Sir Richard

English poet *baptised* Ware Park, Hertfordshire 12 June 1608 *died* 26 June 1666

Educated at Cambridge and the Inner Temple, Fanshawe supported the Royalist side on the outbreak of the Civil War and was secretary of war to the Prince of Wales. He fought at Worcester where he was taken prisoner then released on bail. After the Restoration he became Ambassador in Portugal and in Spain, where he died. He was an excellent linguist who translated Virgil, Horace, Camoens and Guarini. A Metaphysical poet, his 'Ode on His Majesty's Proclamation, Commanding the Gentry to Reside on their Estates, 1630' begins 'Now war is all the world about, / And everywhere Erynnis reigns, / Or else, the torch so late put out, / the stench remains.'

Fearing, Kenneth

American poet *born* Oak Park, Illinois 28 July 1902 *died* 1961

Fearing studied at the University of Wisconsin then moved to New York as a freelance writer, achieving major commercial and critical success with his suspense novel *The Big Clock* (1946). His *New and Selected Poems* appeared in 1956. Fearing uses a conversationally expansive style to portray the characters who dominate the everyday life of America. His 'Dirge', for example, contains this address: 'O executive type, would you like to drive a floating-power, knee-action, silk-upholstered six? Wed a Hollywood star? Shoot the course in 58? Draw to the ace, king, jack / O fellow with a will who won't take no, watch out for three cigarettes on the same, single match'.

Felltham, Owen

English poet *born* Suffolk *c*1602 *died* 1668

Felltham was eighteen when he published the first version of his *Resolves, Divine, Moral, and Political*, a collection of essays. As a young man he visited the Low Countries. He entered the service of the Earl of Thomond at Great Billing, Northamptonshire, where he is buried. An Anglican and royalist, he referred to Charles I (in a poetic tribute) as 'Christ the Second'. His 'Song' in

the Metaphysical mode, is an address to his 'Dearest': 'The waving
sea can with such flood / Bathe some high palace that hath stood /
Far from the main up in the river: / Oh think not then but love
can do / As much, for that's an ocean too, / That flows not every
day, but ever.'

Fenton, Elijah

English poet *born* Newcastle, Staffordshire 20 May 1683
died 1730

Fenton had to leave Cambridge without a degree as he would not
swear allegiance to William and Mary. He was in Flanders as Lord
Orrery's secretary and subsequently became a tutor in the house
of Lady Trumbull. He edited Waller and Milton and translated
Books I, IV, XIX and XXII of Pope's version of Homer's *Odyssey*.
His verse, such as 'An Ode to the Right Hon Lord Gower' (1716)
is formal though there are occasionally individual flourishes: 'But
here, no clarion's shrilling note / The Muse's green retreat can
pierce; / The grove, from noisy camps remote, / Is only vocal with
my verse'. Fenton's tragedy *Mariamne* (1723) was successful in
its time.

Fenton, James

English poet *born* Lincoln 1949

Educated at Oxford, Fenton worked as a journalist in England,
Vietnam and Germany before becoming theatre critic of the
Sunday Times. His selected poems 1968–82 were published as *The
Memory of War* (1982). The title poem of *Children in Exile* (1983) is
a sustained meditation, in quatrains, of the victims of war. Like
early Auden, Fenton has a journalistically taut command of detail
and a thematic depth: 'From five years of punishment for an
offence / It took America five years to commit / These victim–
children have been released on parole. / They will remember all
of it.' The poem ends: 'Let them dream / Of Jesus, America,
maths, Lego, music and dance.'

Ferguson, Samuel

Irish poet *born* Belfast 10 March 1810 *died* Dublin 9 August 1886

An Irish Protestant of Scottish stock Ferguson was called to the
Irish Bar in 1838, to the Inner Bar in 1859. For his work as
Deputy Keeper of the Irish Records he was knighted in 1878. His
scholarship was celebrated and he enthusiastically supported the
Gaelic revival. 'The Forging of the Anchor' shows the linguistic
surge of his verse: 'Come, see the Dolphin's anchor forged – 'tis at
a white heat now: / The bellows ceased, the flames decreased
though on the forge's brow / The little flames still fitfully play
through the sable mound, / And fitfully you still may see the grim
smiths ranking round, / All clad in leathern panoply, their broad

hands only bare: / Some rest upon their sledges here, some work the windlass there.'

Fergusson, Robert
Scottish poet *born* Edinburgh 5 September 1750
died Edinburgh 17. October 1774

Described by Burns as 'my elder brother in Misfortune, / By far my elder Brother in the muse' Robert Fergusson raised Scots verse to a new expressive level by applying his robust style to the subject of his native city where he was employed as a clerk after an education at St Andrews University. In 'Auld Reekie', Edinburgh comes alive in brilliantly described detail: 'Now Morn, wi' bonny purple smiles, / Kisses the air-cock o' Saunt Giles; / Rakin their een, the servant lasses / Early begin their lies an' clashes.' Allied to his descriptive gift Fergusson had a fine poetic sense of humour; he was, however, given to fits of depression. After falling down a flight of stairs he was taken to the Edinburgh Bedlam where he died, a victim of contemporary ignorance about mental breakdown.

Ferlinghetti, Lawrence
American poet *born* Yonkers, New York 1919

Educated at Columbia and the Sorbonne, Ferlinghetti co-founded, in 1953, the City Lights Bookshop at 261 Columbus Avenue, San Francisco. From this base he operated as a publisher (of Ginsberg and others) and as a promoter of Beat poetry – a rawly emotional mode full of topical references and political protest. *A Coney Island of the Mind* (1958) expresses his vision of 'suffering humanity' in contemporary America; 'They are the same people / only further from home / on freeways fifty lanes wide / on a concrete continent / spaced with bland billboards / illustrating imbecile illusions of happiness'. His *Endless Life: Selected Poems* appeared in 1981.

Fiacc, Padraic
Irish poet *born* Belfast 1924

Fiacc's father emigrated to the USA and the poet was educated in New York. He returned to Belfast in 1946, and became the first Ulster poet to receive the AE Prize – for his unpublished collection *Woe to the Boy* (1957). His *Odour of Blood* appeared in 1973. In several poems he reflects on the nature of the Ulster experience, as in 'Tears': 'After the bombing the British soldier / Looks up into the barbwired Irish / Twilight. His unflinching open eyes / Deaden, yet involuntarily flood / With the colour of tea / Drenches his combat jacket sleeve. // Now he is hugging, / Now he is giving / his male love / To a screaming fellow being, he does / Not know if it is a man or a woman.'

Fiamengo, Marya
Canadian poet *born* Vancouver 1900

Born into a Serbo–Croatian family, Marya Fiamengo was
educated at the University of British Columbia where she later
taught. She published *North of the Cold Star* in 1978. Her work
shows an obvious humanity as well as an international range of
reference. Her poem 'for Osip Mandelstam', inspired by a tragic
victim of Stalinism, expresses the author's anguish and states:
'Remorseless, implacable destiny / where pogroms fall through
the air / like programmes at a Sunday concert, / I would give up
everything / especially history / for mercy and justice, / a little
tender sanity.' The linear arrangement of the poem is
appropriately abrupt.

Field, Eugene
American poet *born* St Louis 3 September 1850
died 4 November 1895

A lawyer's son,was educated at the University of Missouri.
He married the sixteen-year-old Julia Sutherland Comstock in
1873 and had eight children by her. He became a columnist with
the Chicago *Morning News* from 1883 until his death, contributing
a regular 'Sharps and Flats' feature. A man with a highly
developed sense of humour he was acclaimed as 'childhood's born
laureate'. One of his best remembered poems is 'Little Boy Blue'
which describes a child's love for his toy dog and toy soldier: 'And
they wonder, as waiting the long years through / In the dust of
that little chair, / What has become of our Little Boy Blue, / Since
he kissed them and put them there.'

Field, Michael
see below

'Michael Field' was the joint pseudonym of Katherine Harris
Bradley (born Birmingham 27 October 1848, died 26 September
1914) and her niece Edith Emma Cooper (born Kenilworth,
Warwickshire 12 January 1862, died 13 December 1913). From
the age of four, Edith lived with her Aunt Katherine, the
daughter of a tobacco manufacturer. In collaboration they wrote
27 tragedies and eight volumes of poetry. Their work is sensitive
and aesthetically alert. Their poetic description of 'La Gioconda,
by Leonardo Da Vinci, in the Louvre' ends: 'Behind her, crystal
rocks, a sea and skies / Of evanescent blue on cloud and creek; /
Landscape that shines suppressive of its zest / For those
vicissitudes by which men die.'

Finch, Anne (Countess of Winchelsea)
English poet *born* near Southampton 1661 *died* 1720

Like Anne Killigrew, Anne Kingsmill Finch was a Maid of Honour to Mary of Modena at the court of James II. After the Revolution of 1688 her husband, Heneage Finch, refused to swear allegiance to William and Mary. As a result Anne and Heneage (5th Earl of Winchelsea) lived largely in the country. In poems, such as 'Ardelia's Answer to Ephelia', she contrasted her rural retreat with London: 'We parted thus, the night in peace I spent, / And the next day, with haste and pleasure went / To the best seat of fam'd and fertile Kent. / Where lett me live from all detraction free / Till thus the World is criticis'd be mee'.

Finch, Robert
Canadian poet *born* Freeport, Long Island 1900

Educated at the University of Toronto then at the Sorbonne, Finch was Professor of French at the University of Toronto. His work was included in the *New Provinces* anthology of 1936 and he was thus associated with the move to introduce a more modern tone into Canadian poetry. His 'Jardin de la Chapelle Expiatoire' combines the two languages most readily at his command: 'Newspapers crackle and hoops roll. / The bench unfurls its slatted scroll / To let a Latin lover's arm / Perturb the Saxon sense of form. // Je t'aimerai toujours! – Toujours? – / Toujours, voilà ce qu'est l'amour. / The obedient clock across the park / Marks time all day to that remark.' His collection *Has and Is* appeared in 1981.

Finlay, Ian Hamilton
Scottish poet *born* Nassau, Bahamas 28 October 1925

Raised in Scotland, Finlay became internationally known in the 1960s as a leading exponent of 'concrete poetry' – using the visual possibilities of typography to shape poems as spatial patterns on the page. In 1969 he moved to Stonypath, Dunsyre, Lanarkshire and there he translated his ideas into physical form, collaborating with pictorial artists, photographers, sculptors and craftsmen to make objects embodying his conceptual conclusions. He also developed his garden into an artistic event, regarding this as a direct collaboration with nature. Autumn becomes, in a stone inscription, 'One (Orange) Arm Of The World's Oldest Windmill' and a swallow is 'The Cloud's Anchor'.

Fitzgerald, Edward
English poet *born* near Woodbridge, Suffolk 13 March 1809 *died* 14 June 1883

Son of a country gentleman, Fitzgerald was educated at Cambridge. While recovering from the breakdown of his marriage, he read the poems of Omar Khayyám and began to render them into English. Though the original quatrains (*rubáiyát*) amount to a series of short poems, Fitzgerald organised them as a sequence moving reflectively from dawn to dusk. With its stanzaic novelty and hedonistic tone, *The Rubáiyát of Omar Khayyám* (1859, 4th edition 1879) became a Victorian bestseller: 'Here with a Loaf of Bread beneath the Bough, / A Flask of Wine, a Book of Verse – and Thou / Beside me singing in the Wilderness – / And Wilderness is paradise enow.'

Fitzgerald, Robert

American poet *born* Geneva, New York 1910

Raised in Springfield, Illinois, Fitzgerald was educated at Harvard and studied Classics and Philosophy at Cambridge. He was a reporter for the *New York Herald Tribune* from 1933–5 and for the following seven years was on the staff of *Time* magazine. After three years' service in the Navy he taught at Sarah Lawrence College until 1953. With Dudley Fitts he made distinguished translations of Euripides and Sophocles. In his poem 'History' he is expansive: 'Into this mountain shade everything passes. / The slave lays down his bones here, and the hero, / Thrown, goes reeling with blinded face; / The long desirèd opens her scorched armpits.'

Fitzgerald, R D

Australian poet *born* Hunter's Hill, Sydney 1902

Robert D Fitzgerald was educated in Sydney (where he read science at the University), and subsequently qualified as a land surveyor. After working in Fiji as a Government Surveyor, he returned to Australia as senior surveyor in the Commonwealth Department of the Interior. Fitzgerald writes a slow stately verse whose gravity is influenced by Yeats. In 'The Wind at Your Door' he reflects on his Irish connexions: 'These are the Irish batch of Castle Hill, / rebels and mutineers, my countrymen / twice over: first, because of those to till / my birthplace first, hack roads, raise roofs; and then / because their older land time and again / enrolls me through my forebears'.

Flecker, James Elroy

English poet *born* London 5 November 1884
died Davos, Switzerland 3 January 1915

A clergyman's son, Flecker was educated at Oxford and Cambridge where he studied Persian and Arabic before entering the Consular Service. In 1910 he was posted to Constantinople and, while on leave, married a Greek girl, Helle Skiaderessi. He was vice-consul at Beirut from 1911–13; he died, in a sanatorium, of tuberculosis. Drawing on his knowledge of oriental literature and his love of the English classics, he attempted to combine exoticism with formal perfection. His *The Golden Journey to Samarkand* (1913) has an incantatory quality: 'Sweet to ride forth at evening from the wells / When shadows pass gigantic on the sand / And softly through the silence beat the bells / Along the Golden Road to Samarkand.'

Fletcher, Giles
English poet *born* 1585 *died* Alderton, Suffolk 1623

Called Giles Fletcher the Younger, to distinguish him from his father Giles Fletcher (1546–1611), he was educated at Cambridge where he obtained a readership in Greek grammar and was, in 1617, appointed to a college living. A year after being elected reader in Greek language, in 1618, he became rector of Alderton, Suffolk. His finest work is 'Christ's Victorie and Triumph in Heaven and Earth' (1610) which includes a memorable description of the Celestial City: 'A heavenly feast no hunger can consume, / A light unseen, yet shines in every place, / A sound no time can steal, a sweet perfume / No winds can scatter, an entire embrace / That no satiety can e'er unlace.'

Fletcher, John
English poet *born* 1579 *died* 1625

Son of Richard Fletcher (Bishop of London in 1594), and cousin of Giles and Phineas Fletcher, Fletcher was educated at Cambridge. He first established a literary reputation by writing plays in collaboration with Francis Beaumont after whose death, in 1616, Fletcher wrote alone and sometimes in collaboration with, for example, Philip Massinger. His tragedy *Valentinian* contains the spirited song beginning: 'Now the lusty spring is seen; / Golden yellow, gaudy blue, / Daintily invite the view: / Everywhere on every green / Roses blushing as they blow / And enticing men to pull, / Lilies whiter than the snow, / Woodbines of sweet honey full'.

Fletcher, John Gould
American poet *born* Little Rock, Arkansas 3 January 1886
died Little Rock 10 May 1950

After studying at Harvard, Fletcher decided to become a fulltime poet when he inherited money on the death of his father. He went to England in 1908 and attached himself, first, to Pound's Imagist school, then to Amy Lowell's 'Amygist' group. Returning to America he became a member of the Fugitives and contributed to the agrarian anthology *I'll Take My Stand* (1930). In 1936 Fletcher returned to Little Rock and, eleven years after winning the Pulitzer Price for his *Selected Poems* (1938), drowned in a pond near his home. His best poems, such as 'Green Symphony', show a flair for extravagant images: 'The glittering leaves of the rhododendrons / Balance and vibrate in the cool air'.

Fletcher, Phineas
English poet *born* 1582 *died* 1650

The brother of Giles Fletcher the Younger and the cousin of John Fletcher, Phineas Fletcher was educated at Eton and Cambridge. He took orders and was Sir Henry Willoughby's chaplain at Risley, Derbyshire. He wrote (for example) *Brittains Ida* (1628) and *The Purple Island* (1633) as well as prose works and Latin poems. His reputation has been eclipsed by that of his brother John though Phineas was capable of such finely cadenced lines as those beginning: 'Drop, drop, slow tears / and bathe those beauteous feet, / Which brought from heaven / the news and prince of peace: / Cease not, wet eyes, / his mercies to entreat; / To cry for vengeance / sin doth never cease'.

Fleming, Marjorie
Scottish poet *born* Kirkcaldy 15 January 1803
died Kirkcaldy 19 December 1811

Called 'Pet Marjorie' by Dr John Brown and 'The Wonder Child' by Mark Twain, Marjorie Fleming was the daughter of an accountant. In 1808 she went to Edinburgh with her cousin, Isabella Keith, and lived with the Keith family for three years. The prose and poems in her three-volume journal show an exceptionally lively personality and a passion for rhyme. 'The Life of Mary Queen of Scots', Pet Marjorie's most ambitious work, begins: 'Poor Mary Queen of Scots was born / With all the graces which adorn / Her birthday is so very late / That I do now forget the date / Her education was in France / There she did learn to sing and dance'. Pet Marjorie died of meningitis.

Foley, Michael
Irish poet *born* Derry 1947

Educated at St Columb's College and Queen's University, Belfast, Foley became a Computer Science Lecturer in Dublin. He published *The GO Situation* in 1982. His work is humorous and his characteristic stance is to project himself as a realist surrounded by hopeless romantics. 'I remember Adlestrop' is a criticism of the mass of poetry written in admiration of Edward Thomas's poem 'Adlestrop': 'Yes, I remember Adlestrop. / Such an innocent vague / Neither-here-nor-there poem / – Yet it started so much crap.' The poem ends: 'All the vaguely mysterious / Bogusly sonorous / Phoneyly resonant slop! / Oh I remember Adlestrop.'

Ford, R A D
Canadian poet *born* Ottawa 1915

Educated at the University of Western Ontario and Cornell, Ford was Canadian Ambassador to the Soviet Union. He translated

impressively the work of Spanish and Russian poets and
published his *Selected Poems* in 1983. After his retirement from the
Canadian Embassy he settled in France. His poems tell of his
travels abroad, but in a critical rather than a touristic tone.
'Roadside near Moscow', for example, begins with a description
of 'Trees, gathered in profane / Assembly to watch over the
slow / passing of the almost human–like / Column of prisoners,
waiting for the snow / to fill in their tracks – strange / Judges of
evil done / In many ways.'

Forrester, Charles Robert
English poet *born* 1803 *died* 1850

Forrester was a public notary at the Royal Exchange in London
where his brother Alfred (1804–72) was in business with him. He
published *Castle Baynard* (1824), a novel; and *Sir Roland* (1827), a
medieval romance. He and Alfred (who did the drawings)
collaborated on *Absurdities of Prose and Verse* (1827), published
under the pseudonym Alfred Crowquill. He contributed to the
Ladies Magazine, *Comic Offering*, the *New Monthly Magazine* and
Bentley's Magazine (under the pseudonyms Hal Willis and Alfred
Crowquill). 'The Bill of Fare' is one of the best examples of his
light verse: 'For Capitalists – men of crumbs! / I've puddings made
of choicest plums'.

Foss, Sam Walter
American poet *born* Candia, New Hampshire 19 June 1858
died 26 February 1911

Foss was brought up on his father's farm and was educated at
Brown University. He was a journalist who became editor of the
Boston *Yankee Blade* and from 1898 onwards was librarian of the
Somerville Public Library. A humorist who contributed light
verse to various newspapers, he celebrated the American
infatuation with money in 'The Rattle of the Dollar': 'Though the
winter storms assault his path, and drift his way, and blow, / In his
heart he feels the sunshine of an endless summer-time; / For he
listens to the music of the money in his pocket – / To the rattle of
the dollar, and the jingle of the dime.' His *Songs of the Average Man*
appeared in 1907.

Fowler, William
Scottish poet born Edinburgh 1560 *died* London 1612

Educated at St Andrews University, Fowler was for some time in
France as a Protestant spy. Back in Scotland he became, in 1584,
minister in Hawick. He was popular at the court of James VI and
served as Queen Anne's secretary. He also helped in the
preparation of the King's *Basilicon Doron*. He translated Petrarch's
Triofni in 1587 and produced a sonnet sequence *The Tarantula of*

Love. 'In Orknay' begins: 'Upon the utmost corners of the warld, / and on the borders of this massive round, / quhaire fates and fortoune hither hes me harld, / I doe deplore my greiffs upon this ground'. He also published a prose description of his arrangements for the baptism of Henry, Prince of Wales.

harld drawn

Fox, George
Irish poet
19th century, dates unknown

Very few biographical facts are known about Fox. He was, like Samuel Ferguson, one of the members of the Ulster Gaelic Society (founded 1830) and took an enthusiastic interest in the Irish language. He graduated from Trinity College, Dublin, in 1847 and emigrated to America in 1848. His poem 'The County of Mayo' is an effective song of farewell: 'They are altered girls in Irrul now; 'tis proud they're grown and high, / With their hair-bags and their top-knots – / for I pass their buckles by. / But it's little now I heed their airs, for God will have it so, / That I must depart for foreign lands, and leave my sweet Mayo.'

Frame, Janet
New Zealand poet *born* Dunedin 1924

Raised in Oamaru, Janet Frame was educated at Otago University; she worked as a teacher and a nurse-companion in Dunedin. From 1956–61 she lived in London. After suffering a mental breakdown she wrote *Faces in the Water* (1962), a novel that contrasts personal with social insanity. She visited, on several occasions, the Yaddo Foundation, the writers' colony in Saratoga Springs, New York. Though best known as a novelist she has written poems as poignant as 'The Clown': 'dear lonely man in torn world of nobody, / it is for this waste that we have hoarded words over so many / million years since the first, groan, / and look up at the stars. Oh oh the sky is too wide to sleep under!'

Fraser, G S
Scottish poet *born* Glasgow 8 November 1915
died 3 January 1980

Educated at St Andrews University, George Sutherland Fraser served in the Middle East during the Second World War and was (from 1959–79) a lecturer in English at Leicester University. A gifted critic, he conveyed his passion for poetry in such books as *The Modern Writer and his World* (1953) and *Vision and Rhetoric* (1959). His reasons for leaving Scotland are indicated in his poem 'Meditation of a Patriot': 'He sings alone who in this province sings. / I kick a lamp-post, and in drink I rave: / With Byron and with Lermontov / Romantic Scotland's in the grave.' His tone is resigned, often apologetic as in 'Problems of a Poet': 'They shall say, his basket was emptied early, / He bowed, but did not come for the curtain call.'

Frere, John Hookham

English poet *born* London 21 May 1769 *died* Malta 7 January 1846

An antiquary's son, Frere was friendly with Canning (the future Prime Minister) at Eton. He was a Fellow of Caius College, Cambridge, and a clerk in the Foreign Office. He became a Member of Parliament in 1796, helped Canning to found the *Anti-Jacobin* in 1797, and served as Under Foreign Secretary. In 1817 he published his mock-heroic poem on *King Arthur and his Round Table*, using ottava rima so effectively that Byron followed his example in *Beppo* (1818). Here is Frere's description of Sir Gawain: 'A word from him set everything at rest, / His short decisions never fail'd to hit; / His silence, his reserve, his inattention, / Were felt as the severest reprehension'.

Frost, Robert

American poet *born* San Francisco 26 March 1874
died 29 January 1963

On his father's death, the ten-year-old Frost moved to New England. After studying at Harvard and farming in New Hampshire he went to England where he befriended and greatly encouraged Edward Thomas. When Frost returned to the USA he settled in New Hampshire and wrote the poems in *New Hampshire* (1923). His lucid praise of nature was allied to a folksy philosophy that seemed quintessentially American: 'The woods are lovely, dark, and deep, / But I have promises to keep, / And miles to go before I sleep, / And miles to go before I sleep.' ('Stopping By Woods on a Snowy Evening'). President John F Kennedy greatly admired Frost and invited him to read 'The Gift Outright' at his inauguration.

Fry, Christopher

English poet *born* Bristol 1907

Fry was three when his father, an Anglican lay-preacher, died. He became an actor in 1927 and worked in various repertory companies. During the Second World War he served with the Pioneer Corps. Influenced by the verse plays of T S Eliot, Fry wrote *A Phoenix Too Frequent* (1946) and the hugely successful *The Lady's Not for Burning* (1949). He was acclaimed as a dramatist of Elizabethan power though his reputation subsequently declined after the enthusiasm of the 1950s. Speeches, such as Dynamene's Lament, from *A Phoenix Too Frequent*, retain their verbal energy:

'What a mad blacksmith creation is / Who blows his furnaces
until the stars fly upward / And iron Time is hot and politicians
glow'.

Fuller, John
English poet *born* Ashford, Kent 1 January 1937

Son of the poet Roy Fuller, John Fuller was educated and later
taught at Oxford, which plays an atmospheric part in his poetry.
His poem 'The College Ghost', for example, is a supernatural
story set in the university and invokes the confusion that follows
a convivial evening: 'My black tie carelessly telling the
approximate time, / The claret filling my toes, the toes my shoes /
And the shoes knowing more or less the way to go'. Fuller's
poems exude contentment: his world of town and gown, of 'wine
buff' and committees meeting to 'discuss a new bottle', is an
academic utopia where there is drama in the sight of a girl sitting
an examination.

Fuller, Roy
English poet *born* Failsworth, Lancashire 11 February 1912

Roy Fuller left school at sixteen to train as a solicitor in which
capacity he worked for many years with the Woolwich Equitable
Building Society. His first collection *Poems* (1939) showed his debt
to the didactic style of Auden. During the Second World War,
Fuller served in the Fleet Air Arm of the Royal Navy and the
experience made him question the poetic posture of infallibility.
In the title poem of *The Middle of a War* (1942) he sounded the self-
critical note that was to become characteristic of his mature
poetry: 'My photograph already looks historic. / The promising
youthful face, the matelot's collar, / Say "This one is remembered
for a lyric, / His place and period – nothing could be duller."'

Garioch, Robert
Scottish poet *born* Edinburgh 9 May 1909
died Edinburgh 26 April 1981

From 1942–5 Garioch was a prisoner of war in Italy and
Germany; he spent most of his working life as a schoolteacher. As
an Edinburgh man, Garioch decided to take as his poetic model
Robert Fergusson who had previously inspired the young Robert
Burns. Like Fergusson, Garioch wanted his poems to reflect the
life of the city and he recorded his impressions and opinions in a
series of Edinburgh sonnets which can be read as individual items
or as related parts of a comic vision of Edinburgh. 'Elegy', one of
the sonnets, recalls two headmasters he had known: 'Ane sneerit

quarterly – I cuidna square / my savings bank – and sniftert in his
spite. / Weill, gin they arena deid, it's time they were.'
cuidna could not; *sniftert* sniff; *gin* if

Garlick, Raymond
Welsh poet *born* London 1926

Though born into an English family, Garlick was brought up in
Wales and subsequently identified with his adopted country.
After leaving school at fifteen he became a factory worker, near
London, then studied at Leeds University and University College,
Bangor. He taught in several schools before settling in the
Netherlands in 1960 as a staff member of the International
School, Eerde Castle, Overijssel. In 1967 he returned to Wales to
teach Welsh Studies at Trinity College, Carmarthen. He was one
of the founders of the *Anglo–Welsh Review* (originally called *Dock
Leaves* until the name was changed in 1957) and edited it from
1949–60. His own work affirms (in, for example, 'Consider
Kyffin') 'voyages to where Wales joins / the world's end'.

Garrigue, Jean
American poet *born* Evansville, Indiana 8 December 1914
died 1972

Jean Garrigue was educated at Chicago University and
subsequently taught at several colleges including Iowa, Bard
and Queen's. She wrote articles for the *Kenyon Review*, *New
Republic*, the *Saturday Review of Literature*, and other journals. Her
collections include *The Ego and the Centaur* (1947) and *Country
Without Maps* (1964). Her best poems, such as 'Lightly Like Music
Running', have an energetic rhythm and an Edenic mood: 'Lightly
like music running, our blood / In and out of the cloud's woven
pastures, / It was all in the shade of the vines and meadows /
Where Adam delves, in the green fables / Of the dogdays, in early
youth.'

Garth, Sir Samuel
English poet *born* 1661 *died* 1719

Garth was a distinguished doctor who became physician-in-
ordinary to George I. He was friendly with Dryden and
encouraged Pope. His *The Dispensary* (1696), a mock-heroic poem,
attacks the apothecaries who were opposed to the issue of free
medicine to the poor: 'Speak, goddess! since 'tis thou that best
canst tell / How ancient leagues to modern discord fell; / And why
physicians were so cautious grown / Of others' lives, and lavish of
their own; / How by a journey to the Elysian plain / Peace
triumphed, and old Time returned again.' Later in the first canto,
Garth observes 'But now no grand inquiries are descried, / Mean
faction reigns where knowledge should preside'.

Gascoigne, George

English poet *born* Cardington, Bedfordshire *c*1525
died near Stanford 7 October 1577

Educated at Cambridge and Gray's Inn, Gascoigne was a Member
of Parliament for Bedford (1557-9) and also served as a soldier in
the Low Countries (1572-4). Deprived of his inheritance because
of his disreputable behaviour, he married the mother of Nicholas
Breton and lived as a country gentleman; nevertheless he
continued to get into trouble by accumulating debts. His *Notes of
Instruction Concerning the Making of Verse* (1575) is regarded as the
first English critical essay. A representative figure of the English
Renaissance, he wrote provocative poems such as the one
beginning '"And if I did, what then? / Are you aggrieved
therefore? / The sea hath fish for every man, / And what would
you have more?"'

Gay, John

English poet *born* near Barnstaple, baptised 16 September
1685 *died* 4 December 1732

As Gay's parents died when he was a child he became an
apprentice silkmaker but abandoned this work to take up a
literary life. He became friendly with Pope and with Swift who
assisted him in the writing of *Trivia* (1716) and also encouraged
him to write *The Beggar's Opera* (1728), a hugely successful musical
pastoral. It includes songs like that beginning: 'Youth's the
season made for joys, / Love is then our duty, / She alone who
that employs, / Well deserves her beauty. /Let's be gay, / While
we may, / Beauty's a flower despised in decay.' Gay earned £800
from this work and published a sequel *Polly* (1729). In his final
years Gay lived in the home of his patron, the Duke of
Queensberry.

Geddes, Alexander

Scottish poet *born* Ruthven, Banffshire 1737
died 26 February 1802

Born into a Roman Catholic family, Geddes trained for the
priesthood in Paris. His scholarly translation of the *Satires* of
Horace impressed his contemporaries but his liberal
interpretation of Hebrew Scripture led to his suspension from the
Church. He moved to London where Lord Petre encouraged him
to translate the Bible for English Roman Catholics and this
version (as far as Ruth) appeared in three volumes (1792-6). His
best-known Scots poem is his 'Epistle to . . . the Scottish Society
of Antiquaries': 'For tho' 'tis true that Mither-tongue / Has had
the melancholy fate / To be neglekit by the great, / She still has
fun an open door / Amang the uncurruptit poor'.

Ghose, Zulfikar
Pakistani poet *born* Pakistan 1935

Ghose, who was raised in British India, came to England in 1952 and studied at Keele University. For five years he was cricket and hockey correspondent of the *Observer*. In 1969 he moved to the USA as an associate professor of English at the University of Texas at Austin. He is a highly imaginative novelist; *A New History of Torments* (1982) uses the El Dorado myth to comment on the modern world. His expressive use of language is shown in 'Flying over India': 'India lies still in primeval / intactness of growth. The great alluvial / plains are sodden with trees; neither city / nor village intrudes with temples and towers / in this sprawling virgin-land decked with flowers // and trees, trees.'

Gibbon, Monk
Irish poet *born* Dublin 1896

Educated at St Columba's College, Dublin and at Oxford, Gibbon won the Silver Medal for Poetry at the 1928 Tailteann Games. He published several collections of poetry including *This Insubstantial Pageant* (1951). His affirmative attitude to nature is shown in his pursuit of an elusive creature in 'Salt': 'All was well. / It was a delight merely to sniff the morning / And know the wood was haunted by her. Others had said / she hung, in safety caged, above a hundred doorways, / Twittering her daily reassurance. / Oh mystery of existence, shy as air'. By the end of the poem Gibbon concludes that Truth 'Hops, out of reach, a yard or so away, / Or perches in the branch her soul has chosen.'

Gibson, Wilfred
English poet *born* Hexham, Northumberland 2 October 1878 *died* 26 May 1962

Gibson did social work in London before going to the Western Front as a private. His collection *Battle* (1916) was one of the first to indicate the real conditions of the war. 'The Bayonet', for example, rejects patriotic sentiment in favour of a grimly realistic situation: 'This bloody steel / has killed a man. / I heard him squeal / As on I ran.' After the war he lived in Gloucestershire near his friend Lascelles Abercrombie. As both of them had (with Walter de la Mare) been willed a share of the posthumous royalties of Rupert Brooke's poems they were able to devote most of their time to poetry. Though he wrote many rural poems he also sustained his interest in the plight of the urban poor.

Gilbert, Sir W S
English poet *born* London 18 November 1836 *died* 29 May 1911

William Schwenck Gilbert, son of a novelist, was educated at King's College, London. In 1855 he was entered at the Inner

Temple and was called to the Bar in 1863. To supplement his income he contributed to *Fun* and to *Punch* which rejected his 'Yarn of the *Nancy Bell*', one of the best of the *Bab Ballads* (1869): 'And I eat that cook in a week or less, / And – as I eating be / The last of his chops, why, I almost drops, / For a wessel in sight I see.' Subsequently Gilbert collaborated with Arthur Sullivan to create some classic comic operas such as *Trial by Jury* (1875), *The Pirates of Penzance* (1879) and *The Gondoliers* (1889). He died of heart failure after rescuing a lady visitor from his swimming pool at Harrow. He was knighted in 1907.

Gilman, Charlotte Perkins
American poet *born* 1860 *died* 1935

Related to Harriet Beecher Stowe, Charlotte Perkins Gilman left her husband and thereafter attempted to put her feminist principles into practice. She wrote an influential study of *Women and Economics* and in her poems expressed the same radical commitment to the women's movement. One of her feminist poems runs as follows: 'She walketh veiled and sleeping, / For she knoweth not her power; / She obeyeth but the pleading / Of her heart, and the high leading / Of her soul, unto this hour. / Slow advancing, halting, creeping, / Comes the Woman to the hour! – / She walketh veiled and sleeping, / For she knoweth not her power.' Ill from cancer, she eventually took her own life.

Gilmore, Mary
Australian poet *born* near Goulburn, New South Wales *died* 1962

Born Mary Cameron, the poet began her working life as a schoolteacher and later turned to journalism. Passionately attached to radical ideals, she was one of the group, led by William Lane, who went to Paraguay in the 1890s to establish New Australia. In Paraguay, she married William Gilmore, another of Lane's supporters; when New Australia disintegrated, the Gilmores returned to Australia and Mary edited the Woman's Page in the Sydney *Worker*. In 1937 she was made a Dame Commander of the Order of the British Empire. Her poems are earnest expressions of her ideals, as in 'Nationality': 'I have grown past hate and bitterness, / I see the world as one; / Yet, though I can no longer hate, / My son is still my son.'

Gilpin, Catherine
English poet *born* Scaleby Castle, near Carlisle 1738
died Carlisle 29 April 1811

Catherine Gilpin's father commanded Scaleby Castle and her brothers were artistically accomplished: William was the celebrated literary exponent of the 'picturesque', Sawrey was a painter. She lived for some time at 14 Finkle Street, Carlisle, with her friend Susanna Blamire, the 'Muse of Cumberland'. Under the influence of Susanna, Catherine wrote lyrics as lively as 'The Village Club': 'I lives in a neat little cottage; / I rents me a neyce little farm; / On Sundays I dresses me handsome; / On Mondays I dresses me warm. // I goes to the sign of the Anchor; / I sits myself quietly down, / To wait till the lads are all ready, / For we hev a club i' the town.'

Ginsberg, Allen

American poet *born* Newark, New Jersey 3 June 1926

Son of the poet Louis Ginsberg, Ginsberg was raised in Paterson, New Jersey, and educated at Columbia University. Fascinated by the visionary poetry of Blake and Whitman, Ginsberg regarded himself as the anarchic embodiment of America's 'Beat' generation of the 1950s. He used drugs to explore levels of consciousness and became an international celebrity as a result of his hypnotic stage performances. *Howl* (1956) retains its power as an extraordinary verbal assault on complacency: 'I saw the best minds of my generation destroyed by madness, starving hysterical naked, / dragging themselves through the negro streets at dawn looking for an angry fix'.

Glassco, John

Canadian poet *born* Montreal 1909 *died* 1981

Educated at McGill University, Glassco edited *The Poetry of French Canada in Translation* (1970) and published the prose works *Memoirs of Montparnasse* (1970) and *The Fatal Woman* (1974). Ten years before his death he published his *Selected Poems* (1971). Unlike some of his contemporaries he acknowledged the Canadian tradition of affirmative nature poetry and in 'Quebec Farmhouse' revived it, though with obviously ironic overtones: 'This is the closed, enclosing house / That set its flinty face against / The rebel children dowered with speech / To break it open, to make it live / And flower in the cathedral beauty / Of a pure heaven of Canadian blue'.

Glover, Denis

New Zealand poet *born* Dunedin 1912 *died* 1980

Educated at the University of Canterbury, where he won a boxing blue, Glover became a journalist then returned to the university as an English lecturer from 1936-8 and 1946-8. He founded the Caxton Press in 1938 and brought out *The Wind and the Sand* (1945) and *Sings Harry* (1951) under its imprint. Glover's character Harry, the bard, expresses himself sceptically about social pretensions. 'Themes' begins with Harry asking what should be sung: 'Sing truthful men? Where shall we find / The man who cares to speak his mind: / Truth's out of uniform, sings

Harry, / That's her offence / Where lunacy parades as common sense.'

Glover, Richard
English poet *born* London 1712 *died* 1785

Son of a merchant, Glover followed in his father's commercial footsteps and also wrote prolifically from the age of sixteen (when he produced a poem about Sir Isaac Newton). He was twenty-five when he published the first nine books of his epic *Leonidas* – which was well received. In 1770 he enlarged *Leonidas* from nine to twelve books, and produced a sequel *The Athenians*. Glover's epic is cluttered with the conventions of extravagantly heroic verse, as this extract from Book XII shows; 'Back to the pass in gentle march he leads / The embattled warriors. They, behind the shrubs, / Where Medon sent such numbers to the shades, / In ambush lie.'

Gogarty, Oliver St John
Irish poet *born* Dublin 17 August 1878 *died* 22 September 1957

The original of Joyce's Buck Mulligan in *Ulysses* (1922), Gogarty went to Trinity College, Dublin, and studied medicine. Because of his financial advantages, he tended to patronise Joyce; when Joyce left Ireland, Gogarty pursued a distinguished career as a surgeon. In 1922 he was made a Senator of the Irish Free State but when his country adopted the name Eire in 1936, Gogarty expressed disapproval of new political developments and three years later moved to the USA. He was a witty prose writer – for example *Tumbling in the Hay* (1939) – and a poet who (after reading Tolstoy) wrote 'Ringsend': 'I will live in Ringsend / With a red-headed whore, / And the fan-light gone in / Where it lights the hall-door'.

Goldsmith, Oliver
Irish poet *born* Pallas, Longford 10 November 1731
died London 4 April 1774

Disfigured by smallpox at the age of eight, Goldsmith was educated at Trinity College, Dublin, and at Edinburgh where he studied medicine in 1752. In London he became a member of Dr Johnson's circle. He produced a masterly work in three different modes with his novel *The Vicar of Wakefield* (1776), his play *She Stoops to Conquer* (1773) and his discursive poem *The Deserted Village* (1770) from which the following lines are taken: 'Sweet was the sound when oft at evening's close, / Up yonder hill the village murmur rose; / There as I past with careless steps and slow, / The mingling notes came softened from below; / The swain responsive as the milk-maid sung, / The sober herd that lowed to meet their young . . .'

Goldsmith, Oliver
Canadian poet *born* St Andrew's, New Brunswick 1794 *died* 1861

Grandnephew of the above, he worked for the government and rose to the position of Deputy Commissary General, a post that made him a much-travelled man. Under the influence of his Irish namesake's *The Deserted Village*, he fashioned his *The Rising Village* which was published in England in 1825 then, in a revised text, in Canada in 1834. Although *The Rising Village* is derivative it has lively descriptive touches: 'See! from their heights the lofty pines descend, / And crackling, down their pond'rous lengths extend. / Soon from their boughs the curling flames arise, / Mount into air, and redden all the skies; / And where the forest once its foliage spread, / The golden corn triumphant waves its head'.
as the milk-maid sung, / The sober herd that lowed to meet their young . . .'

Gordon, Adam Lindsay
Australian poet *born* Fayal, the Azores 19 October 1833
died 24 June 1870

Gordon settled in Australia in 1853 and set about several careers. As well as writing poetry, he became a celebrity as a jockey and cultivated a dashingly romantic image. Tragically he came out of retirement in 1870, because of financial problems, and was badly injured in a fall from a horse. Defeated, so he thought, as well as depressed he shot himself. In Australia he is regarded as a Byronic figure and in 1934 a bust of Gordon was placed in Poet's Corner in Westminster Abbey. His dramatic monologue 'The Sick Stockrider' expresses some of the poet's own attitudes: 'This I know – / I should live the same life over, if I had to live again; / And the chances are I go where most men go.'

Gower, John
English poet *born* Kent *c*1330 *died* 1408

Born into a wealthy family, Gower was known as a benefactor of churches. He was friendly with Chaucer and entered the service of the future Henry IV to whom he dedicated the revised (1393) version of *Confessio amantis* (originally written for Richard II). From 1377 Gower lived in semi-retirement in the priory of St Mary's Overeys, Southwark, where he married his nurse Agnes Groundolf. His *Confessio* contrasts courtly love with Christianity. Towards the end of the poem the author laments 'That I am feble and impotent, / I wot nought how the world is went.' Gower himself ended his days in distress caused by the onset of blindness.

Graham W S
Scottish poet *born* Greenock 19 November 1918

William Sydney Graham trained as an engineer in Scotland but later settled, as a fulltime writer, in Madron, Penzance, Cornwall. He is an ecstatic poet who celebrates the sea in a lucid and affirmative language. His poems move in mood between childhood memories and details of his life in Madron. 'To My Mother' explains: 'The flowing strongheld Clyde / Rests me my earliest word / That has ever matchlessly / Changed me towards the sea.' 'The Fifteen Devices' is set in Cornwall: 'My fifteen devices of shadow and brightness / Are settling in and the Madron / Morning accepts them in their place.' Graham has protected his privacy though he has read his poems and lectured in the USA.

Grainger, James
English poet *born* 1721 *died* 1767

Grainger was an army surgeon who later settled in London as a doctor. His 'Ode to Solitude' was published in 1755 and impressed Dr Johnson with its 'very noble' opening: 'O solitude, romantic maid! / Whether by nodding towers you tread, / Or haunt the desert's trackless gloom, / Or hover o'er the yawning tomb, / Or climb the Andes' clifted side, / Or by the Nile's coy source abide, / Or starting from your half-year's sleep / From Hecla view the thawing deep'. In 1759 Grainger went to the West Indies where he set up a practice in St Christopher's and married the Governor's daughter. Dr Johnson found Dr Grainger 'an agreeable man, a man that would do any good that was in his power'.

Graves, Alfred Percival
Irish poet *born* Dublin 22 July 1846 *died* 27 December 1931

Graves, whose father became Bishop of Limerick and Fellow of the Royal Society, was educated at Trinity College, Dublin. He worked as a clerk in the Home Office before pursuing a career as an inspector of schools – in Manchester, Taunton and Southwark. Involved in the Irish Renascence, he published *Father O'Flynn and Other Lyrics* in 1889. His autobiography *To Return to All That* (1930) responds to his son Robert's *Good-bye to All That* (1929). 'Father O'Flynn' is recognised as a comic classic: 'Och, Father O'Flynn, you've the wonderful way wid you, / All the ould sinners are wishful to pray wid you, / All the young childer are wild for to play wid you, / You've such a way wid you, Father avick!'

Graves, Robert Ranke
English poet *born* London 24 July 1895

Graves is the son of a schools inspector who wrote the song 'Father O'Flynn'. After a scholarship to Charterhouse, Graves planned to go to Oxford but instead enlisted when England declared war on Germany. On 24 July 1916 he was reported dead of wounds received at the Somme and was thus able to read his own obituary in *The Times*. Graves (twice-married and once close to the poet Laura Riding) believes that the survival of poetry depends on the celebration of women as earthly representatives of the eternal Muse – the White Moon Goddess who is formally evoked in 'To Juan at the Winter Solstice': 'Her sea-blue eyes were wild / But nothing promised that is not performed.'

Gray, Sir Alexander

Scottish poet *born* Dundee 6 January 1882
died Edinburgh 17 February 1968

Educated at the universities of Edinburgh, Göttingen and Paris, Gray was a Civil Servant and then Professor of Political Economy at the University of Aberdeen until 1934. In 1956 he became Emeritus Professor of Political Economy at Edinburgh University. He was a prominent figure in educational affairs and did distinguished work as a translator from German and the Scandinavian languages. He is best remembered for his patriotic poem 'Scotland': 'This is my country, /The land that begat me. / These windy spaces / Are surely my own. / And those who here toil / In the sweat of their faces / Are flesh of my flesh, / And bone of my bone.'

Gray, David

Scottish poet *born* near Kirkintilloch, Dunbartonshire
29 January 1838 *died* 3 December 1861

Son of a handloom weaver, Gray was educated at Glasgow University where he studied divinity. He went to London in 1860, with his friend Robert Buchanan, and was encouraged by Monckton Milnes (later Lord Houghton). *The Luggie* (1862) is a long poem about the river that flowed past his birthplace. The sonnet sequence 'In the Shadows' anticipates his early death from consumption: 'If it must be; if it must be, O God! / That I die young, and make no further moans; / That, underneath the unrespective sod, / In unescutcheoned privacy, my bones / Shall crumble soon, – then give me strength to bear / the last convulsive throe of too sweeth breath!' His *Poetical Works* appeared in 1874.

Gray, John

English poet *born* Woolwich 1866 *died* Edinburgh 1934

John Gray is arguably the original of the protagonist of Oscar Wilde's *The Portrait of Dorian Gray* (1891). Introduced to Wilde at a session of the Rhymers' Club in 1889, Gray impressed by his good looks and poetic posturing. After Wilde met Lord Alfred Douglas in 1891 he lost interest in Gray but still paid for the cost of publishing Gray's *Silverpoints* (1892). After Wilde's arrest in 1895, Gray entered the priesthood and became Father John Gray of St Peter's Church, Edinburgh. In poems such as 'Les Demoiselles De Sauve' Gray shows a delicately descriptive touch: 'Beautiful ladies through the orchard pass; / Bend under crutched–up branches, forked and low; / Trailing their samet palls o'er dew–drenched grass.'

Gray, Thomas

English poet *born* Cornhill 26 December 1716
died Cambridge 30 July 1771

The son of an eccentric scrivener, Thomas Gray was educated at Cambridge and returned to the university as a Fellow in 1742. A scholarly, retiring man, Gray refused the Poet Laureateship in 1757. His poetry combines classical control with a romantic feeling for nature that impressed both Wordsworth and Coleridge. He excelled at the composition of Odes but his greatest poetic triumph was the publication, on 15 February 1751, of the 'Elegy Written in a Country Churchyard'. As a melancholy meditation on death the elegy is one of the glories of the English language: 'The curfew tolls the knell of parting day, / The lowing herd wind slowly o'er the lea, / The plowman homeward plods his weary way, / And leaves the world to darkness and to me.'

Grenfell, Julian

English poet *born* 30 March 1888 *died* near Ypres 26 May 1915

Son of Lord Desborough, Grenfell was educated at Eton and Oxford before becoming an officer in the Royal Dragoons in 1910. 'I *adore* War', he admitted, and his ability to outwit and kill enemy snipers single-handed won him the D.S.O. He died after being hit by a shell splinter and two days after his death his poem 'Into Battle' appeared in *The Times* with a note regretting his death. It is a work that affirms the act of war; 'And life is colour and warmth and light, / And a striving evermore for these; / And he is dead who will not fight; / And who dies fighting has increase.' The poem then goes on to insist 'The fighting man shall from the sun / Take warmth, and life from the glowing earth'.

Greville, Fulke

English poet *born* Beauchamp Court, Warwickshire 3 October 1554 *died* 30 September 1628

Fulke Greville – or Lord Brooke as he became when James I made him a baron in 1621 – went to Shrewsbury School at the same time as Philip Sidney. After an education at Cambridge, he became one of Elizabeth I's favourites and Member of Parliament for Warwickshire. From 1614 to 1622 he was Chancellor of the

Exchequer. He was stabbed to death by a disgruntled servant. His tragedy *Mustapha* (1609) contains passages as powerful as the 'Chorus Sacerdotum': 'Oh wearisome condition of Humanity! / Born under one law, to another bound: / Vainly begot, and yet forbidden vanity; / Created sick, commanded to be sound: / What meaneth Nature by these diverse laws?'

Grier, Eldon
Canadian poet *born* London 1917

Grier was educated in Montreal and established himself as a painter who, fascinated by verbal as well as visual colour, published *Selected Poems* (1971) and *Assassination of Colour* (1978). Grier's poems are acutely observant but go beyond description to comment. 'View from a Window' opens with a vision of a poor girl with flies settled in her hair. It ends: 'Beauty complicates the average squalor, / carries the unpredictable like fallout / into the brutal levels, burns about / the ruin and the green vine with its yearning. // She hangs around; she says she's eight. / Her name is tuned for ceremonial complaint; / mine is, that dozy flies can travel here without restraint / in the gentlest of hatchures.'

Griffith, Wyn
Welsh poet *born* Dolgellau 1890 *died* 1977

Griffith was an officer in C Company, the 15th Battalion Royal Welsh Fusiliers, in the First World War. He worked as an officer of the Inland Revenue in London and in 'Office Window' contemplates the natural world in images drawn from his daily routine: 'Beyond the waste of commerce there are hills / and a cool evening caught in the uplands / where ledger lines hold up the clouds. / No figures but the ciphers of the tarns, / no balance but a hawk poised waiting its profit / where small creatures scurry in the grass.' Griffith's memoir *Up to Mametz* appeared in 1931. He was fluent in Welsh as well as English.

Grigson, Geoffrey
English poet *born* Pelynt, Cornwall 1905

An industrious anthologist and, with *New Verse* in the 1930s, an influential champion of Auden's poetry, Grigson writes an extremely opinionated poetry. In his poems he airs his views on, for example, the assassination of Martin Luther King and the paintings of Dufy, yet his main theme is the quality of literary life. He writes about the burial of Thomas Hardy's heart, the death of Louis MacNeice, the career of Clere Parsons. He addresses Auden on his sixtieth birthday and writes a nursery rhyme for T S Eliot: 'Tom, Tom, the pedants' father, / Master of perhaps and rather'. He has, in his best poems, a genuine feeling for the virtues of rural England.

Gunn, Thom
English poet *born* Gravesend 29 August 1929

A journalist's son, Gunn was educated at Trinity College, Cambridge. While still an undergraduate he published his first book *Fighting Terms* (1954) which established him as a combative new voice in English verse. After spending some time in Rome on a studentship he moved to the USA where he taught; then settled in San Francisco as a fulltime writer. His 'On the Move', from *The Sense of Movement* (1957), is set in the San Francisco Peninsula and describes, in existential terms, a gang of motorcyclists: 'On motorcycles, up the road, they come: / Small, black, as flies hanging in heat, the Boys, / Until the distance throws them forth, their hum / Bulges to thunder held by calf and thigh.'

Gurney, Ivor
English poet *born* Gloucester 28 August 1890
died Dartford, Kent 26 December 1937

A tailor's son, Ivor Gurney won a scholarship to the Royal College of Music, London, in 1911. He was a prodigiously gifted songwriter but as early as 1912 began to display signs of mental instability. Wounded at the Somme he began, after the war, to pester the police for a gun with which he could shoot himself. In 1922 he was committed to a private asylum for the insane and spent the rest of his life as a mental patient. He wrote about the war, about his beloved Gloucestershire, and about his own anguish. As he said in 'An Appeal for Death', 'a maker of song / Asks, desires, has prayed for mercy of Death / To end all, lie still, quiet green turf beneath'.

Gustafson, Ralph
Canadian poet *born* Eastern Townships, Quebec 1909

Educated at Bishops's University and Oxford, Gustafson was professor and poet in residence at Bishop's when he retired in 1979. He edited the influential *Penguin Book of Canadian Verse* and published the most recent revision in 1984. A music critic as well as a poet, his selected poems appeared in 1984 as *The Moment is All*. Although he was critical of the romantic style of Canadian poetry, his own 'In the Yukon' has the virtues of Canadian descriptive verse: 'Moose came down to the water edge / To drink and the salmon turned silver arcs. / At night, the northern lights played, great over country / Without tapestry and coronations, kings crowned / With weights of gold.'

Habbington, William
English poet *born* Hindlip, Worcestershire 4 November 1605 *died* 30 November 1654

Born into a Roman Catholic family, Habington was educated at

St Omer's but rejected Jesuit discipline. He married Lucy
Herbert, daughter of Lord Powis, and projected her as a symbol
of chastity in his sequence *Castara* (1634). His tragi-comedy *The
Queen of Aragon* (1640) includes songs that display his metrical skill
and wit: 'Fine young folly, though you were / That fair beauty I
did swear, / Yet you ne'er could reach my heart. / For we
courtiers learn at school / Only with your sex to fool: / Y'are not
worth the serious part.' Habington closes the song with an
epitome of the amorous impulse: 'Bedlam! this is pretty sport.'

Haines, John
American poet *born* Virginia 1924

Haines studied painting and sculpture in Washington and New
York then, in 1947, went to Alaska to live in a cabin of his own
construction, located some seventy miles from Fairbanks. His
work too rejects the solutions imposed on humankind by urban
organisation and instead describes a particular relationship
between one man and his immediate environment. In 'The
Tundra' Haines suggests 'The tundra is a living / body, warm in
the grassy / autumn sun'. In 'Foreboding' he indicates his
suspicion of the outside world as he describes a vision that haunts
him: 'manlike figures approach, cover / their faces, and pass on, /
heavy with iron and distance.'

Hall, Donald
American poet *born* Connecticut 1928

Educated at Harvard and Oxford, Hall settled in Ann Arbor,
Michigan. With his Penguin anthology of *Contemporary American
Poetry* (1962) he helped create a climate of approval for the
intellectually sophisticated verse he favours. 'The Alligator Bride'
shows his ability to improvise ingenious scenarios on everyday
incidents: 'The clock of my days winds down. / The cat eats
sparrows outside my window. / Once, she brought me a small
rabbit / which we devoured together, under / the Empire Table /
while the men shrieked / repossessing the gold umbrella.' His
collection *The Alligator Bride* appeared in 1969, *The Yellow Room
Love Poems* in 1971.

Hall, Joseph
English poet *born* Ashby-de-la-Zouch 1574
died Higham, near Norwich 1656

Educated at Cambridge, Hall took orders and became chaplain to
Prince Henry. In 1618 he was a Deputy to the Synod of Dort and
became Bishop of Exeter in 1627 then Bishop of Norwich in
1641. He upheld the principles of episcopacy against Milton and
was imprisoned, sequestrated (1643) then expelled to a small
farm (1647) near his palace. His satirical muse is energetically

exercised in *Virgidem iarum sex libri* (Six Books of Lashes, 1597–8).
Hall contrasts the glorious past with the squalid present: 'Now
man, that erst hail-fellow was with beast, / Wox on to ween
himself a god at least. / Nor aery fowl can take so high a flight, /
Though she her daring wings in cloud have dight'.

Hall, Richard
Welsh poet *born* Brecon 1817 *died* 1866

Hall became a pharmacist in his native town. He published *A Tale
of the Past and Other Poems* in 1850. A poet with an impressive
descriptive gift, he wrote ingenious acrostics such as 'Pontypool':
'Pontypool! thou dirtiest of dirty places; / Often have I bewailed,
when wandering through thee, / New garments which then bore
the filthy traces / That those can ne'er escape who wish to view
thee: / Yet thou dost show to us some wondrous phases; /
Pouring forth their thick smokes curling to the skies, / Out-
belching scalding steam and scorching blazes, / On every side
huge furnaces arise; / Learn we from them man's skill and
vigorous enterprise.'

Halleck, Fitz-Greene
American poet *born* Guildford, Connecticut 8 July 1790
died Guildford 19 November 1867

With Joseph Rodaman Drake, 'the American Keats', Halleck
wrote the satirical *Croaker Papers* (1819). Like other members of
the Knickerbocker School of poets, he was influenced by Sir
Walter Scott and Byron. His *Marco Bozzaris* (1825) is a Byronic
poem about the struggle for Greek independence. Its urgent lines
include instructions such as 'Strike – for your altars and your
fires; / Strike – for the green graves of your sires; / Gold – and
your native land!' Halleck visited Europe in 1822 and wrote
admiring lines on such subjects as Robert Burns and Alnwick
Castle. He also published *Fanny* (1819), a satirical poem
influenced, inevitably, by Byron.

Hamburger, Michael
English poet *born* Berlin 22 March 1924

An outstanding translator of German poetry and a sophisticated
man of letters, Hamburger has spent his creative life in search of
the elusive area 'where the boundary of dreams / Meets memory'
(as he says in his tribute to T S Eliot). After military service,
Hamburger lived for a while in the USA as an academic. He has
always written a poetry of exploration, presenting himself as a
displaced person seeking a spiritual home. 'From the Notebook
of a European Tramp', an early poem, succinctly states his
position: 'As for my heart, it broke some time ago / When, in the

towns of Europe, I still tried / To live like other men and not to know / That all we lived for had already died.'

Hamilton, William
Scottish poet *born* Bangour, West Lothian 25 March 1704
died Lyons 25 March 1754

Hamilton was two when his father died and his mother remarried Sir Hew Dalrymple, the President of the Court of Session. Educated at Edinburgh University, he contributed poems to Allan Ramsay's *Tea-Table Miscellany*. On a visit to Italy, Hamilton met Bonnie Prince Charlie and in 1745 he served in the Jacobite army. After the defeat of the Scottish clans at Culloden, in 1746, he went into exile in France. His best known poem is the literary ballad 'The Braes of Yarrow': 'Weep not, weep not, my bonny bonny bride, / Weep not, weep not, my winsome marrow! / Nor let thy heart lament to leave / Pouing the birks on the braes of Yarrow.'

Hammond, James
English poet *born* 1710 *died* 1742

The second son of Anthony Hammond, Sir Robert Walpole's brother-in-law, Hammond was educated at Westminster School and became equerry to the Prince of Wales. When a lady called Dashwood rejected his advances, he became mentally ill for a while though the writing of elegies apparently helped him to recover. He became Member of Parliament for Truro, Cornwall, in 1741. His 'Elegy XIII', in which he imagines himself married to 'Delia', has an obvious obsession with the subject: 'Oh, when I die, my latest moments spare, / Nor let thy grief with sharper torments kill, / Wound not thy cheeks, nor hurt that flowing hair, / Though I am dead, my soul shall love thee still'.

Hard, Walter
American poet *born* Manchester, Vermont 3 May 1882
died Manchester, Vermont 21 May 1966

Hard ran his father's drugstore in his home town and made the soda fountain a literary gathering-place. With his wife he also ran the Johnny Appleseed Bookshop, founded by his daughter in 1930. He wrote a column for the Rutland *Herald* and served in both the Vermont Assembly (one term) and the Vermont Senate (four terms). His verse, narrative and descriptive, celebrates the character of life in Vermont. 'A Health Note' is a portrait of one Ezra Perrin; 'Ezra used to putter around the woodpile / And, working a little at a time, / He'd get up enough for the winter. / In summer he did a little in the garden. / He spent much of his time in a rocker / On the front porch, when it was warm enough.'

Hardy, Thomas

English poet *born* Higher Bockhampton 2 June 1840
died Max Gate, near Dorchester 11 January 1928

Though his novels are now regarded as classic works of English
fiction Hardy wrote them, he said, for the money and always
regarded poetry as his first calling. In his lifetime the epic verse
drama *The Dynasts* (1903-8) was acclaimed for its narrative sweep.
Yet his greatest poetic strength is a stark simplicity of expression
in short poems that convey, through a highly personal mood of
resignation, the enduring qualities of the English countryside.
Hardy used familiar stanzaic forms with singular force, as in 'In
Time of "The Breaking of Nations"': 'Yonder a maid and her
wight / Come whispering by: / War's annals will cloud into night /
Ere their story die.'

Harper, Frances E W

American poet *born* Maryland *died* 1911

The child of black parents who died before she was three, Frances
E W Harper was brought up by an uncle who ran a school for
black children. She was eloquent in denouncing the evils of
slavery: in the 1850s she gave lectures on the subject and in the
1860s, after the Civil War, she visited the South and proposed
educational programmes for the emancipated slaves. She wrote
for various anti-slavery periodicals and donated money to help
black people. Her poem 'The Slave Mother' depicts a child
clinging to his mother: 'He is not hers, for cruel hands / May
rudely tear apart / The only wreath of household love / That
binds her breaking heart.'

Harpur, Charles

Australian poet *born* Windsor, New South Wales 1813 *died* 1868

Harpur's parents were convicts and the poet perceived Australia
not as a penal colony but as a modern Eden. He worked as a
schoolteacher, sheep farmer and gold commissioner for the
Government; his determination to shape a distinctively
Australian style of poetry made him the first in a long line of
Australian poets. Harpur had a flair for descriptive verse as well as
passion for the country he lived in and his evocative approach is
seen to advantage in 'A Midsummer Noon in the Australian
Forest': 'Not a sound disturbs the air, / There is quiet
everywhere; / Over plains and over woods / What a mighty
stillness broods!'

Harris, Max

Australian poet *born* Adelaide 1921

After studying at the University of Adelaide, Harris established
the publishing house of Reed and Harris, and founded and edited

the periodical *Angry Penguins* in the 1940s. Devoted to modernism *Angry Penguins* was eventually discredited when Harris devoted an issue to the work of a nonexistent poet 'Ern Mallay' whose poems were concocted by James McAuley and Harold Stewart from random texts. Although he was fined £5 for publishing 'indecencies' Harris survived the hoax and the police court to continue with his ironic and often tender poems, as in 'A Window at Night' which ends: 'Be easy, then, to love without intent, / To shelter from the darkness on a heath / In some calm innocence or deed of faith. / In which I'll join, to mirror your content.'

Harrison, Tony
English poet *born* Leeds 1937
Educated at Leeds University, Harrison spent four years in Northern Nigeria, one year in Prague (as a teacher at Prague University), and some time in Cuba, Brazil, Senegal and The Gambia (as a UNESCO Travelling Fellow). His *Selected Poems* appeared in 1984. His work is rooted in his experience of Leeds and he celebrates the collective character of his family, frequently implying a contrast between the vitality of the North of England in contrast to the smooth South. 'Background Material' begins 'My writing desk. Two photos, mam and dad. / A birthday, him. Their ruby wedding, her. / Neither one a couple and both bad. / I make out what's behind them from the blur.'

Hart-Smith, William
Australian poet *born* Tunbridge Wells, Kent 1911
Born in England and educated in New Zealand, Hart-Smith is nevertheless a poet closely associated with Australia. From 1936 to 1947 he lived in Australia as a journalist and writer for radio; during the Second World War he served in the Australian army. In the 1940s Hart-Smith was identified with the Jindyworobaks, a group of poets anxious to express the aboriginal experience of Australia. Later he evolved a more individual style. His best poems have an elliptical quality as the poet tries to extract the maximum of meaning from the minimum of words. 'Razor Fish' informs the reader that a straight line drawn on a page 'wouldn't be / as thin / as a / Razor Fish / seen / edge / ways / on'.

Hatton, Julia Ann
Welsh poet *born* 1764 *died* 1838
Born Julia Ann Kemble, 'Ann of Swansea' (as she was called), was a member of a celebrated family of actors and younger sister of Sarah Siddons. She ran the Swansea Bathing House and published *Poetic Trifles* in 1811. Her 'Swansea Bay' shows her somewhat melodramatic style: 'In vain by various griefs oppressed / I vagrant roam devoid of rest, / With aching heart, still lingering

stray / Around the shores of Swansea Bay. // The restless waves that lave the shore, / Joining the tide's tumultous roar, / In hollow murmurs seem to say – / Peace is not found at Swansea Bay.' 'Ann of Swansea' was a prolific writer of English verse.

Hawker, Robert Stephen

English poet *born* Plymouth 3 December 1803 *died* 1875

Son of a curate, Hawker was vicar of Morwenstow, Cornwall, from 1835 to 1874 and known as 'the sailor's friend' on account of his involvement in local events. He wrote a long poem *The Quest of the Sangraal* (1863) but was best known for 'The Song of the Western Men'. 'The Fatal Ship' records the loss of HMS *Captain* on 6 September 1870: 'Down the deep sea, full fourscore fathoms down, / An iron vault hath clutched five hundred men! / They died not, like the nations, one by one: / A thrill! a bounding pulse! a shout! and then / Five hundred hearts stood still, at once, nor beat again!' Hawker is also remembered for his creation of the Harvest Festival.

Hay, George Campbell

Scottish poet *born* Elderslie, Renfrewshire 1915 *died* Edinburgh 25 March 1984

Son of John MacDougall Hay, the minister who wrote the novel *Gillespie* (1914), Hay was educated at Oxford where he studied modern languages. During the Second World War he served in North Africa and the Middle East and had a mental breakdown after attempting unsuccessfully to get out of the army. Hay wrote fluently in Gaelic, Scots and English and his lyrical gift is seen to advantage in 'The Old Fisherman' (which was memorably set to music by Francis George Scott): 'The old boat must seek the shingle, / her wasting side hollow the gravel, / the hand that shakes must leave the tiller; / my dancing days for fishing are over.' His collection *Wind on Loch Fyne* appeared in 1948.

Hay, John Milton

American poet *born* Salem, Indiana 8 October 1838 *died* 1 July 1905

Hay, who was educated at Illinois University and Brown University, was a lawyer who became President Lincoln's Secretary and Aide-de-Camp, rising to colonel during the Civil War. He was later Ambassador to England and Secretary of State (in 1898). With J G Nicolay he produced *Abraham Lincoln: A History* (10 vols, 1890). His collection *Pike Country Ballads* (1871) contains his best-known poem, 'Little Breeches'. The narrative tells of a natural survivor, a child who is found alive in a storm after being given up for dead; 'How did he git thar? Angels. / He

could never have walked in that storm: / They jest scooped down
and toted him / To whar it was safe and warm.'

Hayden, Robert
American poet *born* Detroit 1913

Educated at the universities of Wayne State and Michigan,
Hayden became Professor of English at Fisk University. He won
the Hopgood Award in 1938 and 1942; a Rosenwald Fellowship in
1947; and a Ford Foundation grant in 1954. In 1965 his collection
A Ballad for Remembrance won the Grand Prize for Poetry at the
first World Festival of Negro Arts, held in Dakar, Senegal. In his
anthology *Kaleidoscope* (1967) he declared himself 'opposed to the
chauvinistic and doctrinaire' and argued that the black poet
should not be classified by colour. 'In Light Half Nightmare and
Half Vision' begins: 'From the corpse woodpiles, from the ashes
and staring pits of Dachau and Buchenwald they come'.

Heaney, Seamus
Irish poet *born* County Derry 1939

Educated at St Columb's College, Derry, and Queen's University,
Belfast, Heaney established his reputation with *Death of a
Naturalist* (1966). He has since been greatly in demand for
readings in the USA and elsewhere. Regarded by many as the
authentic voice of Ulster, he has written movingly of spiritual and
physical violence. In 'Whatever you say, say nothing' he describes
a camp for internees: 'There was that white mist you get on a low
ground / and it was *déjà-vu*, some film made / of Stalag 17, a bad
dream with no sound. // Is there a life before death? That's
chalked up / in Ballymurphy. Competence with pain, / coherent
miseries, a bite and sup, / we hug our little destiny again.'

Heath-Stubbs, John
English poet *born* London 9 July 1918

After reading English at Oxford, John Heath-Stubbs worked as a
schoolteacher and in publishing. Subsequently he was visiting
Professor of English at the universities of Alexandria and
Michigan. He is an erudite poet who approaches a variety of
subjects with irony and scholarly intelligence. He has a fondness
for traditional forms and is an advocate of technical expertise in
verse. In 'Ars Poetica' he says a poem is 'Like an iceberg – cold,
hard, / Jagged and chaste, glittering / With prismatic colours, as it
drifts / On unpredictable deep-sea tides. Against it also / The
titanic folly of the age / May shatter itself as it goes through its
joyless night.'

119

Heavysege, Charles
Canadian poet *born* Huddersfield, England 1816 *died* 1876

Heavysege settled in Montreal in 1853 and earned his living as a cabinet-maker and journalist. His most acclaimed work was *Saul* (1857, revised 1869), a drama reworking in iambic pentameters the biblical story. Saul's soliloquies have a discursive tone: 'O life, how delicate a thing thou art, / Crushed with the feathery edge of a thin blade! / Frail! – why wert thou not made inviolable? / Why are thou irrecoverable as frail? / Thou, noblest guest, art all as much exposed / To foul ejectment from the flesh as is / The spider from its web by maiden's broom.' Heavysege published another verse drama, *Count Filippo* (1860).

Hecht, Anthony
American poet *born* New York 1922

At Kenyon College, Hecht studied under John Crowe Ransom and later taught at Smith College, Bard, and the University of Rochester. His collection *The Hard Hours* (1967) was awarded the Pulitzer Prize. Hecht is a polished performer of his own work and cleverly sustains an ironic tone. His 'The Dover Bitch' is a humorous rejoinder to Matthew Arnold's 'Dover Beach'. Hecht sees Arnold through the eyes of an imaginary girlfriend; 'To have been brought / All the way down from London, and then be addressed / As sort of a mournful cosmic last resort / Is really tough on a girl, and she was pretty.' 'The Dover Bitch' has been recognised as a contemporary classic of poetic humour.

Helwig, David
Canadian poet *born* Toronto 1938

Before taking up his post in the English Department of Queen's University, Kingston, Ontario, David Helwig studied at the universities of Toronto and Liverpool. A novelist and short-story writer, he has published selected poems under the title *The Sign of the Gunman* (1968); and *Atlantic Crossings* (1977). His poems make scenarios out of incidents he has observed. 'The Jockeys', for example, opens on an observation then speculates on the jockeys: 'Without them, the horses would not follow / the track, nor race, but run only / to heat the air, galloping in arabesques, / wheeling and turning. Or would be still / as the wind shaped itself around their haunches.'

Hemans, Felicia
English poet *born* Liverpool 25 September 1793
died Dublin 16 May 1835

Felicia Browne, whose father was a Liverpool merchant, married Captain Hemans in 1812. Six years later he left her and their five sons. She lived in Wales until 1831 then moved to Dublin where she was acclaimed as a literary celebrity. A derivative poet, she was influenced by Byron and fond of Scott – who welcomed her at Abbotsford during her visit to Scotland. Poems such as 'The Diver' show a power to evoke unusual scenes; 'Thou has been where the rocks of coral grow, / Thou has fought with eddying waves; – / Thy cheek is pale, and thy heart beats low, / Thou searcher of ocean's caves!'

Hemingway, Ernest

American poet *born* Oak Park, Illinois 21 July 1898
died Ketchum, Idaho 2 July 1961

One of the great figures of modern American literature, Hemingway was the son of a doctor. A brilliant reporter, he wrote novels such as *The Old Man and the Sea* (1952) which earned him the Nobel Prize for Literature in 1954. Although only twenty-five of Hemingway's poems were published during his lifetime, he preserved the verse he wrote and it was posthumously collected in *88 Poems* (1979). Poems such as 'To Chink whose Trade is Soldiering' have something of the verbal panache of his prose: 'We've drunk too much good beer / Watched the sun rise / And cursed the rain / That spoiled the piste / Or turned the river brown / So flies were useless.'

Henderson, Hamish

Scottish poet *born* Blairgowrie 11 November 1919

Educated at Cambridge, Henderson was an intelligence officer with the Highland Division in North Africa during the Second World War. In 1951 he began to work for the School of Scottish Studies, Edinburgh University, collecting traditional Scottish songs and stories and establishing an important archive. His *Elegies for the Dead in Cyrenaica* (1948), drawing on the North African desert campaign, is a powerful indictment of war. The First Elegy begins: 'There are many dead in the brutish desert, who lie uneasy / among the scrub in this landscape of half-wit / stunted ill-will. For the dead land is insatiate / and necrophilous. / The sand is blowing about still.' He has also written political songs.

Henderson, Paul

New Zealand poet *born* Leithfield, Canterbury 1913 *died* 1957

Ruth France, who published fiction under her own name and verse under the pseudonym Paul Henderson, spent most of her life in Christchurch. She published *Unwilling Pilgrim* in 1955, *The Halting Place* in 1961. Her powerfully descriptive talent is demonstrated in the first stanza of 'Elegy': 'The mountains to the north stood up like sepulchres / Rising white-boned out of a black sea. / The flat hymnal of light lay asleep in the sky / And sang morning in a minor key / To wake the wheeling flights of birds / That, curious, mark down all drifting wrack / And disabled drowned bodies.'

Henley, W E

English poet *born* Gloucester 23 August 1849 *died* 11 June 1903

Son of a bookseller, William Ernest Henley had his left leg amputated and when English doctors recommended the amputation of his right leg, after his tubercular infection became active, he moved to Edinburgh to be treated by Joseph Lister at the Royal Infirmary. Lister saved Henley's leg, and probably his sanity, by his expertise and example. Henley's sequence 'In Hospital', included in *A Book of Verses* (1888), describes an operation: 'You are carried in a basket, / Like a carcase from the shambles, / To the theatre, a cockpit / Where they stretch you on a table.' Henley was friendly with Robert Louis Stevenson who used him as the model for Long John Silver in *Treasure Island* (1883).

Henri, Adrian

English poet *born* Birkenhead, Cheshire 1932

Henri began his creative life as a painter who studied Fine Arts at the University of Durham. In the 1960s, when the music of the Beatles brought new cultural life to Liverpool, Henri emerged as one of the 'Liverpool Poets' who documented everyday urban life in an idiom influenced by the lyrics of popsongs. He has supported himself by writing and performing his own work and has an instant appeal through his nostalgic poems about his childhood and adolescence. His verse *Autobiography* dwells lovingly on the past: 'flags and bright funnels of ships / walking with my mother over the Seven Bridges / and being carried home too tired / frightened of the siren of the ferryboat'.

Henryson, Robert

Scottish poet *born c*1420 *died c*1490

Little is known of Henryson's life except that he was a schoolmaster in Dunfermline. Dunbar, in his 'Lament for the Makaris', includes him in his catalogue of dead poets: 'In Dunfermlyne he hes done roune, / With maister Robert Henrisoun'. Henryson's masterpiece is *The Testament of Creisseid* (1593) which takes up the story of Creisseid after her desertion by Diomeid and describes her death from leprosy. Henryson's use of rhyme-royal and his reference to 'worthie Chaucer' has allowed critics to classify him as a Scottish Chaucerian but he is a highly individual poet with a warm human touch: 'I mend the fyre and beikit me about, / Than tuik ane drink my spreitis to comfort, / And armit me weill fra the cauld thairout'.

beikit warmed; *spreitis* spirits

Herbert of Cherbury, Lord Edward
English poet *born* Eyton, Shropshire 3 March 1583
died London 20 August 1648

Son of the sheriff of Montgomeryshire, Edward was the brother of George Herbert. He was a sixteen-year-old Oxford student when he married his cousin Mary, four years his senior. He had several children but abandoned his family in 1608 and went to France where, in 1619, he became ambassador to the French court. In 1629 Charles I made him Baron of Cherbury and during the Civil War he supported the royalist side before surrendering to parliament in 1644. A distinguished philosopher, he wrote Metaphysical poems such as 'Elegy over a Tomb': 'Doth the sun now his light with yours renew? / have waves the curling of your hair? / did you restore unto the sky and air / The red, and white, and blue?'

Herbert, George
Welsh poet *born* Montgomery Castle, Wales 3 April 1593
died Bemerton, Wiltshire 3 March 1633

The fifth son of Sir Richard Herbert and Lady Magdalen Herbert, George Herbert was educated at Trinity College, Cambridge which made him first a Fellow (1616) then Reader in Rhetoric then Public Orator. His election to Parliament in 1624 reinforced his secular ambitions; he married Jane Danvers in 1629 and became rector of Bemerton a year later. His posthumously published collection *The Temple* (1633) shows the intellectual strength of his religious faith. 'Giddiness' ends with a plea: 'Lord, mend or rather make us: one creation / Will not suffice our turn: / Except thou make us daily, we shall spurn / Our own salvation.'

Herbin, John Federic
Canadian poet *born* Windsor, Nova Scotia 1860 *died* 1923

Educated at Acadia University, Herbin published *Canada and Other Poems* in 1891 and *The Marshlands* in 1899. He earned his living as a jeweller in Wolfville, Nova Scotia, and his sonnet 'Haying' is an intricately made product of Canada's agrarian muse: 'From the soft dyke-road, crooked and waggon-worn, / Comes the great load of rustling scented hay, / Slow-drawn with heavy swing and creaky sway / Through the cool freshness of the windless morn. / The oxen, yoked and sturdy, horn to horn, / Sharing the rest and toil of night and day, / Bend head and neck to the long hilly way / By many a season's labour marked and torn.'

Herrick, Robert
English poet *born* London, baptised 24 August 1591
buried 15 October 1674

A goldsmith's son, Herrick initially pursued his father's trade
then went to Cambridge and was ordained in 1623. Charles I
appointed him, in 1629, to the living of Dean Prior, Devonshire;
he was ejected in 1647 but reinstated after the Restoration of
1660. In 1648 he published *Hesperides* and thus established
himself as one of the greatest of English lyric poets, and perhaps
the most frankly sensual. His poem 'To Dianeme' is fairly typical:
'Show my thy feet; show me thy legs, thy thighs; / Show me
those fleshy principalities; / Show me that hill (where smiling love
doth sit) / Having a living fountain under it. / Show my thy waist;
then let me there withal, / By the ascension of thy lawn, see all.'

Hervey, J R
New Zealand poet *born* Southland 1889 *died* 1958

Hervey was ordained an Anglican priest and served in several
parishes in Canterbury from 1915–38. Several of his collections
were published by the Caxton press, including *New Poems* (1942),
Man on a Raft (1949), *She was my Spring* (1955). He suffered from
ill–health over a long period. His poems are contemplative, for
example 'Two Old Men Look at the Sea' which ends: 'How shall
we live and hold, how love and handle / To the last beach the dark
and difficult gleanings? / For so must we come, hugging our
recompense, / To the unfeeling shore, to the bleak admonitory
tide, / Our fear being as a hand that cups a candle / Against the
winds that whiff away pretence, / And the sea whose sentence
strikes like a leaden wave.'

Hewitt, John
Irish poet *born* Belfast 1907

Educated at Queen's University, Belfast, Hewitt left Ireland to
live in Coventry where he ran the Herbert Art Gallery and
observed the various political developments in Ireland with a
shrewd intelligence. His poem 'An Irishman in Coventry'
explores several Irish myths and describes a people 'endlessly
betrayed / by our own weakness, by the wrongs we suffered / in
that long twilight over bog and glen, / by force, by famine and by
glittering fables / which gave us martyrs when we needed men, /
by faith which had no charity to offer, / by poisoned memory and
by ready wit, / with poverty corroded into malice / to hit and run
and howl when it is hit.' He returned to Belfast on his retirement.

Hewlett, Maurice
English poet *born* Weybridge, Surrey 22 January 1861
died 15 June 1923

Son of a civil servant of Huguenot extraction, Hewlett was educated at the International College, Isleworth. Called to the Bar in 1891 he never practised but succeeded, in 1897, to his father's post in the Record Office. He published historical novels, such as *Richard Yea-and-Nay* (1900) and essays. His finest poetic achievement is *The Song of the Plow* (1916), a celebration of the indigenous English peasantry as personified by the hero Hodge who champions the cause of the Angles. The poem opens: 'I sing the Man, I sing the Plow / Ten centuries at work, and Thee, / England, whom men not christen'd now / May live to call Home of the Free.'

Heyrick, Thomas
English poet *born* Market Harborough, Leicestershire 1649 *died* Market Harborough 1694

Son of a tradesman, Heyrick was a great-nephew of Robert Herrick. He was educated locally and at Cambridge before coming back to his native town as curate. A Metaphysical poet, he wrote ingeniously on a number of subjects in *Miscellany Poems* (1691). His lines 'On a Sunbeam' end: 'Thou'rt quickly born and dost as quickly die: / Pity so fair a birth to fate should fall! / Now here and now in abject dust dost lie; / One moment 'twixt thy birth and funeral. / Art thou, like angels, only shown, / Then to our grief for ever flown? / Tell me, Apollo, tell me where / The sunbeams go, when they do disappear?'

Higgins, F R
Irish poet *born* 1896 *died* 1941

Higgins, who was a director of the Abbey theatre from 1935 to 1940, endorsed many of the poetic ideals of Yeats – who reciprocated the interest in his work. He published *Island Blood* (1925), *The Dark Breed* (1927) and *The Gap of Brightness* (1940). In poems such as 'The Old Jockey' he combines an elegiac quality with an impressive insight into character. The poem ends: 'But O you should see him gazing, gazing / When solemnly out on the road / The horse-drays pass overladen with grasses, / Each driver lost in his load; / Gazing until they return; and suddenly, / As galloping by they race, / From his pale eyes, like glass breaking, / Light leaps on his face.'

Hill, Geoffrey
English poet *born* Bromsgrove 1932

Hill was educated at Oxford and became a professor at Leeds University. One of the most individual voices in contemporary poets, he specialises in sequences such as *The Mystery of the Charity of Charles Péguy* (1983). Péguy, a patriotic French poet, was killed on the first day of the first battle of the Marne in September

1914. Hill confronts the known facts of Péguy's death with notions about the place of heroism and conflict in the modern world. His protest against war includes a condemnation of armchair warriors, intellectual or otherwise: 'We are the occasional just men who sit / in gaunt self-judgement on their self-defeat, / the élite hermits, secret orators / of an old faith devoted to new wars.'

Hillyer, Robert

American poet *born* East Orange, New Jersey 3 June 1895
died 1961

Educated at Harvard and the University of Copenhagen, Hillyer was an ambulance driver with the French army at Verdun in 1917 and was awarded the Verdun Medal by the French Government. He had a distinguished academic career, becoming (at the age of forty-two) Boylston Professor of Rhetoric and Oratory at Harvard. He retired from teaching in 1944 and moved to Old Greenwich, Connecticut. For *Collected Verse* (1933) he was awarded the Pulitzer Prize. Reflecting on the academic life in 'Letter to James B Munn' he wrote: 'How often do I see in our profession / Learning a mere extraneous possession, / A self-sufficient mass of dates and sources / Rolled round in academe's diurnal courses, / Where scholars prepare scholars, not for life / But gaudy footnotes and a threadbare wife'.

Hobsbaum, Philip

English poet *born* London 29 June 1932

Educated at the universities of Cambridge and Sheffield, Philip Hobsbaum formed the London 'Group' of poets in the 1950s and advocated traditional English values in verse. As a lecturer at Queen's University, Belfast, in the 1960s he encouraged Irish poets such as Seamus Heaney. He subsequently became Reader in English Literature at Glasgow University. An erudite critic of poetry, he published such collections as *In Retreat* (1966) and *Coming Out Fighting* (1969). 'A Lesson in Love' shows how he contains emotion in strictly measured terms: 'None, none. The awkward pauses when we talk, / The literary phrases, are a lie. / It was for this your teacher ran amock: / Truth lies between your legs, and so do I.'

Hodgson, Ralph

English poet *born* Darlington, Durham 9 September 1871
died 3 November 1962

Hodgson ran away from school and worked as a journalist in London before the First World War. The poems he contributed to Edward Marsh's *Georgian Poetry* led some critics to believe that he had the potential to be a major modern poet but Hodgson disliked publicity and did nothing to promote his own cause. He worked as a lecturer in English at the University of Sendai, Japan, and later settled in America. There is always a strong narrative element in Hodgson's work, for example 'Eve' which retells a familiar story: 'Eve, with her basket, was / Deep in the bells and grass, / Wading in bells and grass / Up to her knees'.

Hogg, James

Scottish poet *born* Ettrick Forest, baptised 9 December 1770 *died* 21 November 1835

The 'Ettrick shepherd' was first a farmworker then became a shepherd at the age of twenty. After meeting Sir Walter Scott he moved to Edinburgh in 1810 and, when he published his collection *The Queen's Wake* (1813), the Duke of Buccleuch presented him with a rent-free home (Altrive Farm, Yarrow) for life. His prose masterpiece *The Private Memoirs and Confessions of a Justified Sinner* appeared in 1824 and has remained a classic study of Scottish guilt. Hogg's songs, in *Songs by the Ettrick Shepherd* (1831), draw on the vigorous tradition of Scottish folksong. 'When the Kye Comes Hame' is one of his best: 'What is the greatest bliss / That the tongue o' man can name? / 'Tis to woo a bonny lassie / When the kye comes hame.'

kye cattle

Holbrook, David

English poet *born* Norwich 9 January 1923

Educated at Cambridge, Holbrook became a Fellow of King's College, Cambridge (1961–5) and a Fellow of Downing College, Cambridge. He published literary criticism and books on adult, school and university education. He is a poet given to airing his opinions in technically controlled verse. 'My First Visit to a Communist Country' describes a trip to Prague in August 1969 and the author's disgust at the ubiquitous Soviet presence: 'After we escaped to Vienna / Old Marx on his pedestal looked so complacent / Among the gay fruit stalls and the lively colourful crowd; / I lean out of the car and shout, "Communism is a flop!" / Nobody arrests me. The fact is indefinite, as if eroded.'

Holland, Hugh

Welsh poet *born* Denbigh 1569 *died* 1633

Holland, a much-travelled man, was a member of the Mermaid Club in London. He was an accomplished writer in both Latin and English. In his sonnet 'On William Shakespeare' he acknowledges the genius of his great contemporary: 'Those hands which you so clapped, go now and wring / You Britons brave, for done are Shakespeare's days; / His days are done that made the dainty plays / Which made the Globe of heaven and earth to ring: /

Dried is that vein, dried is the Thespian spring, / Turned all to tears, and Phoebus clouds his rays. / That corpse, that coffin, now bestick those bays / Which crowned him poet first, then poet's king.'

Holland, Sir Richard
Scottish poet *born c*1420 *died c*1485

A member of the court of James II he was associated with the Douglas faction after whose fall, in 1455, he may have retired to Shetland to pursue his ecclesiastical career. *The Buke of the Howlat* (first published in 1823), his only surviving work, is an allegorical and alliterative account of an owl ('howlat') who dresses up in the feathers of other birds with unfortunate consequences. Here Sir James Douglas reacts to Bruce's deathbed request that he take his heart to the Holy Land: 'I love you mair for that louiss ye lippyn me till, / Than only lordschipe or land, so me our Lord leid! / I sall waynd for no wye to wirk as ye will, / At wiss, gif my werd wald, with you to the deid.'

louiss honour; *lippyn* entrust; *me till* to me; *waynd* hesitate; *wye* man; *wiss* (your) wish; *werd* fate; *wald* would

Holmes, Oliver Wendell
American poet *born* Cambridge, Massachusetts 29 August 1809 *died* Boston, Massachusetts 7 October 1894

Brought up in Boston, among 'the Brahmin caste of New England', Holmes was indignant when Calvinists removed his father from his Cambridge parish; thereafter Holmes never lost an opportunity to denounce Calvinism. A graduate of Harvard, Holmes was, from 1847 to 1853, Professor of Anatomy at Harvard Medical School. He was a brilliant lecturer and raconteur, a wit who nevertheless made important contributions to medicine, a poet who mocked hypocrisy as in 'Contentment': 'I care not much for gold or land; – / Give me a mortgage here and there, / Some good bank-stock, some note of hand, / Or trifling railroad share, – / I only ask that Fortune send / A *little* more than I shall spend.'

Hood, Thomas
English poet *born* London 23 May 1799 *died* London 3 May 1845

Son of a bookseller who died in 1811, Hood was tubercular and was sent, for the sake of his health, to Dundee where he began to write for the local journals. Returning to London he continued his prolific journalistic career and made a reputation as a writer of light verse. As a protest against appalling working conditions he published 'The Song of the Shirt' (1843) anonymously, in *Punch* whose fortunes flourished as a result. The poem retains its didactic power: 'With fingers weary and worn, / With eyelids

heavy and red, / A Woman sat, in unwomanly rags, / Plying her
needle and thread – / Stitch! stitch! stitch! / In poverty, hunger,
and dirt, / And still with a voice of dolorous pitch / She sang the
"Song of the Shirt!"'

Hook, Theodore
English poet *born* London 22 September 1788
died London 24 August 1841

Son of James Hook, the music-hall composer, Hook was educated
at Harrow and Oxford. When he was seventeen he produced the
comic opera *The Soldier's Return* (1805) which was followed by
Catch Him Who Can (1806). Appointed Accountant-General of
Mauritius in 1812, he returned home in disgrace in 1818 when he
was sent to prison over his alleged part in a financial scandal.
Subsequently he was released when it was shown that his deputy
had been the most guilty party. He edited *John Bull* and the *New
Monthly Magazine* and wrote several novels including *Gilbert Gurney*
(1836). His love of puns is shown in his 'Cautionary Verses to
Youth of Both Sexes': 'For instance, *ale* may make you *ail*, your
aunt an *ant* may kill'.

Hope, A D
Australian poet *born* Cooma, New South Wales 1907

Educated at the universities of Sydney and Oxford, Alec Derwent
Hope was, until his retirement in 1967, Professor of English at
the Australian National University. His contributions to
periodicals established him as a satirist but the appearance of *The
Wandering Islands* (1955) revealed a deeper involvement with the
subjects of his verse. Hope, whose influence on Australian poetry
has been considerable, always writes incisively and his poem
'Australia' is a bittersweet evocation of his native land: 'They call
her a young country, but they lie: / She is the last of lands, the
emptiest, / A woman beyond her change of life, a breast / Still
tender but within the womb is dry'.

Hopegood, Peter
Australian poet *born* near Billericay, Essex 1891 *died* 1967

Hopegood was educated in England, then went to Canada (in
1909) where he worked as a fur-trader. During the First World
War he was awarded the Military Cross as well as a pension for
injuries. He settled in Australia in 1924 and did various jobs,
including a spell in the pearling industry. His poetry is
unsentimental and observant, often with humorous undertones.
His 'Why Poets Tell the Moon' opens with a comment on the
emotional self-indulgence of poets: 'I am a dog-skin bag, says the
poet: / In me there is a howl for every grief in the gamut, / And
one or two that fit no common sorrow.'

Hopkins, Ellice

English poet *born* Cambridge 1836 *died* 1904

Ellice Hopkins spent much of her life helping the economically underprivileged. She lived among navvies and wrote pamphlets urging an improvement in working conditions for those she felt were exploited by Victorian society, particularly factory children. Her single volume *Autumn Swallows* (1883) showed the more subjective side of her character and 'Life and Death' is a contemplation of renewal: 'The upward stroke rang out glad life and breath / And still dead winters changed with spring, / And graves the new birth's cradle were; / And still I grasped the flying skirts of Death, / And still he turned, and, beaming fair, / The radiant face of Life was there.'

Horovitz, Frances

English poet *born* London 13 February 1938
died London 2 October 1983

Poet and actress Frances Horovitz died at the age of forty-five after courageously enduring cancer of the ear. She was married to the poet Michael Horovitz. She is a writer who can draw deeply personal conclusions from acute observations. Her 'London Summer' opens with a verbal picture of 'high flying / tattered flags' and attributes the same movement to human beings 'stretched frail and luminous / by the passionate freedom of the air'. She explored two related emotions – an ecstatic love of life and a corresponding terror of death. Towards the end of her life, inevitably, the figure of death became a dominant presence in her poetry.

Horovitz, Michael

English poet *born* Frankfurt 1935

The youngest of ten children, Horovitz notes he was 'descended from cantors, rabbis, vintners and Chasidim of Hungary, Czechoslovakia and Bohemia'. He arrived in England at the age of two and was educated at Oxford. He founded the magazine *New Departures* and promoted a style of performance-poetry indebted to the American Beats and to the visionary style of Blake. An accomplished reader, Horovitz has an ecstatic style. 'Glad Day', inspired by an engraving by Blake, begins: 'A dawn of agitating winds / dapples leaves afresh on skylit space / awakening alps of cloud to race / and drop out, giving way to sun / as firm in its good morning beams'. Horovitz was married to the poet Frances Horovitz.

Housman, A E

English poet *born* Fockbury, Worcestershire 26 March 1859
died 30 April 1936

Educated at Bromsgrove and Oxford, Alfred Edward Housman wrote most of the poems in *A Shropshire Lad* (1896) when employed as a clerk in HM Patents Office 1881–92. He became Professor of Latin at University College, London, in 1892 and at Cambridge in 1911. He was an outstanding Latinist and a fiercely critical essayist. A complex man, he wrote apparently simple verses that nevertheless contain descriptive power and emotional depth. Poem XLIX from *A Shropshire Lad* expresses his ideal of adolescent innocence: 'Oh, 'tis jesting, dancing, drinking / Spins the heavy world around. / If young hearts were not so clever, / Oh, they would be young for ever: / Think no more, 'tis only thinking / Lays lads underground.'

Howe, Julia Ward

American poet *born* New York 1819 *died* Portsmouth, Rhode Island 17 October 1910

Julia Ward Howe was one of the most progressive women of her time, advocating prison reform and female suffrage. She was one of the founders of the New England Woman Suffrage Association (despite her husband's distaste for the notion of married women as political activists) and spent much of her time in pursuit of her ideals. In 1862, the *Atlantic Monthly* published 'The Battle Hymn of the Republic' which ensured her literary immortality: 'Mine eyes have seen the glory of the coming of the Lord; / He is trampling out the vintage where the grapes of wrath are stored; / He hath loosed the fateful lightning of His terrible, swift sword; / His truth is marching on.'

Howell, James

Welsh poet *born* Abernant, Carmarthen 1594 *died* 1666

Howell was a man of many gifts who worked as a diplomat and excelled as a linguist, including Welsh among his accomplishments. His lines 'Upon Dr Davies's British Grammar' were sent, as a verse-letter, to Ben Jonson in 1629. The poem contains a remarkable linguistic credo: 'This is the tongue the bards sung in of old, / And Druids their dark knowledge did unfold; / Merlin in this his prophecies did vent, / Which through the world of fame bear such extent. / This spoke that son of Mars and Britain bold / Who first amongst Christian worthies is enrolled. / This Brennus who, to his desire and glut, / The mistress of the world did prostitute.'

Hughes, Langston

American poet *born* Joplin, Missouri 1 February 1902
died New York 22 May 1967

Hughes worked on his father's ranch then as a sailor and a cook until Vachel Lindsay encouraged him to devote himself to writing. His first collection, *The Weary Blues* (1926), began a distinguished career as the doyen of black American poets. Hughes used rhythms drawn from jazz and the blues and projected personal dignity rather than abstract indignation. He could be incisive, though, and also employed a somewhat folksy irony, as in 'Cross'; 'My old man died in a fine big house, / My ma died in a shack. / I wonder where I'm gonna die, / Being neither white nor black?' Among his best work is a Harlem sequence, *Montage of a Dream Deferred* (1951).

Hughes, Ted
English poet *born* Mytholmroyd, West Yorkshire 17 August 1930

When Hughes was seven his family moved to Mexborough, Yorkshire, a coal-mining town where his parents took a newsagent's shop. Before going up to Pembroke College, Cambridge, he did two years' national service as an RAF ground wireless mechanic. In 1956 he married the American poet Sylvia Plath and the following year published *The Hawk in the Rain*. *Crow* (1970), a major sequence, established him as the ascendant figure among his contemporaries. Crow is a subhuman creature who mocks the biblical creation. In 'A Childish Prank' Crow invents sex by biting the Worm into two: 'He stuffed into man the tail half / With the wounded end hanging out. // He stuffed the head half head first into woman'. In 1985 he succeeded Sir John Betjeman as Poet Laureate.

Hughes, Thomas
Welsh poet flourished 1818–65

Hughes was Rector of Clocaenog, Ruthin, and a linguist of some distinction. His *Poems by Hughes* (1865) collects Welsh, Latin and English poems by himself and his father. 'A Cheese for the Archdeacon' is a eulogy of a favourite food: 'It's moist and it's mild, and without too much boasting / I think it's a capital cheese for toasting. / It's not much decayed, nor strong in its savour: / Though for some it is rather too flat in its flavour. / And because it's too weak for to please every palate, / It perhaps may suit better when eaten with salad. / When cold or when toasted its taste is so mild / It will please the most delicate lady or child.'

Hulme T E
English poet *born* Endon, North Staffordshire 1883
died near Nieuport 28 September 1917

Thomas Ernest Hulme was sent down from St John's College, Cambridge, for fighting and spent some time abroad before returning to Cambridge in 1912. Unsuited to the academic routine, he left university and settled in London where his anti-romantic philosophical ideas impressed Ezra Pound and A R

Orage who published his articles in the *New Age*. Five of his poems appeared, as 'The Complete Poetical Works of T E Hulme', at the end of Ezra Pound's *Ripostes* (1912). His Imagist approach is evident in 'Autumn' which begins: 'A touch of cold in the Autumn night – / I walked abroad, / And saw the ruddy moon lean over a hedge / Like a red-faced farmer.' He was killed while serving with the British Army.

Hume, Alexander
Scottish poet *born c*1556 *died* 4 December 1609

The second son of the fifth Lord Polwarth, Hume was educated at St Andrews University and in France. Returning to Scotland he was part of the court of James VI but left to become minister of Logie, Stirlingshire, and a man who put his faith in the Reformation. His greatest poem 'Of the Day Estivall' (meaning 'Of a summer's day'), is a masterly piece of descriptive writing using the sun as a symbol of God: 'O perfite light, quhilk schaid away, / Ehe darkenes from the light, / And set a ruler ou'r the day, / Ane uther ou'r the night. // Thy glorie when the day foorth flies, / Mair vively dois appeare, / Nor at midday unto our eyes, / the shining Sun is cleare.'

Humphreys, Emyr
Welsh poet *born* Trelawynd, Flintshire 1919

Son of a schoolmaster, Humphreys was educated at the University Colleges of Aberystwyth and Bangor. During the Second World War, he was a member of a relief mission and later he became a BBC producer of radio and television drama. His novels – such as *A Man's Estate* (1955) and *Flesh and Blood* (1974) – have been much admired. In poems in English, he considers the persistence of the past, as in 'From Father to Son': 'There is no limit to the number of times / Your father can come to life, and he is as tender as ever he was / And as poor, his overcoat buttoned to the throat, / His face blue from the wind that always blows in the outer darkness'.

Hunt, Leigh
English poet *born* Southgate, Middlesex 19 October 1784
died 28 August 1859

Leigh Hunt, the son of a preacher, got a job in the War Office in 1805. Three years later he left to edit *The Examiner* and in 1813 was sentenced to two years' imprisonment for libelling the Prince Regent. He visited Byron and Shelley in Italy in 1822 and consistently championed their poetry. In 1847 he was given a Civil List Pension. His six-part poem *Captain Sword and Captain Pen* (1835) is a plea for peace, an idea also implicit in his best known poem 'Abou Ben Adhem': 'Abou Ben Adhem (may his tribe increase!) / Awoke one night from a deep dream of peace, / And saw, within the moonlight in his room . . . An angel writing in a book of gold'.

Hutchinson, Pearse
Irish poet *born* Glasgow 1927

Born in Scotland of Irish parents, Hutchinson lived for some time in Spain. He established himself as a skilled translator of Catalan poetry and as a writer in both Irish and English. His English verse is included in *Expansions* (1969) and *The Frost is All Over* (1975). His verbal energy is demonstrated effectively in 'Connemara': 'In kelp cormorant fuchsia foxglove country, / collies and black-faced cream-wooled sheep, / drystone walls at once darker and brighter after the rain, / the quartz gleaming whiter in the gloaming, / I name Ben Gorm, Blue Peak, tingling day-luminous blue / in the distance, green close-to at Leenaun'.

Huxley, Aldous
English poet *born* Godalming, Surrey 26 July 1894
died 22 November 1963

Grandson of the great biologist Thomas Henry Huxley, Aldous Huxley was educated at Eton and Oxford. His intention to become a doctor was thwarted by an eye infection which left him almost blind for a while. He wrote brilliant satirical novels such as *Point Counter Point* (1928) and the dystopia *Brave New World* (1932). His mystical philosophy was expressed in the influential *Doors of Perception* (1956). The poetry he published in *Leda* (1920) is a modern application of the Metaphysical mode, as in 'Fifth Philosopher's Song': 'A million million spermatozoa, / All of them alive: / Out of their cataclysm but one poor Noah / Dare hope to survive.'

Hyde, Robin
New Zealand poet *born* Cape Town 19 January 1906
died 23 August 1939

Iris Guiver Wilkinson ('Robin Hyde') was educated at Wellington Girls' College. An attack of rheumatic fever left her permanently lame and she subsequently suffered from periodic attacks of mental illness. She worked as a journalist and published her first collection, *The Desolate Star*, in 1929. In 1938 she decided to travel to England via Siberia and became involved in the Chinese war; after the battle of Hsüchow she was arrested as a spy and badly treated by Japanese troops. She arrived in an England about to enter a Second World War and committed suicide. In 'The Deserted Village', set in China, she notes where 'the women ran outside to be slain.'

Ignatow, David
American poet *born* New York 1914

David Ignatow left college during the Depression and worked as a businessman in New York; as editor of the *Beliot Poetry Journal* from 1949–59; and as poetry editor of the *Nation* from 1962–3. In his various volumes of poetry he deals with a wide variety of subjects from a radical viewpoint. 'East Bronx', for example, depicts the hopelessness created by economic hardship for while 'two children sharpen / knives against the curb' adults 'sit on the toilet seat / with locked door' to read escapist literature. 'All Quiet' is an ironic comment on the unexpected outbreak of peace in the Vietnam War: 'How come nobody is being bombed today?' he asks in the opening line.

Ingelow, Jean
English poet *born* Boston, Lincolnshire 17 March 1820 *died* 20 July 1897

A banker's daughter, Jean Ingelow settled in London where she was on friendly terms with Tennyson, Browning and Christina Rossetti. She wrote children's stories and novels including *Fated to be Free* (1875) and *Sarah de Berenger* (1879). Her literary ballad, 'the High Tide on the Coast of Lincolnshire (1571)', which comes complete with archaic spelling, tells of the drowning of the speaker's daughter-in-law: 'That flow strewed wrecks about the grass, / That ebbe swept out the flocks to sea; / A fatal ebbe and flow, alas! / To manye more than myne and mee: / But each will mourn his own (she saith), / And sweeter woman ne'er drew breath / than my sonne's wife Elizabeth.'

Ingamells, Rex
Australian poet *born* Orroroo, South Australia 1913 *died* 1955

After graduating from Adelaide University, Ingamells was a schoolteacher in Adelaide then, in 1946, went to Melbourne to work in publishing as an educational representative. In 1938 he founded the Jindyworobak Club which insisted on the importance of the Australian aboriginal experience; as a result a poetic school of Jindyworobaks came into being. Ingamells attempted to give a poetic voice to the Australian continent in such works as 'History': 'These are the images that make my dreams, / strong images but frail; dimmed-with-glow yet clear: / Pioneer ships lumbering in the sunset, / lumbering along our sombre eastern coastline, / swaying, awkward but beautiful, north to Port Jackson'.

Ireland, Kevin
New Zealand poet *born* Auckland 1933

Ireland lived for a long period in London, then moved to Ireland.

He published *Face to Face* in 1963 and *Educating the Body* in 1967.
He also wrote the libretti for the operas *The Snow Queen* (1982)
and *The Man who made Good* (1982). His 'Parade: Liberation Day' is
a vivid townscape complete with the ominous appearance of
soldiers: 'Now picture the infantry, / cold, damp, / measuring
with hobnails / the way back to camp. / Yet make their tread trail
from the distance, / though they are near: / gently imagine
them, / their future is not clear.' A shorter poem, 'Striking a
pose', also introduces a threat: 'if death still comes / we'll strike a
pose / and hold our breath / until he goes'.

Iremonger, Valentin
Irish poet *born* 1918

A diplomat, Iremonger represented Ireland in London,
Stockholm and India. His first collection of poems, *Reservations*,
won the AE Memorial Award in 1945. His *Horan's Field and Other
Reservations* appeared in 1972. His work is descriptively precise
and in 'This Houre Her Vigil' he movingly mourns a lady called
Elizabeth: 'Next morning, hearing the priest call her name, / I
fled outside, being full of certainty, / And cried my seven years
against the church's stone wall. / For eighteen years I did not
speak her name / Until this autumn day when, in a gale, / A
sapling fell outside my window, its branches / Rebelliously
blotting the lawn's green. Suddenly, I thought / Of Elizabeth,
frigidly stretched.'

Irwin, Thomas Caulfield
Irish poet *born* 1823 *died* 1883

Educated privately, Irwin was an accomplished linguist. He wrote
frequently for the *Dublin University Magazine* but was eccentric, so
his contemporaries thought, to the point of insanity. His sonnets
are extremely inventive and often superbly atmospheric: 'A
roadside inn this summer Saturday: / The doors are open to the
wide warm air, / The parlour, whose old window views the bay, /
Garnished with cracked delph full of flowers fair / From the fields
round, and whence you see the glare / Fall heavy on the hot slate
roofs and o'er / The wall's tree shadows drooping in the sun.' So
begins one of the best.

Jackson, Alan
Scottish poet *born* 1938

Educated at Edinburgh University, Jackson was at his most active
in the 1960s when he was secretary of the Scottish Committee of
100 and a leading figure in organising poetry readings during the
Edinburgh International Festival. Influenced by the American
'Beat' poets, he applied their conversational style to Scottish
culture and produced several satirical poems denouncing the

Presbyterian negativity he observed in Scotland. In 'Knox (2)' he wrote new words to the tune of the song 'Johnny Lad': 'O Knox he was a bad man / he split the Scottish mind. / The one half he made cruel / and the other half unkind.' Jackson has supported himself by performing his work.

Jackson, Helen Hunt

American poet *born* Amherst, Massachusetts 15 October 1830 *died* Colorado Springs 12 August 1885

Helen Maria Fiske went to school with her friend Emily Dickinson and later moved, for health reasons, to Colorado Springs where she married, in 1875, her second husband William Jackson. In 1882 she visited the Cahuilla Indian Reservation in San Jacinto, California, gathering material used in her novel *Ramona* (1884). Her exposure of the condition of the American Indians made her a prominent figure and her poems were praised by such authorities as Emerson. Her sonnet 'Danger' ends: 'The mighty are brought low by many a thing / Too small to name. Beneath the daisy's disk / Lies hid the pebble for the fatal sling.'

Jackson, Michael

New Zealand poet *born* Taranaki 1940

Educated at the universities of Auckland and Cambridge, Jackson became an anthropologist on the teaching staff of Massey University, Palmerston North. He published *Latitudes of Exile* in 1976 and *Wall* in 1980. He is a compassionate poet whose professional skill enables him to put humankind in a contemplative context. His 'Neanderthal' opens with a description of the ancient impulse to bury the dead 'with care'. The poet warns the reader not to categorise prehistoric people as another species: 'do not imagine them / with brutish hands, / crag-browed, unkempt, ill- / spoken, who nursed and minded / these unlucky ones.'

Jacob, Violet

Scottish poet *born* Montrose 1863 *died* 9 September 1946

Daughter of the eighteenth Laird of Dun, Violet Kennedy-Erskine married Arthur Otway Jacob, an army officer, and lived for a while in India. She wrote lively poems in Scots, including 'Mistress Mackay' –from *The Northern Lights* (1927) – which is a comical portrait of a Scotswoman: 'She wadna bide oot an' she wadna bide in, / The tea was infused but she wadna begin, / There were jeelies an' bannocks tae welcome her doon / And a bottle o' whuskey they'd bocht i' the toon / And the hale o' the neebours hurrayin' like ane / When Mistress Mackay got a flicht in a plane.'
bide stay; *jeelies* jellies

James I

Scottish poet *born* Dunfermline 25 July 1394
died Perth 21 February 1437

Son of Robert III, James was captured by English pirates and
spent eighteen years as a prisoner of the English. In 1423, his final
year of captivity, he fell in love with Lady Joan Beaufort – an
experience recorded poetically in his *The Kingis Quair* (published
1783) – and married her the following year when released on a
ransom of 60,000 merks. He restored respect for the monarchy
and founded what was to become the Court of Session. However
conspirators (who hoped to win the throne for the younger son of
Robert II) murdered James I. *The Kingis Quair* reveals a genuine
poetic gift: 'Worship, yet that loveris bene, this May, / For of
your bliss the kalendis are begonne, / And sing with us, away,
winter, away!'
kalendis first day

James VI

Scottish poet *born* Edinburgh Castle 19 June 1566
died London 27 March 1625

Son of Mary Queen of Scots, James VI was crowned, according to
Protestant rites, on 29 July 1567. He was tutored by the great
Latinist George Buchanan and in 1589 married Anne of Denmark
(by whom he had seven children, including the future Charles I).
He believed in the Divine Right of Kings and achieved his
greatest ambition when he became king of England on the death
of Elizabeth I in 1603. He returned to Scotland only once, in
1617 when he failed to force episcopacy on the kirk. His 'Reulis
and Cautelis' (1585) is a treatise on verse and his Scottish court
sustained a Castalian Band of poets including Alexander
Montgomerie. The King's 'Admonition to Montgomerie'
addresses a 'maistre of our art'.

James, Clive

Australian poet *born* Sydney 1939

James's public reputation was made, first, as a television critic and
then as a television performer specialising in the cannibalisation
of other television programmes. He is thus representative of an
age that lives vicariously by the light of a bulb in the corner of a
room. Television is his primary source of information and he
acknowledges this in satirical sequences that ridicule public
personalities. His *Poems of the Year* (1983) is a commentary, in
ottava rima, on the year 1982. When discussing the Falklands war
he turns from that topic to think of snooker on television: 'It is a
pitiless yet bloodless quarrel / Racking the nerves behind the
deadened pan.'

Jarrell, Randall
American poet *born* Nashville, Tennessee 6 May 1914 *died* 1965

Educated at Vanderbilt University, Jarrell served in the US air force in the Second World War. He was a consultant in poetry at the Library of Congress and, from 1947 until his death, taught at the Women's College of the University of North Carolina in Greensboro. Robert Lowell described him as 'the most heartbreaking English poet of his generation'. His work is intensely personal and searchingly observant. 'Women on a Bus', composed the year before his death, is characteristic; 'Old women and old men, / Approaching each other in life's pilgrimage, / In their neutral corner, their third sex, / Huddle like misers over their bag of life / And look with peasant cunning, peasant suspicion, /At every passer-by, who may be Death.'

Jeffers, Robinson
American poet *born* Pittsburg, Pennsylvania 10 January 1887 *died* Carmel Point, California 20 January 1962

Son of a theologian, Jeffers was educated in Europe and at Occidental College, California. Left a legacy by an uncle, in 1914, he settled with his wife Una at Carmel Point where he built Tor House, some of it with his own hands, from granite boulders. For forty-three years Jeffers remained at Tor House, pronouncing poetic judgement on the folly of humanity. Though his work is pessimistic, its qualities of clarity and passion suggest a creative heroism. He was drawn to archetypal images and dramatic flourishes. In *The Women at Point Sur* (1927) he wrote: 'I have seen and not fallen, I am stronger than the idols, / But my tongue is stone how could I speak him?'

Johnson, Georgia Douglas
American poet *born* Atlanta, Georgia 1886 *died* 1967

Educated at the University of Georgia and at Oberlin Conservatory, Georgia Douglas Johnson became a schoolteacher then moved to Washington where she worked in government agencies. In 1918 she established herself as the most important black poet since Frances Harper with her collection *The Heart of a Woman*, the title poem of which ends with a poignant reflection on the position of women: 'The heart of a woman falls back with the night, / And enters some alien cage in its plight, / And tries to forget it has dreamed of the stars / While it breaks, breaks, breaks on the sheltering bars.' Her home in Washington was a meeting place for black intellectuals.

Johnson, James Weldon
American poet *born* Jacksonville, Florida 1871 *died* 1938

Educated at Atlanta University, Johnson was the first black to pass the Florida Bar examination. He wrote lyrics for his brother Rosamond's songs and they both went to New York in 1901 where they created successful musical comedies. As a member of the US diplomatic service, he served as a consul in Venezuela then in Nicaragua. His novel *The Autobiography of an Ex-Colored Man* appeared in 1912. From 1916–20 he was Field Secretary of the National Association for the Advancement of Colored People whose General Secretary he became from 1920–30. He was appointed Professor of Creative Literature at Fisk University in 1930. In 'The Creation' he describes God, 'Like a mammy bending over her baby', making a man.

Johnson, Lionel
English poet *born* Broadstairs, Kent 15 March 1867
died London 4 October 1902

Son of an army officer, Johnson was educated at Winchester and Oxford. He moved to London, supporting himself by literary journalism, and became a convert to Roman Catholicism in 1891. An alcoholic, he died of a fall in Fleet Street; Ezra Pound's *Hugh Selwyn Mauberley* (1920) mentions 'how Johnson (Lionel) died / By falling from a high stool in a pub'. He was greatly interested in Irish poetry and Celtic myth but his best-known poem is 'By the Statue of King Charles at Charing Cross': 'The splendid silence clings / Around me: and around / The saddest of all kings / Crowned, and again discrowned. / Comely and calm, he rides / Hard by his own Whitehall: / Only the night wind glides: / No crowds, nor rebels, brawl.'

Johnson, Louis
New Zealand poet *born* Wellington 1924

Raised in the New Zealand provinces, Johnson returned to Wellington in 1944. In 1959 he moved to Hastings then came back to Wellington in 1964, becoming an assistant editor at the School Publications branch of the Education Department. His collections include *The Dark Glass* (1955), *New Worlds for Old* (1957), *Bread and a Pension* (1964). In 'Before the Day of Wrath' – from the sequence 'Four Poems from the Strontium Age' – he reflects on humankind's capacity for destruction: 'Today the rain draws blood; the winds / Burn out our eyes; the barbarous / Plants tear flesh that never mends: / Sweet water-holes turn suddenly poisonous.'

Johnson, Pauline
Canadian poet *born* Stratford, Ontario 1861 *died* 1913

Pauline Johnson's father was a Mohawk chief married to an Englishwoman and Pauline adopted the Mohawk name Tekahionwake. A skilled performer, she gave readings in the USA and England. Her collected poems appeared in 1912 under the title *Flint and Feather*. 'The Corn Husker' shows her concern for a persecuted people: 'Age in her fingers, hunger in her face, / Her shoulders stooped with weight of work and years, / But rich in tawny colouring of her race, / She comes a-field to strip the purple ears. // And all her thoughts are with the days gone by, / Ere might's injustice banished from their lands / Her people, that to-day unheeded lie, / Like the dead husks that rustle through her hands.'

Johnson, Samuel
English poet *born* Lichfield 18 September 1709
died 13 December 1784

A bookseller's son, Johnson was too poor to complete his education at Oxford. His marriage to Elizabeth Porter, however, gave him some financial security and when he came to London, in 1737, he was determined to succeed. His great *Dictionary* appeared in 1755 and in 1763, the year he met his biographer James Boswell, he founded 'the Club' (later, 'The Literary Club'). A formidable man and conversationalist of genius, Johnson satirised *The Vanity of Human Wishes* (1749) in his poem of that name: 'See nations slowly wise, and meanly just, / To buried merit raise the tardy bust. / If dreams yet flatter, once again attend, / Hear Lydiat's life and Galileo's end.'

Johnston, George
Canadian poet *born* Hamilton, Ontario 1913

Educated at the University of Toronto, Johnston taught at Carleton University in Ottawa. His poems were collected in *Auk Redivivus* (1981). Johnston uses traditional techniques, preferring rhyme to the other options available in modern verse. He can be an effective ironist, however, counterpointing the tensions of domestic life with the terror implicit in modern society. 'War on the Periphery', for example, ends: 'My little children eat my heart; / At seven o'clock we kiss and part, / At seven o'clock we meet again; / They eat my heart and grow to men. // I watch their tenderness with fear / While on the battlements I hear / The violent, obedient ones / Guarding my family with guns.'

Jonas, George
Canadian poet *born* Budapest 1935

Hungarian by birth, George Jonas came to Toronto in 1957 and has earned his living freelancing and working for the Canadian Broadcasting Corporation. His collection *Cities* came out in 1973. His verse is discursive in approach and ironic in tone. The sequence 'The Happy Hungry Man' comes to some subjective conclusions on the quality of individual life: 'We are slowly coming of age. / Time does the only thing it can do for us in passing. / We'd have to look at some fixed object to notice / it passes at the same speed as we do / Only much faster. // But there are no objects outside of ourselves. / We learn our lessons wrinkle by wrinkle, / Humbly planting behind us now and then / The milestone of a missing tooth.'

Jones, David

Anglo–Welsh poet *born* Brockley, Kent 1 November 1895
died Calvary Nursing Home 28 October 1974

The son of a printer, David Jones studied painting before serving as a private on the Western Front from 1915–1918. After the war he returned to the practice of painting and in 1921 was received into the Roman Catholic church. His masterpiece, *In Parenthesis* (1937), was hailed as a work of genius by T S Eliot. Set in the period 1915–16 it combines a realistic description of battle with ritualistic elements from Celtic myths and Welsh traditions. When Private John Ball is wounded 'it came as if a rigid beam of great weight flailed about his calves, caught from behind by ballista-baulk let fly or aft-beam slewed to clout gunnel-walker'.

Jones, D G

Canadian poet *born* Bancroft, Ontario 1 January 1929

Douglas Gordon Jones studied at the universities of McGill and Queen's, Kingston. He taught at Bishop's University and in the Department of English at the University of Sherbrooke. His *Butterfly on a Rock* (1970) is a critical exploration of Canadian literature. He won the Governor General's Award for Poetry in 1977 and published *A Throw of Particles* in 1983. Like many Canadian poets he responds to his natural environment. 'Tremor' reflects that 'here in Quebec the snow / drifts and the pit / of an avocado splits // in a glass jar'. Similarly, 'Annunciation' alludes to the snow and asserts that 'The air is not air, it is an arctic / Confidence of flowers.'

Jones, Ebenezer

Welsh poet *born* London 20 January 1820
died Brentwood 14 September 1860

Son of a Welsh Calvinist, Jones was badly treated at school before becoming a clerk. He published *Sensation and Event* in 1843 and was politically sympathetic to the Chartist movement. He had an unhappy marriage which ended in separation and revealed, in his verse, a melancholy temperament. 'A Development of Idiotcy' is a characteristically sombre narrative: 'She is dead within that bed; and never more / Will she hearken to his dreams of paradise, / And wind her arms around him, sweetly paling / With excess of happiness. / Three days and nights he haunted a near mountain; / The sky was cloudless, and the sunshine strong, / And not one mournful breeze ever stole to him, / Loosening his tears.'

Jones, Glyn
Welsh poet *born* Merthyr Tydfil, Glamorgan 1905

Son of a post-office worker, Jones was trained as a teacher in Cheltenham, and taught all his life in Glamorgan until he retired in 1965. His highly descriptive short stories, in such volumes as *The Blue Bed* (1937), earned him much admiration. He was made an honorary Doctor of Literature by the University of Wales in 1974. A bilingual Welshman, he has written poems in English full of the same rich detail that distinguishes his stories. In 'Merthyr' he refers to 'this glorying in all / Created things, the golden sun, the small / Rain riding in the wind, the silvery shiver / Of the dawn-tongued birches, and the chromium river'.

Jones, Harri
Welsh poet *born* Llanafan Fawr 1921 *died* Newcastle, New South Wales 29 January 1965

During the Second World War, Jones served in mine-sweepers in the Mediterranean. He then graduated from University College, Aberystwyth and, in 1959, emigrated to Australia where he worked as a lecturer at Newcastle University College, New South Wales. He was drowned; his fourth collection, *The Colour of Cockcrowing* was posthumously published in 1966. In 'Back?', a poem dedicated to R S Thomas, he comments provocatively on his experience of exile: 'Of course I'd go back if somebody'd pay me / To live in my own country / Like a bloody Englishman. // But for now, lacking the money, / I must be content with the curlew's cry / And the salmon's taut belly // And the waves, of water and of fern / And words, that beat unendingly / On the rocks of my mind's country.'

Jones, John
Welsh poet *born* Llanasa, Flintshire 1788 *died* 1858

Known as 'Poet Jones', John Jones spent most of his working life in factories. In 1856 he published *Poems by John Jones*. In 'Holywell' he describes the impact of industrialisation on Wales: 'Industry's children are the sons of Wales, / No real starvation through their land prevails: / Their hills, though sterile, and their portion scant – / They ask no affluence and they know no want; / No bounds they crave for but their native sod, / With leave to labour and to worship God. / Yet will they not oppression bear too long, / But burst their fetters – a resistless throng, / And prove that spirit not extinguished quite / Which shone conspicuous on the fields of fight'.

Jones, John

Welsh poet *born* Llanfairtalhaearn, Denbighshire 1810 *died* 1869

Known as *Talhaiarn*, John Jones was a building supervisor who worked in England and France as well as Wales. A bilingual poet, he wrote prolifically in Welsh and *Gwaith Talhaiarn* (1869) included his song 'Watching the Wheat' in English: 'While I watch the yellow wheat / I wander by the river, / To dream a day-dream of my love, / For I must love her ever: / I see her in the glassy stream, / Her eyes with sweetness beaming: / Oh, how delicious 'tis to me / To be thus ever dreaming'. The poem ends with a declaration of fidelity: 'With ardent joy I'll love my love, / She steals my heart and fancy; / Of all the girls that grace the land, / There's none like winsome Nansi.'

Jones, Sally Roberts

Welsh poet *born* London 1935

A librarian by profession, Sally Jones associated with other Welsh poets in London and then returned to Wales in the 1960s at a time when there was a renewal of Welsh cultural consciousness. She became a secretary of the English language section of *Yr Academi Gymreig* (The Welsh Academy, founded 1959) when that was established in 1968. She also formed her own publishing house, Alun Books. She is at her best in discursive poems such as 'Community': 'There has been a death in the street; / We are less by that much. Statistics / Cannot say what we lose, what we give: / Questionnaires for the Welfare Department / Tell industrious lies.'

Jong, Erica

American poet *born* New York, 26 March 1942

Before achieving bestsellerdom with her novel *Fear of Flying* (1973) Erica Jong was recognised as a poet who could reconcile her feminist conscience with an irreverent approach to sexuality. She conveys the feminine condition with intelligence and an inventive wit, bringing a sense of playfulness to modern poetry. Her brief, brittle lines often, as in 'The Truce Between the Sexes', develop autobiographical details: 'My life and my poems lived apart: / I had to marry them, / and marrying them / meant divorcing him, / divorcing the lie.' Her first marriage, to Allan Jong, ended in divorce and she subsequently married the writer Jonathan Fast.

Jonson, Ben

English poet *born* Westminster 11 June 1572 *died* 6 August 1637

One of the most brilliant figures in English drama, Jonson was descended from the Scottish Johnstones of Annandale. Educated at Westminster School, he worked as a bricklayer, served as a soldier, and became an actor. He married Anne Lewis in 1594 and four years later, when put on trial for the murder of another actor in a duel, successfully pleaded benefit of clergy. A number of masterly plays – including *Volpone* (1605) and *The Alchemist* (1610) – established him as a major figure. His poem 'On my Son' ends: 'Rest in soft peace, and, asked, say here doth lie / Ben Jonson, his best piece of poetry. / For whose sake, henceforth, all his vows be such / As what he loves may never like too much.'

Joseph, Jenny
English poet *born* 1932

Jenny Joseph read English at Oxford and later worked as a journalist and a lecturer. To convey her sense of concern about the world her poems offer images of injustice: 'Dirty well-fed men carve up with knives / That people sit in factories to make' she writes in 'Beyond Descartes'. Her style is headlong and rhetorical and imposes itself with some urgency on the reader who is told tales of horror about 'Man as matter': 'Man to live must get his teeth in flesh, / Tastiness oozing round his itching canines, / Aroma and sweet slap of roast on tongue.' Her feminist poems are composed with anger as she surveys the world Man has created.

Joseph, M K
New Zealand poet *born* 1914 *died* 1981

Educated at the universities of Auckland and Oxford, Joseph (who was born in England) served in the British Army during the Second World War. Subsequently he returned to New Zealand and taught English at Auckland University. He published *Imaginary Islands* in 1950, *The Living Countries* in 1959. His deep indignation over injustice is expressed emphatically in 'Mercury Bay Eclogue': 'Over the sea lie Europe and Asia / The dead moulded in snow / The persecution of nuns and intellectuals / The clever and the gentle / The political trials and punishment camps / The perversion of children / Men withering away with fear at the end.'

Joyce, James
Irish poet *born* Dublin 2 February 1882
died Zurich 13 January 1941

Recognised as the most outstanding experimental novelist of the twentieth century, Joyce established the modernist mode in prose with *Ulysses* (1922) and lifted prose to a new level of linguistic complexity with *Finnegans Wake* (1939). At the age of twenty-two Joyce left Ireland and created his masterpieces in Continental exile. His poetry exhibits none of the verbal daring of his prose but effectively cultivates a romantic Irish lyricism. Joyce published two slim volumes of poetry, *Chamber Music* (1907) and *Pomes Penyeach* (1927) which includes 'A Flower Given to my Daughter': 'Frail the white rose and frail are / Her hands that gave / Whose soul is sere and paler / Than time's wan wave.'

Junkins, Donald
American poet *born* Saugus, Massachusetts 1931

Educated at Boston University, Donald Junkins subsequently taught at Boston University, Emerson College, Chico State College (California) and the University of Massachusetts, Amherst. Technically sophisticated and drawn to fluent free verse, Junkins continues the American poetic fascination with the individual as a disturbing part of a natural element, as in 'Walden, 100 Years After Thoreau': 'I was the only one / at the pond; a nervous / chipmunk / hurried in the leaves; / on a wooden marker / pointing to the stones / at the site of Thoreau's hut / a solitary bluebird / waited'. The poem is included in *Crossing by Ferry* (1978).

Justice, Donald
American poet *born* Miami, Florida 1925

Educated at the universities of Miami, Stanford and North Carolina, Justice taught at the State University of Iowa. His style ranges from a lushly romantic love of detail – 'Here in Katmandu' has 'flowers, / Tremulous, ruddy with dew' – to an abrupt way of dealing with disturbing experiences. 'Counting the Mad', for example, uses the rhythms of a nursery rhyme to convey the child-like insecurity of the subjects of the poem: 'This one was put in a jacket, / This one was sent home, / This one was given bread and meat / But would eat none, / And this one cried No No No No / All day long.' Justice is a considerable craftsman whose collection *The Summer Anniversaries* was the Lamont Poetry Selection in 1959.

Kavanagh, Patrick
Irish poet *born* Monaghan 1905 *died* 1967

Son of a cobbler, Kavanagh worked as a farmer and a shoe-maker. He came to Dublin in 1939 and wrote literary journalism and the autobiography *The Green Fool* (1938). In 1955 he joined the Board of Extra-Mural Studies, University College, Dublin. His novel *Tarry Flyn* was published in 1948. His long poem *The Great Hunger* (1942) is a masterly evocation of the hardships of Irish rural life: 'Poor Paddy Maguire, a fourteen-hour day / He worked for years. It was he that lit the fire / And boiled the kettle and gave the cows their hay. / His mother tall hard as a Protestant spire / Came down the stairs barefoot at the kettle-call / And talked to her son sharply'.

Kazantzis, Judith
English poet *born* Oxford 1940

A history graduate, Judith Kazantzis has lived in London and
Sussex. She has written educational texts (on 'Women in Revolt'
for example), and contributed to the London *Evening Standard* and
the feminist magazine *Spare Rib*. Her work describes, with wit as
well as indignation, the exploitation of women in a society shaped
by men. 'The love of the nude for the little man' asserts: 'We
surround you, the slender giraffe women / your herd, in our
barest skin – you have / the full run of our suspenders, bras,
panties / necklaces, dolls; all accessories to / tickle a poor man's
fancy, but / no fact – which would break your gaze.'

Kearns, Lionel
Canadian poet *born* Nelson, British Columbia 1937

After an education at the University of British Columbia, Lionel
Kearns became a lecturer in English at Simon Fraser University.
His collection *Ignoring the Bomb* appeared in 1982. Kearns writes
poems that present a simple situation which he then undermines
with irony. 'International Incident', for example, begins with the
poet sounding off to an American, who has bought him beer,
about the iniquity of the Government of the USA. There is a neat
reversal of roles at the end of the poem: 'yes I was drinking the
American's beer / and reminding him that it sure takes guts / to
be so hostile to your host, but he / thought I was talking about
myself.'

Keats, John
English poet *born* London 31 October 1795
died Rome 23 February 1821

In the three years before his death, from consumption, Keats
completed the work that confers classic status on this most
Romantic of poets. Though licensed to practise as a surgeon and
apothecary he opted for the precarious life of a fulltime writer.
Keats was a passionate man, as much in love with the luxury of
language as with the inspirational figure of his beloved Fanny
Brawne; his notion of 'negative capability', formulated in 1817,
advocates a constant readiness to respond to beauty.
Appropriately his long poem *Endymion* (1818) begins with his
aesthetic credo: 'A thing of beauty is a joy for ever: / Its loveliness
increases; it will never / Pass into nothingness.'

Keene, Dennis
English poet *born* London 10 July 1934

A critic and translator of Japanese literature, Keene is a poet who
divides his life between Tokyo and Oxford. His most ambitious
work is the title poem of his collection *Universe* (1984). This

impressive poem of some length counterpoints autobiographical facts with the various assumptions of science. 'Real life was in the streets,' writes Keene as he reflects on urban chaos. The notion of social turmoil leads him to speculate about scientific laws: 'A singularity occurs when laws break down, as particles dissolve to more / unstable and elusive forms'. He is one of the few poets imaginatively to combine scientific terms with poetic insights.

Kendall, Henry
Australian poet *born* Kirmington, New South Wales
18 April 1839 *died* 1 August 1882

From Charles Harpur, the father of Australian poetry, Kendall absorbed the idea of creating an antipodean poetry from indigenous elements. His poem 'The Last of His Tribe', for example, attempts to convey an aboriginal experience by using essentially Australian terms: 'The wallaroos grope through the tufts of the grass, / And turn to their covers for fear; / But he sits in the ashes and lets them pass / Where the boomerangs sleep with the spear: / With the nullah, the sling, and the spear.' Although his poems have optimistic moments Kendall was a man who suffered frequently from depression and his personal life was chaotic.

Kennedy, Walter
Scottish poet *born* c1460 *died* c1508

The third son of the first Lord Kennedy, Kennedy was related (through his mother) to Robert III. Educated at Glasgow University, he became Depute-Bailie of Carrick. He was praised by both Sir David Lindsay and Dunbar with whom he conducted the 69-stanza 'The Flyting of Dunbar and Kennedy' (1500–5). His 'Honour with Age' begins: 'At matyne houre in midis of the nicht, / Walknit of sleip I saw besyd me sone / Ane aigit man semit sextie yeiris of sicht / This sentence sett and song it in gud tone: / "Omnipotent and eterne God in trone, / To be content and lufe the I haif caus / that my licht youtheid is opprest and done; / Honour with age to every vertew drawis."'
in trone enthroned; *youtheid* youth

Kennedy, X J
American poet *born* New Jersey 1929

After an education at the universities of Seton Hall and Michigan, Kennedy taught at Tufts University. His first collection *Nude Descending a Staircase* (1961) was the Lamont Poetry Selection for 1961. His work has a bittersweet quality as he fashions poignant narratives from everyday events. 'In a Prominent Bar in Secaucus One Day' is a literary ballad about a lady past her prime. After she has told the sad tale of her decline, the poem ends: 'All the house

raised a cheer, but the man at the bar / Made a phonecall and up
pulled a red patrol car / And she blew us a kiss as they copped her
away / From that prominent bar in Secaucus, N J'.

Keyes, Sidney
English poet *born* Dartford, Kent 27 May 1922 *died* 29 April 1943

Son of an army officer, Keyes was put under the care of his
eccentric grandfather when his mother died shortly after his
birth. Educated at Tonbridge School and Oxford, he joined up in
April 1942 and the following April went to North Africa with the
Queen's Own Royal West Kent Regiment. While on patrol he
was captured and presumably killed by the enemy. His
posthumously published poems show a linguistically sharp and
tragic response to the wastage of war, as in 'The Promised
Landscape': 'We lie in a ruined farm / Where rats perform /
Marvels of balance / Among the rafters. / And rain kisses my lips /
Because you are the sky / That bends always over me.'

Killigrew, Anne
English poet *born* 1660 *died* 1685

Anne Killigrew was a Maid of Honour to Mary of Modena and
flourished as one of the most accomplished ladies at the court. As
Dryden noted in his Ode on Anne Killegrew, she was known to be
'excellent in the two Sister-Arts of Poesie, and Painting'. Her
father, Dr Henry Killigrew, was himself a writer (as well as a
theologian) and probably encouraged her literary work. Her
poem 'Upon the Saying that My Verses Were Made by Another'
bitterly records that 'The envious age, only to me alone, / Will
not allow what I do write, my own; / But let them rage, and 'gainst
a maid conspire, / So deathless numbers from my tuneful lyre /
Do ever flow'. She died of smallpox.

King, Henry
English poet *born* London baptised 16 January 1592
died Chichester 30 September 1669

Son of Donne's friend John King, Henry King enjoyed a
successful ecclesiastical career becoming Dean of Rochester in
1638 and, in 1642, Bishop of Chichester which diocese he was
forced to abandon by the Puritan army. After the Restoration he
recovered his bishopric and preached at the court of Charles II.
His poems were published, anonymously and without his
consent, in 1657. He worked within the Metaphysical tradition
and became Donne's literary executor. 'The Exequy' movingly
recalls his wife Anne Berkely who died in 1624: 'Dear loss! since
thy untimely fate / My task hath been to meditate / On thee: thou
art the book, / The library whereon I look / Though almost
blind.'

Kingsley, Charles

English poet *born* Holne Vicarage, near Dartmoor 12 June
1819 *died* 23 January 1875

Educated at Cambridge, Kingsley became curate then rector of
Eversley, Hampshire. A Christian socialist, his novels *Yeast* (1848)
and *Alton Locke* (1850) earned him the nickname 'the Chartist
clergyman'. From 1860–9 he was Professor of Modern History at
Cambridge and became Canon of Westminster in 1873. Though
best remembered for his novels *Westward Ho!* (1855) and the
children's classic *The Water Babies* (1863) he also wrote ruggedly
romantic lines in, for example, 'Young and Old': 'When all the
world is young, lad, / And all the trees are green: / And every
goose a swan, lad / And every lass a queen; / Then hey for boot
and horse, lad, / And round the world away: / Young blood must
have its course, lad, / And every dog his day.'

Kinnell, Galway

American poet *born* Rhode Island 1927

Educated at Princeton University, Kinnell lived in France and
Iran for a while and translated several French poets. Back in the
USA he settled in a farmhouse in Vermont and alternated writing
with periods of teaching. His collection *What a Kingdom It Was*
(1960), contains his 'The Avenue Bearing the Initial of Christ into
the New World', a sustained poem rich in incidental detail:
'Fishes are nailed on the wood, / The big Jew stands like Christ,
nailing them to the wood, / He scrapes the knife up the grain, the
scales fly, / He unnails them, reverses them, nails them again, /
Scrapes and the scales fly.'

Kinsella, Thomas

Irish poet *born* Dublin 1929

Educated by the Christian Brothers, Kinsella became a civil
servant for the Government of Eire and later taught in
universities in the USA. In *The Tain* (1970) he translated the old
Irish epic Tain Bo Cuailgne. His own collections include
Nightwalker (1968), *Selected Poems* (1973), *Fifteen Dead* (1979). His
poem 'In the Ringwood' draws on folk elements to emphasise the
fragility of human relationships: 'I kissed three times her
shivering lips. / I drank their naked chill. / I watched the river
shining / Where the heron wiped his bill. / I took my love in my
icy arms / In the Spring on Ringwood Hill.' When he adopts a
contemporary tone he invariably dwells on the omnipresence of
death.

Kipling, Rudyard

English poet *born* Bombay 30 December 1865
died Burwash, East Sussex 18 January 1936

Kipling, the son of the curator of Lahore Central Museum, worked as a journalist in India from 1882-9. In London he published *Barrack Room Ballads* (1892) the year of his marriage to Caroline Starr Balestier. After his son was killed in the First World War Kipling helped pay for the Last Post to be sounded nightly at the Menin Gate Memorial at Ypres. The immense popularity of Kipling's verse was due to his ability to suggest strong emotion in a memorably simple style, as in 'If –': 'If you can fill the unforgiving minute / With sixty seconds' worth of distance run, / Yours is the Earth and everything that's in it, / And – which is more – you'll be a Man, my son.'

Kirkup, James
English poet *born* South Shields 1923

Educated at Durham University, Kirkup was the first Gregory Poetry Fellow at Leeds University (1950-2). In the 1960s he settled in the Far East and became Professor of English Literature at Kyoto University. The title poem of *A Correct Compassion* (1952), about a heart operation, attracted much attention for its combination of clinical detail and poetic imagery: 'A garland of flowers unfurls across the painted flesh. / With quick precision the arterial forceps click.' Later poems, such as those in *Zen Contemplations* (1978), are more terse in tone, as in 'The Tao of Water': 'in meditation / empty thought / water flowing / water flowing over water / water flowing / over a stone'.

Klein, A M
Canadian poet *born* Montreal 1909 *died* 1972

Klein was educated in Montreal where he practised law until his retirement in 1954. As one of the poets in the *New Provinces* anthology of 1936, he was associated with the move to introduce a more modern tone into Canadian poetry. He published a novel, *The Second Scroll*, in 1951 and his *Collected Poems* appeared in 1974. His poem 'Heirloom' shows his concern for Jewish culture: 'My father bequeated me no wide estates; / No keys and ledgers were my heritage; / Only some holy books with *yahrzeit* dates / Writ mournfully upon a blank front page – // Books of the Baal Shem Tov, and of his wonders; / Pamphlets upon the devil and his crew; / Prayers against road demons, witches, thunders; / And sundry other tomes for a good Jew.'

Knight, Etheridge
American poet *born* Corinth, Mississippi 1933

Knight was wounded in Korea and survived through narcotics. In 1960 he was imprisoned because (so he says in 'The Idea of Ancestry') 'in Memphis I cracked a croaker's crib for a fix'. In Indiana State Prison he began to write poems and in 1968, the year of his release, his collection of *Poems from Prison* was published. A black poet of great power, Knight writes movingly of another prisoner in 'Hard Rock Returns to Prison from the Hospital for the Criminal Insane': 'The WORD was that Hard Rock wasn't a mean nigger / Anymore, that the doctors had bored a hole in his head, / Cut out part of his brain, and shot electricity / Through the rest.' Knight then establishes the truth of the rumours.

Knister, Raymond
Canadian poet *born* near Comber, Ontario 1899 *died* 1932

Educated at Trinity College, Toronto, Knister went to the USA to work on the staff of *The Midland* then returned to Toronto as a freelance writer. He was drowned at the early age of thirty-three. His work was posthumously assembled as *Collected Poems* (1949) and *Selected Stories* (1974). He is known as one of the most persuasive poetic voices of rural Ontario and adhered to the Canadian tradition of delicately descriptive writing, as in 'Lake Harvest' which ends: 'Patient the horses look on from the sleighs, / Patient the trees, down from the bank, darkly ignoring the sun. / Each saw swings and whines in a grey-mittened hand, / And diamonds and pieces of a hundred rainbows as strown around.'

Knowles, James Sheridan
English poet *born* Cork 12 May 1784 *died* 30 November 1862

Son of a schoolmaster who favoured Catholic emancipation, Knowles was taken to London in 1793. He was a precocious youth who wrote 'The Welsh Harper' at the age of fourteen, a feat that impressed Hazlitt, Lamb and Coleridge. He subsequently studied medicine and became resident vaccinator to the Jennerian Society in London; he also attended Rowland Hill's ministry at Surrey Chapel. He wrote successful plays such as *William Tell* (1825) and impressed as an actor. He abandoned the theatre in 1843 and became a Baptist preacher. Like William Tell, in his play, he wanted 'Your prayers – your prayers – and be my witnesses.'

Koch, Kenneth
American poet *born* Cincinnati, Ohio 27 February 1925

Koch served in the Pacific with the US Army and was educated at the universities of Harvard and Columbia. He was associated (with John Ashbery and Frank O'Hara) with the Poet's theatre and also with the Artist's theatre. His long Byronic poem *Ko, or a Season on Earth* (1959) tells, in ottava rima, the story of a devastatingly powerful baseball pitcher who comes from Japan to join the Dodgers: 'As in a dream, / But not the ones he had, Ko

counted ten, / Wound up, and threw the baseball with such
steam / That it went through the backstop, lost till when / The
field would be torn down, and lazy goats / Would ramble through
it gnawing shreds of coats'. Koch's *The Duplications* appeared
in 1977.

Kroetsch, Robert
Canadian poet *born* Heisler, Alberta 26 June 1927

After studying at the universities of Alberta, McGill and Iowa,
Kroetsch taught at the University of Manitoba, Winnipeg and was
a writer in residence at various Canadian universities. A novelist
as well as a poet, he published *But We Are Exiles* (1965) and
received the Governor General's Award for Fiction for *The
Studhorse Man* (1969). His collections of poetry include *The Sad
Phoenician* (1979). In poems such as 'There is a World' Kroetsch
uses a fragmentary form to convey the insecurity of modern life:
'good morning, monday you don't / look so hot yourself you one-
eyed / bastard here in the hard west / we hold each other's
bodies / here / in the coyote night we howl'.

Kumin, Maxine
American poet *born* Philadelphia 1925

Maxine Kumin studied at Radcliffe College and subsequently
taught English at various universities including Princeton and
Columbia. A novelist as well as a poet, she has written movingly
of the persistence of the ancestral past in the mind of a sensitive
woman. After living near Boston for several years she moved to a
farm in New Hampshire and the rural mood of her later poetry
has an affirmative freshness. 'July, Against Hunger' rejoices in the
present: 'Meanwhile, a new life kicks in the mare. / Meanwhile,
the poised sky opens on rain. / The time on either side of *now*
stands fast /glinting like jagged window glass.'

Kunene, Mazisi
South African poet *born* Durban 1932

Educated in Durban, Mazisi arrived in London in 1959 and
worked for African National Congress. An authority on Zulu
poetry he often composes first in Zulu then produces English
versions of the poems. He settled in the USA in the 1970s,
becoming a professor of African Literature at the University of
California. His politically orientated poetry is tempered by a
lyrical approach to language. 'Abundance' begins: 'I possess a
thousand thundering voices / With which I call you from the
place of the sinking sun. / I call you from the shaking of
branches / Where they dance with the tail of the wind. / You are
the endless abundance / Singing with the lips of all generations.'

Kyffin, Morris
Welsh poet *born* near Oswestry *c*1555 *died* 1598

A bilingual poet, Kyffin has been held up as an example to
modern Welsh poets: in 'Consider Kyffin', Raymond Garlick
describes him: 'as Welsh / a word-spinner as you could wish, /
who wove in both tongues'. In his poem 'The Blessednes of
Brytaine' (1587) Morris offers a eulogy of Elizabeth I: 'Let hills
and rocks rebounding echoes yield / Of Queen Elizabeth's long
lasting fame; / Let woody groves and watery streams be filled, /
And creeks and caves, with sounding of the same: / O Cambria,
stretch and strain thy utmost breath, / To praise and pray for
Queen Elizabeth.' Kyffin's poem suggests that he disapproved of
Welsh involvement in the Babington plot against the Queen.

Kynaston, Sir Francis
English poet *born* 1587 *died* 1642

Educated at both Oxford and Cambridge, Kynaston was knighted
in 1618 and elected to the House of Commons in 1621. In 1635
he established, at his Covent Garden home, a private academy, or
Museum Minervae, at which he and friends taught scientific and
literary subjects. Kynaston translated the first two books of
Chaucer's *Troilus and Criseyde* into Latin rhyme royal. His own
poems, in the Metaphysical mode, weave variations on the
perennial theme of love, as in 'To Cynthia. On Concealement of
her Beauty': 'Do not conceal those tresses fair, / The silken snares
of thy curled hair, / Least finding neither gold, nor ore, / The
curious silk worm work no more.'

Laing, Dilys Bennet
American poet *born* 1906 *died* 1960

Daughter of a civil engineer, Dilys Bennettt was widely travelled
as a child. At the age of two she contracted polio and at the age of
twelve became partially deaf as the result of a mastoid infection.
A prolific writer, even as a teenager, she moved to Seattle and
married the poet Alexander Laing. Later she lived in Vermont
and published a novel as well as verse. She died of acute asthma,
leaving behind poems as accomplished as 'Ten Leagues Beyond
the Wide World's End': 'I pursue him, the loved one all
unsolved, / through mines of mercury, salt caves and folded
stone, / down decimal steps of dream and sleep and death, /
through flowering, breaking rocket-head of war / and long
anxious ferment of peace.'

Laing, R D
Scottish poet *born* Glasgow 1927

R D Laing studied medicine at Glasgow University and was, from
1951-3, a psychiatrist in the British Army. He worked in the

Glasgow Royal Mental Hospital; Glasgow University's Department of Psychological Medicine; and the Tavistock Clinic (1957–61). He was director of the Langham Clinic, London, from 1962–5 and in 1964 became Chairman of the Philadelphia Association. Since the publication of *The Divided Self* (in 1960) he has been internationally known as a radical thinker with an innovative explanation of schizophrenia and domestic stress. His poems, in *Do You Love Me?* (1976) for example, express his ideas as incisive rhymes: 'sometimes I am / sometimes I'm not / but which is which / I forgot'.

Lamb, Charles
English poet *born* London 10 February 1775
died 27 December 1834

Lamb's father was confidential clerk to Samuel Salt, an Inner Temple bencher, and the author went, from 1782–9, to Christ's Hospital where he became friendly with Coleridge. In 1796 Lamb's sister Mary murdered her mother with a table-knife and Lamb thereafter devoted himself to Mary's welfare. He published poems, a play, and collaborated with his sister in the successful *Tales from Shakespeare* (1807). As 'Elia' he contributed a brilliant series of essays to the *London Magazine*. Though his light verse is inferior to his prose 'A Farewell to Tobacco' is impressive: 'May the Babylonish curse / Straight confound my stammering verse, / If I can a passage see / In this word-perplexity'.

Lampman, Archibald
Canadian poet *born* Morpeth, Ontario 1861 *died* 1899

A clergyman's son, Lampman spent many of his formative years near Lake Rice. He was educated at Trinity College, Toronto, and worked in the Post Office Department of the Civil Service in Ottawa whose landscape he responded to imaginatively. He published only two collections before dying of a heart condition: *Among the Millet* (1888) and *Lyrics of Earth* (1896). *The Poems of Archibald Lampman* (with a memoir by his friend Duncan Campbell Scott) appeared in 1974. One of the Group of the Sixties, he was an outstanding nature poet. 'A Summer Evening', a sonnet, begins: 'The clouds grow clear, the pine-wood glooms and still / With brown reflections in the silent bay'.

Landon, Letitia E
English poet *born* London 14 August 1802 *died* 15 October 1838

An army sergeant's daughter, Letitia Elizabeth Landon pursued her lachrymose muse with profit in collections such as *The Troubadour* (1825). A scandal led to her breaking off an engagement and marrying George Maclean, Governor of Cape Coast Castle in the Gold Coast. Two months after her arrival in

West Africa, L E L (as she styled herself when writing) was found dead with an empty bottle of prussic acid in her hand. Her poem 'The Little Shroud' reworks a ballad theme without the vigour of the oral tradition: 'One midnight, while her constant tears / Were falling with the dew, / She heard a voice, and lo! her child / Stood by her, weeping too!'

Landor, Walter Savage
English poet *born* Warwick 30 January 1775
died Florence 17 September 1864

Landor, a doctor's son, was expelled from Oxford as a 'mad Jacobin' and driven out of England by a libel writ of 1857. His aristocratic bearing and republican views seemed eccentric to such as Dickens who modelled Boythorn, in *Bleak House*, on Landor. A brilliant classicist, Landor once said 'I am sometimes at a loss for an English word, for a Latin never.' His epic poetry, as in *Gebir* (1802) is classical in temper and Miltonic in tone. He is perhaps best remembered for the brief 'Dying Speech of an Old Philosopher': 'I strove with none, for none was worth my strife; / Nature I loved, and next to Nature, Art; / I warmed both hands before the fire of life; / It sinks, and I am ready to depart.'

Lane, Patrick
Canadian poet *born* Nelson, British Columbia 1939

Patrick Lane did a number of jobs in construction before moving to Vancouver where he helped found Very Stone House Press. His *Poems New & Selected* came out in 1978. There is a refreshingly realistic foundation to Lane's verse so that when he lifts his lines into images he does not lose contact with the human subject of his poem. Thus 'The Carpenter' is equal to his simile as he laughs 'and single strokes the spikes into the joists / pushing the floor another level higher / like a hawk who every year adds levels to his nest / until he's risen above the tree he builds on / and alone lifts off into the wind / beating his wings like nails into the sky.'

Langhorne, John
English poet *born* Kirkby Steven, Westmoreland 1735 *died* 1779

Langhorne's father died when he was four and he was raised by his mother. He took deacon's orders and went to London, in 1764, as the curate of St John's, Clerkenwell. Subsequently he became assistant preacher at Lincoln's Inn Chapel and, in 1777, prebendary in the Cathedral of Wells. In poems, such as 'The Country Justice', he adopts a high moralistic tone: 'The social laws from insult to protect, / To cherish peace, to cultivate respect; / The rich from wanton cruelty restrain, / To smooth the bed of penury and pain; / The hapless vagrant to his rest restore, /

The maze of fraud, the haunts of theft explore; / The thoughtless maiden, when subdued by art, / To aid, and bring her rover to her heart'.

Lanier, Sidney
American poet *born* Macon, Georgia 3 February 1842
died Lynn, North Carolina 7 September 1881

Son of a lawyer, Lanier was a fine flautist as well as a writer. He fought, during the Civil War, for his beloved South and spent five months, in 1864-5, in a Federal prison. He suffered from tuberculosis but his verse is vital as well as expansively romantic. 'The Marshes of Glynn', ends with a characteristic flourish; 'And now from the Vast of the Lord will the waters of sleep / Roll in on the souls of men, / But who will reveal to our waking ken / The forms that swim and the shapes that creep / Under the waters of sleep? / And I would I could know what swimmeth below when the tide comes in / On the length and the breadth of the marvellous marshes of Glynn.'

Larcom, Lucy
American poet *born* Beverly, Massachusetts 1824 *died* 1893

Lucy Larcom's father, a sea captain, died soon after her birth and her mother took the family to Lowell. There Lucy found employment in a textile mill and did various duties, including supervising the girls who stayed in one of the mill dormitories. Her contributions to local periodicals were admired and she finally found a post as a seminary teacher. Her poem 'Weaving' articulates the feelings of a girl at the loom: 'And how much of your wrong is mine, / Dark women slaving at the South? / Of your stolen grapes I quaff the wine; / The bread you starve for fills my mouth: / The beam unwinds, but every thread / With blood of strangled souls is red.'

Larkin, Philip
English poet *born* Coventry 9 August 1922

As an avowed enemy of modernism Philip Larkin is associated with the return to traditional values in English verse. Conservative by nature and cautious in technique he has established himself as a firm poetic voice articulating the English experience as a nostalgia for the past and a dislike of Abroad. He has spent his working life as a librarian and his creative time as a poet intent on establishing exactly what he likes about England. In 'Church Going' it is the sense of continuity 'Since someone will forever be surprising / A hunger in himself to be more serious'. One of the most influential poets of his time, Larkin has restored a regard for order to English verse.

Larminie, William

Irish poet *born* 1850 *died* 1899

Educated at Trinity College, Dublin he lived in London then
returned to Dublin when he retired in 1887. Like many of his
contemporaries he was interested in conveying the rhythm of
indigenous Irish literature in English verse. He published
Glanlua and Other Poems in 1889 and then, in 1892, *Fand and
Moytura*. The epilogue to 'Fand' contains the following
characteristically patriotic lines: 'And though many an isle be
fair, / Fairer still is Inisfallen, / Since the hour Cuhoolin lay / In
the bower enchanted, / See! the ash that waves today, / Fand its
grandsire planted.' His use of myth is strong rather than
sentimental.

Lawrence, D H

English poet *born* Eastwood, Nottinghamshire
11 September 1885 *died* Vence, France 2 March 1930

David Herbert Lawrence, a miner's son, was not only a
controversial novelist but also a gifted painter and poet. Jessie
Chambers, the girlfriend Lawrence portrayed as Miriam in *Sons
and Lovers* (1913), sent some of his early poems to the *English
Review* which duly printed six pages of them in November 1909.
Lawrence's poetry, like his prose, celebrates his erotic philosophy
and view of life as an intense emotional struggle. From Whitman
he derived an egotistical style and wrote expansively, often in free
verse, about animals, flowers and human sexuality. His 'Song of a
Man Who Has Come Through' asserts his essentially romantic
faith: 'Oh, for the wonder that bubbles into my soul, / I would be
a good fountain, a good well-head, / Would blur no whisper, spoil
no expression.'

Lawson, Henry

Australian poet *born* Mudgee, New South Wales 1867 *died* 1922

Son of a Norwegian gold-digger, Lawson was deaf from the age of
nine. When his mother left his father, Lawson went with her to
Sydney and wrote prose in praise of socialism for her periodical
The Republican. He was a loner whose marriage (of 1896) was
disturbed by his heavy drinking. Like 'Banjo' Paterson, Lawson
reached a large audience with his popular ballads celebrating
typically Australian characters. 'Middleton's Rouseabout'
introduces one such: 'Tall and freckled and sandy, / Face of a
country lout; / This was the picture of Andy, / Middleton's
Rouseabout.' Lawson was a prolific writer whose influence on
Australian culture is still evident.

Layton, Irving

Canadian poet *born* Rumania 1912

Educated at McGill University, he founded – with Louis Dudek
and Raymond Souster – Contact Press. He taught in several
Canadian universities and excelled as a performer of his own
poetry, in Canada and abroad. He won the Governor's Award and
published his collected poems, *A Wild Peculiar Joy*, in 1982. His
approach to nature is always affirmative and he is adept at
bringing his poems to a triumphant conclusion, as in 'the Fertile
Muck'; 'Sit here / beside me, sweet; take my hard hand in yours. /
We'll mark the butterflies disappearing over the hedge / with tiny
wristwatches on their wings: / our fingers touching the earth, like
two Buddhas.'

Lazarus, Emma
American poet *born* New York 1849 *died* 1887
Emma Lazarus was brought up as a member of a rich Jewish
family and lived a life of privilege until shocked by the news of
the Russian pogroms of the 1880s. She then immersed herself in
Jewish culture, translating key Jewish texts and speaking
powerfully on behalf of Zionism. A Marxist, she believed in the
common people. Her sonnet 'The New Colossus' celebrates the
Statue of Liberty as 'A mighty woman with a torch' who says (in
words that are inscribed on a plaque at the bottom of the statue)
'Give me your tired, your poor, / Your huddled masses yearning
to breathe free, / The wretched refuse of your teeming shore. /
Send these, the homeless, tempest-tost to me, / I lift my lamp
beside the golden door!'

Lear, Edward
English poet *born* London 12 May 1812
died San Remo 29 January 1888
When Lear was fifteen his father, a stockbroker, was imprisoned
for debt. Lear earned his living from his pictorial skills and was
employed by the Earl of Derby to illustrate an account of the
menagerie and aviary at Knowsley Hall. While living at Knowsley
Hall, Lear produced nonsense verse for the Earl's children. His
narrative poems show a highly inventive use of language and the
limericks, in *A Book of Nonsense* (1845), are imaginatively abrupt:
'There was a Young Lady of Clare, / Who was sadly pursued by a
bear; / When she found she was tired, she abruptly expired; /
That unfortunate Lady of Clare.'

Ledwidge, Francis
Irish poet *born* County Meath 1891 *died* Flanders 31 July 1917
Ledwidge was a farmworker and manual labourer who became a
trade-union secretary. During the First World War, he fought
with the British Army and was killed in action. Lord Dunsany,
who had encouraged his work, wrote a preface to his

posthumously published *Complete Poems* (1919). His quatrains on 'Thomas McDonagh' show his romantic style and patriotic sympathies: 'He shall not hear the bittern cry / In the wild sky, where he is lain, /Nor voices of the sweeter birds / Above the wailing of the rain. //Nor shall he know when loud March blows / Thro' slanting snows her fanfare shrill, / Blowing to flame the golden cup / Of many an upset daffodil.'

Lee, Dennis
Canadian poet *born* Toronto 31 August 1939

Lee has taught at the University of Toronto, where he studied, and at York University, Toronto. He helped found the House of Anansi Press and works as a publisher's consultant, poet and critic. His collections of poems for children have been well received; his adult poems are found in, for example, *The Gods* (1979). His sequence 'Civil Elegies', of 1968, is an ambitious attempt to confront the complex problems of the modern world. In section 6 the poet confesses 'I am one for whom the world is constantly proving too much – / not this nor that, but the continental drift to barbarian / normalcy frightens me'.

Lee, Laurie
English poet *born* Stroud, Gloucestershire 1914

At the age of nineteen Laurie Lee walked to London then travelled on foot through Spain where, as he described in *As I Walked Out One Midsummer Morning* (1969), he was trapped by the outbreak of the Civil War. In the Second World War he worked for the Ministry of Information. The events of his life insinuate their way into his sensuous verse. 'Music in a Spanish town' begins atmospherically with the poet holding his fiddle 'like a gun against my shoulder'. Despite the explosive tension the poem ends with a vision of the triumph of art over atrocity: 'Suddenly there is a quick flutter of feet / and children crowd about me, / listening with sores and infected ears, / watching with lovely eyes and vacant lips.'

Lee-Hamilton, Eugene
English poet *born* London 1845 *died* 1907

After an education in London, France and Germany, Eugene Lee-Hamilton joined the Diplomatic Service. In 1873, however, he was the victim of a cerebro-spinal disorder that made him a bedfast invalid for twenty years. As a form of relief from his sufferings he began to write verse. His *Imaginary Sonnets* (1888) are invariably morbid, as in 'Luca Signorelli to his Son': 'They brought thy body back to me quite dead, / Just as thou hadst been stricken in the brawl. / I let no tear, I let no curses fall, / But signed to them to lay thee on the bed. / Then, with clenched

teeth, I stripped thy clothes soaked red; / And taking up my
pencil at God's call, / All night I drew thy features, drew them
all, / And every beauty of thy pale chill head.'

Le Fanu, Joseph Sheridan

Irish poet *born* Dublin 28 August 1814 *died* 7 February 1873

Son of Dean Le Fanu of the Episcopal Church of Ireland, Le Fanu
was educated at Trinity College, Dublin. He was called to the Bar
in 1839 but took to writing after the success of his ballad 'Shamus
O'Brien: A Tale of '98': 'Jist afther the war, in the year '98, / As
soon as the boys wor all scattered and bate, / 'Twas the custom,
whenever a pisant was got, / To hang him by thrial – barrin' sich
as was shot. – / There was trial by jury goin' on in the light, / And
martial-law hanging' the lavins by night.' Le Fanu contributed to
the *Dublin University Magazine* (which he eventually owned) some
of the novels which made him famous. *Uncle Silas* (1864) is one of
his finest novels.

Leigh, Henry S

English poet *born* London 29 March 1837 *died* 16 June 1883

An artist's son, Leigh was a prolific writer who published *Carols of
Cockayne* in 1869. 'To a Timid Leech' is characteristic of his
playful light verse: 'Nay, start not from the banquet where the red
wine foams for thee, / Though somewhat thick to perforate this
epidermis be, / 'Tis madness, when the bowl invites to linger at
the brink; / So haste thee, haste thee, timid one. Drink, pretty
creature, drink!' He also wrote the poems in *A Town Garland*
(1878) and *Strains from the Strand* (1882). He translated several
French comic operas for the English stage, including *Falsacappa*
(1871) and *Le Roi Carotte* (1872). His *Jeux d'Esprit* appeared in
1877.

Leighton, Robert

Scottish poet *born* Dundee 20 February 1822
died Liverpool 10 May 1869

Raised on his stepfather's farm in Fife, Leighton went to Dundee
Academy then worked in his brother's office in Dundee. In one of
his brother's sailing ships he travelled round the world in 1842-3
and subsequently settled in Preston, Lancashire. In 1854 he went
to Ayr as branch manager of a Liverpool firm; four years later he
went to the head office in Liverpool. His poems are burdened by
a self-consciously poetic diction but in some pieces, such as
'Incense of Flowers', he shows a genuine appreciation of nature:
'This rich abundance of the rose, its breath / On which I almost
think my soul could live, / This sweet ambrosia, which even in
death / Its leaves hold on to give.'

Leonard, Tom
Scottish poet *born* Glasgow 22 August 1944

Educated at Glasgow University, Leonard has used the speech-rhythms of his native city to create conversationally compelling dialect poems. His dramatic monologues introduce the reader to a variety of voices and show the considerable resources of the Glasgow patois. 'The Good Thief', an extremely popular poem, reproduces the voice of a Glasgow Celtic football fan and there is a provocative pun involved in the Glaswegian pronounciation of 'in saying': 'heh jimmy / ma right insane yirra pape / ma right insane yirwanny us jimmy / see it nyir eyes / wanny uz'. The meaning is ambiguous and clearly Leonard is no mere linguistic reporter but an imaginative eavesdropper.

Le Pan, Douglas
Canadian poet *born* Toronto 1914

Educated at the universities of Toronto and Oxford, Le Pan worked as a diplomat and academic. His collection *The Wounded Prince* appeared in 1948 and *The Net and the Sword* (1953) won the Governor General's Award. His novel *The Deserter* was published in 1964. His poem 'Canoe-trip' puts the Edenic ideal of Canada under critical scrutiny. After invoking 'this fabulous country', Le Pan writes: 'It is good, / It is good stock to own though it seldom pays dividends, / There are holes here and there for a gold-mine or a hydro-plant. / But the tartan of river and rock spreads undisturbed, / The plaid of a land with little desire to buy or sell.'

Leslie, Kenneth
Canadian poet *born* Pictou, Nova Scotia 1892 *died* 1974

A man of intellectual authority, Leslie was educated at the universities of Dalhousie, Nebraska and Harvard. In 1971 he published *The Poems of Kenneth Leslie*. Although he was aware of the experimental thrust of modernism, he was also drawn to traditional forms and attracted to the descriptive mainstream of Canadian verse. His sonnets, in 'By Stubborn Stars', show an ability to renew the resources of a well-worn form: 'A warm rain whispers, but the earth knows best / and turns a deaf ear, waiting for the snow, / the foam of bloom forgotten, the rolling crest / of green forgotten and the fruit swelling slow.'

Lever, Charles
Irish poet *born* Dublin 31 August 1806 *died* Trieste 1 June 1872

Educated at Trinity College, Dublin, Lever studied medicine in Göttingen and practised as a doctor in Ireland and Brussels (1840–2). From 1842–5 he edited the *Dublin University Magazine* which had published his first novel, *Harry Lorrequer*, in 1837. His second novel, *Charles O'Malley* (1840), was immensely popular on account of its humour and he continued to produce novels. He went to Italy in 1858 as Consul at Spezzia and was transferred, in 1867, to Trieste. Poems such as 'Mary Draper' are excellent examples of light verse: 'The parson, priest, sub-sherrif, too, / Were all her slaves, and so would you, / If you had only but one view / Of such a face or shape, or / Her pretty ankles'.

Levertov, Denise
American poet *born* Ilford, Essex 1923

During the Second World War, Denise Levertov was a nurse in England. She married Mitchell Goodman, the American writer, and settled in the USA in 1948. She lived in New York for a while and taught at Tufts College, Medford, Massachusetts. Her work is affirmative with a physical approach to imagery. 'Our Bodies', for example, is anatomically precise: 'I have // a line or groove I love / runs down / my body from breastbone / to waist. It speaks of / eagerness, of / distance. // Your long back, / the sand colour and / how the bones show, say // what sky after sunset / almost white / over a deep wood to which / rooks are homing, says.'

Levi, Peter
English poet *born* Ruislip, Middlesex 16 May 1931

Educated at Oxford, Peter Levi was a Jesuit priest until 1977; he then married and, in 1984, became Professor of Poetry at Oxford University. A former member of the British School of Archaeology at Athens, he translated the Russian poems of Yevtushenko and published several collections of his own work including *Collected Poems 1955–1975* (1976). 'Good Friday Sermon 1973', one of his finest poems, uses couplets to explore the central Christian symbols. It ends by asserting: 'Justice shall be like the snow and the sea. / Christ is the end of all calamity, /and what is true and strong shall come to birth. /There shall be no more wickedness on earth.' Levi also published the treatise *The Noise Made by Poems* (1977).

Levine, Philip
American poet *born* Detroit 1928

Levine was educated at Wayne State University and later taught at Fresno State University, California. He is a poet of considerable passion and liberal sympathies who writes in honour of, for example, 'The Poets of Chile Who Died with Their Country'. He often shows an admiration for athletic men of action, like the boxer described in 'Baby Villon'. His abiding theme, though, is human suffering especially as experienced in his native Detroit. 'They Feed They Lion' is a powerful meditation on the 1967 insurrection in Detroit: 'From they sack

and they belly opened / And all that was hidden burning on the
oil-stained earth / They feed they Lion and he comes.'

Lewis, Alun

Welsh poet *born* Cwmaman, near Aberdare 1 July 1915
died Burma 5 March 1944

The son of Aberdare's Director of Education, Lewis studied at the
University of Wales and Manchester University before
schoolteaching. He was called up in 1940, married in 1941 and
published *Raider's Dawn* in 1942. In 1944 he was posted to Burma
with the sixth battalion South Wales Borderers and died after
being accidentally shot. His admiration for Edward Thomas is
acknowledged in the last lines of 'All Day It has Rained' in which
he turns from thoughts of war to a memory of childhood and 'the
shaggy patient dog who followed me / By Sheet and Steep and up
the wooded scree / To the Shoulder O' Mutton where Edward
Thomas brooded long / On death and beauty – till a bullet
stopped his song.'

Lewis, Eiluned

Welsh poet *born* Newtown, Montgomeryshire 1900 *died* 1979

Eiluned Lewis was educated in London where she worked on the
News Chronicle and became assistant editor of the *Sunday Times*.
Her novel *Dew on the Grass* (1934) was awarded the Gold Medal of
the Book Guild; she also published *The Captain's Wife* (1943) and
The Leaves of the Tree (1953). In her delicately phrased poem 'The
Birthright' she contrasts the routine of city life with the variety of
rural living: 'We who were born / In country places, / Far from
cities / And shifting faces, / We have a birthright / No man can
sell, / And a secret joy / No man can tell. // For we are kindred /
To lordly things, / The wild duck's flight / And the white owl's
wings'.

Lewis, Wyndham

English poet *born* Maine 18 November 1884 *died* 7 March 1967

Lewis came to England as a child and was educated at Rugby
School and the Slade School where he polished his considerable
skills as a painter. He was one of the outstanding modernists: a
brilliant satirist, a provocative editor (of *Blast*), an innovative
painter, a formidable propagandist for Vorticism, a powerful
novelist. His satirical poem *One-Way Song* (1933) promotes
himself as the reactionary enemy of English liberalism and uses
couplets with incisive anger: 'The man I am to blow the bloody
gaff / If I were given platforms? The riff-raff / May be handed all
the trumpets that you will. / Not so the golden-tongued.'

Lillard, Charles
Canadian poet *born* California 1944

Lillard was brought up in Alaska, where he worked in the bush, and British Columbia. He taught at the University of Victoria before becoming a freelance writer. He has published several books of poetry including *A Coastal Range* (1983). His poems, written with an insistent rhythm, contrast the fragility of humankind with the durability of nature. 'One View from the Kynoch' begins with men drilling at the forty foot level while three eagles hang off the palisades. At nightfall the eagles are still there: 'They will be here forever / while men like ourselves / come and go, and all our mauling / will leave no more trace than a spray of sunbeams.'

Lindsay, Sir David
Scottish poet *born c*1490 *died c*1555

Son of David Lindsay of the Mount, in Fife, Lindsay became a Gentleman-usher responsible to the young James V whose friend he remained. He became Lyon King of Arms in 1529 and went on various missions as the King's emissary. His sympathy with the common people of Scotland is expressed in such poems as *The Dreme* (1528) in which John the Common-Weill embodies the author's anger: 'Our gentyl men are all degenerate; / Liberalitie and Lawtie, both, are loste; / And Cowardyce with Lordis is laureate; / And knichtlie curage turnit in brag and boste'. John the Common-Weill reappears in Lindsay's masterpiece, *An Pleasant Satyre of the Thrie Estaitis* (1540) in which he condemns the corruption of his country and calls for Reformation.

Lindsay, Maurice
Scottish poet *born* Glasgow 21 July 1918

Son of an insurance manager, Lindsay studied at the Royal Scottish Academy of Music but an injury to his wrist made it impossible for him to achieve his ambition of becoming a professional violinist. After serving with the Cameronians during the Second World War he worked as a journalist and became Controller of Border Television in 1961. Subsequently he was Director of the Scottish Civic Trust. As editor, anthologist and author he did much to promote the cause of Scottish literature. His *Collected Poems* appeared in 1979. In 'Speaking of Scotland' he says 'Scotland's a sense of change, an endless / becoming for which there was never a kind / of wholeness or ultimate category. / Scotland's an attitude of mind.'

Lindsay, Vachel
American poet *born* Springfield, Illinois 10 November 1879 *died* Springfield, Illinois 5 December 1931

From his beloved Springfield, Lindsay tried to reach out to his fellow Americans and enchant them with the populist verse he called the Higher Vaudeville. A prohibitionist with a desire to be 'the great singer of the YMCA Army', he wandered while chanting for his supper from his pamphlet *Rhymes to Be Traded for Bread*. He was a spellbinding performer of poems such as 'General William Booth enters Heaven' in which 'The banjos rattled and the tambourines / Jing-jing-jingled in the hands of Queens.' Lindsay celebrated American heroes like Lincoln and Johnny Appleseed but in later years became a tragically depressed figure who took his own life.

Livesay, Dorothy
Canadian poet *born* Winnipeg 1909

Educated at the University of Toronto and the Sorbonne, Dorothy Livesay participated fully in the cultural life of her country and acted as a writer in residence at Canadian universities. Her poems are highly imaginative and often deal with sombre themes in a fanciful manner. 'Waking in the Dark', for example, contemplates the horror of the modern world then ends abruptly on an arresting image: 'When I see my grandchild running / in a game of football / his helmet is empty / in his right arm / he carries his head.' Her *Collected Poems* appeared in 1972.

Lloyd, David
Welsh poet *born* Llanidloes 1597 *died* 1663

Lloyd became Dean of St Asaph and achieved considerable success with *The Legend of Captain Jones* (1631), a picaresque poem. The hero's encounter with Prester John prompts some lines on the Welsh language: 'Jones, studying how t'express his eloquence / In some strange language which might pose the Prince, / Now trouls him forth a full-mouthed Welsh oration / Boldly delivered as became his nation. / The plot proved right, for not one word of sense / Could be pick from't; which vexed the learned Prince. / His learned linguists are called in to hear, / Who might as well have stopped each other's ear / For aught they understood, and all protest / It was the very language of the Beast.'

Lloyd, Evan
Welsh poet *born* Bala 1734 *died* 1776

An Anglican parson, Lloyd wrote with satirical skill about ecclesiastical anomalies. His 'Portrait of a Bishop' uses the neoclassical couplet with considerable power: 'He in Christ's doctrine deals by way of trade, / Money by preaching poverty is made – / Whose labours were bestowed upon the head, / Whose heart, that found itself neglected, fled, / And now a mere, mere head he lives, with Greek / Carved on his skull and furrowed in his cheek; / Be-greeked, be-latined and be-hebrewed too, / Yet from no tongue has learnt what he should do: / Who lives as if life's business was to write / Learned materials for a schoolboy's kite; / Whose left hand cannot one good action quote, / And all the merit of his right – a Note.'

Lloyd, Ludovic
Welsh poet *born* Shropshire, flourished 1573–1610

A courtier whose poem (from 'Sidanen') in praise of Elizabeth I is formally taut and extravagantly enthusiastic: 'With palm in hand, with laurel crowned, / With olive decked she first was found. / In Parnasse mount with Muses nine / The tenth Sidanen there did shine. // From Brutus brood, from Dardane line, / Sidanen is that Phoenix fine. / From Camber's soil, from Hector's seed/ Sidanen princely doth proceed. // The eagle's youth I wish this queen, / Acanthus-like to flourish green. / As serpents old do cast their skin, / Then she being old may youth begin. // With joyful days and Nestor's years / I wish to her and to her peers / That when Sidanen dyeth I crave / Mausolus tomb Sidanen have.'

Lloyd, Robert
English poet *born* London 1733 *died* 1764

Son of an under-master at Westminster School, Lloyd was educated at Cambridge where he was known for his convivial habits as well as his intellectual powers. He served as an usher under his father but wearied of the work and turned to writing. He was editor of the *St James' Magazine* and when this was a financial failure went to the Fleet Prison. The poet Charles Churchill assisted him by providing an allowance of one guinea per week and raising a subscription on his behalf. Churchill's sister was also devoted to Lloyd. His poem 'The Miseries of a Poet's Life' draws on his own experience: 'By turns protected and caressed, / Defamed, dependent, and distressed.'

Llwyd, Morgan
Welsh poet *born* Cynfal, near Llanffestiniog, Merioneth 1619 *died* 1659

Morgan, who was educated at Wrexham and Brompton Bryan, was a chaplain with the parliamentary army during the Civil War. In 1647 he became a minister at Wrexham. Strongly committed to the ideal of the Commonwealth, he was angry when Cromwell accepted the title 'Lord Protector'. Llywd's work reflects his passionate, provocative character. Poems such as 'Awake, O Lord, Awake Thy Saints' have a combative tone: 'Let Wales and England roused be! / O churches, sleep no more, / and be not

drunk with wealth or wrath – / hark how the nations roar. //
Holland begins to pledge you all / and sip the wrathful cup, / and
peace with them you shall not make / lest you with Ahab sup.'

Llwyd, Richard

Welsh poet *born* Beaumaris, Anglesey 1752 *died* 1835

Richard Llywd, 'the Bard of Snowdon', was a scholar who
specialised in the study of Welsh manuscripts and genealogy. His
'Beaumaris Bay' (1800) puts the landscape under formal pressure
as it is interpreted according to neoclassical conventions: 'The
landscape's various charms the Muse explores, / The druid haunts
and Mona's hallowed shore, / High Arfon soaring o'er the
humbler isle, / The winding Menai, Daniel's mitred pile; / Thy
towers Caernarfon, triple summits Llŷn, / That distant close the
vast and varied scene. / Below amphibious man, as whim
prevails, / Trims up his little bark, and spreads his sails; / Or led
by florid Health, descends to lave, / And skims the surface of the
bracing wave'.

Lochhead, Liz

Scottish poet *born* Motherwell 26 December 1947

Educated at the Glasgow School of Art, Liz Lochhead became a
schoolteacher then a fulltime writer. She has written for the
theatre – *Blood and Ice* (1982) for example – and performed her
own poetry with considerable success. Her verse explores the
world of the modern woman in an anecdotal manner as she
projects images from her own life. 'Poem for My Sister' begins:
'My little sister likes to try my shoes, / to strut in them, / admire
her spindle-thin twelve-year-old legs / in this season's styles. / She
says they fit her perfectly / but wobbles / on their high heels,
they're / hard to balance.' She published *Memo for Spring* in 1972,
The Grimm Sisters in 1981.

Locker-Lampson, Frederick

English poet *born* Greenwich Hospital 29 May 1821 *died* 1895

Frederick Locker's father was civil commissioner at Greenwich
Hospital and the poet was educated at London schools before
becoming a clerk, in 1837, at Mincing Lane. He married the Earl
of Elgin's daughter in 1850 and left his job at the Admiralty. His
first wife died in 1872 and when, two years later, he married
Hannah J Lampson, he added her name to his own. *London Lyrics*
(1857), his single volume of poetry, showed an obvious debt to
the light verse of Praed. In 'Mr Placid's Flirtation' he writes: 'I'll
try and describe, or I won't, if you please, / The cheer that was set
for us under the trees: / You have read the *menu*, may you read it
again; / Champagne, perigord, galantine, and – champagne.'

Lodge, Thomas
English poet *born* London 1558 *died* London September 1625

Son of the Lord Mayor of London, Lodge was educated at Oxford and Lincoln's Inn though he abandoned law for literature. One of the 'University Wits', he wrote plays as well as the prose romance *Rosalyne, Euphues' Golden Legacy* (1590) which supplied Shakespeare with the plot for *As You Like It* and contained lyrics such as Rosalind's madrigal beginning: 'Love in my bosom like a bee / Doth suck his sweet; / Now with his wings he plays with me, / Now with his feet. / Within mine eyes he makes his nest, / His bed amidst my tender breast; / My kisses are his daily feast, / And yet he robs me of my rest. / Ah, wanton, will ye?' In 1597 Lodge turned to medicine and was working as a doctor when he fell victim to the plague.

Logan, John
American poet *born* Iowa 1923

Educated at Coe College and the University of Iowa, Logan was editorial director of the Poetry Seminar in Chicago and taught at the University of Buffalo. His subjective variations on Roman Catholic themes combine ritual and realism, as in 'A Trip to Four or Five Towns': 'A small, slippered priest / pads up. Whom do you seek, my son? / Father, I've come in out of the rain. / I seek refuge from the elemental tears, / for my heavy earthen body runs to grief / and I am apt to drown / in this small and underhanded rain / that drops its dross so delicately / on the hairs of the flowers, my father, / and follows down the veins of leaves / weeping quiet in the wood.'

Logan, William
American poet *born* Boston, Massachusetts 16 November 1950

Logan was raised in a fishing village in Massachusetts and in suburbs of Pittsburgh and New York. He subsequently studied at Yale and Iowa universities. From 1981 to 1983 Logan lived in England as an Amy Lowell Scholar and produced several poetic observations on a disunited kingdom. 'L'Histoire d'Angleterre', for example, reflects on the Irish situation in a violently textured quatrain: 'Petrol tanker wired to border checkpoint, / broken glass in milk, mined hedge, / improvise where older law prevails: / Catholic marries bullets from Catholic guns.' Logan has an admirable determination to draw large conclusions from the subjects he scrutinises in his poems.

Logue, Christopher
English poet *born* Portsmouth, Hampshire 23 November 1926

Logue lived, from 1951-6, in Paris where he published such collections as *Wand and Quadrant* (1953). When he returned to

London he was associated with the dramatic developments at the Royal Court theatre and also established himself as a highly skilled performer of his own poetry. His satirical sense of humour was celebrated in a series of poster poems and in his 'True Stories' column in the magazine *Private Eye*. He has acted in films by Ken Russell and others and the musical *War Music*, based on his versions of Homer, was produced in 1977. *Ode to the Dodo* (1981), his selected poems 1953–78, contains such humorous shorts as 'James Joyce': ''Tis just as well / In the Customs shed / They search my bag / But not my head.'

Longfellow, Henry Wadsworth
American poet *born* Portland, Maine 27 February 1807
died Cambridge, Massachusetts 24 March 1882
On graduating from Bowdoin College in 1825 Longfellow was invited to remain as a teacher of modern languages; in 1834 he was appointed Professor of Modern Languages at Harvard. He was a modest man much affected by the death of his wife in 1835. He married again, in 1843, and was distraught when his second wife was burned to death in 1861. Longfellow's verse uses memorable metres to explore adventurous themes. *The Song of Hiawatha* (1855), in trochaic tetrameters, achieved immense popularity as did the stirringly patriotic 'Paul Revere's Ride': 'So through the night rode Paul Revere; / And so through the night went his cry of alarm / To every Middlesex village and farm, – / A cry of defiance and not of fear.'

Longley, Michael
Irish poet *born* Belfast 1939
Educated in Belfast and at Trinity College, Dublin, Longley became Assistant Director of the Arts Council of Northern Ireland. His *No Continuing City* appeared in 1969, *The Echo Gate* in 1979. His poems describe the Ulster experience in elegiac verse. 'Wounds', for example, is saturated with thoughts of death: 'He collapsed beside his carpet-slippers / Without a murmur, shot through the head / By a shivering boy who wandered in / Before they could turn the television down / Or tidy away the supper dishes. / To the children, to a bewildered wife, / I think "Sorry Missus" was what he said.' In 1971 Longley edited *Causeway*, a survey of the arts in Ulster.

Lovelace, Richard
English poet *born* Woolwich 1618 *died* 1658
Son of a landowner, Lovelace was educated at Charterhouse and Oxford before going to the court. He fought in the Bishops' Wars and in 1642, for presenting to parliament the Kentish petition to restore Charles I to his rights, was imprisoned in the

Gatehouse where he wrote 'To Althea, from Prison' which
concludes: 'Stone Walls doe not a Prison make, / Nor I'ron bars a
Cage; / Mindes innocent and quiet take / That for an Hermitage; /
If I have freedome in my Love, / And in my soule am free; /
Angels alone that sore above, / Injoy such Liberty.' He lost his
Lucasta (Lucy Sacheverall) who married another after false
reports of Lovelace's death; he lost his fortune in pursuit of the
Cavalier cause.

Lover, Samuel
Irish poet *born* Dublin 24 February 1797 *died* 6 July 1868

Son of an English stockbroker, Lover left school to join his father
in business but left to pursue a career as a painter. He became
secretary of the Royal Hibernian Society of Arts in 1831 and in
1832 collected and illustrated *Legends and Stories of Ireland*. His
miniature portraits of such celebrities as Paganini were greatly
admired and he also wrote poems, plays and novels – including
Rory O'More (1837). He wrote words and music for some two
hundred songs, 'Molly Bawn' attaining great popularity; 'Oh!
Molly Bawn, why leave me pining, / All lonely, waiting here for
you? / The stars above are brightly shining, / Because they've
nothing else to do.' He founded *Bentley's Magazine* with Dickens.

Lowe, John
Scottish poet *born* Kenmore, Galloway 1750
died Fredericksburgh 1798

A gardener's son, Lowe studied divinity and became tutor to the
family of a Mr M'Ghie of Airds. One of M'Ghie's daughters was in
love with a surgeon at sea and when this man – Miller – died, Lowe
wrote his best-known poem 'Mary's Dream'. It begins: 'The moon
had climbed the highest hill / Which rises o'er the source of
Dee, / And from the eastern summit shed / Her silver light on
tower and tree; / When Mary laid her down to sleep, / Her
thoughts on Sandy far at sea, / When, soft and low, a voice was
heard, / Saying, "Mary, weep no more for me!"' Lowe intended to
marry a sister of 'Mary' but instead emigrated to America where
he died, apparently, as a result of dissipation.

Lowell, Amy
American poet *born* Brookline, Massachusetts 9 February
1874 *died* Brookline, Massachusetts 12 May 1925

One of the New England Lowells, Amy was twenty-eight when
she felt the poetic call. On reading the early Imagist poems she
declared 'I too am an *Imagiste*' and went to London, in 1913, to
meet the maestro of the movement. However her pushiness
irritated Ezra Pound who felt that Imagism had degenerated into
'Amygism'. She persevered with her work and made an

idiosyncratic poetry of observation, as in 'The Taxi': 'Streets
coming fast, / One after the other, / Wedge you away from me, /
And the lamps of the city prick my eyes / So that I can no longer
see your face.'

Lowell, James Russell

American poet *born* Cambridge, Massachusetts 22 February
1819 *died* Cambridge, Massachusetts 12 August 1891

After studying law at Harvard, Lowell became a successful
journalist who effectively pursued an abolitionist line. He
married Martha White in 1844 and in 1848 collected the first
series of *Biglow Papers*, originally contributed to the Boston
Courier. In these poems Lowell uses Yankee dialect with satirical
vigour and good humour, as in 'The Courtin'': 'He was six foot o'
man, AI, / Clear grit an' human natur', / None could quicker pitch
a ton / Nor dror a furrer straighter.' After the death of his wife in
1853 he became Professor of Belles Lettres at Harvard and (in
1857) editor of the *Atlantic Monthly*. He published a second series
of *Biglow Papers* in 1867.

Lowell, Maria White

American poet *born* 1821 *died* 1853

Raised in New England, where she was educated in an Ursuline
convent, Maria White formed, with her brother William, an
advanced literary circle called 'The Band'. In 1844 she married
James Russell Lowell and persuaded him to support the
abolitionist movement. Three of her four children died and
though she sustained her husband intellectually, she was
physically weak. After her death, her husband published a
memorial edition of her poems. 'An Opium Fantasy' has an
appropriately other-worldly quality: 'Soft hangs the opiate in the
brain, / And lulling soothes the edge of pain, / Till harshest
sound, far off or near, / Sings floating in its mellow sphere.'

Lowell, Robert

American poet *born* Boston, Massachusetts 1 March 1917
died 1977

A member of one of Boston's most famous families, Lowell was
educated at Kenyon College, Louisiana State University and
Harvard. He rejected the establishment stance and Protestant
faith of his family, becoming a Roman Catholic, a conscientious
objector (during the Second World War), and an opponent of the
American involvement in Vietnam in the 1960s. His most
influential volume was *Life Studies* (1959), acclaimed as the
epitome of the Confessional approach to personal experience.
'Central Park', from *Near the Ocean* (1967) ends bleakly: 'We beg
delinquents for our life. / Behind each bush, perhaps a knife; /

each landscaped crag, each flowering shrub, / hides a policeman
with a club.'

Lowry, Malcolm
English poet *born* New Brighton, Merseyside 1909 *died* 1957

Educated at Cambridge, Malcolm Lowry spent some time at sea as
a deckhand and trimmer. He went to Paris in 1934, then lived in
New York and Mexico. He married his second wife, Margerie, in
1939 and settled in a tidal shack in Dollarton, Vancouver: in this,
his home for fourteen years, he completed his masterly novel
Under the Volcano (1947). Though best known as a novelist Lowry
also wrote poems, many of them dealing with his alcoholic
obsessions. 'Comfort' begins: 'You are not the first man to have
the shakes, / the wheels, the horrors, to wear the scarlet
snowshoe, nor yet the invincible harlot / dogged by eyes like
fishnets.'

Lowther, Pat
Canadian poet *born* Vancouver 1935 *died* 1975

Before she was murdered, Pat Lowther was co-chairman of the
League of Canadian Poets. A fourth collection of her poems, *A
Stone Diary*, was published posthumously in 1977. Her poems are
rhythmically brittle and often inquisitive in tone, as she seeks to
make sense of a difficult world. 'The Complicated Airflow'
contemplates the otherness of objects and conveys the
claustrophobic quality of modern domestic life: 'I think
sometimes my passage / through this hall is like a falling / down a
clef into the sea / and where I hit, a hissing / fault springs on the
surface / (warp in a spider web, / spidering of a mirror // What is
whiter than hurt water? / What is more flawed than a broken /
stave of sound?'

Loy, Mina
Anglo–American poet *born* London 1882 *died* 1966

A member of an affluent English family, Mina Loy was
determined to break away from the Victorian attitudes of her
parents and moved to Europe to study painting. In 1916 she came
to New York and became part of an advanced artistic circle; she
lived in Paris in the 1920s and managed a shop specialising in the
sale of painted lampshades. She returned to the USA in 1936. Her
collection *Lunar Baedeker* (1923) contains a modernist tribute to
feminine creativity: 'LIFE / A leap with nature / Into the essence /
Of unpredicted Maternity /Against my thigh / Touch of
infinitesimal motion /Scarcely perceptible / Undulation'.

Lucie-Smith, Edward

English poet *born* Kingston, Jamaica 27 February 1933

Educated at Oxford, Lucie-Smith made his reputation in England as an art critic, anthologist, broadcaster and poet. Although he has encouraged experimentalism in the visual arts and helped launch the pop poetry of the Liverpool Poets by editing *The Liverpool Scene* (1967) his own verse is stylistically restrained. 'The Lesson', from *A Tropical Childhood* (1961), recalls how he reacted to the death of his father when he was ten. It ends with an image of goldfish in a bowl and children at school assembly: 'Somewhere in myself / Pride like a goldfish flashed a sudden fin.' *The Burnt Child* (1975) is his autobiography.

Lydgate, John

English poet *born c*1370 *died* 1452

Lydgate, the 'Monk of Bury', was educated at Oxford and in France and Italy where he studied the work of Dante and Boccaccio. He was prior of Hatfield for eleven years but spent most of his adult life in the Benedictine Abbey of Bury St Edmunds. A prominent figure of his time, he received a royal pension and produced huge amounts of occasional verse as well as translations and verse paraphrases. His lines on how 'Canace, Condemned to Death by her Father Aeolus, Sends to Her Guilty Brother Macareus the Last Testimony of her Unhappy Passion' are emotionally charged: 'This is mine end, I may it not astart; / O brother mine, there is no more to say'.

astart, escape

Lyly, John

English poet *born* Weald of Kent *c*1554
buried 30 November 1606

Educated at Oxford, where he was a Fellow, Lyly also studied at Oxford. He was Member of Parliament successively for Hindon, Aylesbury and Appleby. His most celebrated work is the prose romance *Euphues* (1579, sequel in 1580), a didactic work whose elaborately antithetical and allusive style gave rise to the term 'euphuism'. Lyly also wrote several dramas, including *Campaspe* (1584) which contains the lyric beginning: 'Cupid and my Campaspe played / At cards for kisses, Cupid paid; / He stakes his quiver, bow, and arrows, / His mother's doves, and team of sparrows: / Loses them too; then, down he throws / The coral of his lip, the rose / Growing on's cheek (but none knows how)'.

Lyon, Lilian Bowes

English poet *born* 1855 *died* 1949

Although she was born a wealthy woman and was related to the royal family, Lilian Bowes Lyon was determined to confront the social tensions of her time. She was head of the Women's Voluntary Services in London and during the Second World War worked in the East End of London, helping poor people through the blitz. Wounded, she refused to have immediate treatment and both her legs were amputated after the onset of gangrene. She left a large part of her wealth to help slum children. In her poem 'A Shepherd's Coat' she declares; 'Time tells a marginal story; / Dilates with midsummer that less than leaf / A mute heart, light heart, blown along the pavement.'

Lyttelton, Lord
English poet *born* 1709 *died* 22 August 1773

Educated at Eton and Oxford, George Lyttelton – son of Sir Thomas Lyttelton – entered Parliament where he was a formidable foe to Sir Robert Walpole. He became Secretary to the Prince of Wales and later Lord of the Treasury and Chancellor of the Exchequer. He wrote several books, including a now-forgotten *History of Henry II*, and generally did (in the words of Dr Johnson) 'nothing to be despised and little to be admired'. Lyttelton's wife, Lucy Fortescue of Devonshire, died in 1746 and this loss led to the composition of 'Monody': 'In vain I look around / O'er all the well-known ground, / My Lucy's wonted footsteps to descry; / Where oft we used to walk, / Where oft in tender talk / We saw the summer sun go down the sky'.

Lytton, Robert, Earl of
English poet *born* London 8 November 1831
died Paris 24 November 1891

Son of the first Baron Lytton, the novelist and statesman, Edward Robert Bulwer, First Earl of Lytton, was educated at Harrow and Bonn. He was private secretary to his uncle Sir Henry Bulwer (later Lord Dalling and Bulwer) in Washington and Florence and subsequently obtained diplomatic posts in Europe. He became Viceroy of India in 1876 and in 1887 was appointed ambassador in Paris. His literary works, usually published under the pseudonym Owen Meredith, include *Clytemnestra* (1855), *Lucile* (1860) and *Fables in Song* (1874). *Glenaveril* (1885), a novel in verse, contains some memorable lines: 'There be three hundred different ways and more / Of speaking, but of weeping only one'.

Macaulay, Lord Thomas Babington
English poet *born* Rothley Temple, Leicestershire
25 October 1800 *died* 28 December 1859

Educated at Cambridge, Macaulay was called to the Bar in 1826. As a Member of Parliament, he supported Liberal programmes, calling for parliamentary reform and the abolition of slavery; as a member of The Supreme Council in India, from 1834 to 1838, he was responsible for the Indian penal code. In 1842 he published *Lays of Ancient Rome* and his *History of England* (4 vols, 1848-61) was recognised as a classic. His narrative poems, such as *The Armada*, are vivid and vigorous; 'Far on the deep the Spaniard saw, along each southern shire, / Cape beyond cape, in endless range, those twinkling points of fire. / The fisher left his skiff to rock on Tamar's glittering waves: / The rugged miners poured to war from Mendip's sunless caves.'

MacBeth, George
Scottish poet *born* Shotts, Lanarkshire 19 January 1932

George MacBeth was educated at Oxford and later worked as a poetry producer for the BBC. One of the most prolific poets of his time, he developed a macabre style to express surrealistic scenarios in technically dazzling verse. His use of black comedy generated a genre of 'sick' and (slick) verse. His poem on his own death, 'And I bequeath', offers a typically morbid image: 'And I bequeath my empty head, / My hollow flesh, and leaking bones, / To those well nourished upon groans / Who operate upon the dead.' Increasingly, however, MacBeth has humanised his Gothic imagination through a concern for others, implying that if death is to be defeated the poet must encourage the living.

MacCaig, Norman
Scottish poet *born* Edinburgh 14 November 1910

Norman MacCaig's father owned a chemist's shop in Edinburgh and the poet studied Classics at Edinburgh University. He was a schoolteacher in Edinburgh from 1934-70 and from 1970-9 was Reader in Poetry at Stirling University. His poems are generally set in Edinburgh or around Lochinver (his summer home) and he treats townscapes and landscapes with Metaphysical wit and great technical facility. In his poem 'Return to Scalpay' (his mother was a native of Scalpay) he writes 'I / Have no defence, / For half my thought and half my blood is Scalpay, / Against that pure, hardheaded innocence, / That shows love without shame, weeps without shame, / Whose every thought is hospitality'.

McCarthy, Thomas
Irish poet *born* Cappoquin, County Waterford 1954

Educated at University College, Cork, McCarthy joined the staff of the Cork City Library. He won the Patrick Kavanagh Award in 1977. In 1978, the year *The First Convention* appeared, he was a Fellow of the Iowa University Writing Programme. *The Sorrow-Garden* apeared in 1981. McCarthy writes a bookish style of poetry, building atmospheric scenarios, writing about novelists (Francis Stuart and Isaac Bashevis Singer) and his poem 'My father, reading' suggests a parental reason for this: 'My father became famous on his word-journeys, / sailing (on extended leave), with Scott, avenging / all crime with *Four Just Men*. Every book I open / brings him to the window'.

McCauley, James
Australian poet *born* Lakemba, Sydney 1917 *died* 1976

A graduate of Sydney University and a schoolteacher, McCauley was Director of Research and Civil Affairs in the Military Government of Papua and New Guinea during the Second World War. He edited the quarterly *Quadrant* and was Professor of English Literature in the University of Tasmania. With his friend Harold Stewart, McCauley caused a sensation in 1944 when he successfully submitted to the modernist journal *Angry Penguins* poems, purporting to be the work of the nonexistent poet 'Ern Malley', composed of bits and pieces of random texts. A convert to Roman Catholicism, his own poems are orderly and aphoristic: 'Judgement is simply trying to reject / A part of what we are because it hurts' he wrote in 'Because'.

McCrae, Hugh
Australian poet *born* Melbourne 1876 *died* 1958

Son of the well-known Australian man of letters George Gordon McCrae, Hugh McCrae studied architecture then worked as a contributor (of drawings as well as verse) to the Sydney *Bulletin*. He subsequently worked as an actor and a lecturer; in 1953 he was awarded the Order of the British Empire for his distinguished contribution to Australian literature. McCrae uses his great facility for rhyming to create comic scenarios, as in 'Camden Town'; 'I leap with rage and seize my stick, / Like Hitler turned quite lunatic, / Throw open drawers and cupboards wide, / And canter down the stairs outside, / Exclaiming "Damn!" and "Well, I'm blowed!" / Until I reach Macarthur Road.'

McCrae, John
Canadian poet *born* Guelph, Ontario 30 November 1872 *died* January 1918

Educated at the University of Toronto, McCrae qualified as a doctor and wrote a standard *Text Book of Pathology* (1914). During the First World War he served as a medical officer in the front line during the Second Battle of Ypres. He is still best known for his elegiac war poem 'In Flanders Fields': 'In Flanders fields the poppies blow / Between the crosses, row on row / That mark our place; and in the sky / The larks, still bravely singing, fly / Scarce heard amid the guns below.' Put in charge of a hospital at Boulogne, he died of pneumonia before he was able to take up the appointment.

McCuiag, Ronald
Australian poet *born* Newcastle, New South Wales 1908

After attending school in Sydney, McCuaig went to work in a
warehouse and later gravitated to radio journalism. Later he
worked for newspapers including the *Sydney Morning Herald* and
The Bulletin. Some of his imitations of seventeenth century poetry
have the limitations of pastiche, but his poems on contemporary
subjects are executed with a stylish flair for speech rhythms. 'The
Commercial Traveller's Wife', a dramatic monologue, begins
revealingly: 'I'm living with a commercial traveller; / He's away,
most of the time; / Most I see of him's his wife; as for her: / I'm
just home from a show, / And there I am undressing, in my
shirt . . . The door's opened; it's Gert'.

MacDiarmid, Hugh
Scottish poet *born* Langholm 11 August 1892
died Edinburgh 9 September 1978

Born Christopher Murray Grieve, this postman's son adopted his
pseudonym in 1922. Using the resources of the etymological
dictionary and the oral rhythms acquired as a child on the
Scottish Border, MacDiarmid created 'Synthetic Scots', an
experimental idiom that avoided regionalism and displayed an
international range of reference. His masterpiece, *A Drunk Man
looks at the Thistle* (1926) describes the hero's journey as he begins
under the influence of Scotch spirit and ends with an awareness of
Scottish spirituality. A combative intellectual, MacDiarmid's
credo was uncompromising: 'I'll ha'e nae hauf-way hoose,
but aye be whaur / Extremes meet – it's the only way I ken / To
dodge the curse conceit o' bein' richt / That damns the vast
majority o' men.'

ken know

McDonagh, Donagh
Irish poet *born* Dublin 1912 *died* 1968

Son of Thomas McDonagh, a leader of the Irish Rising of 1916,
McDonagh became a District Justice in Wexford (subsequently in
Dublin). His verse play *Happy as Larry* (1946) was internationally
acclaimed. The title poem of his collection *The Hungry Grass*
(1947) is a morbid meditation on a landscape visited by death:
'Here in a year when poison from the air / First withered in
despair the growth of spring / Some skull-faced wretch whom
nettle could not save / Crept on four bones to his last
scattering, // Crept, and the shrivelled heart which drove his
thought /Towards platters brought in hospitality / Burst as the
wizened eyes measured the miles / Like dizzy walls forbidding him
the city.'

MacDonagh, Thomas

Irish poet *born* Tipperary 1878 *died* Dublin May 1916

Educated at the Royal University of Ireland, where he subsequently lectured, he was executed for his part in the Easter Rising of 1916. He published an important critical work on *Literature in Ireland* (1916) expounding his idea of the 'Irish Mode' which consists of a long line with an anapaestic beat and a wavering movement counterpointing the anapaestic rhythm. His 'John-John' uses the style of folksong: 'I dreamt last night of you, John-John, / And thought you called to me; / And when I woke this morning, John, / Yourself I hoped to see'. He also produced a splendid version of 'The Yellow Bittern' from the eighteenth century Irish of Cathal Buidhe Mac Giolla Ghunna.

MacDonald, George

Scottish poet *born* Huntly, Aberdeenshire 10 December 1824 *died* 18 September 1905

A farmer's son, MacDonald was educated at King's College, Aberdeen and at Highbury Technical College. He became a Congregationalist minister in 1850 but resigned five years later when he turned to journalism. In 1859 he became a professor at Bedford College London. He published *Poems* (1857) then explored an imaginative world of fantasy in *Phantastes* (1858) and *Lilith* (1895), romances that influenced the work of J R R Tolkien and C S Lewis. There is an ecstatic quality in poems such as 'Longing': 'White dove of David, flying overhead, / Golden with sunlight on thy snowy wings, / Outspeeding thee my longing thoughts are fled / To find a home afar from men and things'.

McDonald, Nan

Australian poet *born* Sydney 1921 *died* 1973

An Arts graduate of Sydney University, Nan McDonald worked as an editor with a Sydney publishing house. Her contemplative verse has great dignity and emotional force. 'The Bus-Ride Home' begins with a reflection on the death of a miner, Old Jack, and closes with a personal response to the fragility of life; 'My hand lay / Across my bag, I saw how white the bone / Shone through the skin; and round us the weak light / Gave way before a stealthy tide of darkness / That scoured the hollows out in face and throat / And filled the sockets of the eyes with shade. / A cold breath drifted inward from the night / And someone shut the glass, as if in fear / Our flesh would crumble at its touch to dust.'

MacDonogh, Patrick

Irish poet *born* 1902 *died* 1961

MacDonogh left Ireland to live in London: nevertheless he retained the Irish Revivalist approach to language, seeking to simulate Gaelic rhythms in his verse. 'The Widow of Drynam' is a memorable dramatic monologue: 'I stand in my door and look over the low fields of Drynam. / No man, but the one man has known me, no child but the one / Grew big at my breast, and what are my sorrows beside / That pride and that glory? I come from devotions on Sunday / And leave them to pity or spite, and though I who had music have none / But crying of seagulls at morning and calling of curlews at night, / I wake and remember my beauty and think of my son / Who would stare the loud fools into silence / and rip the dull parish asunder.'

MacEwan, Gwendolyn
Canadian poet *born* Toronto 1941

Gwendolyn MacEwan decided, early in life, to devote herself to writing and has published novels and stories as well as the poems in *Magic Animals* (1974) and *Earthlight* (1982). Her work has a wide thematic range and she can write ('The Child Dancing') about an incident in the Warsaw ghetto or alter our perception of T E Lawrence by making him say, in the dramatic monologue 'Tall Tales': 'Poets only play with words, you know; they too / are masters of the Lie, the Grand Fiction. / Poets and men like me who fight for something / contained in words, but not words. // What if the whole show was a lie, and it bloody well was – / would I still lie to you? Of course I would.'

McGee, Thomas D'Arcy
Irish poet *born* 1825 *died* 1868

A member of the Young Ireland political party, McGee had to leave Ireland as a result of his political activities. He emigrated to Canada and became Minister for Agriculture. He died at the hands of an assassin. His *Collected Poems* (1869) contains compositions such as 'The Celts' which reveal Irish Revivalist sentiments: 'Long, long ago, beyond the misty space / Of twice a thousand years, / In Erin old there dwelt a mighty race, / Taller than Roman spears; / Like oaks and towers they had a giant grace, / Were fleet as deers, / With wind and waves they made their 'biding place, / These western shepherd seers.'

McGonagall, William
Scottish poet *born* Edinburgh March 1925
died Edinburgh 29 September 1902

McGonagall's father, an Irish cotton weaver, settled in Dundee when the self-styled 'Poet and Tragedian' was eleven. After working as a weaver, McGonagall 'received the spirit of poetry' in 1877. Although his verse was technically crude he was an

enthusiastic performer of his own (and Shakespeare's) work.
Received as a figure of fun by audiences in public houses – which
– he took himself seriously. His 'Poetic Gems' are still immensely
popular on account of their doggerel vigour: 'Oh, thou demon
Drink, thou fell destroyer; / Thou curse of society, and its
greatest annoyer.'

McGough, Roger
English poet *born* Liverpool 9 November 1937

McGough, who was educated at the University of Hull, came to
prominence as one of the leading Liverpool poets of the 1960s – a
time when, due to the impact of the Beatles, Liverpool was a
magical name with the news media. A witty poet and a skilled
performer, he sang with the pop group 'The Scaffold' and toured
the country giving readings of his work. He excells at giving
urban life a romantic gloss, as in 'My Busseductress': 'She is as
beautiful as bustickets / and smells of old cash / drinks guinness
off duty / eats sausage and mash. / But like everyone else / she has
her busdreams too / when the peakhour is over / and there's
nothing to do.'

McGuckian, Medbh
Irish poet *born* Belfast 1950

Educated at Queen's University, Belfast, Medbh McGuckian
became an English teacher at St Patrick's College, Knock. She
published *Portrait of Joanna* and *Single Ladies* in 1980; *The Flower
Master* in 1982. Her work is densely metaphorical, full of arresting
images that put everyday objects in a poetic perspective. 'Power-
cut' observes (in the second of three stanzas): 'My dishes on the
draining-board / Lie at an even keel, the baby lowered / Into his
lobster-pot pen; my sponge / Disintegrates in water like a bird's
nest, / A permanent wave gone west.'

MacInnes, Tom
Canadian poet *born* Dresden, Ontario 1867 *died* 1951

Educated at the University of Toronto, MacInnes was called to
the Bar in 1893. He published *Complete Poems* in 1923 and *In the
Old of my Age* in 1947. A witty poet, he can write elegantly and
ironically of erotic experience, most ingeniously in 'Zalinka': 'I
was glad that she slept for I never / Can tell what the finish will
be: / What enamoured, nocturnal endeavour / May end in the
killing of me: / But, in the moonlit obscuro / Of that silken,
somniferous lair, / Like a poet consumed with a far lust / Of
things unapproachably fair / I fancied her body of stardust – /
Pounded of spices and stardust – / Out of the opulent air.'

Mackay, Charles
Scottish poet *born* Perth 27 March 1814 *died* 24 December 1889

A naval officer's son, Mackay was educated at the Caledonian Asylum in London – where he settled in 1834 as a journalist and author of books of verse and prose. He became editor of the *Illustrated London News* in 1852 and reported on the American Civil War for *The Times*. His hugely popular lyrics were set to music by Sir H R Bishop. One of them, 'The Good Time Coming', had a circulation of almost half a million: 'There's a good time coming, boys, / A good time coming; / We may not live to see the day, / But earth shall glisten in the ray / Of the good time coming. / Cannon-balls may aid the truth, / But thought's a weapon stronger; / We'll win a battle by its aid – /Wait a little longer.'

McKay, Claude
American poet *born* Jamaica 1891 *died* 1948

McKay – whose father was a peasant proprietor who cultivated coffee, cocoa, bananas and sugarcane in Jamaica – came to the USA in 1912. He was educated at Kansas State University then moved to New York. He visited London in 1919, the Soviet Union in 1922, and lived in Europe for ten years, coming into contact with the American expatriate writers of the 1920s. His first novel *Home to Harlem* (1928) was a critical and commercial success. His *Selected Poems* appeared in 1953. In 'The Negro's Tragedy' he wrote; 'It is the Negro's tragedy I feel / Which binds me like a heavy iron chain, / It is the Negro's wounds I want to heal / Because I know the keenness of his pain.'

McKay, Don
Canadian poet *born* Owen Sound, Ontario 1942

After an education in Ontario and Wales, Don McKay took a teaching job in London. He published *Long Sault* in 1975 and *Birding, or Desire* in 1983. McKay's poems often display a sardonic attitude towards life and (for example in 'Alias Rock Dove, Alias Holy Ghost') reduce humankind to 'the poor sons of bitches'. In 'March Snow' he reverses the traditional Canadian affirmation of the snowscape by asserting 'The snow is sick' and ending with 'the atrocity of tulips thrusting up / dog-penis red and raw.'

McKellar, J A R
Australian poet *born* Dulwich Hill, Sydney 1904 *died* 1932

After attending Sydney High School, John Alexander Ross McKellar went to work for the Bank of New South Wales where he established himself as a future general manager. While pursuing his cultural interests (including a passion for music and painting) he also demonstrated an athletic talent as a footballer and cricketer. After a game of rugby, he became ill with pneumonia which led to his early death. His athletic and aesthetic interests are combined in his thoughtful poem 'Football Field: Evening': 'To strain and struggle to the end of strength; / To lean on skill, not ask a gift of chance, / To win, or lose, and recognise at length / The game the thing; the rest, a circumstance.'

Mackenzie, Kenneth
Australian poet *born* Perth, Western Australia 1913
died Tallong Creek, near Goulburn (NSW) January 1955

After studying law at the University of Western Australia, Mackenzie worked as a film and drama critic in Sydney. He was with the Australian military forces during the Second World War; as his novel *Dead Men Rising* (1951) recalls, he was a member of the garrison at Cowra prison-camp when there was a mass-escape of Japanese. He drowned at the age of forty-two. Mackenzie's verse is concerned with the quality of poetic consciousness, a subject he approaches in 'Caesura': 'Sometimes at night when the heart stumbles and stops / a full second endless the endless steps / that lead me on through this time terrain / without edges and beautiful terrible / are gone never to proceed again.'

McKuen, Rod
American poet *born* Oakland, California 29 April 1933

McKuen worked as a labourer, a radio disc-jockey, a newspaper columnist and (during the Korean War) a psychological-warfare scriptwriter. He has enjoyed enormous popular success: his film score for *The Prime of Miss Jean Brodie* earned him an Academy Award Nomination and his books of verse sold more than seven million copies in a four-year period. He has written songs for some of America's most popular singers, including Frank Sinatra who recorded *A Man Alone*. His sentimental appeal is obvious in, for example, 'Corners': 'I turn each corner still / hoping for the Virgin Mary to appear. / She'll be dressed in cardboard blue / the way she was in Sunday school'.

McLachlan, Alexander
Canadian poet *born* near Glasgow, 1818 *died* 1840

McLachlan left Scotland and settled in Ontario in 1840. Beginning with one acre of land at Erin, he became a successful farmer, eventually moving to Amaranth. His *Poetical Works*, published in 1900, shows his enthusiasm for his adopted country. 'O! come to the greenwood shade', in particular, expresses a deep distrust of urban life and a love of the open air: 'O! come to the greenwood shade, / Away from the city's din, / From the heartless strife of trade, / And the fumes of beer and gin; / Where commerce spreads her fleets, / Where bloated luxury lies, / And Want as she prowls the streets, / Looks on with her wolfish eyes.'

MacLean, Sorley
Scottish poet *born* Osgaig, Raasay 26 October 1911

Regarded as the most gifted Gaelic poet of the century, MacLean was educated at Edinburgh University. In 1940 he joined the Signals Corps, was posted to Egypt and was seriously injured at the Battle of El Alamein. He subsequently taught in Edinburgh then became headmaster of Plockton Secondary School, Wester Ross. In 1972 he retired to Skye. His sequence *Dàin do Eimhir* (1943) sets an intense love affair against the background of the Spanish Civil War. Something of MacLean's quality comes through his own translations of his selected poems, *Spring Tide and Neap Tide* (1977), as in 'Ebb': 'I am not striving with the tree that will not bend for me, / and the apples will not grow on any branch'.

MacLeish, Archibald
American poet *born* Glencoe, Illinois 7 May 1892 *died* 1982

Educated at Yale and Harvard, MacLeish became a lawyer. He was a captain in the Field Artillery in the First World War and in 1923 abandoned his law practice to live in Paris among the expatriate artistic community there. When he returned to the USA he became a prominent public figure, editing *Fortune*, acting as Librarian of Congress (1939-44) and serving in the US Government (1941-5) – eventually as assistant secretary of state. He received many honours, gaining the Pulitzer Prize in 1932 for his long poem *Conquistador* and becoming, in 1949, Professor of Rhetoric at Harvard. In 'Ars Poetica', a fanciful declaration of his poetic faith, he said 'A poem should not mean / But be.'

Macleod, Norman
Scottish poet *born* Campbeltown, Argyll 3 June 1812
died 16 June 1872

A minister's son, Macleod was educated at Glasgow and Edinburgh universities and was ordained in 1838. During Scotland's theological Disruption of 1843, he remained faithful to the Church of Scotland and from 1851 he ministered in Glasgow where he put his philanthropic theories into practice. He became chaplain to Queen Victoria in 1857 and Moderator of the General Assembly of the Church of Scotland in 1869. From 1860, until his death, he edited the religious magazine *Good Words* in which his most famous work, 'Trust in God', first appeared: 'Courage, brother! do not stumble, / Though thy path is dark as night; / There's a star to guide the humble – / Trust in God and do the right.'

MacNeice, Louis
Irish poet *born* Belfast 12 September 1907
died 3 September 1963

Son of the Protestant Bishop of Down, MacNeice was educated at
Marlborough and Oxford. He was a Lecturer in Classics at
Birmingham University from 1930–1936. With Auden he went
to Iceland, a trip that provided the material for their *Letters from
Iceland* (1937). From 1941–1949 he worked with the BBC in
London, producing radio drama and features. MacNeice was
linked with Auden, Spender and Day Lewis as one of the 'Pylon
Poets' of the 1930s but his work was always more lyrical than that
label suggests. His lively sense of humour is evident in 'Bagpipe
Music': 'It's no go the Government grants, it's no go the
elections, / Sit on your arse for fifty years and hang your hat on a
pension.'

Macpherson, James
Scottish poet *born* Ruthven 27 October 1736
died 17 February 1796

Macpherson's supposed translations of Ossian, son of Fingal,
were among the most popular works of the eighteenth century. A
crofter's son, Macpherson claimed he had translated the Gaelic
poems of Ossian when actually he had improvised a Celtic epic on
the basis of a few authentic fragments. *Fingal* (1761) and *Temora*
(1763) are written in an ecstatic style that influenced the
Romantic movement. Macpherson's Ossianic poems are
impressive works of fantasy. He also published poems under his
own name, for example 'The Hunter' with its combative
Highland hero; 'His country's love the youthful hero warms, /
And vengeance strung his almost wearied arms.'

Macpherson, Jay
Canadian poet *born* 1931

Jay Macpherson came to Canada from England and studied at the
universities of Carleton and Toronto where she became a
lecturer. She uses rhyme in an effective manner, containing her
expansive imagination in formally tight poems. 'The Fisherman'
is an example of her ability to lift verse beyond description: 'Old
Adam on the naming-day / Blessed each and let it slip away: / The
fisher of the fallen mind / Sees no occasion to be kind, // But on
his catch proceeds to sup; / Then bends, and at one slurp suck
up / The lake and all that therein is / To slake that hungry gut of
his, // Then whistling makes for home and bed / As the last
morning breaks in red; / But God the Lord with patient grin /
Lets down his hook and hoicks him in.'

McWhirter, George
Canadian poet *born* Ulster 1939

Moving to Canada from Ulster, McWhirter became a member of the Department of Creative Writing at the University of British Columbia and managing director of *Prism International* magazine. He has published collections of short stories and the poems in, for example, *Fire Before Dark* (1984). He has an obsessive style of writing, scrutinising a subject until he forces a conclusion. 'Reminder' begins as an encounter with a spider which spins a spell, as well as a web, round the poet who eventually approaches his wife; 'Seeing the fine / incarceration of my face, she screams. / I blow the web off with a kiss that clings.'

Magnan, James Clarence
Irish poet *born* Dublin 1805 *died* Dublin 1849

Without a formal education, Magnan learned various languages and worked in a scrivener's office then in the library at Trinity College. His addiction to drugs and alcohol reduced him to poverty and he died of cholera in Meath Hospital. In 'Shapes and Signs' he gives a compelling form to his fancies: 'I exult alone in one wild hour – / That hour in which the red cup drowns / The memories it anon renews / In ghastlier guise, in fiercer power – / *Then* Fancy brings me golden crowns, / And visions of all brilliant hues / Lap my lost soul in gladness, / Until I wake again, / And the dark lava-fires of madness / Once more sweep through my brain.'

Mahon, Derek
Irish poet *born* Belfast 1941

Educated at Trinity College, Dublin, Mahon worked as a teacher and writer in Ireland, Canada, the USA and England. He settled in London and was, for a while, poetry editor of the *New Statesman*. *Night Crossing* appeared in 1968, *Poems 1962–78* in 1979. His verse, full of telling descriptive detail, displays a craftsman's concern with stanzaic form, as in 'A Garage in Co Cork': 'Surely you paused at this roadside oasis / In your nomadic youth, and saw the mound / Of never-used cement, the curious faces, / The soft-drink ads and the uneven ground / Rainbowed with oily puddles, where a snail / Had scrawled its slimy, phosphorescent trail.'

Mahoney, Francis Sylvester
Irish poet *born* Cork 1804 *died* Paris 18 May 1866

Son of a wool manufacturer, Mahoney was educated at the Jesuit College, Clongoweswood, County Kildare, where he became Professor of Rhetoric before being expelled from the Order. He moved to London, wrote for *Fraser's Magazine*, and under the pseudonym Father Prout produced his humorous *Reliques* (1836 and 1876). The man who described himself as 'an Irish potato seasoned with Attic salt' was eventually reconciled with the Church. His 'The Bells of Shandon' reveals his metrical ingenuity: 'With deep affection and recollection / I often think of the Shandon bells, / Whose sounds so wild would, in days of childhood, / Fling round my cradle their magic spells.'

Mair, Charles
Canadian poet *born* Lanark, Ontario 1838 *died* 1927

Educated at Queen's University, Kingston, Ontario, Mair published *Dreamland and Other Poems* (1868) and the poetic drama *Tecumseh* (1886). His poems are composed in praise of Canada and though his verse is technically conventional it has, at its best in 'Winter', a physical feeling for the environment: 'When gadding snow makes hill-sides white, / And icicles form more and more; / When niggard Frost stands all the night, / And taps at snoring Gaffer's door; / When watch-dogs bay the vagrant wind, / And shiv'ring kine herd close in shed; / When kitchens chill, and maids unkind, / Send rustic suitors home to bed – / Then do I say the winter cold, / It seems to me, is much too bold.'

Maitland, Sir Richard
Scottish poet *born* East Lothian 1496 *died* 20 March 1586

Maitland studied law in St Andrews and Paris and served James V, Mary Queen of Scots and James VI as Privy Councillor, judge and (from 1562–7) keeper of the Great Seal. His greatest service to Scottish literature was his compilation of the Maitland Manuscript, a folio containing forty-one of his own poems and 141 poems by Scottish poets of the fifteenth and sixteenth centuries. He became blind in middle age, a fact he reflects on in his 'Solace in Age': 'Quhone young men cumis fra the grene, / At the futball playing had bene, / With brokin spald, / I thank my god I want my ene, / And am so ald.'

Quhone when; *spald* collar-bone; *ene* eyes; *ald* old

Mallet, David
Scottish poet *born* Crieff, Perthshire *c* 1705
died London 21 April 1765

Born David Malloch, the poet changed his name after the critic John Dennis ridiculed him as 'Molloch'. He came to London in 1723 and set about building a literary career through various contacts: he was, for example, first friendly with Pope but later criticised him on behalf of Lord Bolingbroke who left Mallet all his works and manuscripts. He married into a fortune when he took a second wife and he generally cultivated the rich and influential so that he lived from several sinecures. Mallet's best-remembered work is the literary ballad 'William and Margaret' which begins: ''Twas at the silent, solemn hour /When night and morning meet; / In glided Margaret's grimly ghost, / And stood at William's feet.'

Mandel, Eli
Canadian poet *born* Estevan, Saskatchewan 3 December 1922

Educated at the universities of Saskatchewan and Toronto, Mandel became a professor at York University, Toronto. He has published much critical work including a book on *Irving Layton* (1969) and anthologies including *Poets of Contemporary Canada* (1972). His selected poems, *Dreaming Backwards*, appeared in 1981. Mandel's best poems, such as 'The Madwomen of the Plaza de Mayo', use a conversationally clear language heightened by indignation: 'in the Plaza the Presidential palace / reveals soldiers like fences with steel spikes / the rhythm of lost bodies / the rhythm of loss // A soldier is a man who is not a man. / A fence, a spike / A nail in somebody's eye. / Lost man.'

Manifold, J S
Australian poet *born* Melbourne 1915

John S Manifold was educated at Cambridge, worked as a teacher, and went to Europe and West Africa with the British army in the Second World War. His poem 'The Tomb of Lieut John Learmonth, A I F', in terza rima, is a moving tribute to a friend. It demonstrates the emotional strength and verbal control possessed by Manifold; 'He also spun his pistol like a toy, / Turned to the hills like wolf or kangaroo, / And faced destruction with a bitter joy. / His freedom gave him nothing else to do / But set his back against his family tree / And fight the better for the fact he knew / He was as good as dead.' Subsequently Manifold did much to revive the indigenous bush-ballad.

Mansfield, Katherine
New Zealand poet *born* Wellington 14 October 1888
died 9 January 1923

Daughter of a banker, Katherine Mansfield Beauchamp came to London and established herself as a forceful critic and formidable intellectual. She married George Bowden in 1909, left him after a few days, and in 1911 met Middleton Murry whom she married in 1918 on obtaining a divorce from Bowden. Illness, caused by a lung complaint, made her travel in search of a suitable climate. She was friendly with D H Lawrence who portrayed her as Gudrun in *Women in Love* (1920). Her short stories are masterly; her *Poems* (1923), such as 'Sanary', vivid; 'The shimmering, blinding web of sea / Hung from the sky'.

Marlowe, Christopher
English poet *born* Canterbury February 1564
died Deptford 30 May 1593

Son of a shoemaker, Marlowe was educated at Cambridge.
Deciding against an ecclesiastical career he moved to London
where he became famous as a playwright, with *Tamberlaine the
Great* (1587), and infamous as a blasphemer and brawler. His
alleged atheism was denounced by the Privy Council and he was
stabbed to death by Ingram Frizer after an argument in a tavern.
His non-dramatic verse, as in the unfinished *Hero and Leander*,
shows a mastery of the Italianate style. His best-known lyric is
'The Passionate Shepherd to his Love': 'Come live with me and be
my love, / And we will all the pleasures prove / That hills and
valleys, dates and fields, / Woods, or steepy mountain yields.'

Marshall, Tom
Canadian poet *born* Niagara Falls 1938

After an education at Queen's University, Tom Marshall became a
lecturer at his alma mater. His collection *The Elements* appeared in
1980. His work shows a strongly developed social conscience and
in 'Politics' he considers the contours of the Canadian Eden: 'An
almost monochrome snowscape / is the beginning of our myth. /
Against it I have set / the brown and gold richness / of a room, a
large room / with three large windows. Snow / flickers like cinema
in all of them.' At the end of the poem he asserts that 'no
mythology finally will matter / (theirs or ours) unless it is true / to
a single room with its large windows / a single room made of
many windows / opening and closing their eyes of cold snow.'

Marvell, Andrew
English poet *born* Winestead-in-Holderness, Yorkshire 31 March
1621 *died* London 18 August 1678

Son of a Calvinist clergyman, Marvell was educated at Cambridge
and was later tutor to some of the leading Puritans, including
Cromwell's ward William Dutton. He became Milton's assistant
in the Latin Secretaryship in 1657 and from 1659–78 he was
Member of Parliament for Hull. Marvell was equally adept at
using private and public poetic modes. His 'Horatian Ode' of
1650 celebrates 'restless Cromwell' and records the execution of
Charles I. His erotic poem 'To his Coy Mistress' arouses passion
through elaborately expansive metaphysical conceits: 'An
hundred years should go to praise / Thine eyes, and on thy
forehead gaze. / Two hundred to adore each breast: / But thirty
thousand to the rest.'

Masefield, John

English poet *born* Ledbury, Hertfordshire 1 June 1878
died 12 May 1967

A solicitor's son Masefield was fourteen when he went to sea as an
apprentice on a windjammer sailing round Cape Horn. The next
year he gave up the life of a sailor and did various jobs in New
York until 1897 when he returned to England. His long narrative
poems, such as *The Everlasting Mercy* (1911) and *Reynard the Fox*
(1919) were both critically and commercially successful and in
1930 Masefield succeeded Robert Bridges as Poet Laureate. His
long poems are now unfairly neglected in favour of admittedly
adroit anthology pieces like 'Sea Fever': 'I must go down to the
seas again, to the lonely sea and the sky, / And all I ask is a tall
ship and a star to steer her by'.

Mason, R A K

New Zealand poet *born* near Auckland 1905

A classics graduate of Auckland University, Ronald Allison Kells
Mason worked as a teacher, company secretary, public works
foreman and landscape gardener. From 1945–1955 he was a
trade union official in Auckland. As editor of the periodical
Phoenix (1932–3) he expressed a Marxist indignation with social
anomalies and in his study of New Zealand administration in the
Cook Islands, *Frontier Forsaken* (1946), he came to polemical
conclusions. His 'Sonnet of Brotherhood' begins: 'Garrisons pent
up in a little fort / with foes who do but wait on every side /
knowing the time soon comes when they shall ride / triumphant
over those trapped and make sport / of them'.

Mason, William

English poet *born* 1725 *died* 1797

Mason is best remembered as the biographer and literary
executor of Thomas Gray. A royal chaplain, he held the living of
Ashton and was precentor of York Cathedral. His tragedies,
Elfrida and *Caractacus*, made little impression and he wrote a
number of portentous occasional poems. Yet his 'Heroic Epistle
to Sir William Chambers, Knight, Comptroller-General of His
Majesty's Works' contains some spirited couplets: 'Let David
Hume, from the remotest north, / In see-saw sceptic scruples hint
his worth; / David, who there supinely deigns to lie / The fattest
hog of Epicurus' sty / Through drunk with Gallic wine, and Gallic
praise, / David shall bless Old England's halcyon days'.

Massey, Gerald

English poet *born* near Tring, Hertfordshire 29 May 1828
died 29 October 1907

The son of a canal boatman, Massey was sent to work, at the age

of eight, in a silk mill; subsequently he worked as a straw-plaiter.
When he was fifteen he went to London and was encouraged by
Charles Kingsley under whose influence Massey became a
dedicated Christian Socialist. His collection *Babe Christabel* (1854)
established his reputation and he was described as the 'poet of
liberty, labour, and the people'. He became a journalist and
lectured on spiritualism in the USA. His somewhat sentimental
'Little Willie' was a popular poem. After describing the death of
the eponymous hero, Massey writes: 'The storms they may beat, /
The winter winds may rave; / Little Willie feels not / In his
workhouse grave.'

Masters, Edgar Lee
American poet *born* Garnet, Kansas 23 August 1868
died Melrose Park, Philadelphia 5 March 1950
Brought up in Petersburg and Lewiston, Illinois, Masters was
familiar from boyhood with the Spoon River area that features in
his masterpiece. He earned his living as a lawyer in Chicago then
in 1920 retired to New York where he stayed, in the Hotel
Chelsea, as a fulltime writer with a faith in agrarianism. His *Spoon
River Anthology* (1915) comprises free verse monologues spoken
by 244 dead citizens of a mid-Western town. 'Percival Sharp'
speaks for the author when he says: 'It is all very well, but for
myself I know / I stirred certain vibrations in Spoon River /
Which are my true epitaph, more lasting than stone.'

Mathews, Aidan Carl
Irish poet *born* Dublin 1956
Educated at Trinity College, Dublin, Mathews received the *Irish
Times* Award for poetry in 1974, the Patrick Kavanagh Award in
1976, the Macaulay Fellowship in Literature in 1978. His
collection *Windfalls* was published in 1979. He is adept at evoking
the anxiety of modern life and the isolation of the individual. His
poem 'Night' begins: 'I switch off the light, afraid / Of what
comes after night prayer. / Even on knees beside the bedside, /
Half-way through a Hail Mary, / No crucifix can halt / The
thought or the suggestion. // I think of bulking rock, / The blunt
knock of mallets. / A soldier threw the dice, / Another picked his
nails. / A shape slung on a cross; / Wrists, ribcage slackened.'

Mathias, Roland
Welsh poet *born* Talybont-on-Usk, Breconshire
4 September 1915
Educated at Oxford, Mathias was a headmaster in Birmingham
and editor of the *Anglo-Welsh Review*. His work, in such volumes as
Absalom in the Tree (1971), is highly sensitive and concerned about
the changes imposed on the Welsh landscape. His 'The Flooded

Valley' begins 'My house is empty but for a pair of boots: / The
reservoir slaps at the privet hedge and uncovers the roots / And
afterwards pats them up with a slack good will: / The sheep that I
market once are not again to sell. / I am no waterman, and who of
the others will live / Here, feeling the ripple spreading, hearing
the timbers grieve? / The house I was born in has not long to
stand: / My pounds are slipping away and will not wait for
the end.'

Mayne, Seymour
Canadian poet *born* Montreal 18 May 1944

Seymour Mayne, educated at McGill, taught at the Hebrew
University of Jerusalem and the University of Ottawa. He
published several books of verse including *The Impossible Promised
Land* (1981). He has written poignantly of the Jewish Wars (in
'Birthday' where he commemorates 'a young man who will never
age') and his 'Before passover' brings the Jewish experience to
Montreal: 'From afar now hear / the voices of aging women, /
smell the shawl hugging / the wizened *bobeh* / who never begged
but lived / for the conception of the ordinary, / bartering in the
bazaar of genes and death.'

Melville, Hermann
American poet *born* New York 1 August 1819
died New York 28 September 1891

Melville's father went bankrupt then insane and the author did
various jobs before going to sea as a cabin boy (in 1839) and
enduring the experiences that became the basis of his masterly
fiction. Misunderstood by the American reading public, Melville
worked from 1868 to 1885 as a customs inspector in New York
and spent his creative time on his poetry. *Clarel* (1876), inspired
by Melville's three-week visit to Palestine in 1857, is the narrative
of a quest by an American divinity student. At the end of the
poem the author tells Clarel to persevere: 'Emerge thou mayst
from the last whelming sea, / And prove that death but routs life
into victory.'

Menai, Huw
Welsh poet *born* 1887 *died* 1961

Menai was raised in Caernarvonshire and subsequently went south
to work in the Rhondda collieries. He became a checkweighman
for the Cambrian Coal Combine at Golfach Goch. A bilingual
poet, working in Welsh and English, he wrote imaginative
responses to such subjects as 'Rooks (December)': 'Gleaners of
grain they did not sow / Four rooks are standing in a row / Upon a
rusty, upturned plough, /Whose blunted shares now wear a
cloak / As brown as the brown earth they broke, / Far too well-fed

to know unrest – / Each beak reclining on each breast, / When every bulging gizzard hath / Known surfeit of the aftermath, / Mute, living monuments are these / Of even darker mysteries'.

Meredith, George
English poet *born* Portsmouth 12 February 1828 *died* Boxhill, Surrey 18 May 1909

Son of a tailor and naval outfitter, Meredith absorbed European intellectual ideas during his education in Germany. In 1849 he married Mary Ellen Nicholls, widowed daughter of Thomas Love Peacock, but in 1858 she eloped with the painter Henry Wallis. From the time of the breakdown of his marriage until Mary's death in 1861, Meredith worked on his 50-poem sequence *Modern Love* (1862). The work is partly autobiographical and depicts the failure of a marriage. Most of the 16-line 'sonnets' (as Meredith called the individual poems) are spoken by the husband and Meredith's modernity is everywhere apparent (as in XXII) 'What may the woman labour to confess? / There is about her mouth a nervous twitch.'

Merrick, James
English poet *born* 1720 *died* 1769

Merrick was a Fellow of Trinity College, Oxford, and as such taught Lord North, the future Prime Minister. He took holy orders but was too ill (from headaches, apparently) to carry out a regular ecclesiastical routine. He produced a version of the Psalms, a collection of Hymns and 'The Chameleon', a moral tale with a well-portrayed central character: 'Oft has it been my lot to mark / A proud, conceited, talking spark, / With eyes that hardly served at most / To guard their master 'gainst a post; / Yet round the world the blade has been, / To see whatever could be seen. / Returning from his finished tour, / Grown ten times perter than before'.

Merrill, James
American poet *born* New York 1926

Educated at Amherst College, Merrill worked as a university teacher. For his collection *Nights and Days* he was given the National Book Award in 1967. His verse is rich in cultural references and has a self-conscious relish for the act of literary creation, as in 'An Urben Convalescence': 'There are certain phrases which to use in a poem / Is like rubbing silver with quicksilver. Bright / But facile, the glamour deadens overnight. / For instance, how "the sickness of our time" // Enhances, then debases, what I feel. / At my desk I swallow in a glass of water / No longer cordial, scarcely wet, a pill / They had told me not to take until much later.'

Merwin, W S

American poet *born* New York 1927

Brought up in Pennsylvania and educated at Princeton, William Stanley Merwin lived in Spain, England and France for periods away from the USA. He published several collections including *The First Four Books of Poems* (1975). His verse engages itself with the natural world in a highly imaginative manner so that description dissolves into discourse. 'Views from the High Camp' begins 'In the afternoon, while the wind / Lies down in its halcyon self, / A finger of darkness moving like an oar / Follows me through the blinding fields; in the focus / Of its peculiar radiance I have found / Treasures I did not know I had lost, several, / Perhaps still in the future.'

Mew, Charlotte

English poet *born* London 15 November 1869
died London 24 March 1928

After the death of her father – an architect – Charlotte Mew saw a brother and sister go insane. She and her sister Anne survived only by renting out part of their house. She was understandably unhappy, yet her work was admired by Thomas Hardy, Walter De la Mare and John Masefield on whose joint recommendation she was awarded a Civil List pension in 1923. However she could not endure the death of her sister Anne and poisoned herself. Her poems have a stark and chilling quality, for example 'Domus Caedet Arborem': 'Ever since the great planes were murdered at the end of the gardens / The city, to me, at night has the look of a Spirit brooding crime'.

Meynell, Alice

English poet *born* Barnes, near London 22 September 1847
died 27 November 1922

Brought up in Italy, Alice Meynell was converted to Roman Catholicism in 1872, brought out her collection *Preludes* in 1875 and married Wilfred Meynell in 1877. She and her husband participated in the Catholic Literary Revival and befriended poets such as Francis Thompson who was saved from drug-addiction by the Meynells. Acclaimed by Coventry Patmore as England's leading literary lady, she refused to be patronised and pursued her feminist convictions. Her poem 'A Father of Women' considers the spectacle of war before closing thus: 'The crippled world! Come then, / Fathers of women with your honour in trust, / Approve, accept, know them daughters of men, / Now that your sons are dust.'

Mickle, William Julius

Scottish poet *born* Langholm 28 September 1735
died Oxford 28 October 1788

Son of a minister, Mickle was a clerk, then partner, in an
Edinburgh brewery but when this ran into financial difficulties he
went to London, in 1764, to work as a proofreader with the
Clarendon Press. His translation of Camoes's *Lusiad*, published
1771-5 by subscription, was a considerable success. He went to
Portugal in 1781 as a naval secretary then later settled at
Foresthill farm, near Oxford. He is credited with the composition
of the song 'There's nae luck aboot the house' and his 'Cumnor
Hall' suggested the subject of *Kenilworth* to Scott: 'The dews of
summer night did fall, / The moon, sweet regent of the sky, /
Silvered the walls of Cumnor Hall, / And many an oak that grew
thereby.'

Middleton, Christopher

English poet *born* 1926

Middleton served with the RAF in Germany from 1944-48 then
went to Oxford. He taught English at Zürich University then
German at King's College, London and is an authoritative
translator of German poetry. His own work does metaphorical
violence to the English language in order to startle the reader into
a fresh appraisal of reality, hence he can be one of the most
unsettling of modern poets. 'Razzmatazz' contemplates atrocity
thus: 'O the bleeding hole / Torn in the flesh / Heart, the hungry
people / Beaten down by the winds / Bayonets, rifle butts'.
Several of his poems similarly dwell on the most horrific aspects
of the twentieth century.

Millay, Edna St Vincent

American poet *born* Rockland, Maine 22 February 1892
died Austerlitz, New York 19 October 1950

Success came early to Edna St Vincent Millay, a celebrity as a
student at Vassar College and one of the best-known names
associated with New York's Greenwich Village. In 1923 she
married the businessman Eugen Bousevain and moved to
Steepletop, a big house in the Berkshire Hills. She was a
sophisticated poet with a brilliant command of traditional forms
such as the sonnet, as in her sequence *Fatal Interview* (1931). In
her later years she became increasingly isolated but never lost the
passion for literary immortality expressed in 'The Poet and His
Book': 'Lift this little book, / Turn the tattered pages, / Read me,
do not let me die!'

Miller, Joaquin
American poet *born* Liberty, Indiana 10 November 1841
died Oakland, California 17 February 1913

Born Cincinnatus Hiner Miller, the 'Poet of the Sierras' took the
name 'Joaquin' in honour of a Mexican rebel he admired.
Infatuated with the idea of poetry, Miller came to London,
printed *Pacific Poems* (1871), and delighted the literari with his
supreme self-confidence and Wild Western panache. In 1886
Miller settled in Oakland and built a house called the Abbey, after
his wife Abbie. Though sentimental in tone and sometimes
primitive in technique, he created some memorable lines like
those in 'The Bravest Battle': 'The bravest battle that ever was
fought; / Shall I tell you where and when? / On the maps of the
world you will find it not; / It was fought by the mothers of men.'

Milliken, Richard Alfred
Irish poet *born* County Cork 1767 *died* County Cork 1815

Millikin, a Corkman all his life, was known for his light-hearted
pastiches of folksongs such as 'De Groves of De Pool' which
renders his local dialect comically as when the Cork militia return
to Liverpool and drink 'de native / Dat is brewed in de groves of
de Pool.' More lyrically, he produced 'The Groves of Blarney'
which was apparently popular with Garibaldi's soldiers on the
march: 'The groves of Blarney / they look so charming, / Down
by the purling / Of sweet, silent brooks, / Being banked with
posies / That spontaneous grow there, / Planted in order / By the
sweet "Rock Close".'

Milne, Ewart
Irish poet *born* Dublin 1903

Milne worked at several jobs, including schoolteaching and
labouring. He went to Spain, during the Civil War, as a Medical
Aid volunteer on the government side. During the Irish troubles,
he expressed the ideals of the Protestant minority in the Republic
and the Protestant majority in Ulster. His poem 'Under Orion'
contemplates how 'Ulster's Red Hand uplifted / Salutes those
about to die / Oh there will be blood, be vengeance / The raven
will tear with his bitter beak / At Cuchulain's side / And blood's
redundance overflow the Erne / in spate indeed'. His various
volumes include *A Garland for the Green* (1962).

Milton, John
English poet *born* London 9 December 1608 *died* Chalfont St
Giles, Buckinghamshire 8 November 1674

Milton, a scrivener's son, was educated at St Paul's School and
Cambridge. Due to his dislike of ecclesiastical discipline he
decided against taking holy orders and instead prepared himself

to be England's epic poet. After the outbreak of Civil War in 1642 he devoted himself to Puritan propaganda and in 1649 was appointed Latin Secretary to the Commonwealth. By 1652 Milton was completely blind and it was after the death of Katherine Woodcock, his second wife, in 1658 that he began work on *Paradise Lost* (1667): 'What in me is dark / Illumine, what is low raise and support; / That to the height of this great argument / I may assert eternal Providence, / And justify the ways of God to men.'

Mitchell, Adrian
English poet *born* London 24 October 1932
Son of a research chemist, Mitchell went to Oxford University then worked as a journalist. He developed great skill as a reader of his own verse and his poetic style evolved in the context of public performance. His poems are extremely accessible: he either affirms the childhood Eden when 'Milk was warm' ('Sally Go Round . . .'); or assumes the role of poetic conscience of the British Left. 'To Whom It May Concern' is a powerful statement of the poet's opposition to American intervention in Vietnam: 'I was run over by the truth one day. / Ever since the accident I've walked this way / So stick my legs in plaster / Tell me lies about Vietnam.'

Monro, Harold
English poet *born* Brussels 14 March 1879 *died* 16 March 1932
Son of a Scottish engineer, Monro came to England at the age of seven and was educated at Cambridge. In 1913 he founded the Poetry Bookshop, in Bloomsbury, which published the five volumes of Edward Marsh's *Georgian Poetry* (1912–22). He served in an anti-aircraft battery during the First World War and from 1919–25 edited *The Chapbook*. His *Collected Poems*, edited by his wife Alida, appeared posthumously in 1933. Though his verse is characteristically Georgian in tone, being technically cautious and thematically insular, a poem such as 'Living' has an appropriate vitality; 'Heart, Brain and Body, and Imagination / All gather in tumultous joy together, / Running like children down the path of morning'.

Montague, John
Irish poet *born* New York 1929
Montague, who has earned his living teaching literature in Ireland, is a poet of power and passion. When he writes about his father's anguish in exile he explains how, in order to cope, he 'drank neat whiskey until / he reached the only element / he felt at home in / any longer: brute oblivion.' The human touch is typically tender and Montague's work is inhabited by gloriously

individualised characters. 'Like Dolmens Round My Childhood, The Old People' is a catalogue of Irish eccentrics such as Maggie Owens who 'was a well of gossip defiled, / Fanged chronicler of a whole countryside'. Montague also responds fiercely to the political situation as when in 'A New Siege' he dwells on Derry and 'the gates between / Ulster Catholic / Ulster Protestant'.

Montagu, Lady Mary Wortley
English poet *born* London baptised 26 May 1689
died 21 August 1762
Eldest daughter of the first Duke of Kingston, Lady Mary was expected to marry a man chosen by her father; instead she eloped, in 1712, with Edward Wortley, MP. She became friendly with Pope who subsequently ridiculed her as 'Sappho' in the *Dunciad*. After travelling in Turkey with her husband she introduced to England the technique of innoculation against smallpox. From 1739 to 1762 she lived in Italy and Avignon, having parted from her husband. She came home to die, of cancer. Her poems are technically taut and forceful, for example her lines 'In Answer to a Lady Who Advised Retirement'; 'Long since the value of this world I know, / Pity the madness, and despise the show'.

Montgomerie, Alexander
Scottish poet *born c* 1545 *died* 1598
A distant kinsman of James VI, Captain Alexander Montgomerie (as he was styled) entered the service of the Regent Morton during the King's minority. He became the chief poetic ornament of James VI's court, exemplified the metrical virtues the King expounded in his treatise 'Reulis and Cautelis' (1585), and wrote *The Cherry and the Slae* (1597). His Catholic principles led to Spanish connexions that resulted in his exile from Scotland. 'The Night is Neir Gone' shows his lyrical gift: 'Hay! now the day dawis; / The jolie Cok crawis; / Now shroudis the shawis, / Throw Nature anone. / The thissel-cock cryis / On lovers wha lyis / Now skaillis the skyis; / The nicht is neir gone'.
shawis groves; *thissell-cock* mistle-thrush cock; *skaillis* clears

Montgomery, James
Scottish poet *born* Irvine, Ayrshire 4 November 1771
died 30 April 1854
Son of a missionary of the Moravian Brethren, Montgomery was educated at the Moravian School at Fulneck, near Leeds. He settled in Sheffield in 1792 and by 1796 had become editor of the *Sheffield Iris*; as such he went twice to prison for political articles he had published. He published *Prison Amusements* in 1797 and the heroic poem *Greenland* in 1819. 'For ever with the Lord' is the

most endurable of his many hymns. His lines on 'An Indian Mother about to Destroy her Child' close with the mother crushing her child 'With the whole burden of her grief, exclaiming, / "Oh, that my mother had done so to me!" / Then in a swoon forgot, a little while, / her child, her sex, her tyrant, and herself.'

Montrose, James Graham, Marquis of
Scottish poet *born* Old Montrose 1612 *died* Edinburgh 21 May 1650

Educated at St Andrews University, Graham became first Marquis of Montrose in 1644. Initially a supporter of the National Covenant (1638) – which defended Scotland's Presbyterian tradition against Charles I's interference – he fought for Charles I during the Civil War until defeated at the Battle of Philiphaugh in 1645. Returning to Scotland in 1650 to pursue the Royalist cause, he was defeated at Carbisdale and executed. His 'Metrical Prayer on the Eve of His Own Execution' ends optimistically: 'Scatter my Ashes, throw them in the Air: / Lord (since Thou know'st where all these Atoms are) / I'm hopeful, once Thou'lt recollect my Dust, / And confident Thou'lt raise me with the Just.'

Moore, Clement Clarke
American poet *born* New York 15 July 1779 *died* 10 July 1863

Clarke's father was Episcopal Bishop of New York and President of Columbia College where the poet was educated. In 1821 he became Professor of Biblical Learning at the General Theological Seminary, New York and his scholarship was shown in a Hebrew lexicon. Subsequently he became Professor of Oriental and Greek Literature. His poem 'A Visit from St Nicholas' was written for his children at Christmas 1822 and appeared anonymously in the Troy *Sentinel* a year later. It begins ''Twas the night before Christmas, when all through the house / Not a creature was stirring, not even a mouse; / The stockings were hung by the chimney with care, / In hopes that St Nicholas soon would be there.'

Moore, Marianne
American poet *born* St Louis, Missouri 15 November 1887 *died* New York 5 February 1972

After an education at Bryn Mawr, Marianne Moore taught secretarial skills for five years then worked as a library assistant in New York for three years. From 1925-9 she edited the *Dial*. Her first collection of *Poems* (1921) began a distinguished career during which she was often honoured (Bollingen Prize, Pulitzer Prize, Gold Medal for Poetry). As she often uses a syllabic count rather than a metrical pattern she has been classified as a syllabic poet though her verse is never predictable. She whimsically collects odd individuals and animals. In 'Saint Nicholas' she asks for 'a chameleon with tail / that curls like a watch spring'; elsewhere she describes 'The Arctic Ox (or Goat)'.

Moore, Thomas

Irish poet *born* Dublin 28 May 1779 *died* Bromham, Wiltshire 25 February 1852

Moore, a grocer's son, was educated in Dublin then moved to London, in 1799, to study law. He became a popular figure in London where he impressed as a fine drawing-room singer as well as translator of the *Odes of Anacreon* (1800). A pugnacious man, he reacted violently to hostile criticism; Byron, for example, was cast as an enemy before he was accepted as a firm friend. Moore's most memorable work appears in *Irish Melodies* (1808–34). In these song-lyrics his style is sentimental yet touchingly effective, as in 'The Minstrel Boy': 'The Minstrel-boy to the war is gone, / In the ranks of death you'll find him'.

Moore, Tom Inglis

Australian poet *born* Camden, New South Wales 1901 *died* 1978

Educated at Sydney and Oxford universities, Moore became a lecturer in the USA and Manila before returning in 1931 to Sydney where he worked on the *Sydney Morning Herald* as a leader-writer. He was with the Army Education Service during the Second World War then taught Australian literature at the Canberra University College. His poems, elegant in expression, make imaginative use of astronomical imagery, as in 'Star Drill'; 'Comfort me with stars, not apples, / For always the sky was my bright consoler. / To-night I am reconciled to aching feet / Seeing the lights of heaven themselves, / Obedient to reveille blown by sunset, / Go equably marching, in humble squad-drill.'

Moraes, Dom

Indian poet *born* Bombay 1938

Moraes's father was a barrister who became editor of *The Times of India*. The poet was educated in Bombay and Oxford. His collection *A Beginning* (1957) was critically acclaimed as evidence of a renewal of romanticism in English verse. He published *Gone Away*, a travel book, in 1960; and an autobiography, *My Son's Father*, in 1968. In poems such as 'Song' he projects himself as a sinner saved by love: 'Then, with the weather worse, / To the cold river, / I came reciting verse / With a hangover. / You shook a clammy hand. / How could I tell you / Then that wild oats died and / Brighter grain grew?'

Morgan, Edwin
Scottish poet *born* Glasgow 27 April 1920

Morgan's father was director of a firm of iron and steel scrap merchants and the home was 'not a particularly bookish house'. Morgan, however, became fascinated by writing and attended Glasgow University as a student then returned to teach there. He is an eclectic poet who has written in a variety of styles, sometimes influenced by the American Beat poets, sometimes by the experimental idiom of Ian Hamilton Finlay, sometimes by the late work of Hugh MacDiarmid. His essential subject is Glasgow, the city he evokes in the title poem of his collection *The Second Life* (1968): 'Is it only the slow stirring, a city's renewed life / that stirs me, could it stir me so deeply as May . . . ?'

Morgan, Pete
English poet *born* Leigh, Lancashire 1939

Morgan was enlisted in the British Army at the age of eighteen and resigned his commission in 1963. He moved to Edinburgh where he worked in public relations and began to establish himself as a performer of his own poems. For several years he lived in Robin Hood's Bay, Yorkshire, which provides the setting for his collection *A Winter Visitor* (1983) The title poem shows his ability to respond to the environment in an atmospheric manner: 'We slept uneasy as tirades: / Woke to the buffeting at walls, / Woke to the knocking at the door, / Woke at last to breaking glass / And a window coming in.' He left Robin Hood's Bay in 1974 and settled in York.

Morris, George Pope
American poet *born* Philadelphia, Pennsylvania 10 October 1802 *died* 6 July 1864

Morris moved to New York where he worked as a printer and, with Samuel Woodworth, founded the *New York Mirror and Ladies' Literary Gazette* which he edited from 1823–42. He made the newspaper (eventually retitled the *Evening Mirror*) the mouthpiece of the Knickerbocker School of writers who helped put New York on the literary map. His collection *The Deserted Bride* (1838) contains his best-known poem, 'Woodman, Spare that Tree!', an early ecological plea: 'That old familiar tree, / Whose glory and renown / Are spread o'er land and sea – / And wouldst thou hew it down? / Woodman, forbear thy stroke! / Cut not its earth-bound ties; / Oh, spare that aged Oak / Now tow'ring to the skies.'

Morris Lewis
Welsh poet *born* Llanfihangel Tre'r Beirdd, Anglesey 1701 *died* 1765

Morris, known as *Llewelyn Ddu o Fôn*, was a surveyor and Welsh scholar. His lively wit is evident in his nautical ballad 'The Fishing Lass of Hakin' which celebrates a girl called Betty: 'Her fishing dress was clean and neat, / It set me all a-quaking, / I loved her and could almost eat / This maiden ray of Hakin; / If ere you saw a cuttle fish, / Her breasts are more inviting, / Like shaking blubbers in a dish, / And tender as a whiting. // Her cheeks are as a mackerel plump, / No mouth of mullet moister, / Her lips of tench would make you jump, / They open like an oyster; / Her chin as smooth as river trout, / Her hair as rockfish yellow, / God's Sounds! I view her round about / But never saw her fellow.'

Morris, Sir Lewis
Welsh poet *born* Carmarthen 23 January 1833
died 12 November 1907

Grandson of the poet Lewis Morris, he was educated at Oxford and called to the Bar. In 1880 he became active in the development of higher education in Wales, helping to establish the University of Wales in 1893. He was knighted two years later. He published *Songs of Two Worlds* in 1871, *The Epic of Hades* in 1876-7. His work was widely read on account of the Tennysonian fluency he shows in, for example, 'Lydstep Caverns': 'Yet ere today is done, / Where now these fairy runnels thread the sand, / Five fathoms deep the swelling tides shall run / Round the blind cave and swallow rock and strand, / And this discovered breast on which I lie / Shall clothe itself again with mystery.'

Morris, William
English poet *born* Walthamstow 24 March 1834
died 3 October 1896

Morris was a Victorian version of the Renaissance man – a writer, designer, typographer and political activist with a vision of an England transformed by socialism. Educated at Oxford and friendly with the Pre-Raphaelites, he attempted to combat the vulgarities of contemporary commercialism. He founded the Socialist League in 1884 and published, in 1891, his *News from Nowhere*, a revolutionary plan for England. Often caricatured as a Utopian dreamer, Morris was always attentive to detail, even in political poems such as 'All for the Cause': 'Here a word, a word in season, for the day is drawing nigh, / When the Cause shall call upon us, some to live, and some to die!'

Morrison, Blake
English poet *born* Burnley, Lancashire 8 October1950

Educated at Nottingham University, Morrison taught at Goldsmith's College, London, and with the Open University. He was Poetry and Fiction Editor of *The Times Literary Supplement* and became Deputy Literary Editor of *The Observer*. He published a critical study of *The Movement* in 1980 and his collection *Dark Glasses* in 1984. Morrison is a thoughtful poet who presents a sense of loss as an abiding emotion in, for example, 'The Renunciation': 'The garden with its nightshade nags like some / Vague guilt and the rooms look so untidy, / But there is nothing we know of to be done.' With Andrew Motion, Morrison edited *The Penguin Book of Contemporary British Poetry* (1982).

Motion, Andrew
English poet *born* London 26 October 1952

Educated at Oxford, Motion lectured in English at the University of Hull from 1977–80. Subsequently he has worked in publishing. He has written warmly of Edward Thomas and Philip Larkin and, though he has not their fondness for rhyme, he is clearly in the conservative English tradition. Motion's verse avoids contemporary issues and instead reaches back nostalgically to the past. His poem 'The Letter', which won him the £5,000 Arvon/Observer Poetry Prize, is atmospheric and conveys a mood that resolves into a precise picture of a heroic fighter-pilot: 'Goggles pushed up, / a stripe of ginger moustache, and his eyes /fixed on my own'.

Mtshali, Oswald
South African poet *born* Vryheid, Natal 1940

Mtshali worked at menial jobs and later settled in Soweto. *Sounds of a Cowhide Drum*, his first collection, appeared in 1971 and revealed him as an eloquent voice of black South African consciousness. Two years later he participated in the Poetry International festival in London. His angry poems have an elemental power as they express the agony of an oppressed people. 'Handcuffs', for example, asserts 'Handcuffs / have steel fangs / whose bite is more painful / than a whole battalion / of fleas' and continues 'my wrists / are manacled. / My mind / is caged. / My soul / is shackled' before concluding on an attack on defeatism.

Mudie, Ian
Australian poet *born* Hawthorn, South Australia 1911 *died* 1976

Mudie was educated at Scotch College in Adelaide where he lived for most of his life, working as a journalist and becoming manager of a real estate agency. He was one of the leading figures among the Jindyworobaks, a group of nationalist poets anxious to express the aboriginal experience of Australia. His poem 'They'll Tell You About Me' gives voice to the archetypal Australian: 'Me – yesterday I was rumour, / today I am legend, / tomorrow, history. / If you'd like to know more of me / inquire at the pub at Tennant Creek / or at any drover's camp / or shearing-shed / or

shout any bloke in any bar a drink / or yarn to any bloke asleep
on any beach, / they'll tell you about me'.

Muir, Edwin

Scottish poet *born* Deernes, Orkney 15 May 1887
died Cambridge 3 January 1959

When Muir was two his father rented a farm on the tiny Orkney
island of Wyre and the six idyllic years spent there gave Muir his
vision of Eden. The Muirs were driven out of Wyre by their
landlord and, in 1901, moved to Glasgow which the poet
regarded as a Fall into a nightmarish labyrinth. Muir worked in a
bone factory and a shipbuilding office and despaired as his father,
mother and two brothers died in Glasgow. In 1918 Muir married
Willa Anderson and began to regain his faith in life. His poetry
asserts his vision of the childhood Eden. His poem 'The Horses'
describes a return, after atomic war, to a rural idyll in the
company of animals 'new as if they had come from their own
Eden'.

Muldoon, Paul

Irish poet *born* County Armagh 1951

Educated at Queen's University, Belfast, Muldoon became a
producer for the BBC in Belfast. He published *New Weather* in
1973, *Mules* in 1977, *Why Brownlee Left* in 1980. His long poem
'Immram' shows both narrative power and rhythmic assurance. It
begins ominously: 'I was fairly and squarely behind the eight /
That morning in Foster's pool-hall / When it came to me out of
the blue / In the shape of a sixteen-ounce billiard cue / That lent
what he said some little weight. / "Your old man was an ass-hole. /
That makes an ass-hole out of you." / My grand-father hailed
from New York State. / My grand-mother was part Cree. / This
must be some new strain in my pedigree.'

Munday, Anthony

English poet *born* London 1553 *buried* 10 August 1633

A draper's son, Munday was orphaned around 1570 and became a
boy actor then an apprentice printer. He went to Rome in 1578
to spy on English Catholic Refugees and subsequently produced a
number of anti-Catholic pamphlets. After warning about the
possibility of a plot against Elizabeth I in *A Watchword to England*
(1584) he was given a minor position at Court. He wrote several
plays including *The Downfall of Robert, Earl of Huntingdon* (1601), a
Robin Hood tale; and a sequel *The Death of Robert, Earl of
Huntingdon* on which Munday collaborated with Henry Chettle.
From *England's Helicon* (1600) comes his lyric beginning 'Beauty
sat bathing by a spring / Where fairest shades did hide her'.

Murphy, R D

Australian poet *born* Cooma, New South Wales 1910

The son of Irish immigrants, Redmond D Murphy was educated at the Marist Brothers' High School, Darlinghurst, Sydney, and himself became a Marist Brother. He has taught English in schools established by the Marist Brothers in New South Wales, Victoria and South Australia. He cultivates a self-consciously literary diction and adopts a sardonic tone, as in 'Speak to Strangers': 'Step through the gate and see / My collection of illusions. My grandfather's name / Was Adam. We may discover a thing or two / In common, tastes the same. This is your place? / I'd not pick your purse or kinsey at the keyhole, / But merely borrow a match to see your face.'

Murphy, Richard

Irish poet *born* Galway 1927

For several years Murphy ran a fishing boat in County Galway – the 'hooker' featured in his volume *The Last Galway Hooker* (1961). He is capable of sustained narratives and evocatively explores the lives of his ancestors. 'The God Who Eats Corn' recalls his father, William Lindsay Murphy, who retired from the British Colonial Service as Governor of the Bahamas and settled in Southern Rhodesia in 1950. 'The Woman of the House' describes his grandmother, Lucy Mary Ormsby: 'On a patrician evening in Ireland / I was born in the guest-room: she delivered me. / May I deliver her from the cold hand / Where now she lies, with a brief elegy?' The brief elegy runs for twenty-six quatrains

Murray, Charles

Scottish poet *born* Alford, Aberdeenshire 28 September 1864 *died* Banchory, Kincardineshire 12 April 1941

At the age of twenty-four Murray emigrated to South Africa where he worked as an engineer with a gold-mining company. During the Boer War he was a lieutenant with the Railway Pioneer Regiment then became (1912) Secretary of Public Works in the Government of the Union of South Africa. He returned to Scotland in 1924. Murray's use of his native Aberdeenshire dialect was immensely popular: when 'There's aye a something' appeared in the Aberdeen *Press and Journal* in 1933 the first edition sold out by 9am and two extra editions had to be printed. His masterpiece is 'The Whistle' which begins: 'He cut a sappy sucker from the muckle rodden-tree / He trimmed it, an' he wet it, an' he thumped it on his knee'.

rodden-tree rowan tree

Murray, Les A

Australian poet *born* New South Wales 1938

Educated at Sydney University, Murray worked as a translator at the Australian National University and as an officer of the Prime Minister's Department before deciding, in 1971, to concentrate on his writing. Many of his poems begin with an observation, spin off into a meditation, then come back to earth with a commonsense conclusion. He is an adroit versifier with a wide range of formal effects at his disposal and a broad approach to everyday experience. He is fond of recalling his Scottish roots and describing the surprises of life in Australia. 'Sydney and the Bush' begins: 'When Sydney and the Bush first met / there was no open ground / and men and girls, in chains and not, / all made an urgent sound.'

Murray, Paul
Irish poet *born* Newcastle, County Down 1947

Educated at St Malachy's College, Belfast, Murray entered the Dominican Order in 1966 and was ordained to the priesthood in 1973. His *Ritual Poems* appeared in 1971, *Rites and Meditations* in 1982. His exploration of Roman Catholic themes is made accessible by the fine descriptive detail of his verse. 'Death of a priest' ends: 'A black breviary propped between his / Chest and chin, a cold / Hand closing his eyes, touching / Without chrism his wrinkled forehead; / Only then could he believe / She was neither fantasy of daydream / Nor temptation: Death.' His critical book on *The Mysticism Debate* appeared in 1978.

Nash, Ogden
American poet *born* Rye, New York 19 August 1902
died Baltimore 1971

Nash's poetry is technically primitive and aesthetically absurd yet is informed by such an intelligent appeal to the emotions that it deserves its immense popularity. Most of Nash's work displays the mentality of a man who deeply resented the process of growing old but had enough art to make light of it. He was obsessed with age and felt an urgent need to regain the outlook of the infant. Nash's verse constantly clings to the past and when he discusses the present it is an area to escape from, as in 'Away From It All': 'I wish I were a Tibetan monk / Living in a monastery. / I would unpack my trunk / And store it in a tronastery'.

Nashe, Thomas
English poet *born* Lowestoft 1567 *died* 1601

A minister's son, Nashe was an argumentative man whose various controversies, and endless attacks on Puritanism, destroyed his hopes of finding a wealthy patron. With *The Unfortunate Traveller, or the Life of Jack Wilton* (1594) he contributed to the development ·

of the English novel. His comedy *The Isle of Dogs* (1597) led to his imprisonment on account of its seditious content. Another comedy, *Summer's Last Will and Testament* (1600), contains the song beginning: 'Spring, the sweet spring, is the year's pleasant king; / then blooms each thing, then maids dance in a ring, / Cold doth not sting, the pretty birds do sing; / Cuckoo, jug-jug, pu-we, to-wiita-woo!'

Neill, William
Scottish poet *born* Prestwick 22 February 1922

Neill joined the RAF in 1938 and left in 1967 with the rank of Warrant Officer. In 1967 he went to Edinburgh University as a mature student and graduated in Celtic studies. He subsequently taught English, in Galloway, for ten years then retired. His verse, as in *Wild Places* (1985), is a direct expression of his personality. 'Inde Cadunt Mortes' begins with an observation then reaches a conclusion: 'While rabbits, like their betters, take no heed / but risk swift death for a mere whimsy's sake, / Mankind to mankind less indifference shows: / we kill for spite as well as feeding crows.'

Neilson, Shaw
Australian poet *born* Penola 1872 *died* Melbourne 1942

Neilson's gently lyrical poems give no indication of the hard life endured by their author. The son of Scottish immigrants, he had little formal education and earned his living through manual work, as a bushworker. Towards the end of his life, when he was unable to indulge in labouring, he was given a post as a messenger working for the Government in Melbourne. When Neilson's collection *Heart of Spring* (1919) appeared, the poet was acclaimed for the tender quality of lyrics such as 'May': 'Shyly the silver-hatted mushrooms make / Soft entrance through, / And undelivered lovers, half awake, / Hear noises in the dew.'

Nelson, Alice Dunbar
American poet *born* New Orleans 1875 *died* 1935

Educated at Straight College, New Orleans, Alice Moore married the black poet Paul Lawrence Dunbar in 1898. With her husband she promoted the cause of black literature, arranging stage presentations of key works. She earned her living as a schoolteacher and contributed prose as well as poems to periodicals. Her poem 'I Sit and Sew' is a protest against the passive role of women: 'The little useless seam, the idle patch; / Why dream I here beneath my homely thatch, / When there they lie in sodden mud and rain, / Pitifully calling me, the quick ones and the slain! / You need me, Christ! It is no roseate dream / That beckons me – this pretty futile seam, / It stifles me – God, must I sit and sew?'

Nemerov, Howard
American poet *born* New York 1920

Nemerov was educated at Harvard and during the Second World War served with the Royal Canadian Air Force. He taught at Hamilton College and Bennington, wrote novels such as *The Melodramatist* (1949), and was active as a literary critic. His several volumes of verse, including *Collected Poems* (1977), show a contemplative approach to experience. 'The View from an Attic Window' recalls 'I cried because life is hopeless and beautiful. / And like a child I cried myself to sleep / High in the head of the house, feeling the hull / Beneath me pitch and roll among the steep / Mountains and valleys of the many years / Which brought me to tears.'

Newbolt, Sir Henry
English poet *born* Bilston, Staffordshire 6 June 1862
died 19 April 1938

A vicar's son, Newbolt was educated at Oxford and called to the Bar in 1887. He enjoyed a successful career as a lawyer, naval historian, editor of the *Monthly Review* (from 1900–1904), Comptroller of Telecommunications during the First World War and was knighted in 1915. As a poet he enjoyed immense popularity: in one year *Admirals All* (1897) went through twenty-one editions of a thousand each. The collection contains his most memorable poem, 'Drake's Drum', with its ringing rhymes and patriotic appeal: 'Drake he's in his hammock an' a thousand mile away, / (Capten, art tha sleepin' there below?), / Slung atween the round shot in Nombre Dios Bay, / An' dreamin' arl the time o' Plymouth Hoe.'

Newcastle, Margaret, Duchess of
English poet *born* 1625 *died* 7 January 1674

Daughter of Sir Thomas Lucas, Margaret became (in 1645) the second wife of William Cavendish, Marquis (subsequently 1st Duke) of Newcastle. Her *Life* (1667) of her husband was attacked by Samuel Pepys as 'the ridiculous history of my Lord Newcastle writ by his wife, which shows her to be a mad, conceited, ridiculous woman, and he an ass to suffer her to write what she writes to him and of him.' Poems such as 'Nature's Cook', however, show an imaginative gift: 'Death is the cook of nature, and we find / Creatures drest several ways to please her mind; / Some Death doth roast with fevers burning hot, / And some he boils with dropsies in a pot; / Some are consumed for jelly by degrees, / And some with ulcers, gravy out to squeeze'.

Newlove, John
Canadian poet *born* Regina, Saskatchewan 1938

Newlove studied at his local university and became a writer in
residence at various Canadian universities. For his collection *Lies*
he won the Governor General's Award for Poetry in 1972. His
selected poems came out in 1977 under the title *The Fat Man*.
Although his diction has a distinctly modern tone, his work – for
example 'The Double-Headed Snake' – draws on the Canadian
tradition of enlightenment through an affirmation of one's native
environment. The poem observes: 'The plains / seem secure and
comfortable / at Crow's Nest Pass; in Saskatchewan / the
mountains are comforting / to think of; among / the eastwardly
diminishing hills / both the flatland and the ridge / seem easy
to endure.'

Nichol, John
Scottish poet *born* Montrose 8 September 1833
died 11 October 1894

Son of John Pringle Nichol, Professor of Astronomy at Glasgow,
Nichol was educated at Glasgow University and Oxford. In 1861
he became the first Professor of English Literature at Glasgow
University. His principal work, the poetic drama *Hannibal* (1873),
is an account of the Second Punic War and a sympathetic
portrayal of the eponymous hero. As Hasdrubal says, in the first
Act, 'I see / Warrior ghosts, that beckon me and point / To
Hannibal, around his head a flame, / Your leader that shall be in
mightier fields, / Planting your standards o'er the hills that
bound / My work, not wholly vain.' Nichol also published critical
books and lives of Burns, Carlyle and Byron.

Nicholson, Norman
English poet *born* Millom, Cumberland 8 January 1914

Nicholson's life and work are wholly concerned with an
exploration of his part of the world; like Wordsworth before him
he suggests the universal in a closely-observed series of local
particulars. He has written verse plays on biblical themes and a
Christian consciousness informs his poetry which is, however,
never dogmatic but alive to the subtleties of experience. His
poems often recreate, in finely textured descriptions, rare
autobiographical moments. 'Comprehending It Not' recalls the
Christmas of 1921: 'My Grandma / Banged on the floor with her
stick to greet me, / Tossed me a humbug and turned again to the
goose, / Spluttering on the kitchen range.'

Norris, John
English poet *born* Oxford 1657 *died* Bemerton 1711

A rector's son, Norris was educated at Oxford where he became a

Fellow of All Souls in 1680. Ordained in 1684, he married five years later and was appointed, in 1692, Rector of Bemerton, George Herbert's parish. As a philosopher he pursued a Christian Platonist ideal. As a Metaphysical poet he displayed intellectual agility, as in 'Hymn to Darkness': 'Haill thou most sacred venerable thing, / What Muse is worthy thee to sing? / Thee, from whose pregnant universal womb / All things, even Light thy rival, first did come. / What dares he not attempt that sings of thee, / Thou first and greatest mystery. / Who can the secrets of thy essence tell? / Thou like the light of God art inaccessible.'

Norris, Leslie
Welsh poet *born* Merthyr Tydfil 21 May 1921

Norris was invalided out of the RAF in 1940 and worked for a while in the Borough Treasurer's department in his native town. He later graduated from the University of Southampton and joined the staff of Bognor Regis College of Education. He published several volumes of verse, including *Mountains, Polecats, Pheasants* (1974). His work is formal in tone and evocative in mood as when he recalls a boxer in 'The Ballad of Billy Rose' and sees a childhood hero reduced to pathos: 'We all marched forward, all, except one man. / I saw him because he was paradoxically still, / A stone against the flood, face upright against us all, / Head bare, hoarse voice aloft, blind as a stone.'

Nortje, Arthur
South African poet *born* Oudtshoorn, Cape Province 1942 *died* Oxford 1973

Nortje was educated at a government high school 'for Coloureds' and became a teacher. In 1965 he went to Jesus College, Oxford, to read English. He taught in Canada and returned to Oxford but committed suicide. His poems convey, with a factual clarity, his distress at the predicament that disturbed him. In 'Autopsy' he contemplates an inhuman condition: '36,000 feet above the Atlantic / I heard an account of how they had shot / a running man in the stomach. But what isn't told / is how a warder kicked the stitches open / on a little-known island prison which used to be / a guano rock in a sea of diamond blue.'

Norton, Caroline Elizabeth Sarah
English poet *born* 1808 *died* 15 June 1877

The beauty of Caroline Sheridan, granddaughter of Richard Brinsley Sheridan, is preserved in a portrait by William Etty. Her marriage, of 1827, to Hon George Norton, a commissioner of bankruptcy, was the source of much unhappiness and she challenged him in the courts for several years after their separation. Her action resulted in legislation recognising some of the rights of married women. 'The Arab's Farewell to His Steed' reveals her romantic approach: 'Evening shall darken on the earth: and o'er the sandy plain, / Some other steed, with slower pace, shall bear me home again.' She married Sir William Stirling Maxwell shortly before her death.

Nowlan, Alden
Canadian poet *born* Windsor, Nova Scotia 1933 *died* 1983

A news editor by profession, Nowlan became writer in residence at the University of New Brunswick. For his collection *Bread, Wine and Salt* he won the Governor General's Award for Poetry in 1967. Drawing on his journalistic experience, Nowlan presents extraordinary incidents and allows them to speak, eloquently, for themselves. 'The Bull Moose' presents an animal suddenly asserting its indifference to mankind. At sunset the bull moose 'straightened and lifted his horns / so that even the wardens backed away as they raised their rifles. / When he roared, people ran to their cars. All the young men / leaned on their automobile horns as he toppled.'

Oakes, Philip
English poet *born* the Potteries 1928

In 'Neutrals' Philip Oakes writes: 'Born between wars / I missed the golden age / When art and action fused / Into a single voice.' He was a child when his father died and as his mother was ill he was given an orphan's education, first at the Bluecoats School, Wolverhampton, from which he was expelled. He later earned his living as a journalist. He has a quiet unassuming style that enables him to recreate autobiographical incidents with a descriptive precision. 'In the Kitchen' renders a particular memory poignantly: 'My mother's soup had beads / Of fat like seed pearls, strung / On the surface, jewelling the spoon. / "Not grease" she always said, / "But goodness", rendering down all creeds / To one affirmative'.

O'Curry, Eugene
Irish poet *born* 1796 *died* 1862

O'Curry was Professor of Irish History and Archaeology at the Catholic University, Dublin, and was one of the great Gaelic scholars of his day. He supplied, for example, James Clarence Mangan with literal versions of Irish poetry so he could make his imaginative translations. His *Lectures on the Manuscript Material of Ancient Irish History* appeared in 1861. His 'Do You Remember That Night?', derived from a seventeenth century Irish source, shows a lively linguistic flair: 'Beloved of my inmost heart, / Come some night, and soon, / When my people are at a rest, / That we may talk together.'

O'Dowd, Bernard
Australian poet *born* Beaufort, Victoria 1866 *died* 1953

The son of Irish immigrants, O'Dowd studied law and was called
to the Victorian Bar. He worked as librarian of the Melbourne
Supreme Court, then as State Parliamentary draftsman. A radical,
he advocated an independent Australian republic. O'Dowd was
interested in a whole range of religious movements and his work
is often ostentatiously allusive. His sonnet 'Australia' begins with
a series of questions which are resolved in the sextet: 'The
cenotaphs of species dead elsewhere / That in your limits leap and
swim and fly, / Or trail uncanny harp-strings from your trees, /
Mix omens with the auguries that dare / To plant the Cross upon
your forehead sky, / A virgin helpmate Ocean at your knees.'

O'Hara, Frank
American poet *born* Baltimore, Maryland 27 June 1926
died Fire Island, New York 24 July 1966

An energetic figure whose career was tragically ended when he
was accidentally run down by a taxicab, O'Hara was educated at
Harvard and Michigan then moved to New York. In 1951 he
joined the Museum of Modern Art and became assistant curator
responsible for exhibitions of Action Painters, including Jackson
Pollock on whom O'Hara published a monograph in 1959. Like
the painters he admired and encouraged, O'Hara attempted to
convey the visual vitality of America. His poem 'Steps' ends 'oh
god it's wonderful / to get out of bed / and drink too much
coffee / and smoke too many cigarettes / and love you so much'.
O'Hara's *Collected Poems* appeared in 1971.

Okara, Gabriel
Nigerian poet *born* 'beside the River Nun', Niger Delta 1921

Okara was the first Nigerian poet to appear in the periodical *Black
Orpheus* (in 1957) and the first editor of the *Nigerian Tide*
newspaper. Trained as a binder he took a job with the
Government Printery at Enugu. His first success was as a radio
writer and he has published a novel *The Voice* (1964). He takes a
delight in transforming the Nigerian landscape into evocative
images. In 'Adhiambo' he writes 'Maybe I'm mad, / for the voices
are luring me, / urging me from the midnight / moon and the
silence of my desk / to walk on wave crests across a sea. / Maybe
I'm a medicine man / hearing talking saps, / seeing behind trees; /
but who's lost his powers / of invocation.'

Oldys, William
English poet *born* 1696 *died* 1761

Oldys was an antiquary and author who wrote the 'Life of Sir
Walter Raleigh' in the 1736 edition of Ralegh's *History of the World*

and contributed several entries to the first edition of the
Biographia Britannica (1747-60). He co-edited, with Dr Johnson,
The Harleian Miscellany (1744-6). His best-known work is the
anacreontic 'Song, Occasioned by a Fly Drinking Out of a Cup of
Ale': 'Busy, curious, thirsty fly, / Drink with me, and drink as I; /
Freely welcome to my cup, / Couldst thou sip and sip it up. /
Make the most of life you may – / Life is short, and wear away.'

Oliver, W H
New Zealand poet *born* Fielding 1925

Educated at the universities of Victoria and Oxford, Oliver
founded and edited *Comment*, a quarterly dealing with current
affairs and the arts. He became Professor of History at Massey
University, Palmerston North, published *The Story of New Zealand*
(1960) and edited *The Oxford History of New Zealand* (1980). His
poem 'In the Fields of My Father's Youth' is a meditation on the
meaning of belonging. It begins: 'In the fields of my father's
youth, now bountiful and green, / I walked and stared, half-
recollecting each / New but anticipated emblem of a past / once
legendary, now more remote than legend / remembering all he
had told for the delight of children'.

Olson, Charles
American poet *born* Worcester, Massachusetts
27 December 1910 *died* 1970

Educated at the universities of Yale, Harvard and Wesleyan,
Olson was – from 1951, until it closed in 1956 – instructor and
rector at Black Mountain College, the experimental educational
centre near Asheville, North Carolina. Olson influenced a
generation of poets (for example Edward Dorn and Robert
Creeley) with his aesthetic. His influential essay on 'Projective
Verse' (1950) insisted on 'open' verse in which the poetic line
comes 'from the breath, from the breathing of the man who
writes, at the moment that he writes'. Olson's *Maximus* poems
(1953-75) celebrate Gloucester, Massachusetts in a major
sequence: 'one loves only form / and form only comes / into
existence when / the thing is born'.

Ondaatje, Michael
Canadian poet *born* Colombo, Sri Lanka 1943

Michael Ondaatje left Sri Lanka and lived in England then in
Canada where he became a Canadian citizen. He was educated at
Bishop's University and the University of Toronto before
working in Glendon College, Toronto. He won the Governor
General's Award for *The Collected Works of Billy the Kid* (1970) in
which poetry, pictures and prose combine to explore the legend
of the celebrated American outlaw. Billy is treated

sympathetically as a victim and dies with a poem on his lips: 'The end of it, lying at the wall / the bullet itch frozen in my head // my right arm is through the window pane / and the cut veins awake me / so I can watch inside and through the window'.

Opie, Amelia
English poet *born* Norwich 12 November 1769
died 2 December 1853

Amelia Alderson, a doctor's daughter, married the painter John Opie in 1798. With her husband's enthusiastic approval she wrote sentimental poems and novels that were read and appreciated by such as Sir Walter Scott. In works such as *Temper* (1812) and *Tales from Real Life* (1813) she charted the triumph of virtue. Becoming a Quaker in 1825, she devoted herself to charitable work. Characteristic of her moralistic approach is 'The Orphan Boy's Tale', a metrical tearjerker: 'Yet I was once a mother's pride, / And my brave father's hope and joy; / But in the Nile's proud fight he died, / And now I am an orphan boy.'

O'Reilly, John Boyle
Irish poet *born* Dowth Castle, near Drogheda 28 June 1844
died 10 August 1890

A schoolteacher's son, O'Reilly was, at eleven, an apprentice newspaper compositor. After joining the Fenians, he enlisted, in 1863, in the 10th Hussars with the purpose of spreading sedition. When his activities were exposed he was first condemned to death; the sentence was then commuted to 20 years' penal servitude in Western Australia, beginning in 1868. He escaped to the USA on a whaler in 1869 and became editor and part owner of the Boston *Pilot* newspaper in 1874. His novel *Moondyne* (1880), about Australian convicts, was a great success. In poems such as 'A White Rose' he reveals his romanticism: 'For the love that is purest and sweetest / Has a kiss of desire on the lips.'

Ormond, John
Welsh poet *born* Dunvant, Swansea 1923

Son of the village shoemaker, Ormond was educated at University College, Swansea, and became a staff writer on *Picture Post* from 1945-9. From 1955 he worked as a documentary filmmaker/producer with the BBC for whom he made films on Vernon Watkins, Dylan Thomas, Alun Lewis and R S Thomas. His collection *Definition of a Waterfall* appeared in 1973. Like Dylan Thomas, he is a compulsive craftsman sometimes producing hundreds of worksheets before finalising a text. His energetic evocation of nature is seen to advantage in 'Salmon': 'The river sucks them home. / The lost past claims them. / Beyond the headland / It gropes into the channel / Of the nameless sea. / Offshore they submit / To the cast, to the taste of it.'

O'Shaughnessy, Arthur
Irish poet *born* London 14 March 1844 *died* 30 January 1881

Privately educated, O'Shaughnessy spent his working life in the British Museum Library and the Natural History Museum where he specialised in fish and reptiles. Friendly with D G Rossetti, he identified with many of the Pre-Raphaelite ideals. Not all his work has worn well but his celebrated 'Ode' continues to impress through its euphonic power: 'We are the music-makers / And we are the dreamers of dreams, / Wandering by lone sea-breakers, / And sitting by desolate streams; – / World-losers and world-forsakers, / On whom the pale moon gleams: / Yet we are the movers and shakers / Of the world for ever, it seems.'

O'Sullivan, Seamas
Irish poet *born* Dublin 1879 *died* Dublin 1958

Educated in Dublin, James Sullivan Starkey (who wrote under the pseudonym Seamas O'Sullivan) was an actor with the Irish National Theatre company, performing in London as well as Dublin. In 1913 he founded the influential *Dublin Magazine* and edited it until his death. He published several collections including *Collected Poems* (1940) and his prose appeared in *Essays and Recollections* (1944). In 'Nelson Street' he shows his skill at assembling domestic images: 'There is hardly a mouthful of air / In the room where the breakfast is set, / For the blind is still down though it's late, / And the curtains are redolent yet / Of tobacco smoke, stale from last night.'

O'Sullivan, Vincent
New Zealand poet *born* Auckland 1937

Educated at the universities of Auckland and Oxford, O'Sullivan was an academic for a long period. He promoted the cause of his country's verse in his *Anthology of Twentieth Century New Zealand Poetry* (1971). His collections include *Our Burning Time* (1965), *Bearings* (1973), and *The Butcher Papers* (1982). He is an observant poet fascinated by the emotional connotations of the environment as in his memory of his father's death in *Brother Jonathan, Brother Kafka* (1980): 'On the day my father died a flame-tree / with its stiff immaculate flares cupped over / the leafless branches outside the hospital window / said for us several things voice could not get round to'.

215

Outram, George
Scottish poet *born* Glasgow 1805
died Rosemore, Holy Loch 1851

Born at Clyde Ironworks where his father was manager, Outram
became in 1837 editor of the *Glasgow Herald*. Under his influence
the newspaper became one of Scotland's great institutions and his
name is preserved in the title of its managing company. His verse
is occasional and amusing, as in 'The Annuity': 'I gaed to spend a
week in Fife – / An unco week it proved to be – / For there I met a
waesome wife / Lamentin' her viduity. / Her grief brak out sae
fierce and fall, / I thought her heart wad burst the shell; / And – I
was sae left to mysel' – / I sell't her an annuity.'

unco strange; *waesome* woesome; *sell't* sold

Owen, Wilfred
English poet *born* Oswestry, Shropshire 18 March 1893
died Sambre Canal, France 4 November 1918

Wilfred Owen was the poet who most poignantly conveyed the
horror of warfare in verse that has both rich verbal texture and
startling descriptive precision. He enlisted in 1915 and two years
later, when invalided home after fighting at the Somme, met
Siegfried Sassoon in Craiglockhart War Hospital, near
Edinburgh. Fascinated by the technical details of poetry, Owen
made a major technical innovation when he invented the
pararhyme, matching consonants before and after different
vowels. When he returned to France, where he won the MC, he
was killed by machine-gun fire. As he wrote, in 'Strange Meeting',
'Courage was mine, and I had mystery, / Wisdom was mine, and I
had mastery'.

Padgett, Ron
American poet *born* Tulsa, Oklahoma 1942

Padgett moved from Tulsa to New York where he was one of a
group of poets associated with Ted Berrigan's *'C' Magazine* in the
1960s. As such he wrote self-consciously playful poems and
collaborated with Berrigan on *Bean Spasms* (1967). His poem 'The
Sandwich Man' shows him teasing the reader by interrupting the
narrative with amusing asides: 'A dog barks outside the window /
Either that or the window's silent in the dog / – You'll say I'm
playing the overture / And finale off against each other, after all, /
There's no other way to locate the middle, / Which is more
elusive than it might seem'.

Page, P K
Canadian poet *born* Swanage, England 1916

Page was educated in England and at schools in Winnipeg and
Calgary. A member of the 'Preview' group of poets in Montreal,

Page published *Poems Selected and New* (1974) and *Evening Dance of the Grey Flies* (1981). The poems that reveal Page as an imaginative writer are those that identify with natural vitality. 'Element' has the poet 'as fish returned by dream into the stream'. 'Summer' opens on another abrupt metamorphosis: 'I grazed the green as I fell / and in my blood / the pigments flowed like sap. / All through my veins the green / made a lacey tree. / Green in my eye grew big as a bell / that gonged and struck / and in a whorl of green in my ear / it spun like a ball.'

Palgrave, F T

English poet *born* Great Yarmouth 28 September 1824
died 24 October 1897
Son of the historian Sir Francis Palgrave, Francis Turner Palgrave was educated at Oxford where he was friendly with Matthew Arnold and Arthur Hugh Clough. He was, briefly, assistant secretary to Gladstone then Vice-Principal of Kneller Hall, a teacher's training college. His poems were published in *Idylls and Songs* (1854), *Visions of England* (1881) and *Amenophis* (1892). His classic anthology, *The Golden Treasury of Songs and Lyrics*, appeared in 1861 and from 1885-95 he was Professor of Poetry at Oxford. His faith in lyrical poetry is reflected in his own poems, such as 'Eutopia': 'There is a garden where lilies / And roses are side by side; / And all day between them in silence / The silken butterflies glide.'

Parker, Dorothy

American poet *born* West End, New Jersey 22 August 1893
died New York 7 June 1967
Dorothy Rothschild (who kept her married name after her divorce from Edwin Pond Parker II) was acclaimed during her lifetime, as one of America's wittiest women. She was educated at a Catholic convent school, became drama critic of *Vanity Fair*, and was the most quoted member of the literary circle known as the Algonquin Hotel Round Table. Some of the trenchant humour, for which she was famous, animates her formally elegant poems. *Enough Rope* (1926), her bestselling collection, contains her characteristically bittersweet thoughts on suicide; 'Guns aren't lawful; / Nooses give; / Gas smells awful; / You might as well live.'

Parnell, Fanny

Irish poet *born* 1854 *died* 1882
Fanny was the sister of the great Irish patriot Charles Stewart Parnell (1846-91) and, like him, endlessly involved in Irish politics and the notion of the regeneration of the Irish nation. She contributed to *The Nation* newspaper. In 'After Death' she writes euphorically of the triumphant march of Irish history: 'I

should turn and rend the cere-cloths round me – / Giant sinews I should borrow – / Crying, "Oh, my brothers, I have also loved her / In her loneliness and sorrow! // "Let me join with you the jubilant procession, / Let me chant with you her story; / Then, contented, I shall go back to the shamrocks, / Now mine eyes have seen her glory."'

Paterson, Andrew Barton
Australian poet *born* 1864 *died* 1941

Paterson practised law in Sydney and also wrote, under the pseudonym 'The Banjo', bush ballads for the *Bulletin*; collected as *The Man from Snowy River* (1895), his vigorously Australian verse achieved great popularity. He turned from law to journalism and was a war correspondent during the Boer War. Paterson's poems celebrate an Australian ideal of manhood as various heroes endure against adversity. 'Saltbush Bill' is a characteristic tale of raw courage: 'Now Saltbush Bill was a drover tough as ever the country knew / He had fought his way on the Great Stock Routes from the sea to the big Barcoo; / He could tell when he came to a friendly run that gave him a chance to spread, / And he knew where the hungry owners were that hurried his sheep ahead'.

Patmore, Coventry
English poet *born* Woodland, Essex 23 July 1823
died Lymington 26 November 1896

Son of the writer P G Patmore, Coventry Patmore was privately educated and became an assistant in the printed book department of the British Museum. His *Poems* (1844) were admired by the Pre-Raphaelites and the four volumes of *The Angel in the House* (1854–62) consider conjugal love, as in Book II, Canto VI: 'He makes his sorrow, when there's none; / His fancy blows both cold and hot; / Next to the wish that she'll be won, / His first hope is that she may not; / He sues, yet deprecates consent; / Would she be captured she must fly; / She looks too happy and content, / For whose least pleasure he would die'. He became a Roman Catholic in 1864 and published *The Unknown Eros* in 1877.

Paton, Sir Joseph Noel
Scottish poet *born* Dunfermline, Fife 13 December 1821
died 26 December 1901

Paton became a student at the Royal Academy, London, in 1843; in 1845 and 1847 he gained the premiums awarded by the Royal Commission at the Westminster Hall competitions. He became a Royal Scottish Academician in 1850 and the Queen's limner

(Scotland) in 1865. He was knighted in 1867. His visual work is allegorical and ornamental. In *Poems by a Painter* (1861) and *Spindrift* (1867) he shaped his pictorial imagination into formal verse: 'Young Love that was so fond, so fair, / With his mouth of rosy red, / Argent wing and golden hair, / And those blue eyen, glory-fed / From some fount of splendour, far / Beyond or moon or sun or star – / And can it be that he is dead?'

Patten, Brian
English poet *born* Liverpool 7 February 1946

Like Adrian Henri and Roger McGough, Patten was identified by the press as one of the 'Liverpool Poets' who followed lyrically in the footsteps of the Beatles when the group's fame drew international attention to their native city in the 1960s. He lives by writing and performing his own work which recreates, with imaginative embellishments, the events of his own youth. Thus his dislike of school is recast in satirical form in 'Little Johnny's Confession': 'This morning / being rather young and foolish / I borrowed a machinegun my father / had left hidden since the war, went out, / and eliminated a number of small enemies. / Since then I have not returned home.'

Paulin, Tom
Irish poet *born* Leeds 1949

The child of Scottish presbyterian parents who settled in Belfast, Paulin was brought up in Belfast and educated at the universities of Hull and Oxford. He became a lecturer in English at the University of Nottingham. He has published a critical study of *Thomas Hardy* (1975) and collections of verse including *Liberty Tree* (1983). The Ulster experience is evident in his work. 'Settlers', from his first collection *A State of Justice* (1977), describes how his parents came to Belfast: 'They cross from Glasgow to a black city / Of gantries, mills and steeples. They begin to belong. / He manages the Iceworks, is an elder of the Kirk; / She becomes, briefly, a cook in Carson's Army.'

Peacock, Thomas Love
English poet *born* Weymouth 18 October 1785
died 23 January 1866

Son of a glass-merchant, Peacock was the original of Dr Middleton in Meredith's *The Egoist* (1879) where he is described as 'a strong man, an athlete in his youth, a keen reader of facts and no reader of persons, genial, a giant at a task, a steady worker besides, but easily discomposed'. He entered, in 1819, the service of the East India Company and was Chief Examiner from

1837–56. His novels, such as *Nightmare Abbey* (1818), are highly imaginative and in (for example) *Maid Marian* (1822) he punctuates the prose with lyrics like 'Robin Hood': 'Bold Robin has robed him in ghostly attire, / And forth he is gone like a holy friar, / Singing hey down, how down, down, derry down!'

Pearse, Patrick
Irish poet *born* 1879 *died* Dublin May 1916

'I write it out in a verse – / MacDonagh and Macbride / And Connolly and Pearse' wrote W B Yeats (in 'Easter 1916') of those executed by the English for their part in the Easter Rising of 1916. Pearse was a prolific writer and also founder of St Enda's School, Dublin. During the Easter Rising, Pearse called on the spirit of Cuchulain to rally the rebels in the Post Office. While many of his poems have an urgent political message, 'I am Ireland' aspires to a mythical quality: 'I am Ireland: / I am older than the Old Woman of Beare. // Great my glory: / I that bore Cuchulainn the valiant. / / Great my shame: / My own children that sold their mother. // I am Ireland: / I am lonelier than the Old Woman of Beare.'

Peele, George
English poet *born* London *c*1558 *died c*1597

A salter's son, Peele was educated at Oxford and returned to London to earn himself a reputation as the most outrageously behaved writer associated with the 'University Wits': in 1579 he was ejected from Christ's Hospital, where his father lived, by the governors. He worked as an actor and wrote successful plays, most of them with excellent incidental lyrics. From *The Old Wife's Tale* (1595) come the lines beginning: 'Fair maid, white and red, / Comb me smooth, and stroke my head; / And thou shalt have some cockle bread. / Gently dip, but not too deep, / For fear thou make the golden beard to weep.'

Percival, James Gates
American poet *born* Berlin, near Hartford, Connecticut 18 September 1795 *died* Hazel Green, Wisconsin 2 May 1856

Son of a medical man, Percival graduated from Yale then qualified as a doctor. He was not content, however, to pursue one profession so switched from medicine to journalism then worked as a chemistry teacher and a geological surveyor. He was a skilled translator from various languages and a popular poet but found little peace. At the end of his life he went to Wisconsin to take up a post as state-geologist and fell into a decline. Poems of his often pursue the calm that so often eluded him. 'The Coral Grove' ends: 'Then, far below, in the peaceful sea, / The purple mullet and gold-fish rove, / Where the waters murmur tranquilly, / Through the bending twigs of the coral grove.'

Perrie, Walter
Scottish poet *born* Quarter, Lanarkshire 5 June 1949

Educated at Edinburgh University where he studied philosophy, Perrie co-founded the magazine *Chapman* in 1970. Deriving his Marxist aesthetic from a study of the poetry of Hugh MacDiarmid, Perrie's long poem *A Lamentation for the Children* (1977) explored the emotions of Lanarkshire miners. His collection *Concerning the Dragon* (1984) shows his command of a variety of forms and ends with the elegiac 'All to the Dark' in which he links himself with the Scottish tradition (Grieve being MacDiarmid's real name): 'Dunbar and Grieve – and Perrie, / *all to the dark go down*, / eat of the lotus berry / and in its darkness, drown.'

Philips, Ambrose
English poet *born* Shropshire *c*1675 *died* 18 June 1749

On account of the sickly sentimentality of some of his poems, Philips was described by Henry Carey as 'Namby-Pamby', a sobriquet Pope included in his *Dunciad*: 'And Namby Pamby be prefer'd for wit'. The nickname passed into the English language as a synonym for childish sentimentality. Philips was educated at Cambridge but fell foul of Pope in London, with disastrous consequences for his reputation. His lines 'To Miss Charlotte Pulteney in Her Mother's Arms' are representative of his style; 'Timely blossom, infant fair, / Fondling of a happy pair, / Every morn, and every night, / Their solicitous delight, / Sleeping, waking, still at ease, / Pleasing, without skill to please'.

Philips, John
English poet *born* Bampton, Oxfordshire 30 December 1676 *died* 15 February 1708

Son of the archdeacon of Salop, Philips was educated at Cambridge where he took a special interest in botany. *The Splendid Shilling* (1703), a parody of Milton's *Paradise Lost*, compares the possessor of the shilling with the problems of the poet: 'But I, whom griping Penury surrounds, / And Hunger, sure attendant upon Want, / With scanty offals, and small acid tiff, / (Wretched repast!) my meagre corpse sustain: / Then solitary walk, or doze at home / In garret vile, and with a warming puff / Regale chill'd fingers; or from tube as black / As winter-chimney, or well-polish'd jet, / Exhale mundungus, ill-perfuming scent!'

Philips, Katherine
English poet *born* London 1631 *died* London 1664

A merchant's daughter, Katherine Fowler was educated as a
presbyterian though later abandoned her 'presbyterian
principles'. In 1647 she married James Philips, a Welshman, and
helped him run his financial affairs. Her literary salon, the Society
of Friendship, brought her into contact with poets such as
Cowley and Henry Vaughan; her translation of Corneille's *Pompey*
brought her to the attention of the literary public. In her work
she speaks as 'Orinda', a persona that encouraged candid lines
like those in 'Orinda to Lucasia': 'Thou my Lucasia are far more
to me, / Than he to all the under-world can be; / From thee I've
heat and light, / Thy absence makes my night.' She died of
smallpox.

Pickthall, Marjorie
Canadian poet *born* Gunnersbury, England 1883 *died* 1922

Marjorie Pickthall was educated at Bishop Strachan School,
Toronto, and wrote novels and short stories with some success.
Her *Complete Poems* appeared in 1936. While her Canadian
contemporaries were intent on creating a national style, she
adhered to traditional English values in verse. Her work often has
a religious tone. 'Mary Tired', for example, tenderly retells a
familiar story: 'through the starred Judean night / She went in
travail of the Light: / With the earliest hush she saw / God beside
her in the straw. / One small taper glimmered clear, / Drowsing
Joseph nodded near'.

Picot, James
Australian poet *born* Baldock, Hertfordshire 1906
died Burma 1944

Picot came to Australia in 1923 and did farm work in the Darling
Downs in south-east Queensland. He studied theology though he
decided not to be ordained as an Anglican priest. During the
Second World War, he was captured by the Japanese in Singapore
and died in a prison-camp. His poetry is vividly descriptive and
excitedly impressionistic. 'Elegy for Liebe' þegins: 'Yield, utter,
offer, (you, her Darling Downs) / All Beauty – tender corn or late
the sheaves, / Whether alfalfa in October crowns / Your fences
heaving purple, or the leaves / Golden from willow into April
pool, / All down Dalrymple whirl, her memory / Be wild leaf
sweet, that early touch and cool. / Woodpecker, call, hill-bird!'

Pierpont, John
American poet *born* Litchfield, Connecticut 6 April 1785
died Medford, Connecticut 1866

Pierpont (whose great-grandfather was one of the founders of

Yale and whose grandson was the multimillionaire John Pierpont
Morgan) graduated from Yale in 1802. He practised law in Boston
then studied theology before returning to Boston as a minister.
His abolitionist views and anti-slavery poems offended his
congregation and after twenty-six years as pastor of the Hollis
Street Church, Boston, he was forced to resign. In his late
seventies he volunteered for the Civil War as a chaplain to the
troops; he died in poverty. His poem on 'The Fourth of July'
displays his fervour and hymn-like verse: 'O let freemen be our
sons / And let future Washingtons / Rise, to lead their valiant
ones / Till there's war no more!'

Pitter, Ruth
English poet *born* Ilford, Essex 1897
A schoolteacher's daughter, Ruth Pitter was educated in London
and worked, during the First World War, with the War Office.
She later joined an arts and craft firm then, in 1930, established
with a friend a Chelsea-based craft business. Though her work
appeared in *The New Age* and other prestigious places, she was
subsequently neglected as a poet. Though she is a skilled writer of
light verse, she can also bring dignity to simple subjects like 'The
Old Woman', a sonnet that ends with the villagers being
comforted: 'They live, they sleep, take comfort, knowing her /
Handmaid to love, priestess of life and death.'

Planché, James Robinson
English poet *born* London 27 February 1796 *died* 30 May 1880
Son of a watchmaker of Huguenot descent, Planché was articled
to a bookseller but turned to the stage, managing several theatres
and turning out more than two hundred plays. He also wrote
opera libretti, including the text for Weber's *Oberon* (1826). He
became Rouge Croix pursuivant at the Heralds' College in 1854
and Somerset Herald in 1866. His society verse, such as 'A Song
for the End of the Season', is accomplished: 'Sir John has this
moment gone by / In the brougham that was to be mine, / But,
my dear, I'm not going to cry, / Though I know where he's going
to dine. / I shall meet him at Lady Gay's ball / With that girl to his
arm clinging fast, / But it won't, love, disturb me at all, / I've
recovered my spirits at last.'

Plath, Sylvia
American poet *born* Boston, Massachusetts 27 October 1932
died London 11 February 1963
As the daughter of two German-speaking intellectuals Sylvia
Plath grew up in a close cultural climate; after graduating from
Smith College she won a fellowship to Cambridge University
where she met Ted Hughes then married him in 1956. Her

emotionally intense and rhythmically brittle poetry draws on painful experiences: her father's death when she was eight, her knowledge of atrocities like the concentration camps, the breakdown of her marriage. In 'Lady Lazarus' she says 'Dying / Is an art, like everything else. / I do it exceptionally well.' Her confessional style and suicide made her, for many readers, a symbol of the woman as a victim in a man's world.

Plomer, William
South African poet *born* Pietersburg, North Transvaal
10 December 1903 *died* 1973

Educated, in England, at Rugby School, Plomer returned to Africa as a farmer and trader. He lived for two years in Japan, then came back to England by way of Manchuria, Siberia, Russia, Poland and elsewhere. During the Second World War he worked at the Admiralty. He wrote novels, libretti for operas by Benjamin Britten (*Gloriana*, for example), and poems. His best poems are satirical and in 'The Playboy of the Demi-World: 1938' he gently mocks a familiar aesthetic type; 'He prances forward with his hands outspread / And folds all comers in a gay embrace, / A wavy toupee on his hairless head, / A fixed smile on his often-lifted face.'

Plunkett, Joseph Mary
Irish poet *born* Dublin 1887 *died* Dublin May 1916

Educated in Roman Catholic schools in Dublin and at Stonyhurst in England, Joseph Mary Plunkett became editor of the *Irish Review* in 1913. Like MacDonagh and Pearse, he was executed for taking part in the Easter Rising of 1916. *The Poems of Joseph Mary Plunkett* appeared in 1916. His poems, for example 'I See His Blood upon the Rose', have a melancholy tone and move with a religious ritual: 'I see his face in every flower; / The thunder and the singing of the birds / Are but his voice – and carven by his power / Rocks are his written words. // All pathways by his feet are worn, / His strong heart stirs the ever-beating sea, / His crown of thorns is twined with every thorn, / His cross is every tree.'

Poe, Edgar Allan
American poet *born* Boston, Massachusetts 19 January 1809
died Baltimore, Maryland 7 October 1849

Poe's parents were both actors who died when he was an infant and he was brought up by John Allan, a merchant. He spent two years in the US Army and later entered the Military Academy at West Point though he was dismissed in 1831. He earned his living as a journalist and as the author of classic tales of horror. His early poetry, published before he was twenty-two, is cast in the manner of the English Romantics. The mature poems he produced, in the last five years of his life, hauntingly express his fascination with death, as in 'Annabel Lee' which recalls 'my bride, / In the sepulchre there by the sea, / In her tomb by the sounding sea.'

Pomfret, John
English poet *born* Luton 1667 *died* London 1703

Son of the rector of Luton, Pomfret was educated at Cambridge and became minister of Malden, Bedfordshire. He died of smallpox. He was a pugnacious character who wrote, in the preface to his 1699 collection of poems, 'It is not the multitude of applauses, but the good sense of the applauders which establishes a valuable reputation'. Pomfret's own reputation was never high though his poem 'The Choice' was once popular: 'If Heaven the grateful liberty would give, / That I might choose my method how to live, / And all those hours propitious fate should lend, / In blissful ease and satisfaction spend, / Near some fair town I'd have a private seat, / Built uniform, not little, nor too great'.

Pope, Alexander
English poet *born* London 22 May 1688
died Twickenham 30 May 1744

Physically deformed and socially handicapped (on account of his Roman Catholic religion) Pope was aware from an early age of his own vulnerability. A victim of the cruelty of others he accordingly developed a powerful literary armoury to make the most of 'This long disease, my life' (as he called it in his 'Epistle to Dr Arbuthnott'). His mastery of rhyme, his exquisite sense of verbal balance and his brilliant epigrammatic wit made him one of the greatest satirists in verse, as he powerfully demonstrated in *The Dunciad* (1728). His view of the world combined cynicism with an appreciation of natural and manmade order, as he explained in *An Essay on Man* (1733): 'All nature is but art, unknown to thee; / All chance, direction which thou canst not see . . . One truth is clear, Whatever is, is right.'

Porter, Peter
Australian poet *born* Brisbane, Australia 1929

Son of a warehouseman, Porter settled in London in 1951 and worked at various jobs including advertising and literary journalism. His work played a part in the cultural shaping of the 1960s since *Once Bitten, Twice Bitten* (1961) was one of the most forceful books of the decade. Porter's style is satirical, his lines incisive; rather than seething with moral indignation he offers exact observations that speak for themselves. His main target is indifference which he considers in 'Annotations of Auschwitz':

'London is full of chickens on electric spits, / Cooking in windows where the public pass. / This, say the chickens, is their Auschwitz, / And all poultry eaters are psychopaths.'

Pound, Ezra
American poet *born* Hailey, Idaho 30 October 1885
died Venice 1 November 1972

Pound's father was an assayer in the Philadelphia Mint and the poet's passionate interest in economics is evident in the *Cantos* he composed from 1917 onwards. After studying Romance languages at Hamilton College, Clinton, he taught for a time before arriving in London in 1908. His impact on England was enormous and he was largely responsible for creating the cultural climate for the modernism of James Joyce and T S Eliot (whose *The Waste Land* is dedicated to Pound who helped shape it). His own poetry is erudite and allusive, often multilingual in manner. In his eighty-first Canto he declared: 'error is all in the not done, / all in the diffidence that faltered.'

Praed, Winthrop Mackworth
English poet *born* London 26 July 1802 *died* 15 July 1839

A lawyer's son, Praed was educated at Eton and Cambridge where he was twice winner of the Chancellor's Medal for English verse. Called to the Bar in 1829, he became a Member of Parliament but lost his seat when the Reform Bill was passed in 1832. He returned to Parliament and became Peel's Secretary of the Board of Control. His elegantly witty society verse is seen to advantage in 'Our Ball': 'You'll come to our Ball; – since we parted, / I've thought of you more than I'll say; / Indeed, I was half broken-hearted / For a week, when they took you away.' The poem ends: 'And you'll think of the spell that once bound you; / And you'll come – won't you come? – to our Ball?'

Pratt, E J
Canadian poet *born* Western Bay, Newfoundland
4 February 1883 *died* 1964

Edwin John Pratt, a Methodist minister's son, was educated at the University of Toronto where he studied theology and psychology. In 1920 he was appointed Professor of English at Toronto and remained in the city after retiring in 1953. He edited the *Canadian Poetry Magazine* from 1936 to 1943 and was an example to, and influence on, other Canadian poets who recognised him as a major figure. His *Collected Poems* appeared in 1972. In poems as sustained as 'The Titanic' (1935) he shows his ability to combine narration with comment: 'The quick return, the will to save, the race / Of snapping oars to put the realm of space / Between the half-filled lifeboats and the wreck.'

Price, Jonathan
English poet *born* 1931 *died* 10 February 1985

After National Service in the RAF, Jonathan Price read English at
Oxford. He was, from 1954–64, an editor in London, working for
a trade magazine and several book publishers. He joined Oxford
University Press in 1964. The best poems in his *Everything Must Go*
(1985) juxtapose different historical periods. 'Kilroy Was Here'
introduces a flint scraper, turned up by the plough, and takes the
poet back to neolithic times and forward to the 'umptieth-
century' with thoughts of the next man to receive the message of
mortality. 'The Old, Old Story' comments on the persistence of
warfare through the centuries, beginning with a man talking
about World War and ending as 'A listener lolled on furs beside
the fire, / Having just fashioned a much better spear.'

Prince, F T
English poet *born* Kimberley 1912

Educated in South Africa and at Oxford, Prince worked in the
USA before the Second World War. During the war he served as a
captain in the Intelligence Corps and afterwards earned his living
as a university professor of English. The title poem of his
collection *Soldiers Bathing* (1954) is an impressive meditative poem
that begins with an evocation of an actual scene and reaches out
for artistic and theological conclusions on the spectacle. In this
poem the couplets complement rather than contain the notion of
life enhanced by aesthetic awareness: 'I feel a strange delight
that fills me full, / A gratitude, as if evil itself were beautiful'.

Prior, Matthew
English poet *born* near Wimborne Minster, Dorset 21 July
1664 *died* Wimpole 18 September 1721

A joiner's son, Prior worked in his uncle's tavern in London
before the Earl of Dorset encouraged his literary talents by
sending him to Westminster School and Oxford. He was
appointed Plenipotentiary to France and helped draft the Treaty
of Utrecht (1713), an action that led to two years' imprisonment
in the Tower of London on the death of Queen Anne. After his
release his admirers brought out the 1718 folio editions of his
Poems which brought him £4,000. He wrote elegantly amusing
poems such as 'To a Child of Quality': 'She may receive and own
my flame, / For, though the strictest prudes should know it, /
She'll pass for a most virtuous dame, / And I for an
unhappy poet.'

Procter, Adelaide Anne
English poet *born* London 30 October 1825 *died* 2 February 1864

Daughter of Bryan Waller Procter – a solicitor, Commissioner of

Lunacy and poet – Adelaide wrote poems from an early age. She contributed pseudonymously to *Household Words* and *All the Year Round* and collected her verse in *Legends and Lyrics* (1858). She became a Roman Catholic in 1851 and was active in advocating women's rights. Her poem 'A Lost Chord' is still in circulation: 'Seated one day at the Organ, / I was weary and ill at ease, / And my fingers wandered idly / Over the noisy keys. // I do not know what I was playing, / Or what I was dreaming then; / But I struck one chord of music, / Like the sound of a great Amen.' She died of consumption.

Procter, Bryan Waller
English poet *born* Leeds 21 November 1787 *died* 5 October 1874

Procter was at Harrow at the same time as Byron then went to London where he was a successful solicitor and barrister. He published volumes such as *Dramatic Scenes* (1819) and his tragedy *Mirandola* (1821) was successfully produced at Covent Garden Theatre. From 1832–61 he was a Commissioner of Lunacy. He survived his daughter, Adelaide Anne Procter, by ten years. Procter (who wrote under the name Barry Cornwall – an approximate anagram of his Christian names) has, in poems such as 'The Sea', an ecstatic quality: 'The Sea! The Sea! the open Sea! / The blue, the fresh, the ever free! / Without a mark, without a bound, / It runneth the earth's wide regions 'round.'

Prowse, William Jeffery
English poet *born* Torquay 6 May 1836
died near Nice 17 April 1870

When Prowse was eight his father died, and he was raised by an uncle in Greenwich. He became a journalist, contributing to *Chamber's Journal*, the *Ladies' Companion*, the *National Magazine* and the *Daily Telegraph* for which he wrote leaders and articles on sport. 'The City of Prague' is one of the best examples of his excellent light verse: 'I dwelt in a city enchanted, / And lonely, indeed, was my lot; / Two guineas a week, all I wanted, / Was certainly all that I got. / Well, somehow I found it was plenty; / Perhaps you may find it the same, / If – *if* you are just five-and-twenty, / With industry, hope, and an aim'. He retired to Devon and, for the sake of his health, wintered at Cirniès, near Nice, where he died of consumption.

Pudney, John
English poet *born* Langley 1909 *died* 1977

A farmer's son, Pudney was educated at Gresham's School where he fell under the spell of his fellow-pupil W H Auden. He worked as a BBC producer and as a journalist and during the Second World War was an RAF Intelligence Officer. Though his postwar poetry was stylistically and thematically varied he remains best-known for his war poem 'For Johnny'. This was written on the back of an envelope during a London air-raid when the poet took refuge in a blacked-out pub in Whitehall. In 1944 the poem was quoted in full in Antony Asquith's film *The Way to the Stars*: 'Do not despair / For Johnny-head-in-air; / He sleeps as sound / As Johnny underground' is the first of three stanzas.

Purdy, Alfred
Canadian poet *born* near Wooler, Ontario 1918

After going to college in Belleville, Purdy became a peripatetic poet, travelling the world from his base in Ameliasburgh, Ontario. His collection *The Cariboo Horses* won the Governor General's Award for poetry in 1965. *Being Alive* collects his poems of the period 1958–78. His account of 'The Country North of Belleville' shows how subjectively he views each landscape he encounters: 'Yet this is the country of defeat / where Sisyphus rolls a big stone / year after year up the ancient hills / picnicking glaciers have left strewn / with centuries' rubble'. At the end of the poem he contemplates a return though 'we must enquire the way / of strangers'.

Quarles, Francis
English poet *born* near Romford 8 May 1592
died 8 September 1644

Quarles was born in the manor house of Stewards owned by his father, a surveyor-general of victualling for the Navy. Educated at Cambridge and Lincoln's Inn he was in Ireland, from 1626–30, as secretary to Archbishop Ussher. He was appointed Chronologer of the City of London in 1639 and supported the royalist side in the Civil War. He was twice married and had eighteen children by his first wife. Quarles wrote in the Metaphysical manner with the passion evident in his poem 'My Beloved is mine, and I am his': 'He is my altar, I his holy place; / I am his guest, and he my living food; / I'm his by penitence, he mine by grace; / I'm his by purchase, he is mine by blood'.

Raine, Craig
English poet *born* Bishop Auckland, County Durham
3 December 1944

Educated at Oxford University where he later taught, Craig Raine made his career in literary journalism and publishing. His wit and unusual powers of observation have created a modern Metaphysical poetry rich in startlingly fresh images. The title poem of his book *A Martian Sends a Postcard Home* (1979) portrays the world as an extra-terrestrial might see it: 'Mist is when the sky is tired of flight / and rests its soft machine on ground: then the

world is dim and bookish / like engravings under tissue paper.'
Raine's distinctive work has encouraged a school of so-called
'Martian' poets but he remains an original, always confronting
reality with the poetic resources of dream.

Raine, Kathleen

English poet *born* 14 June 1908

Brought up in Northumberland and educated at Cambridge,
where she graduated in natural sciences and worked as a research
fellow, Kathleen Raine was converted to Roman Catholicism in
1944. She describes herself as a Platonist and has been an
enthusiastic advocate of the informed mysticism of Blake; her
William Blake and Traditional Mythology (1968) combines
scholarship with a personal statement of her belief in a
transcendent world. In poems such as 'The Island Cross' (from
the sequence 'Eileann Chanaidh') she roots her faith in empirical
observation: 'Against grain of granite / Hardness of crystalline
rock-form mineral / Form spiritual is countergrained. . .'

Ralegh, Sir Walter

English poet *born* Hayes Barton, Devon *c*1552
died Tower Hill, London 29 October 1618

Ralegh began a life of adventure by soldiering in France
and Ireland and serving at sea against the Spaniards. One of
Elizabeth I's favourites, he was knighted in 1584, after an
expedition to North America during which he discovered and
named Virginia. On the death of Elizabeth I he was accused of
conspiring against James I and sentenced to death though he
escaped with imprisonment in the Tower of London. After his
voyage to Guiana he returned to London and James I had him
beheaded. He wrote spirited poems such as 'The Passionate Man's
Pilgrimage': 'Give me my scallop-shell of quiet, / My staff of faith
to walk upon, / My scrip of joy, immortal diet, / My bottle of
salvation'.

Ramsay, Allan

Scottish poet *born* Leadhills, Lanarkshire 15 October 1684
died Edinburgh 7 January 1758

Son of a mine manager, Ramsay went to Edinburgh in 1701 to
work as an apprentice wigmaker and, in 1719, became a
bookseller. His cultural impact on the capital was immense: for
example, he established, in 1725, the first circulating library in
Britain; and, in 1736, he opened a theatre (which was closed
under the Licensing Act of 1737). In *The Tea-Table Miscellany* (five
volumes, 1724–37) he collected Scottish songs. His Scots poetry
influenced Fergusson and Burns and his pastoral play *The Gentle
Shepherd* (1725) is an important contribution to Scottish drama.

'My Peggy is a Young Thing' ends: 'My Peggy sings sae saftly, / And in her sangs are tald, / With innocence the wale of sense, / At wau king of the fauld.'

wale choice; *wau king* watching; *fauld* fold

Randall, Dudley
American poet *born* 1914

Randall became a librarian in Detroit and publisher of the Boardside Press, established to promote the cause of black poetry. Like many other black poets he is concerned with the extension of black consciousness so his work is radical in tone and sustained by the power of indignation. In 'Roses and Revolutions' Randall writes: 'Musing on roses and revolutions, / I saw night close down on the earth like a great dark wing, / and the lighted cities were like tapers in the night, / and I heard the lamentations of a million hearts / regretting life and crying for the grave, / and I saw the Negro lying in the swamp with his face blown off'.

Randolph, Thomas
English poet *born* Newham-cum-Badby, Northamptonshire *died* 17 March 1635

A steward's son, Randolph was educated at Cambridge where he was acclaimed as a writer of English and Latin verse. He became friendly with Ben Jonson and lived somewhat riotously in London. As well as his *Poems* (1638) he wrote six plays including *Amyntas,* a pastoral comedy; and *The Muses' Looking-glass* (1638). His poems are metrically precise and his 'Ode to Master Anthony Stafford' catalogues the pleasures of the countryside: 'Come, spur away, / I have no patience for a longer stay, / But must go down, / And leave the chargeable noise of this great town: / I will the country see, / Where old simplicity, / Though hid in gray, / Doth look more gay / Than foppery in plush and scarlet clad.'

Rands, William Brighty
English poet *born* 1823 *died* 1880

From a poor family, Rands went to work in a warehouse at an early age. He educated himself and wrote under pseudonyms such as 'Henry Holbeach', 'Matthew Browne,' 'Timon Fieldmouse'. After studying stenography he obtained a job as a reporter in the Committee Rooms of the House of Commons and contributed to the *Illustrated Times*, *Good Words* and *Argosy*. In 1869 he published a book on *Chaucer's England*. His volume *Lilliput Lectures* (1871) contains poems, such as 'Beautiful World', which have a touching quality of affirmation: 'Great, wide, beautiful, wonderful World, / With the wonderful water round you curled, / And the wonderful grass upon your breast – / World, you are beautifully drest.'

Ransford, Tessa
Scottish poet *born* Bombay 8 July 1938

Educated in Scotland, Tessa Ransford spent eight years in Pakistan as the wife of a missionary. She returned to Scotland in 1968 and settled in Edinburgh. She published *Light of the Mind* in 1980, *Fools and Angels* in 1984. In 1983 she established the Scottish Poetry Library in Edinburgh – Scotland's first poetry library – and became its director. Her own verse is delicate yet demonstrative as she writes with emotional anguish of the brutality of the modern world and finds an answer in the feminine principle of creativity. 'Woman' begins: 'Woman is / acute angles of feeling; / wires exposed to the world, / connected at the womb.'

Ransom, John Crowe
American poet *born* Pulaski, Tennessee 30 April 1888
died Gambier, Ohio 3 July 1974

One of the most influential American authors, Ransom was one of The Fugitives, a group of Southern poets associated with the *Fugitive* poetry magazine which ran from 1922-5. As such he expressed fundamentally agrarian ideals. His book *The New Criticism* (1941) gave the name to a leading school of American criticism which insisted on the aesthetic autonomy of a literary work. From 1937, Ransom taught at Kenyon College, Ohio, and founded the *Kenyon Review*. His own poems, such as 'Old Mansion (After Henry James)' is attentive to verbal texture: 'As an intruder I trudged with careful innocence / To mask in decency a meddlesome stare'.

Rawlinson, Gloria
New Zealand poet *born* Haapai, Tonga 1918

Gloria Rawlinson came to New Zealand in 1924 and settled in Auckland. She published *Gloria's Book* in 1933, *The Perfume Vendor* in 1936, *Of Clouds and Pebbles* in 1963. The title sequence of *The Islands Where I was Born* (1955) is a vivid evocation of the landscape that shaped the poet's imagination: 'For then I thought we lived on the only route, / In the apple of a heavenly eye, the fond / Providence of flowery oils and fruit, / Kingdom of Joy and Enjoy to the farthest frond. // I was out of all reckoning one last Steamer Day / When I saw the Pacific skyward beyond our coral; / Farewells fluttered . . . palm-trees turned away / And cool on my cheeks the wind from a new littoral.'

Read, Sir Herbert
English poet *born* Kirkbymoorside, Yorkshire 4 December 1893 *died* 12 June 1968

A farmer's son, Read was educated at Leeds University and served as an infantry officer in France and Belgium in the First World War during which he won the DSO and MC. He edited the *Burlington Magazine* (from 1933–9) and was knighted in 1953. Though an advocate of experimentalism in visual art, Read published many poems that show a fine command of the conventions of English verse. His address 'To a Conscript of 1940' reflects on the sacrifice of the First World War: 'We think we gave in vain. The world was not renewed. / There was hope in the homestead and anger in the streets / But the old world was restored and we returned / To the dreary field and workshop, and the immemorial feud / Of rich and poor.'

Reading, Peter
English poet *born* 1946

Peter Reading's fragmentary and frequently surrealistic verse alternates an oddity of perception with a matter-of-factual brutality. In 'Editorial' he is 'having the shakes / uncellophaning fags this crapulous morning' while in 'Dark Continent' he delicately evokes the way 'A rose / finger of dawn caresses a mud hut'. His forceful narrative poems make their impact by simulating the speech of antisocial creatures. 'At Home' presents a crime in counterpoint for after the description of an assault on an old woman there is the maniacal voice of the thug: 'Then we gets this knife thing / what she had hung on the wall like / and we gives her face the old quick / criss-cross with the point.'

Reaney, James
Canadian poet *born* near Stratford, Ontario 1 September 1926

Educated at the University of Toronto, Reaney became a professor of English at the University of Western Ontario. He had success as a dramatist and published, for example, *Apple Butter and Other Plays for Children* (1973). His *Selected Shorter Poems* came out in 1975, *Selected Longer Poems* in 1976. His poems range from the whimsicality of 'The Chough' to the amused eroticism of 'The Oracular Portcullis' which ends: 'Slowly Illyria made / Her delirious epigram: / "It is surely a well-known fact, / My dear, / That women are concave, / And men are convex?" / Thus spake Illyria; this question she posed, / Then quite quickly her portcullis closed.'

Redgrove, Peter
English poet *born* 1932

Redgrove read Natural Sciences at Cambridge and has worked as a research scientist and as a lecturer at the Falmouth School of Art. Stylistically his work harks back to the grand manner of the early Eliot so that metaphorically dense diction is expressed in conversationally fluent rhythms. The rich verbal texture is created out of enjambement, internal rhyme, alliteration and a habit of repeating keywords like musical notes suggesting set responses. His is an ecstatic, affirmative poetry written in celebration of the bewildering variety of the natural world. In 'The Apple-Broadcast' he opens with 'A valley full of doctor apples, / A valley-stream like flaming straw'.

Reed, Henry
English poet *born* Birmingham 1914

Reed attended school and university in his native Birmingham. After working as a schoolteacher he became a freelance journalist until called up in 1941. His sequence 'Lessons of the War', from *A Map of Verona* (1946), begins with 'Naming of Parts' in which the poet counterpoints the official voice of the army instructor with the lyrical reflections of a listener: 'This is the lower sling swivel. And this / Is the upper sling swivel, whose use you will see, / When you are given your slings. And this is the piling swivel, / Which in your case you have not got. The branches / Hold in the gardens their silent, eloquent gestures, / Which in our case we have not got.'

Reed, Whittemore
American poet *born* New Haven, Connecticut 1919

Reed was educated at Yale and taught at Carleton College. In 1964–5 he was consultant in poetry at the Library of Congress and then became a member of the staff of the National Institute of Public Affairs in Washington, DC. His volumes of verse include *Poems New and Selected* (1967). Reed's work is sophisticated in style and poignant in tone. His 'The Walk Home' is a reflection on the process of growing old: 'pipes and slippers / Move to their destined places, swords to theirs; / And one walking home at dusk with the evening paper /Thinks with erosive irreverence that perhaps / He should let his subscription to that sheet lapse.'

Reese, Lizette Woodworth
American poet *born* Waverley (Baltimore), Maryland 9 January 1856 *died* Baltimore, Maryland 17 December 1935

Lizette Woodworth Reese taught in local schools for forty-eight years of her life. Her first collection *A Branch of May* appeared in 1887 and her last collection *Pastures* came out two years before her death. H L Mencken pronounced her the outstanding lyric poet of her generation. She wrote several excellent sonnets, including the poignant tale of 'The Second Wife': 'She knows, being woman, that for him she holds / The space kept for the second blossoming, / Unmixed with dreams, held tightly in the folds / Of the accepted and long-proper thing'. Her memoir *A Victorian Village* (1929) describes the funeral procession of Lincoln passing through Baltimore.

Reeves, William Pember

New Zealand poet *born* Canterbury, New Zealand 1857 *died* 1932

Reeves studied law in New Zealand and was called to the Bar but became a journalist. He subsequently published various volumes of prose and poetry and served as High Commissioner for New Zealand from 1905 to 1909. His patriotic tribute to 'New Zealand' expresses simple sentiments with vigour: 'God girt her about with the surges / And winds of the masterless deep, / Whose tumult uprouses and urges / Quick billows to sparkle and leap. / He filled from the life of their motion / Her nostrils with breath of the sea, / And gave her afar in the ocean /A citadel free.' The poem ends optimistically: 'And clear from her lamp newly lighted / Shall stream o'er the billows upcurled / A light as of wrongs at length righted, / Of Hope to the world.'

Reid, Christopher

English poet *born* Hong Kong 13 May 1949

Reid is usually grouped along with Craig Raine as one of the 'Martian' school of modern Metaphysical poets and there is, in his work, a love of linguistic puzzles and themes that tease the imagination of the reader. Reid's personal strength lies in his ability to transform subjects, normally taken for granted, into something delightfully rich and strange. His 'Folk Tale', for example, is an ingenious portrayal of a golfer: 'And then there was a mad astronomer, / the shepherd of a solitary moon, / who chased his tiny, pock-marked planet / over the hills for half a morning. / The countryside was his enemy: / uncouth heather and highwayman copses / kept taking his jewel and hiding it. / His only friends were the eighteen pickpockets.'

Rendall, Robert

Scottish poet *born* 1898 *died* 1967

Rendall lived in Kirkwall, Orkney, where he was a partner in a drapery firm. Raised as a Plymouth brother he wrote pamphlets about his Calvinist persuasion and also took an energetic interest in the shells of Orkney. He published *Country Sonnets* in 1946, *Orkney Variants* in 1951. He wrote in English, Scots and in the Orkney dialect. 'The Fisherman', perhaps his best composition, was described by George Mackay Brown as 'a perfect poem'. It begins: 'Auld jeems o' Quoys, wha erst wi' leid and line / Keen as

a whitemaa, reaped the Rousay Soond, / And in his weathered
yawl a twalmonth syne / Set lapster-creels the Westness craigs
aroond'.

wha who; *erst* formerly; *whitemaa* gull

Rexroth, Kenneth

American poet *born* South Bend, Indiana 22 December 1905
died Montecito, California 6 June 1982

After being orphaned at the age of thirteen, Rexroth did various
manual jobs and acquired a radical attitude to politics. He moved
to San Francisco in 1927, becoming one of the city's most
prominent cultural figures. He exhibited his paintings and
promoted concerts of poetry-and-jazz; from 1960–8 he was a
columnist with the San Francisco *Examiner*. His work commands a
variety of metrical modes and he can range from a casual
conversational tone to the formal control of his literary ballad
'Song from a Dance Play': 'Her skirt is of green velvet, too, / And
shows her silken thigh, / Purple leather for her shoe, / Dark as her
blue eye.'

Reznikoff, Charles

American poet *born* 1894 *died* 1976

A lawyer by training, Reznikoff did not practise but instead wrote
novels, verse plays and poems. He was one of the Objectivist
poets of the 1930s, extending Pound's aesthetic of sculptural
verse. His major achievement is *Testimony* (1965, 1968), his poetic
account of American life from 1885–1900. It is an anecdotal
narrative insisting on factual precision: 'There were twenty wire-
stitching machines on the floor, worked by a shaft that ran under
the table; / as each stitcher put her work through the machine, /
she threw it on the table.' *The Complete Poems of Charles Reznikoff*
appeared in two volumes in 1978.

Rhys, Ernest

Welsh poet *born* London 17 July 1859 *died* 25 May 1946

Rhys was brought up in Carmarthen, his father's native town, and
trained as a mining engineer. He moved to London in 1885 as a
freelance writer and became friendly with Yeats, Dowson and
Lionel Johnson. He was the editor of Everyman's Library and
made many important works widely available. His own verse, in
such collections as *Rhymes for Everyman* (1933), is metrically
conservative. 'The Ballad of the Homing Man' is an exceptional
evocation of domesticity: '"Three voices in a doorway," he says –
"a woman's form, / And a lighted hearth behind her can make a
desert warm. // And what is Heaven but a house, like any other
one, / Where the homing man finds harbour and the hundred
roads are done?"'

Rich, Adrienne
American poet *born* Baltimore 1929

While a senior at Radcliffe College, Adrienne Rich published her
first collection, *A Change of World* (1951). She later lived in
Cambridge, Massachusetts and Manhattan. She spent a year in
England on a Guggenheim Fellowship and also held an Amy
Lowell Travelling Scholarship. The title poem of her *Diving into
the Wreck* (1977) explores an imaginative territory of her own
making in underwater images: 'the thing I came for: / the wreck
and not the story of the wreck / the thing itself and not the myth /
the drowned face always staring / toward the sun / the evidence of
damage / worn by salt and sway into this threadbare beauty / the
ribs of the disaster / curving their assertion / among the tentative
haunters.'

Riddell, Alan
Scottish poet *born* Townsville, Australia 1927 *died* London 1977

Riddell was the son of Scottish parents and was educated in
Scotland. He worked as a journalist with the *Daily Telegraph* in
London but spent much of his time in Scotland where he came
under the influence of the experimental poet Ian Hamilton
Finlay. Riddell was fascinated by the visual possibilities of
typography and produced a collection of his concrete poems
under the title *Eclipse* (1972). His more conventional poems are
elliptical in effect, as in 'Goldfish at an Angle': 'And even head-
on / curiously they flatten / themselves against glass against eyes
against / – the world.'

Riddell, Elizabeth
Australian poet *born* Napier, New Zealand 1909

After an education in New Zealand, Elizabeth Riddell began her
journalistic career in 1930 with *Smith's Weekly* of Sydney and the
Sydney *Sunday Sun*. She married E N Greatorex in 1935, worked
as a war correspondent during the Second World War, then
returned to Australia in 1945. Her lushly descriptive style is seen
to advantage in 'The Island Graves': 'From out the landless sea
they sailed towards / The Islands swaying on their coral stems, /
To where the great white parrakeets swooped and screamed /
Their witless language, and the coco palms / Streamed all one way
between / The wind's wet fingers.'

Ridge, Lola
American poet *born* 1873 *died* 1941

Lola Ridge moved from Ireland to Australia then came to the
USA in 1907. She earned her living by taking on what work was
available and was a model and factory worker as well as an
illustrator, copywriter and writer of pulp fiction. An anarchist,

she protested, like fellow poets Edna Millay and Dorothy Parker, against the trial of the Italian immigrants Sacco and Vanzetti, believing they were sent to prison and eventually executed for their anarchist views. Her work is radical in tone, as in 'Spires': 'Spires of Grace Church, / For you the workers of the world / Travailed with the mountains.'

Riding, Laura

American poet *born* New York 16 January 1901

After her divorce from Louis Gottschalk in 1925 Laura Riding went to Egypt with Robert Graves and his wife and returned to England with them. She seriously injured herself in a fall, in 1929, from a fourth-storey window then went with Graves to live in Mallorca. Her formidable personality and feminist views greatly impressed Graves whose book *The White Goddess* (1948) is partly inspired by her. She parted from Graves and married Schulyer Jackson in 1941. After the publication of her collected *Poems* in 1938 she renounced poetry. In 'The Virgin' she writes 'My flesh is at a distance from me. / Yet approach and touch it: / It is as near as anyone can come.'

Riley, James Whitcomb

American poet *born* Greenfield, Indiana 7 October 1849
died 22 July 1916

A lawyer's son, Riley left school at sixteen and became a sign and house painter. Later he diversified into writing and acting and achieved great success as an entertainer, giving readings in the Hoosier dialect. He was fond of practical jokes and once published his poem 'Leonainie' over the name of Edgar Allan Poe. One of his most endurable poems is 'Little Orphant Annie': 'You better mind yer parents, and yer teachers fond and dear, / An' churish them 'at loves you, an' dry the orphant's tear, / An' he'p the pore and needy ones 'at clusters all about, / Er the Gobble-uns's'll git you / Ef you / Don't / Watch / Out!'

Roberts, Charles G D

Canadian poet *born* Douglas, New Brunswick 10 January
1860 *died* 26 November 1943

A minister's son, Charles George Douglas Roberts was educated at New Brunswick University and was (from 1885-95) Professor of English at King's College, Nova Scotia. He moved to New York, in 1897, to devote himself to writing and during the First World War served with the Canadian Army, eventually as a major. One of the Canadian poets known as the Group of the Sixties, he was also well known for his novels and books on animal life. His hopes for his country are expressed, emphatically, in 'Canada': 'The Saxon's force, the Celtic fire, / These are thy manhood's heritage! / Why rest with babes and slaves? Seek higher / The place of race and age.'

Roberts, Michael
English poet *born* Bournemouth 1902 *died* December 1948
Educated at Cambridge, Roberts became a schoolteacher in Newcastle upon Tyne. He was an energetic anthologist and his *New Signatures* (1932), *New Country* (1933), and *The Faber Book of Modern Verse* (1936) defined the poetry of the 1930s and established the ascendancy of the school of Auden. In his influential introduction to the Faber anthology, Roberts claimed that 'the need for an evaluating, clarifying poetry has never been greater than it appears to be today.' His own poems, such as 'The Castle', seek such contemporary relevance: 'Suburbs creep up the hill, and the trams are running, /Children find ghostly playmates in the ruins'.

Robinson, Edwin Arlington
American poet *born* Head Tide, Maine 22 December 1869
died New York 6 April 1935
Raised in Gardiner, Maine ('Tilbury Town' in his poems) Robinson had an unhappy upbringing: his father, a merchant, was obsessed by spiritualism; his mother died of diphtheria; his brother was a drug addict. Depressed and given to drinking, he endured poverty until President Theodore Roosevelt came across *The Children of the Night* (1897) and got him a job at the New York Custom House. He achieved success with his verse-novels and received the Pulitzer Prize for his *Collected Poems* of 1921. Robinson's poems invest traditional forms with an ironic intelligence, as in 'New England': 'Joy shivers in the corner where she knits / And Conscience always has the rocking-chair'.

Rochester, Lord
English poet *born* Ditchley, near Woodstock 1 April 1647
died Woodstock 26 July 1680
John Wilmot, second Earl of Rochester, was eleven when he succeeded his father. After an Oxford education he did the Grand Tour then returned to England where he became notorious as a courtier given to drunkenness and debauchery. Of Charles II he wrote a memorable premature epitaph: 'Here lies our Sovereign Lord the King, / Whose word no man relies on; / Who never said a foolish thing, / Nor ever did a wise one.' Rochester's satirical verse is savage and some of his greatest lines are to be found in his outrageously bawdy poems. Before his death Rochester repented his sins but he is remembered as one of the most obstreperous, and gifted, rakes of the Restoration.

Rodgers, W R

Irish poet *born* Belfast 1909 *died* Los Angeles 1968

William Robert Rodgers was educated at Queen's University, Belfast, then became (from 1939–46) minister of Loughall Presbyterian Church, County Armagh. He worked in London as a BBC producer from 1946–52 and was later poet in residence at Claremont College, Los Angeles. The epilogue to 'The Character of Ireland' shows both his wit and verbal vivacity: 'I am Ulster, my people an abrupt people/Who like the spiky consonants in speech / And think the soft ones cissy; who dig / The *k* and *t* in orchestra, detect sin / In sinfonia, get a kick out of / Tin cans, fricatives, fornication, staccato talk, / Anything that gives or takes attack, / Like Micks, Tagues, tinkers' gets, Vatican.'

Roethke, Theodore

American poet *born* Saginaw, Michigan 25 May 1908
died Bainbridge Island, Puget Sound, Seattle 1 August 1963

Roethke's father and uncle owned a large greenhouse in his hometown (ninety miles northwest of Detroit) and the poet's horticultural imagery was thus suggested from an early age. He taught English at the University of Washington from 1947–63 and died after suffering a heart attack while swimming in a neighbour's pool on Bainbridge Island. His *Collected Poems* appeared in 1966. His poems impose a conceptual order on nature and in his 'Meditation at Oyster River' he seems to anticipate his death, wishing to be at one with water, 'The tide rustling in, sliding between the ridges of stone, / The tongues of water, creeping in, quietly.'

Rogers, Samuel

English poet *born* London 30 July 1763 *died* 18 December 1855

Rogers followed his father into a bank of which he became principal partner. A rich man, he enjoyed encouraging authors and artists and his breakfasts became cultural entertainments attended by the leading figures of his time. His own work was accomplished rather than original. *An Ode to Superstition* (1786) contains his lines on rural tranquillity: 'Mine be a cot beside the hill; / A bee-hive's hum shall soothe my ear; / A willowy brook, that turns a mill, / With many a fall shall linger near.' Rogers also wrote *Human Life* (1819) and *Italy* (1822). On the death of Wordsworth he was offered the Poet Laureateship but declined the position.

Rolland, John

Scottish poet *born c*1530 *died c*1580

A presbyter of the diocese of Glasgow and, in 1555, a notary in

Dalkeith, Rolland had connexions with the Scottish court. His allegory *The Court of Venus* appeared in 1575 and his *The Sevin Seages translatit out of prois in Scottish meter* in 1578. The Epilogue to *The Sevin Seages* begins: 'In haist ga hy thee to sum hoill, / And hyde thee, be not callit ane buik; / Ga, cowne thee owir all clene with coill, / Sone smeir thee owir with smiddie smuik, / Or scour pottis to sume creischie Cuik: / Or in sum kitching turne the speit: / Amang Ladeis thou dar not luik, / For thay will on thee with thair feit; / For men of gude thou art not meit: / Thay will thee hald of small availl'.

cowne begrime; *smiddie* smithy; *pottis* pots; *creischie* greasy

Rolls, Eric
Australian poet *born* Grenfell, New South Wales 1923

Son of a farmer, Rolls was taught through the NSW Correspondence School before continuing his education in Sydney. During the Second World War he was with the Australian Imperial Force in New Guinea and Bougainville. Later he farmed his own land near Narrabri, NSW. His poems provide an informative account of his experience as a farmer. 'Sheaf tosser', for example, confronts the brooding figure of the crow: 'My fork grows heavy as the light grows dim. / There are five sheaves left but I've fear of a whim / That one of the crows has an evil eye / And the five sheaves left will be there when I die / For each bird's forgotten how to fly / Till he drives out my soul with the force of his cry'.

Rorie, David
Scottish poet *born* Edinburgh 17 March 1867
died Aberdeen 18 February 1946

David Rorie spent his working life – in Fife and lower Deeside – as a doctor and what leisure time he had as a writer of Scots verse. Though he was a graduate of Edinburgh University's famous Medical Faculty he brought to his writing a penchant for folksy sentiments and proverbial home-truths. Rorie shaped his vigorous verse by reworking the stuff of local legend and current gossip and is at his best when rattling off a good story in the vernacular. His humour is warm and includes his own profession, in 'The Auld Doctor': 'Tak' ony job ye like ava! / Tak' trade, the poopit or the law, / But gin ye're wise ye'll haud awa / Frae medical degree, O!'

ava at all; *poopit* pulpit; *gin* if; *haud* hold

Roscoe, William Caldwell
English poet *born* Liverpool 20 September 1823
died 30 July 1859

Grandson of William Roscoe, the historian of the Medici, Roscoe was educated at University College, London. He entered the Middle Temple and was called to the Bar in 1850. After practising law for two years he went into semi-retirement through ill health. He died of typhoid. His sonnets, such as 'Daybreak in February', are descriptively effective: 'Over the ground white snow, and in the air / Silence. The stars, like lamps soon to expire, / Gleam tremblingly; serene and heavenly fair, / The eastern hanging crescent climbeth higher. / See, purple on the azure softly steals / And Morning, faintly touched with quivering fire, / leans on the frosty summits of the hills'.

Roscommon, Earl of
English poet *born c*1633 *died* 1684

Wentworth Dillon, fourth Earl of Roscommon was the son of James Dillon and Elizabeth Wentworth. He was born in Ireland but sent to Yorkshire by his uncle, the Earl of Strafford, Lord Deputy of Ireland. Educated at the University of Caen, he travelled on the Continent, returned to England at the Restoration of 1660 and became Master of the Horse to the Duchess of York. He was the first critic to publicly praise Milton's *Paradise Lost* and his own *Essay on Translated Verse* (1684, revised 1685) has a moralistic tone: 'Immodest words admit of no defence, / For want of decency is want of sense. / What moderate fop would rake the park or stews, / Who among troops of faultless nymphs may choose?'

Rosenberg, Isaac
English poet *born* Bristol 1890 *died* the Somme 1 April 1918

Born into a poor Jewish family and brought up in London's East End, Rosenberg was apprenticed at fourteen to a firm of engravers then, thanks to the patronage of three Jewish ladies, studied painting at the Slade School. Suffering from tuberculosis he moved to South Africa for health reasons, but returned to enlist with the Suffolk Regiment in May 1915. He was killed in battle. In his war poems, such as 'Dead Man's Dump', he used pictorially precise imagery to evoke the alarming atmosphere of battle: 'The air is loud with death, / The dark air spurts with fire, / The explosions ceaseless are. . . Maniac Earth! howling and flying, / your bowel / Seared by the jagged fire'.

Rosenblatt, Joe
Canadian poet *born* Toronto 1933

Joe Rosenblatt is a visual as well as a verbal artist who lives at Qualicum Beach, British Columbia. For his collection *Top Soil* he won the Governor General's Award for Poetry in 1976; in 1983 he published *The Brides of the Stream*. Pictorially alert, he has a metaphorical, almost Metaphysical, manner. 'All Worlds Lead to the Lobe' ends on an accumulation of images: 'Reflections bounce off the billiard table / solipsist spheres roll into the pockets of ears / and little people in boots of metaphor await the thunders / before the minnows of happiness change into adults.'

Ross, Alan

English poet *born* Calcutta 1922

Ross played cricket and squash for Oxford University and retained his interest in sport, celebrating it in journalism and in poems as compelling as his tribute to 'Stanley Matthews', the great footballer; 'he draws / Defenders towards him, the ball a bait / They refuse like a poisoned chocolate, / retreating, till he slows his gait / To a walk, inviting the tackle, inciting it.' He served on destroyers during the Second World War and became an Intelligence Officer in Germany. He edits the *London Magazine* and publishes books under the journal's imprint. He has written books on travel and cricket and several collections including *To Whom it May Concern* (1958).

Ross, Alexander

Scottish poet *born* Kincardine O'Neil 13 April 1699
died 20 May 1784

Educated at Marischall College, Aberdeen, Ross became parish schoolmaster at Lochlee, Angus. In 1768 he published *Helenore; or, the Fortunate Shepherdess: a Pastoral Tale in the Scottish Dialect, along with a few Songs*. Because of the 'few songs', not the pastoral drama, Ross is remembered as a writer. 'Woo'd, and Married, and A'' is his best-known song: 'Wooed and married and a', / Married and wooed and a'; / The dandilly toast of the parish / Is wooed and married and a'. / The wooers will now ride thinner, / And by, when they wonted to ca'; / 'Tis needless to speer for the lassie / That's wooed and married and a'.'
dandilly over-admired; *speer* enquire

Ross, W W E

Canadian poet *born* Peterborough, Ontario 1894 *died* 1966
Educated at the University of Toronto, Ross worked as a geophysicist with the Agincourt Magnetic Observatory near Toronto. His selected poems, *Shapes & Sounds,* were posthumously published in 1968. Perhaps because of his professional concern with nature, Ross wrote poems protesting against man's assault

on his environment. In some poems he expresses an impulse to merge with nature, in others he expresses an ecological anguish, as in the lines beginning thus: 'The saws were shrieking / and cutting into / the clean white wood / of the spruce logs / or the tinted hemlock / that smells as sweet – / or stronger pine, / the white and the red.'

Rossetti, Christina Georgina
English poet *born* London 5 December 1830
died London 29 December 1894

Christina Rossetti, whose expressively melancholy features were portrayed in the paintings of her brother Dante Gabriel Rossetti, embodied many of the ideals of the Pre-Raphaelite Brotherhood. She was devoted to the Anglican faith and invested her verse (for example, 'In the Bleak Mid-Winter') with spiritual values. She never married though she had her admirers; and she gladly shared the troubles of her sister Maria (who died of cancer) and her brother Dante (who suffered from depression). Her religious verse has both formal control and the emotional anguish seen in 'A Better Resurrection': 'I lift mine eyes, but dimmed with grief / No everlasting hills I see; / My life is in the falling leaf; / O Jesus, quicken me.'

Rossetti, Dante Gabriel
English poet *born* London 12 May 1828
died near Margate 9 April 1882

Son of the former curator of antiquities in Naples Museum Rossetti studied painting and, in 1848, became one of the founders of the Pre-Raphaelite school of painting. When his wife Elizabeth Siddal died in 1862 he buried with her the manuscript of a collection of *Poems* which was recovered and published in 1870. An insomniac he sought relief in the drug chloral which ruined his already poor health. His pictorially vivid poems are often morbid in theme, as in 'The Orchard-pit': 'This in my dream is shown me; and her hair / Crosses my lips and draws my burning breath; / Her song spreads golden wings upon the air, / Life's eyes are gleaming from her forehead fair, / And from her breasts the ravishing eyes of Death.'

Rowbotham, David
Australian poet *born* Darling Downs, Toowomba, Queensland 1924

Rowbotham worked as a teacher in Queensland before serving with the Royal Australian Air Force during the Second World War. Subsequently he studied at the universities of Brisbane and Sydney, took up a career in journalism, and joined the staff of the Brisbane *Courier*. His work is unassuming yet descriptively sound and thematically serious. 'First Man Lost in Space' reaches out imaginatively to infinity: 'I go before, / Before gods grew, / To where none knew / Creation, nor, / Trailing the plume / Of ice and fire, / The rose desire. / Another bloom / Shall summon me, / Shall save us all, / And the past be / Perpetual'.

Rowland, J R
Australian poet *born* Armidale, New South Wales 1925

After studying at Sydney University, John Rowland joined the Department of External Affairs and subsequently represented Australia in his diplomatic duties in Moscow, London, Indo-China and the United Nations. His international experience allows him to put Australia in a global context. 'Canberra in April' gives details of everyday life with 'Golf at the weekend, gardening after five' before evoking 'A sense of the pale curving continent / That, though a cliché, may still work unseen / And, with its script of white-limbed trees, impart / A cure for habit, some beneficent / Simplicity or steadiness of heart.'

Rukeyser, Muriel
American poet *born* New York 15 December 1915
died 17 February 1980

Educated at Vassar College, Muriel Rukeyser was a woman who applied her splendid talents to both literature and political life. She was in Spain during the Civil War and also visited Hanoi during the Vietnam War. She wrote informative books (on Willard Gibbs and Wendell Wilkie), translated the poems of Ocavia Paz (1961), and celebrated (in her poem 'Ann Burlak') such figures as 'the anonymous Negro woman who held off the guns, / the anonymous prisoner, anonymous cotton-picker / trailing her robe of sack in a proud train, / anonymous writer of these and mill-hand, anonymous city-walker'. Her radical tone and feminist philosphy gave her work much ideological power.

Rumens, Carol
English poet *born* London 1946

Rumens went to Catholic schools before reading Philosophy at London University. Despite her religious background she is not confessional by temperament but affirmative by inclination. She is able to consider the fact of her feminity as a gift to be shared rather than a burden to be endured. Her finely structured poem 'The Most Difficult Door' conveys maternal feelings with a sense of surprise that an individual could be so elemental: 'I sometimes think they must have swum like clouds, / My daughters, through those sea-blue attitudes / Of birth, where I was nothing but the dark / Muscle of time. I bear the water-mark / As proof, but that my flesh could be so filled / And concentrated, heart to heart with child'.

Russell, George William

Irish poet *born* Lurgan, Armagh 10 April 1867
died Bournemouth 17 July 1935

'AE', as he styled himself when writing, went to the School of Art, Dublin, where he met W B Yeats. A prolific painter who never exhibited his work, he worked at various jobs (in a brewery, for example) before involving himself in the Home Rule movement and the Irish Literary Renascence. A founder of the Abbey theatre and editor of the *Irish Statesman*, he produced a good deal of mystical verse and was a powerful influence on Irish cultural life. 'Germinal' begins: 'Call not thy wanderer home as yet / Though it be late; / Now is his first assailing of / The invisible gate. / Be still through that light knocking. The hour / Is thronged with fate.'

Sackville, Thomas

English poet *born* Buckhurst, Sussex 1536 *died* 19 April 1608

After an education at Oxford and Cambridge, Thomas Sackville became a barrister at the Inner Temple. In 1558 he entered parliament and in 1567 was created first Earl of Dorset. Later he served as Lord Treasurer of the Privy Council and Chancellor of Oxford University. His finest poetic work is the 79-stanza 'Induction' to the first enlarged edition of *A Mirror for Magistrates* (1563). Sackville's personification of War is devastatingly vivid: 'Cities he sackt and relmes that whilome flowred / In honnor glorie and rule above the best / He overwhelmed and all their fame devoured, / Consumed, destroied, wasted and never cest / Til he their welth their name and al oprest'.

Salkey, Andrew

Caribbean poet *born* Panama 1928

The son of Jamaican parents, Salkey went to school in Jamaica and came to London in 1951. He taught in a secondary school and later moved to the USA as a lecturer. Best known as a novelist, he published his first novel *A Quality of Violence* in 1959; he has also written children's novels such as *Hurricane* (1964) and *Drought* (1966). As a poet he published *Jamaican Symphony* in 1956 and has subsequently written powerful poems of political protest such as 'Images of Nelson Mandela', about the imprisoned black South African leader: 'A country of the mind, where justice peaks / above a tableland of common wealth / and grounding strength, in a sunrise / of common action across the veldt.'

Samwell, David
Welsh poet *born* Nantglyn, Denbighshire 1751 *died* 1798

Samwell was a surgeon on the voyage of the *Discovery* and, as such, witnessed the murder of Captain James Cook at Kealakekua Bay in 1779. A bilingual poet, he wrote in both Welsh and English. His dramatic monologue 'The Negro Boy' is spoken by an African prince who has exchanged a child for a watch: 'When avarice enslaves the mind / And selfish views alone bear sway, / Man turns a savage to his kind / And blood and rapine mark his way. / Alas! for this poor simple toy / I sold a hapless negro boy.' In the closing stanza of the poem, the prince hopes that God will come to the aid of the child and 'destroy / The oppressors of a negro boy'.

Sandburg, Carl
American poet *born* Galesburg, Illinois 6 January 1878 *died* 22 July 1967

Coming from a family of poor Swedish immigrants, Sandburg had to support himself from a variety of manual jobs before serving, in Puerto Rico, in the Spanish–American War. On his return to the USA he worked as a salesman and journalist and spent two years as secretary to the socialist mayor of Milwaukee. His biography of Lincoln won him the Pulitzer Prize in 1939 and his verse was written with a Whitmanesque energy in celebration of the heroic qualities of the American people. *The People, Yes* (1936) is a populist treatise: 'In the daily labor of the people / by and through which life goes on / the people must laugh or go down.'

Sangster, Charles
Canadian poet *born* Kingston, Ontario 1822 *died* 1893

Educated in Kingston, Sangster worked as a journalist before entering, in 1867, the Civil Service, Ottawa. Like many of his Canadian contemporaries, Sangster takes an Edenic view of his country. *The St Lawrence and the Saguenay* (1856) contains ecstatic lines of nature poetry: 'On, through the lovely Archipelago, / glides the swift bark. Soft summer matins ring / From every isle. The wild fowl come and go, / Regardless of our presence. On the wing, / And perched upon the boughs, the gay birds sing / Their loves: This is their summer paradise; / From morn till night their joyous caroling / Delights the ear, and through the lucent skies / Ascends the choral hymn in softest symphonies.'

Sassoon, Siegfried
English poet *born* Kent 8 September 1886 *died* 1 September 1967

247

Born into a wealthy family, Sassoon was educated at public school at Cambridge. He was an enthusiastic officer in the First World War, earning the nickname 'Mad Jack' and the Military Cross for his bravery in battle. After being invalided home in 1916 he began to question the conduct of the war and became a pacifist. In 1917 he refused to serve further in the army and was sent to a hospital, near Edinburgh, where he wrote incisive anti-war poems and met and encouraged fellow-patient Wilfred Owen. His poem, 'Suicide in the Trenches', is characteristically bitter: 'You smug-faced crowds with kindling eye / Who cheer when soldier lads march by, / Sneak home and pray you'll never know / The hell where youth and laughter go.'

Savage, Richard
English poet *born* London 1698 *died* Bristol 1 August 1743

The bastard son of the Earl of Rivers and the Countess of Macclesfield, Savage was sent (by his maternal grandmother) to a school in St Alban's and was later apprenticed to a shoemaker. When he discovered (from letters) the identity of his mother, he contacted her but she showed no interest in him. In fact when he was sentenced to death, on a charge of murder, she unsuccessfully attempted to persuade the authorities to withdraw the royal pardon that eventually saved him. He was later arrested for debt and died in a debtor's prison. His poem 'The Bastard' (1728) is sustained by indignation; 'Mother, miscalled, farewell – of soul severe, / This sad reflection yet may force one tear'.

Saxe, John Godfrey
American poet *born* High Gate, Vermont 2 June 1816
died Albany, New York 31 March 1887

Son of a mill-owner and prominent local politician, Saxe was admitted to the Bar in 1843. A Democrat, he twice ran unsuccessfully for Governor in his loyally Republican home state. His comical collection *Poems* (1861) was extremely popular and he moved to New York; however, he began to be afflicted by misfortune and was devastated when his daughter died and his wife predeceased him. After suffering severe injuries in a train accident, he withdrew from the world and succumbed to sorrow. Poems such as 'My Familiar' preserve his engaging sense of humour: 'I do not tremble when I meet / The stoutest of my foes, / But Heaven defend me from the friend / Who comes – but never goes!'

Schmidt, Michael
English poet *born* Mexico City 2 March 1947

As managing director of Carcanet Press and general editor of *PN Review*, Michael Schmidt is an influential figure in England where he is associated with a school of poetry that values verbal restraint above emotional intensity. Schmidt is a highly accomplished practioner of this poetic idiom which encourages the writer to operate as an eloquent commentator on events he values. His greatest verbal virtue is a concern with clarity and he is engagingly honest about his obsessions. His four-line poem 'A Savage Dream' explains: 'I had a savage dream of destinations: / A ten-foot fence, barbed, and on the wire / Bones and the rags of prisoners. I had / This dream, and woke in the cool English air.'

Schwartz, Delmore
American poet *born* New York 8 December 1931
died New York 11 July 1966

Schwartz's work was greatly applauded by the critics but the poet was a manic–depressive whose instability led to hospitalisation in Bellevue. When the novelist Saul Bellow raised money to pay for psychiatric help, Schwartz turned against his friend in a cycle of jealousy and hatred that is recreated in Bellow's novel *Humboldt's Gift* (1975) in which Schwartz appears as Von Humboldt Fleisher. In fact, as in Bellow's fiction, the poet died, alone, of a heart attack in a dismal hotel. His verse is emotionally vibrant: 'O son of man, the ignorant night, the travail / Of early morning, the mystery of beginning / Again and again, / while History is unforgiven.' ('In the Naked Bed, in Plato's Cave').

Scott, Alexander
Scottish poet *born c*1515   *died c*1583

There are no details about Scott's early life though he probably trained as a musician. In 1539 he became a prebendary at the Chapel Royal, Stirling, and in 1848 was appointed canon and organist at the Augustinian priory of Inchmahome. His thirty-six known poems were preserved in the sixteenth century Bannatyne manuscript and show ingenious variations on the theme of courtly love. 'To Luve Unluvit', supposedly written after his wife had left him, expresses a wish to 'choose ane uther'. He is at his best when combining tight stanzaic patterns with passion as in 'A Rondel of Luve': 'Luve is ane fervent fire, / Kendillit without desire; / Short pleisure, lang displeisure, / Repentence is the hire'.

Scott, Alexander
Scottish poet *born* Aberdeen 28 November 1920

Son of a power-loom tuner, Scott was educated at Aberdeen University and during the Second World War gained the Military Cross for leading a company attack on a German regimental headquarters at the battle of the Reichswald in 1945. He taught at Glasgow University, becoming Reader in Scottish Literature and head of the Department of Scottish Literature. Influenced by

Hugh MacDiarmid's use of Scots, he wrote several collections, including *Selected Poems* (1975). There is a satirical edge and abrasive tone to his best poems in Scots such as 'Calvinist Sang': 'A hundred pipers canna blaw / Our trauchled times awa, / Drams canna droun them out, nor sang / Hap their scarecraw heids for lang.'

trauchled troubled; *hap* cover

Scott, Duncan Campbell
Canadian poet *born* Ottawa 2 August 1862
died 19 December 1947

Son of a Methodist minister, Scott was educated at Stanstead College, Quebec, before entering the Canadian Civil Service where he rose to the position of Deputy Superintendent General of the Department of Indian Affairs. He was, like Archibald Lampman who encouraged him to write, one of the Group of the Sixties and his work shows his concern for the predicament of the Canadian Indians. His sonnet 'The Onondaga Madonna' begins: 'She stands full-throated and with careless pose, / This woman of a weird and waning race, / The tragic savage lurking in her face, / Where all her pagan passion burns and glows.' In 1934 Scott was made a Companion of the Order of St Michael and St George.

Scott, Frederick George
Canadian poet *born* Montreal 1861 *died* 1944

Educated at Bishop's University and King's College, London, Scott pursued an ecclesiastical career. In 1925 he was appointed Archdeacon of Quebec and his verse is an extension of his lifelong concern with religion. Technically, he was drawn to the English Metaphysical manner and his poems often unfold as a series of answers to theological questions. 'Crucifixion', for example, is a dialogue on sacrificial death: 'Lord, must I bear the whole of it, or none? / "Even as I was crucified, My son." // Will it suffice if I the thorn-crown wear? / "To take the scourge My shoulders were made bare." // My hands, O Lord, must I be pierced in both? / "Twain gave I to the Hammer, nothing loth."'

Scott, F R
Canadian poet *born* Quebec City 1899

The son of the poet Archdeacon Frederick George Scott, F R Scott was educated at Bishop's University, Oxford and McGill where he became Dean of the Faculty of Law. As co-editor of the influential *New Provinces* anthology of 1936, he helped introduce a more modern tone into Canadian poetry. A member of the

'Preview' group of poets in Montreal, he published his *Collected Poems* in 1981. His poem 'Conflict' contains quatrains showing his awareness of social tension: 'Between the dagger and the breast / The bond is stronger than the beast. / Prison, ghetto, flag and gun / Mark the craving for the One.'

Scott, John
English poet *born* Southwark 1730 *died* Radcliff 1783

Born into a Quaker family, Scott passed his life in dread of smallpox until he accepted innoculation at the age of thirty-six. Known as 'Scott of Amwell', since he was raised there, he eventually went to London (after his innoculation) and met Dr Johnson and other cultural celebrities. His 'Ode on Hearing the Drum' remains a powerful poem, particularly the second stanza: 'I hate that drum's discordant sound, / Parading round, and round, and round: / To me it talks of ravaged plains, / And burning towns, and ruined swains, / And mangled limbs, and dying groans, / And widow's tears, and orphan's moans; / And all that misery's hand bestows, / To fill the catalogue of human woes.' Scott finally died of a fever.

Scott, Lady John
Scottish poet *born* Spottiswood 24 June 1810
died Spottiswood 12 March 1900

Alicia Anne Spottiswood, who became Lady John Scott on her marriage to the Duke of Buccleuch's brother in 1836, was born into an old Berwickshire family and brought up in the ancestral home at Spottiswood in the Lammermuir hills. She is best known for her version of the song 'Annie Laurie' but also wrote passionately pro-Jacobite lines such as those 'Suggested by the *Hated* Sight of Culloden': 'Curst be Culloden, blasted for ever, / Blossom or verdure, grow there again never! / May storms rage around it, may bitter winds blight it, / May rain never soften, may sunshine ne'er light it!'

Scott, Tom
Scottish poet *born* Glasgow 6 June 1918

Educated at Newbattle Abbey College, under Edwin Muir, and at Edinburgh University , Tom Scott has written sympathetically on *Dunbar* (1966) and has himself produced his best work in Scots. His abrasive approach is partly a product of his early environment: in 1931 Scott's boiler-maker father had to leave Glasgow, during the economic slump, and begin a new life as a builder in St Andrews. Scott portrays such a man in his sequence

Brand the Builder (1975). In the title poem of his collection *The Ship* (1963) he treats the sinking of the Titanic as an allegory for the collapse of European civilisation: 'Union was broken, and unionism born.'

Scott, Sir Walter

Scottish poet *born* Edinburgh 15 August 1771 *died* Abbotsford, Roxburghshire 21 September 1832

As a sick child suffering from polio Scott was sent to the Border country where his health improved and his mind began to dwell on the traditional ballads he subsequently collected. His first major poetic work, *The Lay of the Last Minstrel* (1805), launched him on a successful career as a narrative poet who could dazzle the public, despite his somewhat stilted diction and predictable rhymes, with celebrations of his 'Land of brown heath and shaggy wood, / Land of the mountain and the flood'. When his popularity was eclipsed by that of Byron ('Byron beat me,' Scott admitted) he abandoned poetry for fiction and found in the novel a more flexible form for his romantic impulses.

Scott, William Bell

Scottish poet *born* Edinburgh 12 September 1811
died Penkill Castle, Ayrshire 22 November 1890

Educated in Edinburgh, Scott was a skilful painter who moved, in 1840, to London where he worked as an artist and teacher. A member of the Pre-Raphaelite group, he was friendly with Swinburne and Christina Rossetti. Many of his paintings were commissioned by private patrons such as his friend Miss Boyd of Penkill Castle where Scott painted murals and designed a medieval hall. His poems are derivative though 'The Witch's Ballad' has interesting decorative touches of period detail: 'We walked abreast all up the street, / Into the market up the street; / Our hair with marigolds was wound, / Our bodices with love-knots laced, / Our merchandise with tansy bound.'

Scupham, Peter

English poet *born* Liverpool 1933

After National Service, Scupham was educated at Cambridge. He became a teacher in Hertfordshire and one of the directors of the Mandeville Press. He published *The Snowing Globe* in 1972, *Winter Quarters* in 1983. He is an evocative poet, responding imaginatively to the spectacle of landscape – and seascape, as in 'Atlantic': 'Beyond the ledges of the foam / A dog seal sways an oilskin head; / The Carracks worked old luggers home, / Black rock commemorates the dead. / The sea shouts nothing, and the shores / Break to a tumult of applause.' The poem ends with a terse couplet: 'Rage at the door. Winds twist and drown. / We founder as the glass goes down.'

Sedley, Sir Charles
English poet *born* Aylesford 1639 *died* 20 August 1701

Son of a Kentish baronet, Sedley was a prominent and familiar figure at the court of Charles II. He was well known as a dramatist and infamous as a profligate. His daughter, Catherine, became mistress of James II who created her Countess of Dorchester. Sedley's poems entertainingly express his bawdy character. 'On the Happy Corydon and Phyllis' is an erotic extension of the pastoral tradition: 'A thousand times he kissed her, / Laying her on the green; / But as he farther pressed her, / A pretty leg was seen: / And something else, but what I dare not name.' Dryden praised Sedley as the Tibullus of his time.

Seidel, Frederick
American poet *born* St Louis 1936

Educated at Harvard, Seidel was Paris editor of the *Paris Review* and taught English at Rutgers University. His verse alternates between radical discontent with American society and a sensuous appreciation of physical pleasures. His moralistic tone is evident in his collection *Men and Women* (1984) which refers to the assassination of Robert Kennedy, to the bombing of Vietnam, to Presidents Nixon and Carter. A poem on 'Scotland' is observant as well as indignant: 'Dukes hunt stags, / While Scotsmen hunt for jobs and emigrate, / Or else start seeing red spots on a moor / That flows to the horizon like a migraine.'

Sempill, Robert
Scottish poet *born* c1595 *died* c1665

Robert Sempill of Beltrees, son of Sir James Sempill, was educated at Glasgow University and supported the Royalist side during the Civil War. Otherwise little is known about his life. His literary importance rests on his creation of the six-line stanza that sustains his comic elegy on Habbie Simpson, 'The Life and Death of the Piper of Kilbarchan': 'Kilbarchan now may say alas! / For she hath lost her game and grace, / Both Trixie, and the Maiden Trace: / But what remead? / For no man can supply his place, / Hab Simson's dead.' Classified as the 'Standard Habbie' stanza by Allan Ramsay it was used so brilliantly by Robert Burns that it could justifiably be renamed the 'Standard Rabbie' stanza.

Serote, Mongane Wally
South African poet *born* Sophiatown, Johannesburg 1944

Serote, who moved from Sophiatown to Alexandra, Johannesburg, was imprisoned under the Terrorism Act in June

1969. After nine months he was released without ever being charged. His first collection *Yakhal 'inkomo* (the cry of cattle at the slaughterhouse) was published in 1972. His defiant attitude and direct approach to diction is evident in 'City Johannesburg' which ends; 'Jo'burg City, Johannesburg, / Listen when I tell you, / There is no fun, nothing, in it, / When you leave the women and men with such frozen expressions, / Expressions that have tears like furrows of soil erosion, / Jo'burg City, you are dry like death, / Jo'burg City, Johannesburg, Jo'burg City.'

Service, Robert
Canadian poet *born* Preston 16 January, 1874
died 11 September 1958

Brought up in Glasgow and educated at Glasgow University, Service worked in a bank before emigrating, at the age of twenty-one, to Canada where he worked with the Canadian Bank of Commerce in the Yukon. He then took up journalism and served, during the First World War, as an ambulance driver in France. He had a flair for recreating the atmosphere of the Canadian outdoors and put his narrative gift to profitable use in *Songs of a Sourdough* (1907) and various other volumes. 'The Spell of the Yukon' embodies his adventurous attitude: 'There's a land where the mountains are nameless, / And the rivers all run God knows where; / There are lives that are erring and aimless, / And deaths that just hang by a hair'.

Sexton, Anne
American poet *born* Newton, Massachusetts 1928
died 4 October 1974

Like Sylvia Plath, Anne (Harvey) Sexton grew up in Wellesley, Massachusetts. She married Alfred Sexton in 1948 and worked as a fashion model in Boston in the early 1950s. She and Plath both attended Robert Lowell's poetry class at Boston University and the two women (in Sexton's words) 'talked death with burned-up intensity' as a result of shared suicidal experiences. Sexton's confessional poetry used images of mental breakdown, attempted suicide and hospitalisation. 'Lullaby', a characteristically brittle poem, is clinically taut: 'My sleeping pill is white. / It is a splendid pearl; / it floats me out of myself.'

Shakespeare, William
English poet *born* Stratford-upon-Avon April 1564
died Stratford-upon-Avon 23 April 1616

Son of a wool-dealer, Shakespeare was educated locally and in 1582 married Anne Hathaway by whom he had three children. Shakespeare had established himself in London as a dramatist by 1589 and later, as a member of the Lord Chamberlain's Company, worked in the Globe Theatre. In 1592 the Earl of Southampton became his patron and in 1596 Shakespeare bought a coat of arms. He retired to Stratford in 1611. His plays are the most memorable by any English dramatist and his sonnets have a unique metaphorical density: 'Shall I compare thee to a summer's day? / Thou art more lovely and more temperate: / Rough winds do shake the darling buds of May, / And summer's lease hath all too short a date.' (Sonnet XVIII)

Shange, Ntozake
American poet *born* Trenton, New Jersey, 19 October 1948

A resident of New York, Ntozake Shange is a poet, playwright and performer. Her work has attracted considerable attention and she has been praised as one of the finest black poets of her generation. Her second collection *Nappy Edges* appeared in 1978 and showed her as a writer of considerable range, producing erotic fantasies as well as observations on the condition of black women. The conversationally urgent tone of her poetry comes over in 'Telephones and other false gods': 'the livin' very often have no dime to make / local telephone calls & 911 is a figment of / muggers' imaginations while they bludgeon / faggots' eyes & rape women who have never / been loved or taken out to dinner.'

Shapiro, Karl
American poet *born* Baltimore, Maryland 10 November 1913

Shapiro was educated at Johns Hopkins University, Baltimore, and joined the US Army Air Force in 1942: his reflections on being a Jewish soldier are given in *V-Letter and Other Poems* (1944). He taught at Johns Hopkins in 1947, worked as editor of *Poetry* (Chicago) from 1950-5, and taught at the University of Illinois from 1966-8. In poems such as 'Auto Wreck' he expresses his melancholy conclusions in measured tones: 'Already old, the question Who shall die? / Becomes unspoken Who is innocent? / For death in war is done by hands; / Suicide has cause and stillbirth, logic; / And cancer, simple as a flower, blooms.' His *Collected Poems* appeared in 1978.

Shelley, Percy Bysshe
English poet *born* Warnham, Sussex 4 August 1792
died Leghorn 8 July 1822

Shelley rebelled against his privileged background from an early age. A landowner's son he was unhappy at Eton and expelled from Oxford for his pamphlet *The Necessity of Atheism* (1811). Five months later he married Harriet Westbrook but left her in favour of Mary Wollstonecraft Godwin whom he married in 1816 after Harriet's suicide by drowning. Shelley and Mary settled in Italy in 1818; he drowned in his boat the *Ariel*. Shelley's poetry is delicately lyrical in style but politically radical and scientifically shrewd in content. His ecstatic 'Ode to the West Wind' ends on a typically optimistic note: 'O Wind, / If Winter comes, can Spring be far behind?'

Shenstone, William
English poet *born* Halesowen, Worcestershire 13 November 1714 *died* Halesowen, Worcestershire 11 February 1763

Educated at Oxford, Shenstone inherited in 1735 his father's estates of the Leasowes, Halesowen, and transformed it into a showpiece of the picturesque style in landscape gardening. Like his estate, his poetry was ornate and ostentatious: *The Schoolmistress* (1742) describes a village school in the Spenserian style; *Pastoral Ballad* (1755) is elaborately effective. His work was admired (by such as Robert Burns) for its confident tone, as in his poem 'Written at an Inn at Henley': 'Who'er has travelled life's dull round, / Where'er his stages may have been, / May sigh to think he still has found / The warmest welcome at an inn.'

Shirley, James
English poet *born* London 18 September 1596 *buried* London 29 October 1666

Educated at Oxford and Cambridge, he was ordained as an Anglican but converted to Roman Catholicism. He worked as a schoolmaster, then as chief playwright for the King's Men; he wrote more than thirty plays. In the Civil War he supported the Royalist side and he died of exposure in the Great Fire of London. His drama *The Contention of Ajax and Ulysses* (1659) ends with the dirge beginning: 'The glories of our blood and state / Are shadows, not substantial things; / There is no armour against Fate; / Death lays his icy hand on kings; / Sceptre and Crown / Must tumble down, / And in the dust be equal made / With the poor crooked scythe and spade.'

Shove, Fredegond
English poet *born* Cambridge 1889 *died* 1949

Daughter of the historian F W Maitland, Fredegond Shove published *Dreams and Journeys* in 1918, *Daybreak* in 1922. Her study of *Christina Rossetti* appeared in 1931 and her *Poems* were posthumously assembled in 1956. Her work is obviously indebted to Christina Rossetti and her mood is invariably wistful, as in 'A Dream in Early Spring' which begins: 'Now when I sleep the thrush breaks through my dreams / With sharp reminders of the coming day: / After his call, one minute I remain / Unwaked, and on the darkness which is Me / There springs the image of a daffodil, / Growing upon a grassy bank alone, / And seeming with great joy his bell to fill / With drops of golden dew'.

Shuttle, Penelope
English poet *born* Staines, Middlesex 1947

Penelope Shuttle's poems, in *The Child-Stealer* (1983) notably, are
composed in melancholy tones and convey the feelings of a
mother whose child is growing up and apart from her. Life, so
these poems suggest, is a gift that is quickly withdrawn from the
women who make it all possible. With each night there is another
raid by 'Lilith, the child-stealer' who claims the children, spirits
them away. 'Mother and Child' acknowledges the anxiety the
author feels at this inevitable process which reduces her to a
reluctant onlooker as her daughter goes her own way 'singing one
of [her] own wild unique songs.' The cadences used by Shuttle are
full of dying falls as she dwells on the theme of loss.

Sidney, Sir Philip
English poet *born* Penshurst, Kent 30 November 1554
died Zutphen 17 October, 1586

A versatile man of letters and a celebrated soldier, Sidney was the
son of Sir Henry Sidney (thrice Lord-Deputy of Ireland, also
President of Wales). He was educated at Oxford. To Penelope,
daughter of the first Earl of Essex, he addressed his sonnets
Astrophel and Stella (1591). He married Frances, daughter of Sir
Francis Walsingham, in 1583 – the year after he had been
knighted. He died from a wound in the thigh while fighting the
Spaniards in the Low Countries. His *Apologie for Poetrie* (1595) is
regarded as the earliest work of English literary criticism. His
sonnets are contemplative, as in the example ending 'Then
farewell, world! thy uttermost I see: / Eternal Love, maintain thy
life in me!'

Sigourney, Lydia Howard Huntley
American poet *born* Norwich, Connecticut 1 September
1791 *died* 10 June 1865

Daughter of a gardener, Lydia Huntley married Charles
Sigourney, a hardware merchant, in 1819. She began writing
poems at the age of eight though her husband disapproved of her
publishing her work until financial problems compelled him to
alter his attitude. Her enormously popular verse which earned
her a reputation as 'the American Hemans', appeared in many
volumes – including *Poems, Religious and Elegiac* (1841) – and
showed her tearful tone. 'The Mother's Sacrifice' has God asking
a woman for her child: 'Morn came. A blight had struck / The
crimson velvet of the unfolding bud; / The harp-strings rang a
thrilling strain and broke – / And that young mother lay upon the
earth, / In childless agony.'

Silkin, Jon

English poet *born* London 1930

Silkin was educated at Leeds University where he was Gregory
Fellow in Poetry. He founded and co-edited the magazine *Stand*
and encouraged, in its pages, the translation of European poetry.
He gained a reputation as a poet with a serious social purpose and
a powerful feeling for nature. 'Death of a Son', which describes
the child's death in a mental hospital at the age of one, is a
remarkable poem, intensely emotional and yet objective: 'I have
seen stones: I have seen brick / But this house was made up of
neither bricks nor stone / But a house of flesh and blood / With
flesh of stone // And bricks for blood.' He has published several
volumes including *nature with man* (1965).

Sill, Edward Rowland

American poet *born* Windsor, Connecticut 29 April 1841 *died*
Cuyahoga Falls, near Cleveland, Ohio 27 February 1887

From his mother, who came from a line of ministers, Sill
developed an interest in religion; when his parents died, in the
early 1850s, he came to live with his uncle in Cuyahoga Falls
where he met and married his cousin Elizabeth Sill. He worked in
a Sacramento post office and a Folsom bank then entered
Harvard Divinity School. He did not, however, like the
institutional aspects of religion and preferred teaching to
preaching. From 1874 to 1882 he was Professor of English at the
University of California then returned to Cuyahoga Falls. His
work is sombre in tone and religious in feeling, as in 'Home'
which ends with a vision of an angel who will come and 'Into the
Infinite Love will lead thee home'.

Simpson, Louis

American poet *born* Jamaica, West Indies 1923

Simpson settled in the USA in 1940. He was educated at
Columbia University and served in the US Army. He taught at the
University of California, Berkeley; and at Stony Brook, Long
Island. His collection *At the End of the Open Road* won the Pulitzer
Prize in 1964. A sophisticated poet, he often sets life in a literary
context, making references to his favourite writers. In more
direct poems, such as 'To the Western World', he reflects on the
American experience expansively: 'In this America, this
wilderness / Where the axe echoes with a lonely sound, / The
generations labour to possess / And grave by grave we civilise
the ground.'

Sims, George R

English poet *born* London 2 September 1847
died 4 September 1922

George R Sims, a prolific journalist and writer of popular verse, joined the staff of *Fun* in 1874. From 1877 he contributed, under the pseudonym 'Dagonet', the 'Mustard and Cress' column in the Sunday *Referee*. His *Dagonet Ballads* were collected in 1882. He wrote various books about London and published a collection of crime stories *Dorcas Dene, Detective* (1897). Though his poetic gift was slight his narrative skill sustains 'In the Workhouse: Christmas Day': 'It is Christmas Day in the Workhouse, / And the cold bare walls are bright / With garlands of green and holly, / And the place is a pleasant sight'.

Sinclair, Keith
New Zealand poet *born* Auckland 1922

Educated at Auckland University, Sinclair served in the army and the navy during the Second World War. He became Professor of History at Auckland University and published *A History of New Zealand* in 1959. His collections include *Strangers or Beasts* (1954) and *A Time to Embrace* (1963). In 'Memorial to a Missionary' he reflects on the life of Thomas Kendall (1778–1832), the first resident missionary in New Zealand: 'Seeking the Maori name for sin, for hell, / Teacher turned scholar he sat at Hongi's feet / And guns were the coin he paid for revelation. / To the south men died when Hongi spent his fees'.

Singer, James Burns
Scottish poet *born* New York 29 August 1928
died Plymouth 8 September 1964

James Burns Singer was educated in Scotland where he worked as a marine biologist before moving to London in 1955. In 1956 he married Marie, a black American psychologist, and this relationship helped compensate for a tragic family background for his father had gone insane and his mother had committed suicide. Singer did not live long enough to realise his full potential: he died of heart failure at the age of thirty-six. He used his scientific background to evolve a spare cerebral style, as in 'An Apology': 'It is the unforgivable / Essence of individual acts / Which uncontrollably attracts / Words through the incommunicable.'

Sisson, C H
English poet *born* Bristol 22 April 1914

After serving in the British Army, during the Second World War, Charles Hubert Sisson pursued a distinguished career in the Civil Service until he retired in 1973. He is an imaginative translator – of Dante, for example, and *The Song of Roland* (1983) – and a singular poet who eschews movements and projects his forceful personality. His early poems displayed a dense verbal exterior but gradually he has moved towards a brilliant clarity. His most mature poems confront death courageously. 'Sleep' opens unequivocally; 'The nights are horrible: I lie awake / Caged in a body that is in decay / As are all human things. Night, you are empty / And I am full of ingratitude.'

Sitwell, Dame Edith
English poet *born* Scarborough 7 September 1887
died London 12 December 1964

The eldest child of Sir George and Lady Ida Sitwell, Edith was raised, with her brothers Osbert and Sacheverell, in the family home at Renishaw Hall, Derbyshire. Adept at publicity, she exploited her resemblance to Elizabeth I and gained a reputation as an eccentric aristocratic aesthete; as such she was caricatured as the 'old harpy' Lady Harriet in Wyndham Lewis's *The Apes of God* (1930). However *Façade* (1922) revealed a talent for linguistic experiment and she showed real passion in later poems such as 'The Shadow of Cain', an indignant reaction to the dropping of the atomic bomb on Hiroshima: 'There was great lightning / In flashes coming to us over the floor'.

Sitwell, Sacheverell
English poet *born* Scarborough 15 November 1897

Like his sister Edith, Sacheverell Sitwell experienced a childhood that was financially secure though emotionally tense. Educated at Eton, he fought the First World War and later established himself as an elegant man of letters. His collection *An Indian Summer* (1982) collects poems written since the death of his sister Edith (in 1964). Sitwell's poetic gift was eclipsed by Edith's as he gladly acknowledges: 'To live as a young man in your flowering shade / Was wonderful indeed, / You could read a poem, and inspire one to poetry.' A romantic by nature, his ideal of poetry preserves the Victorian tone as he describes landscapes and great cultural events.

Skelton, John
English poet *born* c1460 *died* 1529

In 1488 Skelton, whose precise origins are unknown, was created *poeta lauratus* of Oxford and the following year Henry VII appointed him tutor to the royal princes – thus he helped educate the future Henry VIII. Skelton took holy orders, became rector of Diss, Norfolk, in 1505 and was appointed Orator Regius after the accession of Henry VIII in 1509. His unorthodox behaviour (though a priest, he married) and vigorous satires on ecclesiastical corruption offended many and he was briefly imprisoned for attacking Cardinal Wolsey in 'Why Come Ye Nat to Court'. His

verse is unusually direct, as in 'Uppon a Deedmans Hed': 'For I
have dyscust / We are but dust, / And dy we must.'

Skelton, Robin

Anglo–Canadian poet *born* Easington, East Yorkshire
12 October 1925

Educated at the universities of Cambridge and Leeds, Skelton was
Professor of Creative Writing at the University of Victoria,
British Columbia, and editor of the *Malahat Review*. An energetic
anthologist he edited *Poetry of the Thirties* (1964) and *The Cavalier
Poets* (1970). He published many collections including *Because of
Love* (1977) in which eroticism is combined with an intelligent
irony as in the poem beginning: 'It's not too much to say / I am
delighted / to find you once lay / in that bastard's arms, / giving
him what you now / give me, exciting / him with those delicate
fingers, / insistent charms.'

Skinner, John

Scottish poet *born* Birse, Aberdeenshire 3 October 1721 *died*
Aberdeen 16 June 1807

A schoolmaster's son, Skinner was educated at Marischal College,
Aberdeen. He taught in a school in Aberdeenshire and tutored in
the Shetlands. Raised as a Presbyterian he was received into the
Episcopalian Church and was a minister at Longside,
Aberdeenshire. After the rebellion of 1745 he was suspected of
Jacobite sympathies and his church was burned to the ground.
For opposing the government's measures against
Episcopalianism, after the Jacobite rebellion, he was imprisoned
in Aberdeen in 1753. He corresponded with Burns who
considered Skinner's 'Tullochgorum' to be 'the best Scotch song
ever Scotland saw': 'Let Whig and Tory all agree / To spend the
night wi' mirth and glee, / And cheerful sing alang wi' me / The
Reel o' Tullochgorum.'

Skipsey, Joseph

English poet *born* Tynemouth 17 March 1832
died 3 September 1903

When Skipsey was four months old his father, a miners' leader,
was shot dead while attempting to stop a policeman firing on
striking miners. Skipsey went down the mines at the age of seven
yet found time to teach himself about literature. He published
Poems in 1859 and was (in 1863) given a job as a librarian in
Newcastle. He returned to the mines from 1854–82, then became
caretaker of a Newcastle school and (from 1889–91) curator of
Shakespeare's birthplace in Stratford. His work was praised by
Wilde and Rossetti. 'The Golden Lot' indicates his optimism: 'I

lilt my heart-felt lay – / And the gloom of the deep, deep mine, /
Or the din of the factory dieth away, / And a Golden Lot is mine.'

Skirving, Adam

Scottish poet *born* 1719 *died* 1803

A tenant farmer in East Lothian, Skirving was well known locally
for his athletic and conversational powers. After Bonnie Prince
Charlie's victory at the Battle of Prestonpans in 1745 he wrote a
song ridiculing the defeated General Cope; 'Hey, Johnnie Cope,
are ye wauking yet? / Or are your drums a-beating yet? / If ye
were wauking I wad wait / To gang to the coals i' the morning. //
Cope sent a challenge frae Dunbar: / "Charlie, meet me an ye
daur, / And I'll learn you the art o' war / If you'll meet me i' the
morning. // When Charlie looked the letter upon / He drew his
sword the scabbard from: / "Come, follow me, my merry, merry
men, / And we'll meet Johnnie Cope i' the morning!"'

wauking waking; *daur* dare

Slessor, Kenneth

Australian poet *born* Orange, New South Wales 1901 *died* 1971

One of the major figures of modern Australian poetry, Slessor
was educated in Sydney where he also worked as a reporter for
The Sun. During the Second World War he was the Australian
Official War Correspondent and travelled with the troops. He
rejoined *The Sun* in 1944, became literary editor of the *Sunday
Telegraph*, then edited the *Southerly*. Slessor absorbed the
modernist influence of Eliot into Australian poetry. His poem
'Five Bells' is a tribute to a friend who was drowned in Sydney
Harbour in the 1930s: 'I felt the wet push its black thumb-balls
in, / The night you died, I felt your eardrums crack, / And the
short agony, the longer dream, / The Nothing that was neither
long nor short'.

Smart, Christopher

English poet *born* Shipbourne, Kent 11 April 1722
died London 21 May 1771

Smart's father died in 1733 and the poet was befriended by the
Vanes, a wealthy family who had employed the poet's father as a
steward. Educated at Cambridge, Smart worked as a journalist in
London and became notorious for his drunkenness. In 1756 he
was confined in St Luke's Hospital and remained there for seven
years; in 1770 he was imprisoned for debt and died in these
distressing circumstances. Though neglected in his lifetime he is
now highly regarded. His 'A Song to David' (1763) is a majestic

expression of his faith: 'Bless ye the nosegay in the vale, / And with the sweetness of the gale / Enrich the thankful psalm.'

Smith, A J M
Canadian poet *born* Montreal 1902 *died* 1980

Educated at the universities of McGill and Edinburgh, A J M Smith taught at Michigan State University. As co-editor of the influential *New Provinces* anthology of 1936 he was associated with the move to introduce a more modern tone into Canadian poetry. His critical essays, *Towards a View of Canadian Letters*, appeared in 1973; his selected poems, *The Classic Shade*, in 1978. His poem 'The Archer' ends with a fatalistic flourish: 'So for a moment, motionless, serene, / Fixed between time and time, I aim and wait; / Nothing remains for breath now but to waive / His prior claim and let the barb fly clean / Into the heart of what I know and hate – / That central black, the ringed and targeted grave.'

Smith, Alexander
Scottish poet *born* Kilmarnock 31 December 1830
died Edinburgh 5 January 1867

Alexander Smith worked, like his father before him, as a pattern designer until he was appointed Secretary to Edinburgh University in 1854. As his early work displayed apparently uncontrolled stretches of verbosity Smith was included in the literary school called 'Spasmodic' by the highly critical W E A Aytoun. In his finest volume, *City Poems* (1857), Smith dropped his extravagant mannerisms and produced a stylistically sound urban poetry full of industrial energy, as in 'Glasgow': 'Draw thy fierce streams of blinding ore, / Smite on a thousand anvils, roar / Down to the harbour-bars; / Smoulder in smoky sunsets, flare / On rainy nights'.

Smith, Charlotte
English poet *born* London 4 May 1749 *died* 28 October 1806

In 1765 Charlotte Turner married Benjamin Smith, a West India merchant whose incompetence led to the couple being imprisoned for debt in 1782. After this experience, Charlotte began to write to support her family. Her novels, *Emmeline* (1788) and *The Old Manor House* (1793), are highly observant. Her *Elegiac Sonnets* (1784) are rich in natural detail, as in the one beginning: 'The garlands fade that Spring so lately wove, / Each simple flower, which he had nurs'd in dew, / Anemonies that spangled every grove, / The primrose wan, and hare-bell, mildly blue.'

Smith, Dave
American poet *born* Portsmouth, Virginia 1942

Educated at the universities of Virginia, Southern Illinois and Ohio, Smith became a teacher of English and Creative Writing and was Director of the Creative Writing Program at the University of Florida at Gainsville. A novelist (*Onliness*, 1981, is a brilliant parody of the Southern novel) as well as a poet, his verse is sensuous and lyrically affirmative. 'Recess', for example, begins: 'I wake late, lingering in our hollowed bed. / Sun, shallow, streams over me, / little shadows darting, tease / of the maple that buds still / at the windows you opened. / I close my eyes and try / to hear the yammering / robins we've watched unfurl / like dreams we cannot hold.'

Smith, Horace
English poet *born* London 31 December 1779 *died* 12 July 1849

A solicitor's son, Smith was a clerk in a counting house then a stockbroker until he retired in 1820. He inherited a considerable fortune and lived for a while in France. He was friendly with Keats, Shelley and Leigh Hunt and collaborated with his brother, James Smith, on *Rejected Addresses* (1812), a bestselling book of parodies. His light verse is consistently entertaining, as in his portrayal of Harry Dashington in 'The Collegian and the Porter': 'That is, he understood computing / The odds at any race or match; / Was a dead hand at pigeon-shooting; / Could kick up rows, knock down the watch – /Play truant and the rake at random – / Drink – tie cravats – and drive a tandem.'

Smith, Iain Crichton
Scottish poet *born* Lewis 1 January 1928

Smith lived on the Outer Hebridean Island of Lewis until 1945 when he left the island to study English at Aberdeen University. He later taught English at Oban High School and in 1977 retired to become a fulltime writer. Bilingual in Gaelic and English, and a novelist as well as a poet, Smith draws extensively on his early life with his mother who developed a morbid fear of illness when the poet's father died of tuberculosis. The first poem in *Thistles and Roses* (1961) is 'Old Woman' which describes a life that has crumbled before the encroachment of age: 'And she, being old, fed from a mashed plate / as an old mare might droop across a fence / to the dull pastures of its ignorance.'

Smith, James
English poet *born* London 10 February 1775
died 24 December 1839

Brother of Horace Smith, with whom he collaborated on *Rejected Addresses* (1812) – the bestselling book of parodies – Smith was a solicitor's son who succeeded his father as solicitor to the Board of Ordnance. His parody of Crabbe, in 'The Theatre', is excellent: ''Tis sweet to view, from half-past five to six, / Our long wax-candles, with short cotton wicks, / Touch'd by the lamplighter's Promethean art, / Start into light, and make the lighter start; / To see red Phoebus through the gallery-pane / Tinge with his beams the beams of Drury Lane; / While gradual parties fill our widen'd pit, / And gape, and gaze, and wonder, ere they sit.' Crabbe himself thought the parody had caught his tone 'admirably'.

Smith, John
English poet *born* Buckinghamshire 1924

Smith joined the literary agency of Christy & Moore in 1946 and became its managing director in 1959. He retired in 1971 and moved to Hove, Sussex, to concentrate on his own writing. His sophisticated and shapely poems operate on the basis of a grave, and Gravesian, irony. In his best poems he turns observations into assertions. 'Advice to Swimmers' begins: 'To clutch at straws is to drown surely; / Better to thresh the unpropitious waves / In mock of swimming than to go thus down. / Though the sea's deep, life's deeper; miracles may, / Before the last breath, drain the encompassing ocean; / All who fall overboard do not, therefore, drown.'

Smith, Ken
English poet *born* Rudston, East Yorkshire 4 December 1938

Smith has worked as a teacher, a reader for the BBC and a freelance writer. From 1969–73 he lived in the USA and he then returned to England and settled in London. He has survived the vagaries of fashion and created a coherent body of work rather than a few isolated poems. His images read as if they were wrenched from the innards of his own experience and his verse communicates on a basic, visceral level. He has moved, gradually, from an obsession with the feel of physical objects to a philosphical ability to distance himself from his material. In 'Tongue' he writes; 'My tongue is a flute / filling all the tunnels of the subway / with its flute sound'.

Smith, Seba
American poet *born* Buckfield, Maine 14 September 1792
died 1868

When Seba Smith was seven, his family moved to Bridgton where he was educated and later taught. He founded the Portland *Courier* and married the author Elizabeth Prince (who wrote as Elizabeth Oakes Smith). Under the name Major Jack Dowling he contributed satirical articles to the *Courier* and was well-known as a humorist. Smith also wrote the melancholy tale of 'The Mother in the Snow-Storm' which concludes in tear-jerking style: 'At dawn a traveller passed by, / And saw her 'neath a snowy veil; / The frost of death was in her eye, / Her cheek was cold, and hard, and pale; / He moved the robe from off the child – / The babe looked up and sweetly smiled!'

Smith, Stevie
English poet *born* Hull 20 September 1902
died Devon 7 March 1971

Florence Margaret Smith – nicknamed Stevie after the jockey Steve Donaghue – was an idiosyncratic author and eccentric character. Shortly after she was born her father 'took one look at me and rushed away to sea'. For most of her life she lived in London where she worked as a secretary and became increasingly popular as a performer of her own poetry. Her poems present life as an amusing farce though her verbal lightness of touch has its serious moments. Her 'Not Waving but Drowning' remains in oral circulation as an apt comment on life: 'Oh, no no no, it was too cold always / (Still the dead one lay moaning) / I was much too far out all my life / And not waving but drowning.'

Smith, Sydney Goodsir
Scottish poet *born* Wellington, New Zealand 26 October 1915 *died* Edinburgh 15 January, 1975

Born in New Zealand, the son of the famous forensic expert Sir Sydney Smith, Sydney Goodsir Smith came to Scotland at the age of twelve. He enthusiastically embraced a Scots muse and became one of Hugh MacDiarmid's most gifted disciples. Smith was a convivial character well-known in the bars of Edinburgh where he selfconsciously assumed the role of the boozy bard of Auld Reekie. His most characteristic theme is the emotional extremism associated with drink and he can be ecstatic, in *Under the Eildon Tree* (1954), or self-pitying (in 'Ma Moujik Lass'): 'I've nocht tae haud but a whusky glass, / A gey wanchancy feast.'
haud hold; *wanchancy* dangerous

Smith, Vivian
Australian poet *born* Hobart, Tasmania 1933

Smith studied at Hobart High School and the University of Tasmania where he subsequently taught French before moving to English studies at the University of Sydney. He is interested in evoking an essentially Tasmanian perception of life as in his highly wrought poem 'Late April: Hobart': 'And now it's this dark brevity of gold / with so much withering as colours glow / as if the frugal with the fecund mates. / The sunlight dazzles with its April cold / and through the red the brown begins to show. / Beneath it all such final bareness waits.'

Smith, Walter Chalmers
Scottish poet *born* Aberdeen 5 December 1824
died Dunblane 20 September 1908

Educated at Aberdeen University, Smith was ordained as a minister of the Free Church of Scotland in 1850. Thereafter he ministered in Orwell, Kinross-shire; in Glasgow; and in Edinburgh. His collection *The Bishop's Walk* (1861) appeared under the pseudonym 'Orwell' and he later used the pseudonym 'Hermann Knott'. In his best poems, such as 'Glenaradale', he reveals an indignant response to Scotland's troubled history. The poem is spoken by one cleared from his native land; 'There is no fire of the crackling boughs / On the hearth of our fathers, / There is no lowing of brown-eyed cows / On the green meadows, / Nor do the maidens whisper vows / In the still gloaming, /Glenaradale.'

Smither, Elizabeth
New Zealand poet *born* New Plymouth 1941

Married to the painter Michael Smither, Elizabeth Smither settled in her native town as a journalist and writer of stories for children. Her collections include *Here Come the Clouds* (1975), *The Sarah Train* (1980) and *Casanova's Ankle* (1981). She is an observant poet with a sardonic sense of humour. Her poem 'The beak', a portrait of a judge, begins: 'He's a little man with a corporation who can say / Private parts as though it's butterfly cakes. / His mouth opens like a scissors and white air / Pours through smelling of ether. He's known for years / And years that words are the killer. / He chooses his carefully then betrays the jury / (Your accumulated experience) to decide.'

Smithyman, Kendrick
New Zealand poet *born* 1922

After the Second World War Smithyman settled in Auckland where he worked as a teacher in primary schools. Later he taught at the University of Auckland. His collections include *The Blind Mountain* (1950), *Inheritance* (1962), *Earthquake Water* (1972), *The Seal in the Dolphin Pool* (1974). His 'Anzac Ceremony' is a meditation on the meaning of conflict: 'I drove my brother bleeding away from my porch. / I, sated, cursed my sister afraid and hungry away. / She took up strength from the blood he gave; / she bound his wound; she brought water to lave / a hurt now healed in them bleeds my reproach. / What difficult word is there which I must say?'

Snodgrass, W D

American poet *born* Wilkinsburg, Pennsylvania 1926

William De Witt Snodgrass was educated at Geneva College and, after service with the US Navy, the State University of Iowa. Later he taught at the universities of Cornell, Rochester, Wayne State, Syracuse. His first collection, *Heart's Needle* (1959), was awarded the Pulitzer Prize. In the title sequence Snodgrass describes his daughter – born during the Korean War ('Child of my winter, born / When the new fallen soldiers froze / In Asia's steep ravines') – and how he lost touch with her after his divorce. The sequence is sustained by a metrical virtuosity and an emotional honesty: 'Child, I have another wife, / another child. We try to choose our life.'

Snyder, Gary

American poet *born* San Francisco 1930

Snyder studied Japanese and Chinese literature at Berkeley and went to Japan to immerse himself in eastern culture. Friendly with Jack Kerouac and other Beat writers, Snyder embodied the ideal of the poet as an individual surviving heroically in a hostile world, a man seeking the spiritual centre of modern life through physical contact with nature, as in 'Piute Creek': 'All the junk that goes with being human / Drops away, hard rock wavers / Even the heavy present seems to fail / This bubble of a heart. / Words and books / Like a small creek off a high ledge / Gone in the dry air. A clear, attentive mind, / Has no meaning but that / Which sees is truly seen.'

Solway, David

Canadian poet *born* Montreal 1941

Solway was educated at McGill and went on to teach poetry at John Abbott College, Montreal. He published *Selected Poems* in 1982 and *Stones in Water* in 1983. In one of his most effective poems, 'The Last Supper', he puts a familiar story under pressure by approaching it with a sceptical contemporary consciousness: 'The problem surely must have been / how to sustain a dialogue / of epigram & parable, / prophecy & confession, / meal after meal year after year / with never a dirty joke, a vulgar reference, /or the salt & leaven of blasphemy / to lighten that attention. //O all those pale blond apostles / but mainly / sneaking Judas in the corner / hungry for the human touch'.

Sorley, Charles

Scottish poet *born* Aberdeen 19 May 1895
died Loos October 1915

Son of a philosophy professor, Sorley was educated at Marlborough School and then, before going up to Oxford, spent

January to July 1914 in Germany. When he left Germany, in August 1914, he enlisted in the Suffolk Regiment. He was shot dead by a sniper and his collection *Marlborough and Other Poems* appeared in 1916. His work takes a contemplative look at war so that the immediate horror is put in perspective. His last poem was probably the sonnet beginning 'When you see millions of the mouthless dead / Across your dreams in pale battalions go, / Say not soft things as other men have said, / That you'll remember. For you need not so.'

Souster, Raymond
Canadian poet *born* Toronto 1921

Educated in Toronto where he worked as an accountant, Souster was – with Louis Dudek and Irving Layton – one of the founders of Contact Press. He has been an active anthologist and published the first volume of his *Collected Poems* in 1980. He is a poet able to suggest imaginative interpretations of seemingly ordinary events. 'On the Edge' invokes the spectacle of a passerby who becomes 'a headless man', leaving the poet to wonder 'if what passed me was headless / or two-headed, friend or foe: / and if this street / this sun – even this world – is real or unreal.'

Soutar, William
Scottish poet *born* Perth 28 April 1898
died Perth 15 October 1943

William Soutar believed that 'if the Doric is to come back alive, it will come first on a cock-horse'. Accordingly he spent much of his creative time shaping his Scots sentiments into 'bairnsangs' that have become increasingly popular in Scottish schools. Soutar was an active young man who enlisted in the navy in 1916. He later contracted an illness which, after an unsuccessful operation in 1930, made him a bedfast invalid in his parents' home in Perth. Poignantly he summed up his predicament in 'Autobiography': 'Into a bed and into a tomb; / And the darkness of the world's womb.' Despite his disability his verse is good-humoured and triumphant in theme.

Southey, Robert
English poet *born* Bristol 12 August 1774
died Keswick, Cumbria 21 March 1843

Southey, a draper's son, was expelled from Westminster school for writing against flogging. After a year in Dublin as a political secretary he moved to Keswick, in 1803, to be near Coleridge. When Scott turned down the Poet Laureateship in 1813 Southey accepted the position. Southey's first wife became insane in 1834 and the poet himself became mentally confused in his later years. His verse displays more ingenuity than emotion though he can, as in 'The Battle of Blenheim', make shrewd comments: 'For many thousand bodies here / Lay rotting in the sun; / But things like that, you know, must be / After a famous victory.'

Southwell, Robert

English poet *born* Horsham St Faith, Norfolk 1561
died London 21 February 1595

Born into a prominent Roman Catholic family, Southwell studied in Paris and Rome and became a Jesuit. In 1586 he came to England with Henry Garnett (who was later executed for his part in the Gunpowder Plot) and became chaplain to the Countess of Arundel. Apprehended when going to celebrate mass in 1592, he was tortured thirteen times during his three years' imprisonment in the Tower of London; he was then hanged at Tyburn. His work has a visionary intensity as in 'The Burning Babe', a poem celebrating Christmas day: 'As I in hoary winter's night stood shivering in the snow, / Surprised I was with sudden heat which made my heart to glow'. The heat comes from 'A pretty Babe all burning bright'.

Soyinka, Wole

Nigerian poet *born* Abeokuta, Western Nigeria 1934

Educated at Government College, Idaban and University College, Ibadan, Soyinka came to England to study at Leeds University. Later he worked in London with the Royal Court Theatre. On his return to Nigeria in 1960 he became an activist opposed to current atrocities and was imprisoned in Northern Nigeria from 1967 to 1969. A dramatist and novelist as well as a poet, Soyinka has one of the most distinctive voices in African poetry. His satirical 'Telephone Conversation' comments on racism in England. The caller tells the landlady he is phoning 'Friction, caused – Foolishly madam – by sitting down, has turned / My bottom raven black.'

Spear, Charles

New Zealand poet *born* Owaka, South Otago 1910

Educated at the universities of Canterbury and Otago, Spear taught for twenty-seven years in the English Department of Canterbury University. On retiring in 1976 he settled in London. His influential collection *Twopence Coloured* appeared in 1951 and established him as an unusually observant poet able to use traditional forms in a highly individual manner. His description of '1894 in London' expertly evokes a precise aesthetic period. 'Old England's blue hour of unmeasured nips, / The Quiet Time for

Dorian Gray, / The day off for the barmaid's hips, / Prayer-Book revision time down Lambeth Way.'

Spence, Lewis
Scottish poet *born* Broughty Ferry, near Dundee
25 November 1874 *died* Edinburgh 3 March 1955

Educated at Edinburgh University, where he studied dentistry, Spence was a prolific and influential Scottish writer. He worked as a journalist with *The Scotsman*, the *Edinburgh Magazine* and the *British Weekly*; founded the Scottish National Movement in 1926 and helped found the National Party of Scotland two years later. In 1919 he became the first Scottish Nationalist to stand for Parliament. After a study of Middle Scots literature, he began to write poems in a revitalised Scots, as witness 'The Prows o' Reekie' which ends: 'A hoose is but a puppet-box / To keep life's images frae knocks, / But mannikins scrieve oot their sauls / Upon its craw-steps and its walls: / Whaur hae they writ them mair sublime / Than on yon gable-ends o' time?'

Reekie Edinburgh; *scrieve* write

Spencer, William Robert
English poet *born* Kensington Palace 9 July 1770 *died* Paris 1834

Youngest son of Lord Charles Spencer, the Hon William Robert Spencer was educated at Harrow and Oxford. While in Germany, at the age of nineteen, he married the daughter of Count Jenison Walworth then visited Italy with his wife. His translation of Burgen's 'Lenore' was praised by Sir Walter Scott and he resigned his parliamentary seat in 1797 to accept the office of Commissioner of Stamps. He published a collection of *Poems* in 1811 and generally lived a wild life in France before dying in poverty. His light verse is elegant and accomplished, as witness 'To My Grammatical Niece': 'Your Mother's a *Verb* from *Anomaly* free, / Though *Indicative* always of learning and sense, / In *all* of *her* moods she's *Potential* o'er me, / And the *Perfect* is still her *invariable Tense!*'

Spender, Stephen
English poet *born* London 28 September 1909

Spender – like Auden, Macneice and Day Lewis – was one of the politically-orientated poets who took up a leftist stance in the 1930s. His poem 'The Pylons', with its exploration of the industrial landscape and reference to 'the quick perspective of the future', typifies the mood of the period. Yet Spender's gift is better suited to the gentler, apolitical poems of his later years. 'To my Daughter' celebrates no symbolic landscape but the experience of love: 'Bright clasp of her whole hand around my finger . . . All my life I'll feel a ring invisibly / Circle this bone with shining'.

Spenser, Edmund
English poet *born* East Smithfield, London *c*1552
died London 16 January 1599

Spenser was educated at Cambridge and later formed, with Sidney and others, a literary circle styled the 'Areopagus'. In 1580 he became secretary to Lord Grey of Wilton, Deputy for Ireland, and began work on *The Faerie Queene* (1589, 1596), his masterpiece. He came to England in 1590 at the suggestion of Sir Walter Ralegh who presented him to the Queen. He celebrated his courtship of Elizabeth Boyle (whom he married in 1594) in his *Amoretti* (1595), a series of erotic sonnets. Number 76 begins: 'Fair bosom fraught with virtue's richest treasure, / The nest of love, the lodging of delight: / The bower of bliss, the paradise of pleasure, / The sacred harbour of that heavenly sprite.'

Speyer, Leonora
American poet *born* 1872 *died* New York 10 February 1956

A violinist, Leonora Speyer played with the New York Philharmonic and the Boston Symphony Orchestra. With her husband and four daughters, she lived in Paris and London; after her divorce she returned to the USA in 1915. Amy Lowell, her friend, encouraged her to write poetry and her collection *Fiddler's Farewell* (1927) won her the Pulitzer prize. 'The Ladder', one of her sensitive sonnets, presents a dream vision of a ladder of femininity: 'And every rung shone luminous and white, / And every rung a woman's body seemed / Out-stretched, and down the sides her long hair streamed: / And you, you climbed that ladder of delight.'

Stafford, William
American poet *born* Kansas 1914

Educated at the universities of Kansas, Wisconsin and Iowa, Stafford taught at Lewis and Clark College, Oregon. For *Travelling through the Dark* he won the National Book Award in 1962. The title poem of that collection shows him contemplating the relationship between mechanised man and vulnerable nature; when he finds the body of a pregnant doe he can 'hear the wilderness listen'. In 'At Cove on the Crooked River' he again contrasts the openness of the countryside with the closed world of the car and longs for the vision that comes 'When people cramp into their station wagons / and roll up the windows and drive away.'

Stafford, William
American poet *born* Kansas 1914

Educated at the universities of Kansas, Wisconsin and Iowa, Stafford taught at Lewis and Clark College, Oregon. For *Travelling through the Dark* he won the National Book Award in 1962. The title poem of that collection shows him contemplating the relationship between mechanized man and vulnerable nature; when he finds the body of a pregnant doe he can 'hear the wilderness listen'. In 'At Cove on the Crooked River' he again contrasts the openness of the countryside with the closed world of the car and longs for the vision that comes 'When people cramp into their station wagons / and roll up the windows and drive awy.'

Stallworthy, Jon
English poet *born* London 18 January 1935

Educated at Rugby and Oxford (where he won the Newdigate prize for poetry in 1958 and represented the university at rugby football), Stallworthy was an editor with Oxford University Press for ten years. He has written on Yeats and translated from the Russian of Alexander Blok. His own poems combine a Yeatsian regard for form with a highly subjective approach to experience, as in 'Two Hands', a poem about his father; 'The phone has sobbed itself to sleep, / but he has articles to read. I curse / tonight, at the other end of the house, / this other hand whose indecisions keep / me cursing nightly; fingers with some style on paper, elsewhere none.'

Stanley, Thomas
English poet *born* Cumberlow, Hertfordshire 1625
died 12 April 1678

Through his mother, a cousin of the poet Richard Lovelace, Stanley got on familiar terms with prominent writers of his time. He was educated at Cambridge and excelled as a scholar – editing Aeschylus and completing a standard *History of Philosophy* (1665–62). His volume of *Poems* (1647) contains 'The magnet', a love lyric in the Metaphysical manner. After giving examples of attraction in nature, Stanley ends; 'Be not then less kind than these, / Or from love exempt alone; / Let us twine like amorous trees, / And like rivers melt in one; / Or if thou more cruel prove / Learn of steel and stones to love.'

Starbuck, George
American poet *born* Columbus, Ohio 15 June 1931

Starbuck grew up in California and Illinois and attended the universities of Chicago and Harvard. He was a Military Police corporal in Germany and then a professor in Boston. He has two styles, one grave, one playful and is a poet capable of combining a neoclassical manner with scientific manner. Anxious to avoid the sentimentalities of the romantic gesture he packs his poetry with facts and waxes empirical rather than lyrical. In 'The Universe Is Closed and Has REMs' he writes: 'With pointy-headed notions of the sphere / A quantum mass might shrink to, to cohere / Into its own black hole, / Invariably sole / And satisfying to the theorist / Who likes his distillations with a twist / Of irreducibility at bottom.'

Stead, C K

New Zealand poet *born* Auckland 1932

Educated at the universities of Auckland and Bristol, Stead became Professor of English at Auckland University. His influential essay 'From Wystan to Carlos: Modern and Modernism in Recent NZ Poetry' (1979) explores the application of modernism to New Zealand verse. His own verse is eclectic though he sometimes succeeds in putting his theories successfully into practice, as in 'This may be your captain speaking' which ends with an image of 'ancient Maoris' and 'a characterising / untranslatable statement under / pohutukawas endlessly / varied endlessly the same'. His *Walking Westward* appeared in 1979.

Stein, Gertrude

American poet *born* Allegheny (Pittsburgh), Pennsylvania 3 February 1874 *died* 1946

Gertrude Stein studied psychology under William James at Radcliffe and medicine at Johns Hopkins. In 1903 she settled in Paris where she met (in 1909) Alice B Toklas, the woman she lived with for the rest of her life. Gertrude Stein not only championed the Cubist paintings of Picasso, Braque and Gris but attempted to write Cubist poetry by disturbing the narrative flow and emphasising the verbal structure of her work. She had a considerable influence on Ernest Hemingway and was a mother-figure to many of the American writers who flocked to Paris. Her 'Patriarchal Poetry' exemplifies her staccato style: 'Let her try. / Let her try. / Let her be / Let her let her be shy. / Let her try.'

Stephen, J K

English poet *born* London 25 February 1859 *died* 3 February 1892

Son of Sir James Fitzjames Stephen, James Kenneth Stephen was educated at Eton, where he excelled at sport; and at Cambridge, where he became a Fellow of King's College in 1885. Called to the Bar in 1885, he turned to journalism and contributed to the *St James's Gazette* and the *Reflector* (which he founded in 1888). His two collections of light verse, *Quo, Musa, Tendis?* and *Lapsus Calami*,

were both published in 1891. A brilliant parodist, he addressed
'The Parodist's Apology' to Browning: 'If I've dared to laugh at
you, Robert Browning, / 'Tis with eyes that with you have often
wept: / You have oftener left me smiling or frowning, / Than any
beside, one bard except.'

Stephens, James
Irish poet *born* Dublin 2 February 1882 *died* 26 December 1950

Stephens grew up in the Dublin slums and when working as a
clerk was discovered by G W Russell. He helped found, in 1911,
the *Irish Review* and in 1912 won the Polignac Prize for *The Crock
of Gold*, a prose fantasy now recognised as a classic. A small man,
under five feet, he was frequently referred to as a leprechaun. His
verbal vitality is shown to advantage in his celebrated poem 'A
Glass of Beer': 'The lanky hank of a she in the inn over there /
Nearly killed me for asking the loan of a glass of beer; / May the
devil grip the whey-faced slut by the hair, / And beat bad manners
out of her skin for a year.' Stephens wrote fine short stories and
(in 1920) published a collection of Irish fairy tales.

Stephens, James Brunton
Australian poet *born* Bowness, Firth of Forth 1835 *died* 1902

Son of a parish schoolmaster, Stephens was educated in
Edinburgh and took a travelling tutorship in France, Italy, Egypt,
Turkey, Sicily and the Holy Land. Back in Scotland he worked as
a schoolteacher then, for reasons of health, moved to
Queensland, Australia, in 1861. He worked as a tutor to the
family of a squatter and in 1866 his *Convict Once* appeared,
establishing him as a distinctively Australian poet; 'Oh for the
sea! 'Twere so easy to cease in its yielding embracement, /
Caught, like a rain-drop, and merged in the hugeness of infinite
rest, / Only the laugh of a ripple o'erbubbling the dimpled
displacement, / Then the great level of calm, and the hush of the
passionless breast.'

Stephens, Meic
Welsh poet *born* Pontypridd 1938

Educated at Aberystwyth, Stephens worked as a teacher and
journalist. In 1965 he founded *Poetry Wales* and in 1968 he was
appointed Literature Director of the Welsh Arts Council. He has
done much to promote interest in Welsh writing and his own
poems draw on a living tradition. 'Elegy for Mr Lewis (Welsh)' is a
portrait of a pedagogic tyrant and his feeling for Welsh: 'Old
bully, ranting forever in my memory, // you've been dead these
twenty years. Well, / I speak and love the language now, no
thanks to you; / so please allow me, late as usual but not far

wrong, / to raise my hand for once and make this reply: / Cymro, I
know what drove you to despair.'

Stevens, Wallace

American poet *born* Reading, Pennsylvania 2 October 1879
died Hartford, Connecticut 2 August 1955

A lawyer's son, Stevens was educated at Harvard and the New
York Law School before practising law in New York until 1916.
He then joined the Hartford Accident and Indemnity Company
whose Vice-President he became in 1934. His first collection,
Harmonium (1923), was indifferently received but Stevens
persisted with his twin career as poet and businessman. His style,
with its interest in the process of perception, was drawn from the
French Symbolists. *The Man With the Blue Guitar* (1937), a
contemplation of creativity, shows a Metaphysical wit: 'They said,
"You have a blue guitar, / You do not play things as they are." /
The man replied, "Things as they are / Are changed upon the
blue guitar."'

Stevenson, Anne

English poet *born* Cambridge 1933

The child of American parents, Anne Stevenson was brought up
in the USA and educated at the University of Michigan. She went
to England and settled in Hay-on-Wye where she works as a
freelance writer. Her work is powerfully descriptive and she uses
domestic detail in an imaginative manner, as in 'With my Sons at
Boarhills': 'Faces I washed and scolded, only / watched as my each
child laboured from his own womb, / bringing forth, without me,
men who must / call me mother, love or reassess me / as their
barest needs dictate, return / dreaming, rarely to this saltpool in
memory, / naked on a morning full of sea-through jellyfish'.

Stevenson, Robert Louis

Scottish poet *born* Edinburgh 13 November 1850 *died* Opolu,
Samoa 3 December 1889

Stevenson came from a family of lighthouse engineers and at first
intended to carry on the family tradition. However he abandoned
engineering to study law, at Edinburgh University, then
subsequently made his living from tales of adventure and novels
such as *Dr Jekyll and Mr Hyde* (1886). His ability to convey the
imaginative euphoria of the child is seen to advantage in *A Child's
Garden of Verse* (1885). *Underwoods* (1887) contains poems in both
Scots and English. 'Requiem' displays both the elegance of his
diction and his gently melancholic tone: 'This be the verse you
grave for me: / *Here he lies where he longed to be; / Home is the sailor,
home from sea, / And the hunter home from the hill.*'

Stewart, Douglas
Australian poet *born* Eltham, New Zealand 1913

After studying law, Stewart came to Australia in 1938 to pursue a career in journalism; he has done important work as the literary editor of the Sydney *Bulletin*. Stewart is perhaps best known for his intelligent extension of the range of the bush-ballad, so dominant in Australian writing for so long. His 'The Dosser in Springtime' adds a romantic note to the narrative: 'That girl from the sun is bathing in the creek, / Says the white old dosser in the cave. / It's a sight worth seeing though your old frame's weak; / Her clothes are on the wattle and it's gold all over, / And if I was twenty I'd try to be her lover, / Says the white old dosser in the cave.'

Stewart, John
Scottish poet *born* c1539 *died* c1606

Son of Lord Innerneith and a kinsman of James VI, John Stewart of Baldynneis (as he was known when his brother settled the lands of Baldynneis, Perthshire, on him in 1580) was educated at St Andrews University. He became a courtier and one of the Castalian Band of poets encouraged by James VI. Under the influence of the King's treatise 'Reulis and Cautelis' (1585) he wrote several ingenious poems showing his technical brilliance. Dedicated to the King, these were collected in *Rapsodies of the Author's Youthfull Braine* (1556). 'To his Darrest Friend' is a contrapuntal poem: 'My luifing hart does weill aggrie / With you to bie / In weill and wo'. He translated Ariosto's *Orlando furioso*.

Stokes, Adrian
English poet *born* London 27 October 1902
died London 13 December 1972

When, at the age of sixty-four, Adrian Stokes took up writing poetry he had four more years to live; in that time, despite suffering from incurable cancer, he managed to produce the 183 items in his *Collected Poems* (1981). Stokes brought to poetry his aesthetic expertise; as an art historian he took a psychological approach to the subject. His poetry, too, is informed by psychoanalytic theory. His daughter was mentally ill and Stokes became distressed by his inability to penetrate into her private world, as he shows in his poem 'Schizophrenic Girl'; 'You have no inner shut-off space / You at the centre; / A sack of potatoes instead / Speckled with tears and holes. / This too is living'.

Strode, William
English poet *born* Plymouth 1602 *died* 11 March 1645
Strode was educated at Oxford where he became, in 1629, Public Orator. After taking orders he became chaplain to the Bishop of

Oxford – the poet Richard Corbet. Subsequently Strode became rector of East Bredenham, Norfolk; rector of Badley, Northamptonshire; and Canon of Christ Church. He supported the Royalist side in the Civil War. His poetry shows a passion for rural landscapes, as in 'On Westwall Downes'; 'Here and there two hilly crests / Amidst them hug a pleasant green, / And these are like two swelling breasts / That close a tender fall between.' He also wrote a play *The Floating Island* (1633) which was criticised for being tiresomely moralistic.

Stuart, Alice V

Scottish poet *born* Rangoon 1899 *died* 1981

Educated at St Hilda's School, Edinburgh, and at Oxford she became a schoolteacher. Subsequently she settled in Edinburgh as a tutor to foreign language students. She helped found the Scottish Association for the Speaking of Verse and was herself an accomplished reader of poetry. Her 'Lintie in a Cage' is a dramatic monologue spoken by an attendant on the poet Robert Fergusson when he was in Darien Madhouse, Edinburgh, in 1774: 'Yon is the laddie lo'ed to daunder far / Whaur the burnie bickers by the Hermitage / That sits at the fit o Braid; or whaur Dunbar, / Reid as its rocks, briests the blae Firth's blawn rage.'

reid red; *briests* breasts; *lintie* linnet; *blae* lead-coloured

Stuart, Francis

Irish poet *born* Australia 1902

Stuart came from Australia to County Antrim where he lived before a period in England followed by a teaching job at Berlin University. He then returned to Ireland and settled in Dublin. His novels are highly regarded and his verse uses rhyme and taut rhythms. 'Criminals' is a tale of three deaths. In the third section, the criminal drowns a woman: 'So where her mother prays / Each Sunday in the church he carved these words: / "I tied her to a cross and on the third day / She descended into Hell but she shall rise / To the sea's edge again and rot away. / Who was her lover once writes this and dies."'

Suckling, Sir John

English poet *born* Twickenham 1 February 1609 *died* Paris 1642

Educated at Cambridge, Suckling was knighted in 1630. After soldiering abroad he returned to England in 1632 and achieved success with his play *Aglaura* (1637) whose expensive costumes he paid for himself. He fought for Charles I in the Bishops' Wars but fled to France after taking part in an abortive plot to save the Earl of Strafford from execution. According to Aubrey, he took his own life. His Cavalier poetry is characteristically charming as in the celebrated song from *Aglaura*: 'Why so pale and wan, fond lover? / Prithee, why so pale? / Will, when looking well can't move her, / Looking ill prevail? / Prithee, why so pale?'

Surrey, Howard Henry, Earl of
English poet *born c*1517 *died* 21 January 1547

Son of the third Duke of Norfolk, Surrey became cup-bearer to Henry VIII and Earl Marshal at Anne Boleyn's trial. He was knighted shortly after the execution of his cousin, Queen Catherine Howard. Imprisoned for brawling in 1542 and 1543 he was eventually executed, on Henry VIII's orders, for allegedly conspiring against the succession of Edward VI. Surrey, like Wyatt, imported Italian models into English verse and excelled as a sonneteer. His sonnet on spring begins: 'The soote season, that bud and bloom forth brings, / With green hath clad the hill and eke the vale. / The nightingale with feathers new she sings; / The turtle to her mate hath told her tale.'

Swift, Jonathan
Irish poet *born* Dublin 30 November 1667
died Dublin 19 October 1745

Educated in his native Dublin, Swift came to England after the abdication of James II in 1688. As secretary to Sir William Temple he met, and taught, Esther Johnson, his 'Stella'. An Anglican priest, he had a disgust for human weaknesses and wrote some of the greatest satirical works in the English language. In 1713 Swift was appointed Dean of St Patrick's, Dublin, and was subsequently distracted by the death of Esther Vanhomrigh, 'Vanessa', in 1723 and 'Stella' in 1728. In 1742 Swift was declared 'of unsound mind'. His poetry shows an incisive wit transcending the confines of neoclassical verse, as in 'Verses on the Death of Doctor Swift': 'Yet malice never was his aim: / He lashed the vice, but spared the name.'

Swinburne, Algernon Charles
English poet *born* London 5 April 1837 *died* 10 April 1909

An admiral's son, Swinburne was educated at Eton and Oxford where he studied the Classics as well as French and German with a view to mastering metrics. After the publication of *Atalanta in Calydon* (1865) he was recognised as one of the most distinctive poets of his time, a man who brought to English verse the verbal colour of the Continent. His technical virtuosity is always impressive and in poems such as 'The Garden of Proserpine' he expounds a poignant view of life: 'From too much love of living, / From hope and fear set free, / We thank with brief thanksgiving / Whatever gods may be / That no life lives for ever; / That dead men rise up never; / That even the weariest river / Winds somewhere safe to sea.'

Sylvester, Joshua

English poet *born* 1563 *died* Middleburg 28 September 1618

In 1608 Sylvester, a Puritan and merchant-adventurer, published a translation of *La Semaine*, an epic by the French poet Du Partas. As Sylvester's publisher, Humphrey Lownes, lived in the same street as Milton's father it is probable that Milton was familiar with the translation which has lines that anticipate *Paradise Lost*: 'O complete creature! who the starry spheres / Canst make to move, who 'bove the heavenly bears / Extend'st thy power, who guidest with thy hand / The day's bright chariot, and the nightly brand'. Sylvester, once a pensioner of Prince Henry, also wrote poems such as 'To Religion': 'Under thy sacred name, all over, / The vicious all their vices cover'.

Symons, Arthur

English poet *born* Milford Haven 28 February 1865
died 22 January 1945

Symons travelled in France and Italy and absorbed the influence of the French Symbolists. Before his breakdown of 1908, he was known as an adventurous and inventive writer and one of the leading figures of the Decadent movement of the 1890s. In, for example 'Bianca', he transforms passion into an erotic fever: 'Life sucks into a mist remote / Her fainting lips, her throbbing throat; / Her lips that open to my lips, / And, hot against my finger-tips, / the pulses leaping in her throat'. He wrote interesting critical studies of *The Symbolist Movement in Literature* (1899) and *The Romantic Movement in English Poetry* (1909) as well as an autobiographical work, *A Study in Pathology* (1930).

Synge, J M

Irish poet *born* Rathfarnham, near Dublin 16 April 1871
died Dublin 24 March 1909

A barrister's son, John Millington Synge was educated at Trinity College and in Paris where he was advised by Yeats to return to Ireland and study the people of the Aran Islands. He did so and became internationally known as a playwright as a result. After his great drama *The Playboy of the Western World* (1907) was criticised by the sister of one of his enemies, he wrote 'The Curse': 'Lord, confound this surly sister, / Blight her brow with blotch and blister, / Cramp her larynx, lung, and liver, / In her guts a galling give her. / Let her live to earn her dinners / In Mountjoy with seedy sinners: / Lord, this judgement quickly bring, / And I'm your servant, J M Synge.'

Szirtes, George

English poet *born* Budapest 1948

Szirtes's family came to England as refugees after the Hungarian

uprising of 1956 and he studied Fine Art in Leeds and London.
He is an entertaining poet who startles the reader by the
incongruities he brings together. In 'Postscript' he imagines how
'St Sebastian, scandalous / In loincloth, sways like Diana Ross'; in
'Tatooist' he portrays a man who 'pricks the skin' and offers
'angels on a pin'. His pictorial imagination enables him to render
objects in an unusual way and his compassion brings him close to
the subject of 'An Old Woman Walks Home': 'How one fears /
for her survival, her immensity, / the enormous effort of
becoming tears.'

Taggard, Genevieve
American poet *born* Waitsburg, Washington 28 November
1894 *died* Jamaica, Vermont 8 November 1948

Born on an apple farm, Genevieve Taggard was brought up on
Oahu Island, Hawaii, where she became friendly with the children
of Chinese, Japanese and Hawaiian plantation labourers and
developed a detestation of white racism. At the University of
California at Berkeley, she became a socialist and feminist and
pursued her ideals in New York. Her poems generally have a
strong physical foundation, for example 'Everyday Alchemy':
'Men go to women mutely for their peace; / And they, who lack it
most, create it when / They make, because they must, loving their
men, / A solace for sad bosom-bended heads. There / Is all the
meagre peace men get – no otherwhere'.

Tarn, Nathaniel
English poet *born* Paris 30 June 1928

Educated at the universities of Cambridge and Chicago, and at the
Sorbonne, Tarn worked for a publisher (Cape) in London and as a
Professor of Comparative Literature in the USA. An
anthropologist by training, his tone is international and in 1966
he produced a brilliant translation of Pablo Neruda's *The Heights
of Macchu Picchu.* His long poem *The Beautiful Contradictions* (1969),
a poetic survey of the state of the world, alternates between
affirmation and indignation: 'I know that the massacre of the
human environment applies to cities too / and that the most
elegant buildings are always the victims' he says in section twelve.

Tate, Allen
American poet *born* Winchester, Kentucky
19 November 1899 *died* 1979

In 1922 Tate graduated from Vanderbilt University where he
associated with the Fugitive group of Southern poets who
contributed to the *Fugitive* (1922-5), upheld agrarian ideals and
evolved the close textual scrutiny of New Criticism. Tate worked
for a while in his brother's coal business, visited Paris in 1928 on a

Guggenheim Fellowship, and taught at various universities. He also edited *Hound and Horn* (1934–4) and *Sewanee Review* (1944–6). His poems, such as 'Ode to the Confederate Dead', are formal and meditative: 'Turn your eyes to the immoderate past, / Turn to the inscrutable infantry rising / Demons out of the earth – they will not last.'

Taylor, Ann

English poet *born* London 30 January 1782
died 20 December 1866

An engraver's daughter, Ann was the sister of the poet Jane Taylor and Isaac Taylor, the philosopher. She was raised in Suffolk from the age of four then moved to Colchester where her father became minister. Ann and Jane collaborated on several collections of children's verse including *Rhymes for the Nursery* (1806). In 1811 her father moved to a church in Ongar where Ann and Jane were known as 'the Taylors of Ongar'. Her well-known children's poems include 'Meddlesome Matty' and 'My Mother' which begins: 'Who fed me from her gentle breast, / And hush'd me in her arms to rest, / And on my cheeks sweet kisses prest? / My Mother.' Ann married, in 1813, the clergyman Joseph Gilbert.

Taylor, Bayard

American poet *born* Kennett Square, Pennsylvania 11 January 1825 *died* Berlin 19 December 1878

After working as an apprentice printer, Taylor went on a walking tour of Europe, an experience recalled in *Views Afoot* (1846). He witnessed the Gold Rush as a journalist, wrote novels as popular as *Hannah Thurston* (1863), performed diplomatic duties on behalf of the USA, taught German literature at Cornell University, and translated Goethe's *Faust* (1870–1). 'The Deserter' is a tale of a soldier shot for deserting, after dreaming that his family was in danger: 'But o'er his sad grave, by the Mexican sea, / Wives and mothers have planted a blossoming tree; / And maidens bring roses, and tenderly say, – / "It was love – sweetest love – led that soldier away."'

Taylor, Edward

English poet *born* Leicestershire 1645 *died* 1729

Taylor left England, arrived in Boston in 1668, lived for some time in Westfield, and graduated from Harvard in 1671, the year he became a minister. He insisted that his poems should remain unpublished and so they did until they were discovered in Yale library in 1937: the *Poetical Works of Edward Taylor* appeared in 1939, more than two centuries after the poet's death. His style is clearly derived from the English Metaphysical poets and he is adept at bringing his clever conceits to a religious conclusion. His eight Meditations end: 'This bread of life dropt in thy mouth, doth cry. / Eat, eat me, Soul, and thou shalt never die.'

Taylor, Jane

English poet *born* London, 23 September 1783
died Ongar, Essex 13 April 1824

An engraver's daughter, Jane was the sister of the poet Ann Taylor and Isaac Taylor, the philosopher. A precocious child, she began writing at the age of eight and collaborated with Ann on *Original Poems for Infant Minds* (1804) which went into fifty editions and was translated into various languages. In 1811 her father became minister in Ongar, Essex, and the sisters were known as 'the Taylors of Ongar'. Ann's marriage, in 1813, ended the sisters' partnership but Jane continued to write such works as *Display, A Tale for Young People* (1815). Her poem 'The Star' is still in circulation: 'Twinkle, twinkle, little star, / How I wonder what you are! / Up above the world so high, / Like a diamond in the sky!'

Taylor, Rachel Annand

Scottish poet *born* Aberdeen 1876 *died* London 15 August 1960

After graduating from Aberdeen University, Rachel Annand married Alexander Cameron Taylor with whom she lived in Dundee and London. Interested in visual as well as verbal art, she published books on *Aspects of the Italian Renaissance* (1923) and *Leonardo the Florentine* (1927). Her mildly erotic imagery and muted diction is seen to advantage in the sonnet 'Art and Women': 'For with the silver moons we wax and wane, / And with the roses love most woundingly, / And, wrought from flower to fruit with dim rich pain, / The orchard of the Pomegranates are we.' The sonnet closes on the couplet: 'And Art, that fierce confessor of the flowers, / Desires the secret spice of those veiled hours.'

Teasdale, Sara

American poet *born* St Louis 8 August 1884
died New York 29 January 1933

Born into a wealthy family, Sara Teasdale was educated privately. In New York she met Vachel Lindsay, who fell in love with her; Sara, however, ended the courtship when she married a St Louis businessman in 1914. After the publication of *Love Songs* (1917) she was awarded the Pulitzer Prize for poetry though the acclaim did little to lift her depression: she divorced her husband in 1929 and moved to New York. After hearing of the suicide of Vachel Lindsay in 1931, Sara fell into a decline and eventually took her life with an overdose of sleeping pills. In 'Central Park at Dusk' she wrote: 'Silent as women wait for love, / The world is waiting for the spring.'

Tennant, William
Scottish poet *born* Anstruther, Fife 15 May 1784
died Anstruther 14 October 1848

Lame from childhood, Tennant used his time to master various languages and became a teacher of classics then, in 1834, Professor of Oriental Languages at St Andrews University. His verse dramas are now forgotten but he is still celebrated for his mock-heroic *Anster Fair* (1812), a poem whose narrative panache and comic eccentricity of rhyme probably influenced Byron's *Don Juan*, also written in *ottava rima*. In the first Canto, Tennant introduces Maggie Lauder: 'Alone she sat, and pensive as may be / A young fair lady, wishful of a mate; / Yet with her teeth held now and then a-picking, / Her stomach to refresh, the breast-bone of a chicken.'

Tennyson, Alfred Lord
English poet *born* Somersby, Lincolnshire 6 August 1809
died Aldworth, Surrey 6 October 1892

A clergyman's son, Tennyson was educated at Cambridge where he formed a deep friendship with A H Hallam who was engaged to the poet's sister. In 1830 he and Hallam went to the Pyrenees to support the revolt against Ferdinand VII of Spain. Hallam's death, three years later, came as an emotional blow from which Tennyson never recovered. The sense of loss led to the composition, in 130 sections, of *In Memoriam A H H* (1850), Tennyson's characteristically melancholy masterpiece: 'But what am I? / An infant crying in the night: / An infant crying for the light: / And with no language but a cry.' In 1845, the year of his marriage to Emily Sellwood, Tennyson was created Poet Laureate; in 1883 he accepted a peerage from Gladstone.

Thackeray, William Makepeace
English poet *born* Calcutta 18 July 1811 *died* 24 December 1863

Thackeray's father, an official with the East India Company, died in 1816 and the author was sent back to England to be educated at Charterhouse School and Cambridge. He studied law, briefly, in the Middle Temple and studied art in Paris. Back in London he wrote for *Fraser's Magazine* and *Punch*. His wife became insane in 1840 and he had to bring up two daughters. His great novel *Vanity Fair* appeared in 1847–8 and he enhanced his reputation with *Pendennis* (1848) and *The Newcomes* (1853–5). His light verse, as witness 'The Ballad of Bouillabaisse', is splendid: 'This Bouillabaisse a noble dish is – / A sort of soup, or broth, or brew, / Or hotchpotch of all sorts of fishes, / That Greenwich never could outdo.'

Thiele, Colin
Australian poet *born* Eudanda, South Australia 1920

Educated at Adelaide University, Thiele was with the Royal Australian Air Force during the Second World War. He then became a teacher working in several schools before taking up a post on the staff of Adelaide Teachers' College. Thiele became well-known for his contributions to the radio and wrote a number of radio plays. He is attracted to traditional techniques of verse which he can effectively put to humorous use, as in 'Up-Country Pubs': 'With breasts and buttocks firm as trees / The barmaid-waitress blooms and sways; / And drinking timber-men appraise / How things grow upwards from the knees; / All day they dream and climb astride / Such satin-smooth and supple forks'.

Thomas, D M
English poet *born* Cornwall 1935

Educated at Oxford and subsequently a teacher and lecturer, Thomas has had great success as a novelist, especially with *The White Hotel* (1981). As a poet he has a direct, sometimes brutal style being not so much a sensitive artist with words as a signpainter who relies on clarity. His work is sometimes disturbing as he has an appetite for the unusual that leads him to grim subjects. His 'Peter Kürten to the Witnesses' is a dramatic monologue in which a mass murderer looks back on his life and the death of his victims: 'I can smell blood a mile off and I'm certain / the hour is at hand when you will say, / Why did we kill good Peter Kürten? / But it's as well.'

Thomas, Dylan
Welsh poet *born* Swansea 27 October 1914
died New York 9 November 1953

In the three years after leaving school in 1931 Dylan Thomas produced more than 200 poems whereas in the last seven years of his life he wrote only eight. Gradually the image of abandon he had built around himself overwhelmed him. After his early success Thomas established himself as a stunning performer of poetry and when America embraced him he was anxious to display his epic talents as a drinker. For all his personal bluster Thomas contrived, with great technical skill, to produce some of the most ecstatic lyrics in the English language. In poems like 'Fern Hill' he gloriously invokes a childhood Eden: 'Now as I was young and easy under the apple boughs / About the lilting house and happy as the grass was green'.

Thomas, Edward

English poet *born* London 3 March 1878 *died* Arras 9 April 1917

As his father expected him to follow him into the Civil Service, Edward Thomas was prepared in the Classics for public school. He preferred, however, to earn his living from writing and was influenced by Richard Jefferies' example to celebrate the English countryside in prose. Then, encouraged by Robert Frost, he shaped his rural observations into lucid lines. Thomas was killed in action and when his *Collected Poems* appeared in 1920 he was recognised as one of the most sensuous nature poets writing, in 'October', of how 'The green elm with the one great bough of gold / Lets leaves into the grass slip, one by one'.

Thomas, John L

Welsh poet *born* Pibwr Lwyd, Carmarthen 1795 *died* 1871

Known as *Ieuan Ddu*, John L Thomas was a schoolteacher. A bilingual poet, he wrote in Welsh and English and in 1867 published *Cambria upon Two Sticks*, a reference to the two languages of Wales. In his 'Harry Vaughan', Thomas regrets his predecessor's ignorance of his native language: 'But Harry, being of rank, was never taught / the melodies that owned his native land; / He little knew what lays with genius fraught / In Ivor's days had cheered the festive band; / Ap Gwilym's fervid strains had never caught / His ear, and had they, such to understand, / He like the rest of Cambria's well-taught gentry / Deemed the distinction of some bygone century.'

Thomas, R S

Welsh poet *born* Cardiff 29 March 1913

Educated in Cardiff and ordained in 1936, the Reverend R S Thomas has been a clergyman all his adult life but he is neither a dogmatic nor a self-righteously rhetorical poet. He is cautious in his conclusions, encouragingly open-minded. Like Hopkins, Thomas is a poet whose theological doubts and ecclesiastical agonies bring a tautness to the texture of his verse. Many of his poems have a shapeliness that is determined by biblical devices such as parallelism and richly visual imagery. In 'Via Negativa' he writes: 'Why no! I never thought other than / That God is that great absence / In our lives, the empty silence / Within, the place where we go / Seeking, not in hope to / Arrive or find.'

Thompson, Francis

English poet *born* Preston 18 December 1859 *died* London 13 November 1907

Son of a doctor, Thompson was a failure as a medical student and left home to live in London where he did undemanding jobs (for example, selling matches) and became an opium addict.

Impressed by his poems, Wilfrid Meynell, editor of *Merrie England*, persuaded Thompson to overcome his drug problem with the assistance of the monks of Storrington Priory. The experience prompted Thompson to write 'The Hound of Heaven', a visionary encounter between man and God as the hunted and the hunter: 'I fled Him, down the nights and down the days; / I fled Him, down the arches of the years; / I fled Him, down the labyrinthine ways / Of my own mind; and in the midst of tears / I hid from Him'.

Thompson, John
Australian poet *born* Melbourne 1907 *died* 1968

Educated at Melbourne University, Thompson went to England for eight years before returning to Australia to work for the Australian Broadcasting Commission in Perth. He was with the Australian Imperial Force, during the Second World War, and later became a writer-producer with the Australian Broadcasting Commission. His poems show a shrewd intelligence, especially in his witty address 'A Latter-Day Polonius to His Sons': 'Excess in moderation! Take / this principle for your health's sake, / Shunning the curst insipidness / Of moderation in excess . . . Be, above all things, straight and kind, /But never stoop or shrink your mind / To wheedle prudes or flatter fools / Who stint their lust with others' rules'.

Thompson, John
Canadian poet *born* 1938 *died* 1976

After an education in England (where he was born) and the USA, Thompson became a member of the English Department at Mount Allison University, Sackville, New Brunswick. Three years before his death he published his collection *At the Edge of the Chopping There Are No Secrets*. His poems have a physical feel as he explores the environment in a hypersensitive manner. 'Coming Back', for example, contemplates the cold and ends with the poet 'bringing / a few fir cones / which have lain for months, / under the snow, // back to the quiet, knowing / those terrible iron tongues / no longer hammer / against the walls of my house.'

Thomson, James
Scottish poet *born* Ednam, Roxburghshire 11 September 1700 *died* Richmond, Surrey 27 August 1748

A minister's son, Thomson studied divinity at Edinburgh University but when his Professor condemned the imaginative tone of his sermons, he abandoned his religious calling and moved to London, in 1725, to work as a tutor and develop as a writer – in the company of Pope, Gay and other poets he met. Thomson's great sequence *The Seasons* (1730) established him as a

major Augustan poet and a master of natural description.
'Winter' has an almost Wordsworthian wealth of detail: 'The
loosened ice, / Lets down the flood, and half dissolved by day, /
Rustles no more; but to the sedgy bank / Fast grows, or gathers
round the pointed stone, / A crystal pavement, by the breath of
heaven / Cemented firm'.

Thomson, James ('B V')
Scottish poet *born* Port Glasgow 23 November 1834
died London 8 June 1882

After the death of both his parents, Thomson was raised in a
London orphanage. Posted to County Cork as an army
schoolmaster in 1851, he fell in love with Matilda Weller; the
shock of her death, two years later, encouraged him to indulge in
the chronic alcoholism that ended his army career in 1862. His
friend, the celebrated atheist Charles Bradlaugh, published
Thomson's 'The City of Dreadful Night' in the *National Reformer*
from March to May 1874. The poem dwells despairingly on a
bleak and godless world: 'Perpetual recurrence in the scope / Of
but three terms, dead Faith, dead Love, dead Hope.' Thomson is
known as 'B V' after his pseudonym Bysshe Novalis (a tribute to
two of his favourite authors, Shelley and Novalis).

Thoreau, Henry David
American poet *born* Concord, Massachusetts 12 July 1817
died Concord, Massachusetts 6 May 1862

Educated at Harvard, Thoreau was devoted to his home town
where he came under the influence of Emerson and became a
member of the Transcendental Club. An outspoken critic of
convention he asserted, in 'Civil Disobedience' (1849), 'that
government is best which governs least' and in his prose
masterpiece *Walden* (1854) affirmed his ideal of rural retreatism.
An advocate of passive resistance to authority, he later advocated
the use of violence against the obscenity of slavery. His poem
'Independence' ends on this characteristic quatrain: 'The life that
I aspire to live / No man proposeth me – / No trade upon the
street / Wears its emblazonry.'

Thornbury, Walter
English poet *born* London 1828 *died* 1876

In the 1850s Thornbury simulated the swaggering mood of
English imperialism in his *Songs of the Cavaliers and Roundheads* but
he was also capable of an elegant irony. His use of the refrain, in
such poems as 'Smith of Maudlin', is inventive. In the poem the
speaker reflects on the impact his death will have on his friends:
'That night in High Street there will walk / The ruffling
gownsmen three abreast, / The stiff-necked proctors, wary-eyed, /

The dons, the coaches, and the rest; / Sly "Cherub Sims" will then propose / Billiards, or some sweet ivory sin; / Tom cries, "He played a pretty game – / Did honest Smith of Maudlin."'

Thorpe, Rose Hartwick
American poet *born* Mishawaka, Indiana 18 July 1850
died San Diego, California 19 July 1939

Rose Hartwick Thorpe was raised in Litchfield, Michigan, and began to write poetry from an early age. After reading, in *Peterson's Magazine*, the story of a young woman who saved her lover's life – by clinging to the church bell clapper so it could not toll curfew, the time of his execution – she wrote her 'Curfew Must Not Ring Tonight'. The poem, often parodied and memorably interpreted in drawings by James Thurber, has an earnest innocence: 'The brave deed that she had done / Should be told long ages after, as the rays of setting sun / Should illume the sky with beauty; agèd sires, with heads of white, / Long should tell the little children curfew did not ring that night.'

Tickell, Thomas
English poet *born* Bridekirk, near Carlisle 1686 *died* Bath 1740

Tickell was educated at Oxford and was a Fellow, at Queen's College, from 1710 to 1726 when he married in Dublin. His poem *On the Prospect of Peace* (1713), supporting the Peace of Utrecht, impressed Addison who encouraged him to contribute to the *Spectator*. Addison took Tickell to Ireland with him and when he was made Secretary of State, Tickell became his Under-Secretary. On the death of Addison, in 1719, Tickell edited his *Works* and prefaced them with an elegy, 'To the Earl of Warwick, on the Death of Mr Addison': 'Can I forget the dismal night that gave / My soul's best part for ever to the grave? / How silent did his old companions tread, / By midnight lamps, the mansions of the dead'.

Todhunter, John
Irish poet *born* 1839 *died* 1916

Todhunter taught English at Alexandra College, Dublin, and was enthused with the idea of simulating the rhythm of Irish in English verse. When he moved to London he became one of the founders of the Irish Literary Society and encouraged the study of Irish mythology. His poems, for example 'Aghadoe', have an incantatory quality: 'There's a glen in Aghadoe, Aghadoe, Aghadoe, / There's a green and silent glade in Aghadoe, / Where we met, my Love and I, Love's fair planet in the sky, / O'er that sweet and silent glen in Aghadoe'. Todhunter's *The Banshee and Other Poems* appeared in 1892.

Tolkien, J R R

English poet *born* Bloemfontein, South Africa 3 January
1892 *died* Bournemouth 2 September 1973

Educated at Oxford, John Ronald Reuel Tolkien was Professor of
Anglo-Saxon at Oxford from 1925–45 and Professor of English
Language and Literature from 1945–9. He began to write verse at
the age of eighteen though he decided to cast his masterpiece,
The Lord of the Rings (1954–5), in prose. His finest poem, *The
Homecoming of Beorhtnoth Beorhthelm's Son* (1953), is an alliterative
postscript to the Anglo-Saxon *The Battle of Maldon*. Tolkien deals
with the squalid aftermath of the battle when honour is seen to be
done to death as two servants look for Beorhtnoth's body.
Tidwald says: 'When the poor are robbed / and lose the land they
loved and toiled on, / they must die and dung it.'

Tolson, Melvin B

American poet *born* Moberly, Missouri 1898 *died* 1966

Educated at the universities of Fisk, Lincoln and Columbia,
Tolson taught at various southern colleges. In Oklahoma, where
he directed the Dust Bowl Theatre and taught as Professor of
Creative Literature, he was associated with Langston Hughes.
Acclaimed as one of the major black American poets by William
Carlos Williams, Robert Frost, Theodore Roethke and others, he
published *Rendezvous with America* (1944) and *Harlem Gallery*
(1965). His political anger is expressed in 'Dark Symphony': 'The
new Negro, / Hard-muscled, Fascist-hating, Democracy-
ensouled, / Strides in seven-league boots / Along the Highway of
Today / Towards the Promised Land of Tomorrow!'

Tomlinson, Charles

English poet *born* Stoke-on-Trent 8 January 1927

A clerk's son, Tomlinson was educated at Cambridge. In 1951 he
spent nine months as private secretary to the author Percy
Lubbock in Italy where he wrote the poems for his first collection
The Necklace (1955). In 1956 he became lecturer and then Reader
in English poetry at Bristol University. His firt major poetic
success was the publication in 1958 of *Seeing is Believing* in the
USA, two years before it appeared in England. Influenced by
Wallace Stevens, Marianne Moore and William Carlos Williams,
Tomlinson cultivated an international tone. 'His 'Swimming
Chenango Lake' begins: 'Winter will bar the swimmer soon. / He
reads the water's autumnal hesitations / A wealth of ways'.

Toomer, Jean

American poet *born* Washington, DC 26 December 1894
died near Philadelphia 30 March 1967

Educated at Wisconsin University and New York City College,

Toomer went to Georgia in 1922 as principal of a school. His book *Cane* (1923) – a miscellany of poems, stories and prose sketches – made a profound impact as it applied the principles of modernism to black subject-matter. Toomer was neglected after this book and began to blame his misfortune on his identification with the material in *Cane*. All his subsequent work was rejected by publishers and he settled in Bucks County, Pennsylvania as a sad figure from the past. He died in a rest home. 'Cotton Song' states: 'Shackles fall upon the Judgement Day / But let's not wait for it.'

Traherne, Thomas
English poet *born* Hereford 1637
died London 27 September 1674
A shoemaker's son, Traherne was educated at Oxford. Ordained in 1660, he was from 1661–9 rector at Credenhill and, from 1672 onwards, chaplain to Sir Orlando Bridgeman, the Lord Keeper. In the 1890s Bertram Dobell identified some manuscripts, found on a London bookstall, as the work of Traherne whose *Poetical Works* thus appeared in 1903. Often compared to Vaughan, Traherne is more predictable than his fellow Metaphysicals. He constantly looks to an ideal Platonic world, like that glimpsed in 'Shadows in the Water' where 'Some unknown Joys there be / Laid up in store for me; / To which I shall, when that thin Skin / Is broken, be admitted in.'

Traill, Henry Duff
English poet *born* London 14 August 1842 *died* 21 February 1900
Son of a Greenwich magistrate, Traill was educated at Oxford and was called to the Bar at Inner Temple in 1869. He became Inspector of Returns at the Education Office in 1871 but later turned to journalism, contributing to the *Yorkshire Post* and joining the staffs of the *Pall Mall Gazette* (1873) then the *St James' Gazette* (1880). His humorous verse appears in *Recaptured Rhymes* (1882), *Saturday Lays* (1890) and *Number Twenty* (1891). His 'Laputa Outdone' expatiates on the absurdities of English society; 'So, off with it! Off with your bee-bearing bonnet, / Illustrious guest from Luggnaggian shores! / And down on your knee, and do homage upon it / Profound to a State that is madder than yours!'

Tregear, Edward
New Zealand poet *born* Southampton 1 May 1846
died Picton 28 October 1931
Edward Tregear arrived in Auckland in 1863 and his work as a surveyor brought him into contact with the language and culture of the Maoris. After active service in the Maori Wars he worked in the North island as a gold miner and engineer. A socialist,

Tregear was, in 1891, appointed head of the new Bureau of Industries in the Liberal administration. He published the *Maori-Polynesian Comparative Dictionary* (1891) and helped found the Polynesian Society. In 1904 he published *The Maori Race* and in 1913 became president of the Social Democratic Party. 'Te Whetu Plains' invokes 'the Evening Land, / Where man's discordant voices pierce no more'.

Tripp, John
Welsh poet *born* Bargoed, Glamorgan 1927

Brought up in Cardiff, Tripp was educated at Morley College, London. A journalist and public relations officer, he worked with the BBC news service, the Indonesian Embassy and the Central Office for Information. In the 1960s he returned to Wales as a freelance writer. His 'Welcome to Wales' takes a critical look at his own country: 'Among the ancient customs, buttering-up tourists / is not one, so beware of the remnant of pride / hanging in corners. If you prick us, / we shall surely bleed. Here you can buy / what you purchase in Selfridges / and cut a small notch in your wallet for every snip. / There are plenty of bogus Tudor / expense-account restaurants'.

Trumbull, John
American poet *born* Westbury, Connecticut 24 April 1750
died Detroit 12 May 1831

A precocious scholar, Trumbull learned Greek and Latin as a child and graduated from Yale at the age of seventeen: with his colleagues at Yale (where he taught literature) he formed the Connecticut Wits. In Boston he studied law in the office of John Adams and supported the patriotic party; on the outbreak of the American Revolution he worked on his mock epic *M'Fingal* (1775–82) which satirised the folly of the English. At the age of fifty he became a Judge of the Superior Court at Hartford. In *M'Fingal*, Trumbull observes of the English: 'Have they not racked their whole inventions / To feed their brats on posts and pensions; / Made their Scotch friends with taxes groan, / And picked poor Ireland to the bone.'

Tuckermann, Frederick Goddard
American poet *born* Boston, Massachusetts 4 February 1821
died Greenfield, Massachusetts 9 May 1873

Tuckermann abandoned his law practice in order to live the contemplative life of the poet. He retired, to Greenfield, and worked on the sonnets in *Poems* (1860), the only collection published in his lifetime. His poems put the natural world under an almost microscopic scrutiny as Tuckermann explores his relationship with his environment. A characteristic sonnet, 'Hast

thou seen reversed the prophet's miracle', ends 'Then come /
With me betimes, and I will show thee more / Than these, of
nature's secrecies the least: / In the first morning, overcast and
chill, / And in the day's young sunshine, seeking still / For earliest
flowers and gathering to the east.'

Tupper, Martin
English poet *born* London 17 July 1810 *died* 29 November 1889

A doctor's son, Tupper was educated at Oxford and called to the
Bar in 1835. He never practised law, however, being convinced he
was a man of literary destiny. His *Proverbial Philosophy* (4 series,
1838-76) was a bestseller – a million copies went to America –
and admired by such eminent Victorians as the Queen herself.
The style, derived from the Bible, offers unrhymed assertions and
advice, as in the lines 'Of Marriage': 'When thou choosest a wife,
think not only of thyself, / But of those God may give thee of her,
that they reproach thee not for thy being: / See that he hath given
her health, lest thou lose her early and weep: / See that she
springeth of a wholesome stock, that thy little ones perish not
before thee'.

Turnbull, Gael
Scottish poet *born* Edinburgh 1928

An anaesthetist, Turnbull has earned his living in Canada,
California, London and (since 1964) Worcestershire. His poems
are executed in an abrupt, staccato manner that displays a
professional concern with the daily trauma of living and the grim
business of dying. His poem 'Residues' comments on disease and
decay: 'riddled with cancer, scarcely able to sit up, / old Charlie
Oliver, as I drove him to the / hospital: "You do realise that
you've ruined / my day? I was planning to go pheasant shooting".'
The thematic gloom of Turnbull's work is relieved by his stoicism
and by moments of humour. He is an observant poet whose
values are always humane.

Tusser, Thomas
English poet *born c*1524 *died* London 1580

Tusser was a courtier in Lord Paget's service and subsequently
became a farmer in Sussex, Ipswich, Essex, Norwich and
elsewhere. Using his experience Tusser published, in 1557, *A
Hundred Good Points of Husbandrie*, a collection of metrical
observations on farming, gardening and housekeeping. His
'Directions for Cultivating a Hop-Garden' are characteristically
clear: 'Choose soil for the hop of the rottenest mould, / Well
dunged and wrought, as a garden-plot should; / Not far from the
water, but not overflown, / This lesson, well noted, is meet to be

known.' Despite his knowledge, Tusser was not financially
successful as a farmer and died in poverty.

Tuwhare, Hone
New Zealand poet *born* Kaikohe 1922

Hone Tuwhare worked as a boilermaker, was an active trade-
unionist, and settled in Dunedin. His collections include *No
Ordinary Sun* (1964), *Sapwood & Milk* (1972), *Something Nothing*
(1974) and *Selected Poems* (1980). His experience as a New Zealand
Maori is evident in his use of language, as in 'Snowfall' which
describes 'white pointillist flakes on / a Hotere canvas – swirling
about on untethered // gusts of air and spreading thin uneven /
thicknesses of white snow-cover on drooping / ti-kouka leaves,
rata, a lonely kauri, pear / and beech tree.'

Vagaland
Scottish poet *born* Westerwick, Shetland 6 March 1909
died 29 December 1973

T A Robertson, who signed all his poems with the pseudonym
Vagaland, was brought up in Waas, Shetland, and educated at the
Anderson Educational Institute, Lerwick, before going to
Edinburgh University. He spent his working life as a teacher of
English in Shetland and wrote in English as well as the Shetland
dialect. His work is traditional in tone and uses dialect to preserve
the cultural presence and natural beauty of Shetland. His poem
'Vaigin On' places the author's biblical memories in the context
of the Shetland seascape: 'An still, nae maitter if da nicht / is mirk
as he can be, / Da licht at sheened ower Bethlehem / still sheens
across da sea.'

Van Toorn, Peter
Canadian poet *born* near The Hague 1944

Peter Van Toorn, born in a bunker, was educated at McGill
University. He was active as an anthologist and musician as well as
teaching at John Abbot College, Montreal. His collection *In
Guildenstern Country* appeared in 1973. Although his verse is
conspicuously modern in its formal fragmentation, Van Toorn
returns thematically to the roots of Canadian poetry. 'Ode', for
example, celebrates the Edenic appearance of the country: 'My
snoweyed country / jabbed / with plenty / pine, maple, oak, ash,
apple, fire, cedar, tamarack / stuffing a poet's belly, stuffing / the
poet in any man / his belly for weather, mountains, water /
friction in colours.'

Vaughan, Henry
Welsh poet *born* Llansaintffraed, Brecknock 17 April 1622
died 23 April 1695
Vaughan went to Oxford with his twin brother Thomas then
studied law in London before becoming a doctor at Brecon and
Newton-by-Usk. An enthusiastic Royalist, he supported the king
in the Civil War and was imprisoned. Around 1649 he
experienced a renewal of his religious impulse and published the
first volume of *Silex Scintillans* in 1650. His work brings a deep
spiritual pressure to the Metaphysical mode, as in 'The World': 'I
saw Eternity the other night / Like a great Ring of pure and
endless light, / All calm as it was bright; / And round beneath it,
Time, in hours, days, years, / Driven by the spheres, / Like a vast
shadow moved, in which the world / And all her train were
hurled.'

Vaughan, Thomas
Welsh poet *born* Llansaintffraed, Brecknock 17 April 1622
died 1666

With his twin brother Henry Vaughan, Thomas was educated at
Oxford where he remained after Henry went to London. Both
brothers were strong Royalists and were imprisoned for a period.
Thomas Vaughan became one of the leading Hermetical
Philosophers of his time. He also wrote occasional poems such as
the lines 'On the Death of an Oxford Proctor'; 'He plundered not
the heavens, nor brought he down / Secrets from thence which
were before unknown; / Yet some there are believe their wits so
ripe / That they can draw a map of the Archetype, / And with
strange optics tutored they can view / The emanations of the
mystic Jew. / In this his pious ignorance was best / And did excel
his knowledge of the rest.'

Very, Jones
American poet *born* Salem, Massachusetts 28 August 1813
died Salem, Massachusetts 8 May 1880
Jones spent part of his childhood sailing with his father, a sea
captain. At Harvard he was a tutor in Greek while studying at the
university's Divinity School; so deeply felt was his religious faith
that he appeared unstable and was committed, briefly, in the
Mclean Asylum in Somerville, Massachusetts. His
Trancendentalist friend Ralph Waldo Emerson, however, insisted
that Very was 'profoundly sane'. He became a Unitarian
clergyman in Maine and Massachusetts then retired to Salem to
live with his sisters. His sonnets (in which an extra foot is added
to the final line) discover, in such objects as 'The Wind-Flower',
'A lesson taught by Him who loved all humankind'.

Waddington, Miriam
Canadian poet *born* Winnipeg 1917

Educated at the universities of Toronto and Pennsylvania, Miriam
Waddington taught at York University, Toronto. A critic and
editor as well as a poet she published her tenth collection, *The
Visitants*, in 1981. She has a fine descriptive gift, in the best
tradition of Canadian poetry, but can also produce bittersweet
poems like 'Thou Didst Say Me' which ends on a jarring note of
regret: 'year curves to ending now / and thou dost say me, wife / I
choose another love, and oh / the delicate del- / icate serpent of
your mouth / stings deep, and bitter / iron cuts and shapes / my
death, I was so fool.'

Wain, John
English poet *born* Stoke-on-Trent 1925

Educated at Oxford, Wain lectured in English at Reading
University from 1947–55. His novel *Hurry on Down* (1953) led to
critics grouping him with Kingsley Amis and others as Angry
Young Men. His appearance in Robert Conquest's *New Lines*
(1956) identified him as a Movement poet and thus technically
traditional and provincial in tone. In *Weep Before God* (1961) he
included his 'Apology for Understatement': 'Forgive me that my
words come thin and slow. / This could not be a time for
eloquence, / For silence falls with healing of the sense.' He was
Professor of Poetry at Oxford from 1973–8 and published the
texts of his lectures as *Professing Poetry* (1978).

Walcott, Derek
Caribbean poet *born* St Lucia, Windward Islands 1930

Educated at the University of the West Indies, Walcott worked as
a teacher and journalist. He wrote plays such as *The Sea at Dauphin*
(1954) and published various collections of verse including *In a
Green Night* (1962) and *The Castaway* (1965). The theme of
enlightenment through travel is evident in *The Fortunate Traveller*
(1982), the title sequence of which suggests the inner nature of
travel: 'There is no sea as restless as my mind. / The promontories
snore. They snore like whales. / Cetus, the whale, was Christ. /
The ember dies, the sky smokes, like an ash heap. / Reeds wash
their hands of guilt and the lagoon / is stained. Louder, since it
rained, / a gauze of sand flies hisses from the marsh.'

Waller, Edmund
English poet *born* Coleshill, Buckinghamshire 3 March 1606
died 21 October 1687

As a child Waller inherited the estate of Beaconsfield and in his
teens became a Member of Parliament. His first wife, Anne Banks
(whom he married in 1631), was a London heiress who increased

his fortune. When she died in 1634 he courted Lady Dorothy Sidney, the 'Sacharissa' of his poems. For his part in a plot, of 1643, to seize London for the King, he was exiled to Paris for seven years. He was pardoned in 1651 and, after the Restoration, again sat in Parliament. Though he has been criticised for his personal faults he wrote flawless lyrics such as that beginning 'Go, lovely Rose – / Tell her that wastes her time and me, / That now she knows, /When I resemble her to thee, / How sweet and fair she seems to be.'

Ward, Raymond
New Zealand poet *born* London 1925

Educated at London University, Ward served with the Royal Navy for three years during the Second World War. He taught for some time then came to New Zealand in 1959, settling in Dunedin. He published *Settler and Stranger* in 1965. 'Watching Snow' imaginatively combines a personal relationship with a mood evoked by the landscape. It begins: 'You were standing at the window, silently / when the first flakes began to fall / between the houses, to settle in the boughs / of the leafless elm and in the yard below; / and so intently were you watching them / spin through the early winter gloom / to catch in fences, heap the window sill, / you did not notice when I spoke to you.

Warner, Francis
English poet *born* Bishopsthorpe, Yorkshire 29 October 1937

Educated at Cambridge, Warner became Fellow and Tutor in English Literature at St Peter's College, Oxford. In 1972 he was awarded America's Messing International Award for distinguished contributions to literature. Though he has a reputation as an experimental playwright, he brings a well-tested English tradition to bear on his verse as he enjoys rhyme, set patterns of rhythm and the challenge of the sonnet form. In introductory quatrains to his *Collected Poems* (1985) he defines himself as a man of two university towns: 'I give a tongue to my accustomed streets, / The buildings two slow rivers wind among; / Cambridge's sun-touched world of youth and song / That mellow Oxford's majesty completes.'

Warner, Sylvia Townsend
English poet *born* Harrow-on-the-Hill 6 December 1893
died Maiden Newton, Dorset 1 May 1978

A schoolmaster's daughter, Warner was privately educated and became an expert editor of Tudor church music. She was a fiercely independent woman who lived with her friend Valentine Ackland for almost forty years and espoused a number of leftist causes: she joined the Communist Party in 1935 and visited Spain

in 1937. Best known for the novel *Lolly Willowes* (1926) she made
her literary debut with *The Espalier*, a collection of poems. Her
verse uses simple forms and strong rhymes to convey her love of
the English countryside, as in 'The Happy Day': 'All day long / I
purpose in yonder / Green meadows to wander / And think
of a song.'

Warr, Bertram
Canadian poet *born* Toronto 1917 *died* 1943

Educated in Toronto, Warr joined the Royal Air Force in 1941
and was killed in action two years later. His poems were collected,
under the title *Acknowledgement to Life*, in 1970. Even when
contemplating the spectacle of a world at war, Warr produces
tender thoughtful poetry. His 'The Heart to Carry On' ends by
asserting the necessity of love with words that assumed a terrible
irony: 'Leaving you now, with this kiss / May your sleep tonight
be blest, / Shielded from the heart's alarms / Until morning I
return. / Pray tomorrow I may be / Close, my love, within these
arms, / And not lie dead in Germany.'

Warren, Robert Penn
American poet *born* Guthrie, Kentucky 24 April 1905

Winner of Pulitzer Prizes for both Fiction and Poetry – with,
respectively, *All the King's Men* (1946) and *Promises* (1957) –
Warren expresses his powerful imagination in intellectually taut
short poems and in extended narratives. *Chief Joseph of the Nez
Perce* (1983) is arguably the angriest poem ever published by a
septuagenarian poet. It records the fate of the Nez Perce Indians,
whose chief died in exile in 1904, and cites 'the Truth that no /
White man can know, how the Great Spirit / Had made the earth
but had drawn no lines / Of separation upon it'. Warren
celebrates the Indians and upbraids all-American heroes like
General Sherman and Buffalo Bill, who 'once sent his wife a
yet-warm scalp'.

Warton, Joseph
English poet *born* Dunsfold, Surrey 22 April 1722
died 23 February 1800

Warton's father was Thomas Warton, vicar of Basingstoke and
Professor of Poetry at Oxford – where the poet himself took holy
orders. He became headmaster of Winchester College and
Prebendary of Winchester and of St Paul's. He was a member of
Johnson's Literary Club and wrote an *Essay on the Writings and
Genius of Pope* (1757, 1782). Nevertheless his own work rejects the
sophisticated social ideals of Pope in favour of a rural vision, as in
'The Enthusiast': 'Happy the first of men, ere yet confined / To
smoky cities; who in sheltering groves, / Warm caves, and deep-

sunk valleys lived and loved, / By cares unwounded'. Warton also published translations of Virgil's *Eclogues* and *Georgics*.

Watkins, Vernon

Welsh poet *born* Swansea 27 June 1906 *died* 1967

Educated at Cambridge, Watkins worked in Lloyds Bank, Swansea. He married Gwendoline Davies in 1944 and was a friend of Dylan Thomas with whom he corresponded from 1936. His first collection,*Ballad of the Mari Lwyd*, was published in 1941 and he established a reputation as an important writer. His carefully crafted work suggests Edenic aspects of Wales, in (for instance) 'Waterfalls': 'Always in that valley in Wales I hear the noise / Of waters falling. / There is a clump of trees / We climbed for nuts; and high in the trees the boys / Lost in the rookery's cries / Would cross, and branches cracking under their knees // Would break, and make in the winter wood new gaps.'

Watkyns, Rowland

Welsh poet *born* Longtown, Herefordshire, flourished 1634–64

Watkyns, who became Rector of Llanfrynach, Breconshire, published his collection *Flamma sine Fumo* in 1662. His work is forceful and comments sardonically on contemporary events and attitudes. His lines on 'The Common People' show his disdain for the mob: 'The many-headed Hydra, or the People, / Now build the church, then pull down bells and steeple: / Today for learned bishops and a king / They shout with one consent – tomorrow sing / A different note. One while the people cry / To Christ Hosanna; then Him crucify. / And thus the wavering multitude will be / Constant in nothing but inconstancy: / When these together swarm, the kingdom fears; / They are as fierce as tigers, rude as bears.'

Watson, Thomas

English poet *born* London *c*1557 *died* 1592

Educated at Oxford, Watson studied law in London. He translated the *Antigone* of Sophocles into Latin, in 1581, and circulated Latin versions of Petrarch. His *Hecatompathia, or Passionate Century of Love* (1582) consists of a series of 18-line poems styled as 'Sonnets' by Watson. One begins thus: 'Actaeon lost, in middle of his sport, / Both shape and life for looking but awry: / Diana was afraid he would report / What secrets he had seen in passing by. / To tell the truth, the self-same hurt have I, / By viewing her for whom I daily die'. His *The Tears of Fancy* (1593) is a collection of sixty sonnets. He knew Marlowe and wrote an elegy for his other friend, Sir Francis Walsingham.

Watts, Isaac
English poet *born* Southampton 17 July 1674
died 25 November 1748

The author of more than five hundred hymns, including 'O God
our Help in Ages Past', Watts was a clothier's son. Educated at a
Nonconformist academy at Stoke Newington, he was minister of
an Independent congregation in Mark Lane but resigned for
reasons of health. Therafter he stayed at Theobald's, the house of
Sir Thomas Abney, and composed his hymns and sacred poems –
such as *Moral Songs for Children* (1715). His quatrains 'Against
Idleness and Mischief' – parodied by Lewis Carroll in *Alice in
Wonderland* ('How doth the little crocodile') – begin 'How doth the
little busy bee / Improve each shining hour, / And gather honey
all the day / From every opening flower!'

Wayman, Tom
Canadian poet *born* Hawkesbury, Ontario 1945

Wayman, who studied at the universities of British Columbia and
California, published several collections of poetry including
Money and Rain: Tom Wayman Live (1975). A lively and entertaining
poet, Wayman has a flair for sophisticated satire. His 'Wayman in
Love' sets up an amorous scenario then undermines it by
introducing two opinionated intruders. The first is Karl Marx
who expatiates on the economics of eroticism. After Marx has
had his say, Sigmund Freud arrives: 'The newcomer straightens
his glasses, / peers at Wayman and the girl. "I can see," he
begins, /"that you two have problems".'

Webb, Francis
Australian poet *born* Adelaide 1925 *died* 1973

After an education in Sydney, Webb went to Canada with the
Royal Australian Air Force during the Second World War.
Subsequently he divided his time between Australia and Canada,
studying for a year at Sydney University then working for a
Canadian publisher. His best known works are the sequences *A
Drum for Ben Boyd* (1948) and *Leichhardt in Theatre* (1952). He is
expert at extracting pertinent questions for a scrutiny of the
world around him, as in 'Wild Honey': 'Are gestures stars in
sacred dishevelment, / The tiny, the pitiable, meaningless and
rare / As a girl beleagured by rain, and her yellow hair?'

Webb, Harri
Welsh poet *born* Swansea 7 September 1920

Educated at Oxford, Webb became Chief Librarian at Mountain
Ash. He was involved in the Welsh Republican Movement and
became a member of Plaid Cymru in 1935. His work is
distinguished by wit and he has a satirical approach to Welsh

problems. His poem 'Israel' urges the Welsh to pay attention to the achievements of the Jewish people: 'They have switched off Mendelssohn / And tuned in to Maccabeus. / The mountains are red with their blood, / The deserts are green with their seed. / Listen, Wales.' His collected poems 1950–69 were published as *The Green Desert* in 1969.

Webster, Augusta
English poet *born* Poole, Dorsetshire 1837 *died* 1894

Daughter of an admiral, Augusta Webster married a Cambridge law lecturer (in 1836) and wrote essays on the social aspects of Victorian life. In 1870 she published *Portraits* which reveals, between passages of self-consciously rich writing, a talent for description, as in 'Circe': 'Oh, look! a speck on this side of the sun, / Coming – yes, coming with the rising wind / That frays the darkening cloud-wrack on the verge / And in a little while will leap aboard, / Spattering the sky with rushing blacknesses, / Dashing the hissing mountainous waves at the stars.'

Webster, John
English poet *born* London c1580 *died* c1625

A tailor's son, Webster was a freeman of the Merchant Taylor's Company and a clerk of the parish of St Andrew's, Holborn. His reputation rests on four plays – *The White Devil* (1612), *The Devil's Law Case* (1623), *The Duchess of Malfi* (1623) and *Appius and Virginia* (1654) – and on collaborations with Dekker and Rowley. Though his work suggests a spectacle of brutality, he was also capable of fine poetic passages as in the dirge from *The White Devil*: 'Call for the robin-redbreast and the wren, / Since o'er shady groves they hover, / And with leaves and flowers do cover / The friendless bodies of unburied men.' Interest in his work was revived in the nineteenth century by Hazlitt and Lamb.

Wedde, Ian
New Zealand poet *born* Blenheim 1946

Wedde, who lived in East Pakistan and England as a child, was educated at Auckland University. After graduating he spent two years in Amman, Jordan. He worked as a labourer and wrote for cabaret. He settle in Wellington. His collections include *Homage to Matisse* (1971), *Pathway to the Sea* (1975), *Spells for Coming Out* (1977), *Castaly* (1980). In *Earthly: Sonnets for Carlos* (1975) he celebrates his sense of belonging: 'It's too hard & far / to any other dreamt-of paradise / & paradise is earthly anyway, / earthly & difficult & full of doubt. // I'm not good I'm not peaceful I'm not wise / but I love you. What more is there to say. / My fumbling voices clap their hands & shout.'

Wellesley, Lady Dorothy (Duchess of Wellington)
English poet *born* 1891 *died* 1956

Dorothy Wellesley was privately educated before she married the Duke of Wellington. The considerable reputation she enjoyed in the 1930s was partly the result of Yeats's enthusiasm for her work; in the introduction to his *Oxford Book of Modern Verse* (1936) he said she was 'at times magnificent in her masculine rhythm, in the precision of her style'. In her address to 'Demeter in Sicily' she ecstatically approaches the Earth-Mother: 'Demeter! I have seen / Thee throned in rock, thy stallion beside, / Gazing in weeping over uplands wide; / In the right hand a dolphin, left a dove – / Dolphin to swim to heaven on, bird for love'.

Westwood, Thomas
English poet *born* Enfield 1814 *died* 1888

Westwood spent most of his working life in Belgium where he was director and secretary of the Tourney and Jurbise railway. As a poet he favoured a descriptively extreme variety of Victorian verse. In his 'The Quest of the Sancgreall' he confronts Sir Galahad with this scene: 'The kraken, demon-eyed, and hundred-armed, / The sea-wolf and narwhal, mermaids and men – / A ghastly crew of scaled and slimy things – / With hiss, and whoop, and hollo, swift they came, – / Dashing the spray in moon-bows overhead, – / And huddled, interlaced, with one combined / Impulsion, snout and fin and fold and tail, / They sent the shallop skimming through the foam, /Into the distance, fleet as shooting star'.

Wheatley, Phyllis
American poet *born* Africa *c*1753 *died* Boston, Massachusetts 1784

At the age of eight Phyllis, a black girl, was brought to Boston and sold as a slave to John Wheatley, a tailor who recognised her intelligence and had her educated by his wife and daughter. She learned English, Latin and Greek in a remarkably short time and wrote poems which attracted much attention. Her *Poems on Various Subjects, Religious and Moral* (1773) was dedicated to the Countess of Huntingdon who introduced her to English society. Later she married John Peters, a free black, and endured poverty and obscurity. Her poem 'On Being Brought from Africa to America' ends on a couplet: 'Remember, Christians,Negroes, black as Cain, / May be refined, and join the angelic train.'

Whitehead, William
English poet *born* Cambridge 1715 *died* 1785

A baker's son, Whitehead was educated at Cambridge. He became tutor to the Earl of Jersey's son and was appointed Poet

Laureate in 1757, on the death of Colley Cibber. His work
adheres to new classical conventions and his 'Variety', subtitled
'A Tale for Married People', is a polished example of verbal
portraiture: 'A gentle maid, of rural breeding, / By Nature first,
and then by reading, / Was filled with all those soft sensations /
Which we restrain in near relations, / Lest future husbands should
be jealous, / And think their wives too fond of fellows. / The
morning sun beheld her rove / A nymph, or goddess of
the grove!'

Whitheford, Hubert
New Zealand poet *born* Wellington 1921
Educated at Victoria University, Whitheford worked at the
Central Office of Information, in London, from 1953–81. He
then returned to Wellington. His collections include *Shadow of the
Flame* (1950), *The Lightning Makes a Difference* (1962), *A
Native, Perhaps Beautiful* (1967). His poems stress the fragility of
life – 'What will have died before I reach a door?' he asks in 'The
Areana' – and the omnipresence of death. 'At the Discharge of
Cannon Rise the Drowned' has a scenario of death-in-life: 'Out of
a port-hole bursts a smear of flame, / A blast of thunder from the
flood rebounds. / With gliding leap, impelled by answering fire, /
Lazarus rises from his restless couch.'

Whitman, Walt
American poet *born* Huntington, Long Island 31 May 1819
died Camden, New Jersey 26 March 1892
Walt Whitman was brought up by Quakers in Brooklyn where he
was apprenticed to a printer. For the rest of his life he retained a
radical outlook and a fascination with the typographical precision
of poetry. After a career in journalism Whitman selfconsciously
assumed the role of the bard speaking with the authentic voice of
America. His *Leaves of Grass*, first published in 1855, eloquently
promoted the poet as the prophet of his country. Whitman's
personality, like his poetry, was expansive and he offered himself
as an example to the rest of mankind (as in 'Song of Myself'): 'I
celebrate myself, and sing myself, / And what I assume you shall
asume, / For every atom belonging to me as good belongs to you.'

Whittier, John Greenleaf
American poet *born* East Haverhill, Massachusetts 17 December
1807 *died* Hampton Falls, New Hampshire 7 September 1892
On his Quaker father's farm Whittier learned the poetry of Burns
whose influence he often acknowledged. He earned his living
from spells on the farm and journalism; his ambition to become a
member of Congress was set back when he identified himself as a
fierce anti-slavery agitator with the pamphlet *Justice and Expediency*

(1833). Whittier's health was poor but he was a passionate observer of events and the Civil War provided him with much material for his verse. 'Barbara Frietchie', from *In War Time* (1864), made a popular heroic myth from an anecdote: 'Up rose old Barbara Frietchie then, / Bowed with her fourscore years and ten; / Bravest of all in Frederick town, / She took up the flag the men hauled down'.

Whyte-Melville, George John
Scottish poet *born* Strathkinnes, Fife 19 January 1821
died 5 December 1878

Whyte-Melville was educated at Eton and commissioned in, first, the 93rd Highlanders then the Coldstream Guards. He commanded a regiment of Turkish irregular cavalry in the Crimean War and retired as a Major in 1859. Thereafter his life was spent as a country gentleman and his twenty-eight novels reflect his passion for hunting. His poems, in *Songs and Verses* (1869) and elsewhere, also show his love of field sports, as in 'The Galloping Squire': 'And the labourer at work, and the lord in his hall, / Have a jest or a smile when they hear of the sport, / In ale or in claret he's toasted by all, / For they never expect to see more of the sort.' He died in a riding accident.

Wickham, Anna
Australian poet *born* Wimbledon 1884 *died* 1947

Brought up in Australia, Anna Wickham's first great ambition was to be an operatic singer. However, she decided instead to devote herself to poetry and wrote prolifically: in four years, after the First World War, she wrote nine hundred poems. A married woman, she displayed great independence and was friendly with leading writers of her time, including D H Lawrence. In poems such as 'Divorce' she protests against the constraints of domesticity: 'Out in the dark, cold winds rush free, / To the rocks heights of my desire. / I smother in the house in the valley below, / Let me out to the night, let me go, let me go!'

Wiggins, Ella May
American poet *born* 1889 *died* 1929

An Appalachian woman, Ella May married a logger at the age of sixteen. When, some years later, he was disabled in an accident, she had to care for nine children and watch four of them die from whooping cough. A spinner in a cotton mill, she became a militant member of the National Textile Workers' Union and wrote songs denouncing the company owners. When she was on her way to a union meeting in Gastonia, North Carolina, she was shot and killed. Her work is direct and didactic, as in 'The Mill Mother's Lament': 'We leave our homes in the morning, / We kiss our children goodbye / While we slave for the bosses / Our children scream and cry.'

Wigglesworth, Michael
American poet *born* 1631 *died* Malden, Massachusetts 1705

Wigglesworth left England at the age of seven and was educated at Harvard. In 1656 he became pastor of the church at Malden where he lived for the rest of his life, also acting as the local doctor. His *The Day of Doom* (1662) expresses, in 224 stanzas, his vision of New England Puritanism. It enjoyed immense popularity and was learned by heart by readers who responded to its theological message. Wigglesworth wallows in his condemnation of sin, as when he writes: 'Vain hopes are cropped, all mouths are stopped, / sinners have nought to say, / But that 'tis just and equal most / they should be damned for aye.' Despite his professed distaste for fleshly delights, Wigglesworth married three times.

Wilbur, Richard
American poet *born* New York 1921

After an education at Amherst College and Harvard, Wilbur taught at Harvard, Wellesley and Wesleyan University. For his collection *Things of this World* (1956) he won, in 1957, the Pulitzer Prize and the National Book Award. He translated *The Misanthrope* (1955) and *Tartuffe* (1963) by Molière. His work investigates, often with an ironic wit, the relationship between the individual and the civilisation that surrounds him. 'Museum Piece' amusingly contrasts the contents of a gallery with those who are paid to watch over them: 'The good grey guardians of art / Patrol the halls on spongy shoes, / Impartially protective, though / Perhaps suspicious of Toulouse.'

Wilcox, Ella Wheeler
American poet *born* Johnstown Center, Wisonsin 5 November 1850 *died* 1919

A poor girl from a rural background, Ella Wheeler Wilcox was determined to achieve fame and fortune and succeeded with both ambitions. From an early age she sold poems to magazines and when a Chicago publisher declared her *Poems of Passion* (1883) morally unfit for human consumption she became a celebrity. Therafter she was regarded as an erotic poet who wrote prolifically. Fascinated by Hindu mysticism she claimed to communicate with her dead husband who, she said, advised her to read her poems to the troops in France during the First World War. Her best-remembered lines are those that open 'Solitude': 'Laugh, and the world laughs with you; / Weep, and you weep alone'.

Wilde, Oscar
Irish poet *born* Dublin 16 October 1854
died Paris 30 November 1900

Wilde's father was an eye surgeon, his mother a minor poet. After Trinity College, Dublin, he went to Oxford where he won the Newdigate poetry prize. His flamboyant lifestyle and histrionic triumphs made him one of the most famous men of his time but his friendship with Lord Alfred Douglas led to a scandal resulting in Wilde being sentenced, in 1895, to two years' imprisonment for homosexuality. After his release he wrote *The Ballad of Reading Gaol* (1898). Whereas his early poems had been exquisitely aesthetic this grim narrative was a work of outrage and anguish: 'Dear Christ! the very prison walls / Suddenly seemed to reel, / And the sky above my head became / Like a casque of scorching steel'.

Wiliam, Richard
Welsh poet flourished 1590–1630

Known as 'Sir Richard the Blackbird' (*Syr Risiart y Fwyalchen*) Richard Wiliam was a bilingual poet who wrote in Welsh as well as English. He was priest of a parish in East Glamorgan. His poem 'Sir Richard's Confession' is verbally vigorous and revealing: 'yt swit jesu, i pray thy vyw / how j awlter, liff and maner / j apeal lord, tw thy konkord / thy wyl by dwn, ffor my pardwn / j wyl never, by a wandrer / in my offys, ffrom thy sarfys / bwt in demywr, godly plesywr / tw lern tw dwel, with thy gosbel / and set my lyms, with pwr pilgryms / tw seck affter my Redymer / thus thy servant, jldeth konstant / tw life and dy, in thy marsy'.

Wilkinson, Anne
Canadian poet *born* Toronto 1910 *died* 1961

Anne Wilkinson was mainly educated in schools outside Canada. Her *Collected Poems and a Prose Memoir* appeared in 1968. Some of her poems affirm the Canadian tradition of delicate description as when she invokes 'a small Ontario farm' in 'In June and gentle over'. A more distinctively feminine approach is evident, however, in 'Lens'; 'My woman's eye is weak / And veiled with milk; / My working eye is muscled / With a curious tension, / Stretched and open / As the eyes of children; / Trusting in its vision / Even should it see / The holy holy spirit gambol / Counterheadwise, / Lithe and warm as any animal.'

Williams, Charles
English poet *born* London 1886 *died* 1945

Educated at University College, London, Williams worked for thirty-six years for the Oxford University Press in London He wrote several 'metaphysical thrillers', including *Descent into Hell*

(1937), and critical works such as *The English Poetic Mind* (1932). From 1938, when his collection *Taliessin Through Logres* appeared, he was obsessed by the Arthurian legends. 'The Calling of Arthur' describes a crucial encounter between Arthur and Merlin: 'Arthur was young; Merlin met him on the road. / Wolfish, the wizard stared, coming from the wild, / black with hair, bleak with hunger, defiled / from a bed in the dung of cattle, inhuman his eyes.'

Williams, Edward
Welsh poet *born* Llancarfan 1747 *died* 1826

Williams, known as *Iolo Morganwg*, was a stonemason, an antiquary and a literary forger. Although most of his poems were composed in the Welsh language, he also wrote, in English, *Poems Lyrical and Pastoral* (1794). His 'Stanzas Written in London in 1773' regret his move to London and anticipate a return to his native Glamorgan: 'Glamorgan, boast thy sky serene, / Thy health-inspiring gales, / Thy sunny plains luxuriant green, / Thy graceful mountains' airy scene, / Their wild romantic vales. // With nature's wealth supremely blessed, / With peace, with plenty crowned; / In thy white cots, a cheerful guest, / Pure joy dilates the glowing breast / And gladness smiles around.'

Williams, Gwyn
Welsh poet *born* Port Talbot 1904

Williams worked at universities in Cyrenaica and Istanbul as a Professor of English. A bilingual Welshman, he did distinguished translations from the Welsh. His own verse in English has a verbal vigour and a fondness for expressions in everyday use as when he writes, in 'City under Snow': 'spittle, pigeon-dung, dogshit and broken / glass, the layer of soot all iced over and / a new fall powders the cleaned crotches / of cobbled alleys.' Even in nature poems, such as 'Wild Night at Treweithan', he uses a direct diction: 'clouds hump and streak, / the starlings are swept off-course in a black spray, / the gale howls and rattles in my wide chimney'.

Williams, Hugo
English poet *born* Windsor 1942

Educated at Eton, Williams was assistant editor of the *London Magazine* from 1966-70 and subsequently became poetry editor of the *New Statesman*. He published *Symptoms of Loss* in 1965, *Some Sweet Day* in 1975, *Love Life* in 1979. Williams's poems are verbally terse and highly subjective, deriving their quality from the poetic art of perception. 'Tides', for example, ends with a speculative definition of happiness: 'to wander alone /

Surrounded by the same moon, whose tides remind us of
ourselves, / Our distances, and what we leave behind. / The lamp
left on, the curtains letting in the light.'

Williams, Taliesin
Welsh poet *born* Cardiff 1787 *died* 1847

Taliesin Williams, known as *Taliesin ab Iolo*, was the son of the
poet Edward Williams. He was, according to rumour, born in
Cardiff Gaol. A schoolteacher by profession, he wrote in both
Welsh and English and edited his father's manuscripts. In 'Cardiff
Castle' (1827) he brings lurid detail to his observations: 'The
drawbridge gained by deadliest foe, / The coarse encumbered
moat below, / Still fed by gushing wounds; / The onset at the
outward gate, / Where carnage reigned in gory state / And
vengeance knew no bounds; / Where serf and chief of high
renown, / Pinned by the barbed portcullis down, / Convulsive
drew their struggling breath / And writhed in all the pangs of
death.'

Williams, William
Welsh poet *born* Llanfair-ar-y-bryn, Carmarthenshire 1717
died 1791

William Williams – known as *Pantycelyn* after the name of his
family's property in Carmarthenshire, entered the Church in
1740. He worked as a curate then became one of the leaders of
the Methodist movement. His many hymns articulate the ideals
of Methodism, as in 'Hymn XLI': 'Now shall cease and wholly
vanish / Every meaner base delight; / Jesus, the desire and object /
Of the black and of the white, / To the chiefest / Sinners, grace
shall more abound. // Come unto the living fountain, / Sinners
therefore haste away; / Hear the call and do not squander /
Precious moments thus away: / Eat and welcome, / Drink the
pure delicious wine.'

Williams, William Carlos
American poet *born* Rutherford, New Jersey 17 September
1883 *died* Rutherford, New Jersey 4 March 1963

Williams practised medicine in his native Rutherford from
1910–52 in which time, it has been estimated, he delivered 2,000
babies. He was also dedicated to the practice of poetry and kept
in touch with contemporaries such as Ezra Pound and Wallace
Stevens. Operating on the principle 'No ideas but in things' he
produced pictorially sharp poems, for example 'The Red
Wheelbarrow' which places the titular object 'beside the white
chickens'. His five-volume epic *Paterson* (1946–58), set in the town
of Paterson, is impressionistic and occasionally rhapsodic: 'With
evening, love wakens / though its shadows / which are alive by

reason of the sun shining – / grow sleepy now and drop away / from desire.' (Book Two)

Wither, George
English poet *born* Bentworth, Hampshire 1588
died London 2 May 1667

Educated at Oxford, Wither (whose surname was once a synonym for 'hack') went to London where he wrote *Abuses Whipt and Stript* (1613), a satirical poem which earned him a period in Marshalsea prison. In prison he collaborated with William Browne on *The Shepherd's Pipe* (1614) then wrote a sequel *The Shepherd's Hunting* (1615) which contains some lively lines: 'But, alas! my Muse is slow; / For thy pace she flags too low. / Yes, the more's her hapless fate, / Her short wings were clipped of late; / And poor I, her fortune ruing / Am myself put up a-muing.' His satirical exposition of his Puritan principles led to further terms in prison (1621–2, 1646–7, 1660–3).

Wolfe, Charles
Irish poet *born* Dublin 14 December 1791 *died* 21 February 1823

Educated at Winchester and Trinity College, Dublin, Wolfe took holy orders and became rector of Donoughmore. He died of consumption. His poem 'The Burial of Sir John Moore' was published anonymously in the *Newry Telegraph* in 1817 and was initially attributed to Moore, Byron and others. The poem's success is a result of its grave elegiac tone: 'Not a drum was heard, not a funeral note, / As his corse to the rampart we hurried; / Not a soldier discharged his farewell shot / O'er the grave where our hero we buried. // We buried him darkly at dead of night, / The sods with our bayonets turning; / By the struggling moonbeam's misty light, / And the lantern dimly burning.'

Woods, John
American poet *born* Martinsville, Indiana 1926

Educated at the University of Indiana, Woods became a lecturer at Western Michigan University. He published several volumes of verse including *The Cutting Edge* (1966) and *Turning to Look Back: Poems 1955–70* (1971). His work projects the world as an endless source of artistic change, a place where the poet is often at the mercy of his own metaphors. 'Looking Both Ways Before Crossing' shows Woods's stylistic agility: 'I set out for the instant, / telling the wind to stop in the trees. / But leaf fires leap into the ash and air, / or sing back along the limb / where the sun picks for its eye / one drop on a leaf.'

Woods, Margaret Louise
English poet *born* Rugby 1856 *died* 29 November 1945

Daughter of G G Bradley, Dean of Westminster, Margaret married H G Woods (later President of Trinity College, Oxford) in 1879. She achieved success with her novel *A Village Tragedy* (1887) and continued to write verse plays, novels and poems. Her *Collected Poems and Plays* appeared in 1913. Her poems, such as 'The Mariners', are poignant in mood and stately in style: 'The mariners sleep by the sea. / The wild wind comes up from the sea, / It wails round the tower, and it blows through the grasses, / It scatters the sand o'er the graves where it passes / And the sound and the scent of the sea.'

Woodworth, Samuel
American poet *born* Sciutate, Massachusetts 13 January 1784 *died* 9 December 1842

With George Pope Morris, Woodworth founded the *New York Mirror and Ladies' Literary Gazette* in 1823 and so encouraged the Knickerbocker School of writers who helped put New York on the literary map. Though he wrote several satirical poems he is remembered for his sentimental account of 'The Old Oaken Bucket' and the part it played in his childhood: 'The wide-spreading pond, and the mill that stood by it; / The bridge, and the rock where the cataract fell; / The cot of my father, the dairy-house nigh it; / And e'en the rude bucket that hung in the well. / The old oaken bucket, the iron-bound bucket, / The moss-covered bucket, which hung in the well.'

Woolner, Thomas
English poet *born* Hadleigh, Suffolk 17 December 1826 *died* 7 October 1892

Woolner studied sculpture at the studio of William Behnes and in 1843 exhibited 'Eleanor Sucking the Poison from Prince Edward's Wound' at the Royal Academy. He was associated with the *Germ*, the Pre-Raphaelite journal that first published his sequence *My Beautiful Lady* (subsequently published as a volume in 1866). In 'Her Shadow' Woolner meditates on the changes wrought by time: 'I then but yearned for Titian's glorious power, / That I by toiling one devoted hour, / Might check the march of Time, and leave a dower / Of rich delight that beauty I could see, / For broadening generations yet to be.' He published several further volumes of verse and continued to develop as a sculptor.

Wordsworth, William
English poet *born* Cockermouth, Cumberland 7 April 1770 *died* 23 April 1850

A lawyer's son, Wordsworth was educated at Cambridge. In 1791, inspired by the Revolution, he went to France where an affair with Annette Vallon produced a daughter. His revolutionary faith broken by Napoleon's ambitions, Wordsworth was consoled by his sister Dorothy. In 1799 he went to Dove Cottage, Grasmere, and in 1802 married Mary Hutchinson. He was made Distributor of Stamps for Westmorland and Cumberland in 1813 and was appointed Poet Laureate in 1843. Whether writing long philosophical reflections in *The Prelude* (1850) or short lyrics as in for instance *The Lyrical Ballads* (1798), he impresses by the imaginative quality of his meditation, as in his Immortality Ode: 'To me the meanest flower that blows can give / Thoughts that do often lie too deep for tears.'

Wotton, Sir Henry
English poet *born* Broughton Hall, near Maidstone 1568
died December 1639

Educated at Oxford, Wotton did secretarial work for the Earl of Essex but moved to Italy at the time of the Earl's arrest. He was knighted by James I in 1604 and served as his ambassador in Venice, an experience that doubtless provoked his observation that an Ambassador was 'an honest man sent to lie abroad for the good of his country'. In 1624 he became Provost of Eton. He was influenced by his friend Donne, whose life he intended to write. His fine poem in praise of the Queen of Bohemia begins 'You meaner beauties of the night, / That poorly satisfy our eyes / More by your number, than your light, / You common people of the skies; / What are you when the moon shall rise?'

Wright, David
English poet *born* Johannesburg 1920

David Wright became deaf, at the age of seven, as a result of scarlet fever. Educated at Oxford, he made his reputation as a poet and editor – of the magazines *Nimbus* and *X* and anthologies including *Longer Contemporary Poems* (1966). He worked as a journalist with the *Sunday Times* and published several collections including *Monologue of a Deaf Man* (1958), the title poem of which unwraps the gift of life: 'In whatever condition, whole, blind, dumb, / One legged or leprous, the human being is, / I affirm the human condition is the same, / The heart half broken in ashes and in lies, / But sustained by the immensity of the divine.'

Wright, James
American poet *born* Martins Ferry, Ohio 13 December 1927
died 1980

Wright studied at Kenyon College under John Crowe Ransom and at the University of Washington under Theodore Roethke. He taught at the University of Minnesota and at Hunter College, New York. For his *Collected Poems* of 1971 he was awarded the

Pulitzer Prize. The variety of his verse is impressive and he can range from satirical work to the lyricism of 'A Blessing' which ends, after an encounter involving two Indian ponies, with the poet caressing the ear of one of the animals, the 'long ear / That is as delicate as the skin over a girl's wrist. / Suddenly I realise / That if I stepped out of my body I would break / Into blossom.'

Wright, Judith

Australian poet *born* Armidale, New South Wales 1915

Educated, by correspondence, on her family's sheep station and then at Sydney University, Judith Wright worked as a secretary and an agriculturist. After her marriage she moved to Mt Tambourine, southern Queensland, where many of her best poems were written. Later she settled in Canberra. She is recognised as one of Australia's finest poets, a writer of sensitivity and obvious artistic intelligence. Her great theme is the creative power of love. In 'Clock and Heart' she meditates on the importance of poetry and passion: 'Set free at last in human time – / that long-rejected tyranny – / I found in ordinary love / the solitudes of poetry.'

Wright, Kit

English poet *born* Kent 1944

Educated at Berkhamsted School and New College, Oxford, Wright subsequently taught in a South London comprehensive school; lectured in English Literature at Brock University, Ontario; worked as Education Secretary to the Poetry Society, London; and held the post of Fellow-Commoner in the Creative Arts at Trinity College, Cambridge. He displays considerable wit and powers of observation, and is skilled at using rhyme to make a poignant point as in 'Song of Burning' from *The Bear Looked Over the Mountain* (1977): 'Surely it need not matter / That fire shall leave no trace / Of friends that later, sooner, later, / One by one, my darling, / Are going, face by face?'

Wright, Richard

American poet *born* Roxie, near Natchez, Mississippi
4 September 1908 *died* 1960

Born on a plantation, Wright went to Chicago in his teens. In New York he was Harlem correspondent of the *Daily Worker* but subsequently expressed his distrust of Communism. His novel *Native Son* (1940), a great critical and commercial success, was the first novel by an American black to become a Book-of-the-Month Club selection and the first to appear in the Modern Library editions. His autobiographical *Black Boy* (1945), about his upbringing in the South, confirmed his literary stature. He moved to Paris where he lived for fifteen years before his death.

His poem 'Between the World and Me' appeared in *Partisan Review* in Summer 1935: 'The grey ashes formed flesh firm and black, entering into my flesh.'

Wyatt, Sir Thomas
English poet *born* Allington Castle, Kent 1503
buried 11 October 1542

Son of Sir Henry Wyatt, who served Henry VII, Wyatt was educated at Cambridge. Henry VIII sent him on diplomatic missions but also imprisoned him in the Tower of London on the downfall of Anne Boleyn – since Wyatt was one of her admirers. Knighted in 1537, he was again imprisoned in the Tower on the death, in 1540, of Thomas Cromwell whose ideals he endorsed. On his release he was sent to meet the Spanish Ambassador at Falmouth but caught a fatal cold on his journey. His lyrical gift is splendidly displayed in the poem beginning: 'They flee from me, that sometime did me seek / With naked foot, stalking in my chamber.' His influence on the development of English poetry was considerable.

Wylie, Elinor
American poet *born* Somerville, New Jersey 7 September 1885 *died* 1928

Educated in Washington, Elinor Hoyt married the lawyer Philip Hichborn in 1906 then left him, in 1910, to live with her lover Horace Wylie in England. Hichborn committed suicide, in 1912, and Elinor and Wylie returned to the USA to marry three years later. As the subject of a scandal, Elinor was initially ostracised in Washington but accepted in the literary world of New York where she lived with her third husband, the poet William Rose Benét, in the 1920s. In poems such as 'Let No Charitable Hope' she poignantly projects her own personality: 'I was, being human, born alone; / I am, being woman, hard beset; / I live by squeezing from a stone / The little nourishment I get.'

Yeats, William Butler
Irish poet *born* Sandymount, County Dublin 13 June 1865
died Cap Martin, France 28 January 1939

The son of a painter, Yeats studied art in Dublin but soon launched himself on an enormously influential literary career. His interest in the indigenous Irish tradition and his love for Maud Gonne, the Irish nationalist, contributed to the leading part he played in the Celtic Revival. His early poetry is mystical and romantic but the collection *Michael Robartes and the Dancer* (1921) shows a more direct style and an imaginative involvement in political events. 'Easter 1916', written shortly after the Easter Rising in Dublin, commemorates the executed men (including

Sean MacBride, Maud Gonne's husband) who 'Now and in time to be, / Wherever green is worn, / Are changed, changed utterly: / A terrible beauty is born.'

Young, Andrew
Scottish poet *born* Elgin 29 April 1885 *died* Yapton, Sussex 1971

After studying theology in Edinburgh, Young was ordained a minister of the United Free Church of Scotland in 1912. He was converted to the Church of England in 1936, became Vicar of Stonegate, Sussex, in 1941, and was made a Canon of Chichester Cathedral in 1948. His short poems evoke the drama of nature through close observation and a subtle euphony. His sustained two-poem sequence *Out of the World and Back* (1958) is a Christian meditation on the meaning of his own death: 'I had no fear, thinking of nothing more / Than the strange novelty of being dead.'

Zukofsky, Louis
American poet *born* New York 1904 *died* New York 1978

For most of his life Louis Zukofsky lived in New York City, near the print shop where Walt Whitman's *Leaves of Grass* was first set in type. This fact, like so many others relating to his productive life, is noted in his masterpiece *'A'* (complete version, 1978): 'Thru running manes of Leaves of Grass / In their first printer's shop, / The house it was in still stands / On Cranberry Street / That I walk nights / I go to teach / In the Eagle building, of old / Brooklyn.' *'A'*, which Zukofsky began in 1928, is one of the great achievements of modern American verse, a meditation on time as it involves the poet in a creative dimension; Zukofsky said he wanted to sound time 'as on an instrument'.